TRAVELLING IN LAKELAND

Front cover illustrations:
Slaters' Bridge – Little Langdale
Glencoyne Farm – Patterdale
Robin Lane – Troutbeck

Back cover illustration:
NT. Hundred Year Stone – Derwentwater

Travelling in Lakeland

ERIC BAVIN

The Pentland Press
Edinburgh – Cambridge – Durham – USA

© Eric Bavin 1999

First published in 1999 by
The Pentland Press Ltd
1 Hutton Close
South Church
Bishop Auckland
Durham

ISBN 1-85821-621-4

Typeset in Bavin 3* 14/16 and
Goudy by
Carnegie Publishing, Carnegie House, Chatsworth Road, Lancaster

Printed and bound by Antony Rowe, Wilts

*The typeface Bavin 3 was typographically prepared
from samples of the author's own handwriting.

Contents

Chapter 2

Chapter 3

Chapter 4

Chapter 5

Abbreviations

Key to Maps

Selective Biliography

Acknowledgements

I gratefully thank Irene and Philip Elders for their generous provision of accommodation in Lakeland over many years.

My thanks are due also to those who staff Tourist Information Centres and to the authors of church history booklets for the valuable information obtained.

For providing a fund of knowledge and ideas I record my appreciation and gratitude to many National Park Voluntary Wardens, local historians who have led me on Special Interest and Town Walks, National Trust Officers, ex-Cumberlander June Davies and to numerous Cumbrian residents and fellow travellers in Lakeland.

For help with the accuracy of the text I am indebted to many officials with different areas of responsibility, especially to Mr Philip Graham, Information Officer at British Nuclear Fuels plc.

For permission to quote from various brochures I thank Tullie House Museum, Carlisle; Levens Hall Estate, Kendal; Dalemain Estates, Penrith; Cumbria Crystal; Miller Howe Hotel and Restaurant.

I wish also to thank the following for permission to quote copyright material from:

A. Wainwright's seven "Pictorial Guides to the Lakeland Fells", "the Outlying Fells of Lakeland", "Old Roads of Eastern Lakeland"' and "Wainwright on the Lakeland Mountain Passes", all the titles being copyright © Michael Joseph 1992.

"Walks from Ratty" by A. Wainwright, published by The Ravenglass and Eskdale Railway Co. Ltd.

"A History of the Writings of Beatrix Potter" by Leslie Linder, copyright © Frederick Warne & Co. 1971.

"The Buildings of England: Cumberland and Westmorland" by Nicholas Pevsner 1967 by permission of Penguin Books Ltd.

"Grasmere Journal" by Dorothy Wordsworth, copyright © The Wordsworth Trust.

"The Fortress," the third volume of the Herries Chronicle by Hugh Walpole 1932, copyright © Sir Rupert Hart-Davies.

"The Just So Stories" at the conclusion of "The Elephant Child" by Rudyard Kipling, copyright © A. P. Watt Ltd, Literary Agents on behalf of the National Trust for Places of Historic Interest and National Beauty.

"The National Trust Handbook" copyright © the National Trust, 1998.

"The Red Hills" by Dave Kelly, copyright © Red Hill Publications 1994.

I thank David Higham Associates Ltd for permission to quote from "Collected Poems" by Norman Nicholson, published by Faber and Faber, 1966.

I also thank Random House UK Ltd for permission to quote from "Arthur Ransome and Captain Flint's Chest" by C Hardyment, published by Jonathan Cape, and to reproduce four maps and two diagrams from "The Lake District" by Ray Millward and Adrian Robinson, published by Eyre and Spottiswoode, 1970.

Finally, I am most grateful for the sketches drawn by my son, James, and for all the help and support of my wife.

Introduction

It is widely accepted that there are very few limits to the delights and attractions of Lakeland. Within this compact, scenic corner of England, enjoyment for everyone is abundantly available.

Many authors have written personal impressions of this area in prose or poetry highly evocative of the place, time, people and events. Other writers have compiled excellent gazetteers or suggested touring or walking routes.

How then can yet another book on Lakeland be justified?

For more than fifty years, my love of Lakeland has driven me to want to know more. Curiosity has urged me to find out all that I could using Rudyard Kipling's approach:

> "I Keep six honest serving men
> (They taught me all I knew);
> Their names are What and Why and When
> And How and Where and Who.

The results of my enquiries have been written down in notebook form, under headings and jottings, as opposed to continuously flowing prose, or an alphabetical arrangement.

Significantly, the text is arranged in the sequence of car, cycle, bus, boat or train journeys on the basis that such travel is an inevitable start to any outing. The information is presented in the order in which places of interest appear on these routes. These are not tours in the accepted sense, but directions for reaching locations worthy of the readers' attention. This sequential format is continued in the town and village trails for which sketch maps are provided. The great advantage is that quick and easy reference to relevant information is readily available along the way for any Lakeland journey.

The text is equally valid for reaching the starting points for the hundreds of walks on the Lakeland fells and in the valleys, as described in the many books and leaflets currently available. By way of example, reference is made at appropriate places within the text to the starting points for the numerous routes of ascent of the 214 fells described by A. Wainwright in his seven "Pictorial Guides to the Lakeland Fells" and for ascending the 56 foothills detailed by him in "The Outlying Fells of Lakeland". Included also are Wainwright's starting points for the 12 walks in "Old Roads in Eastern Lakeland" and for his 10 "Walks from Ratty".

Travel is necessary to reach the starting point of any walk. To make the most of the journey, simply refer to the appropriate route and the sequential guidance.

Presented here is a comprehensive, in depth guide to the best of Lakeland. I tell of the varied lowland routes and point out the interesting features along the way. At the same time I direct you to the innumerable starting points for walkers, from where Wainwright and many other authors take over as guides to the hills and fells, or to the woods and valleys.

Whether wandering on lowlands or highlands the appropriate maps are essential. When starting points recommended in older books, including Wainwright's, are no longer valid, a good map will indicate alternatives.

Every effort has been made to ensure the accuracy of this information, but any corrections, or suggestions for improvement, would be greatly appreciated.

However, with the passing of time, changes relentlessly take place and no responsibility for consequences arising from the use of this material can be accepted.

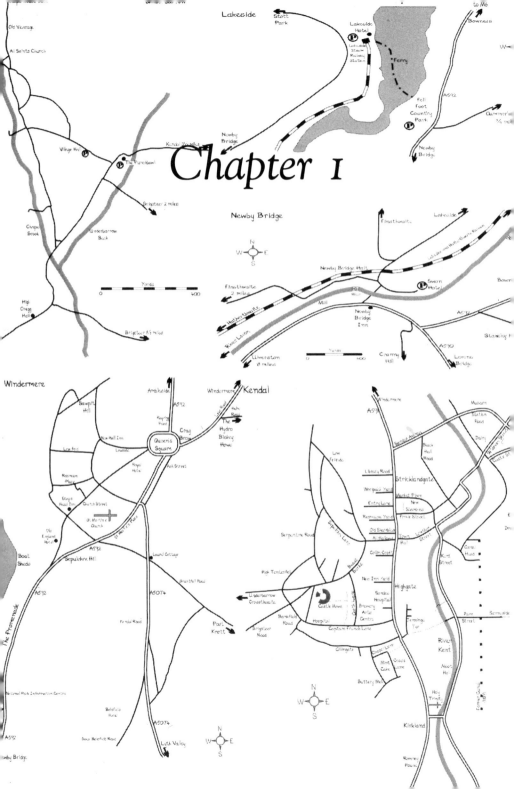

Chapter 1

Kendal

EC. Th. Mkt. W, S. [ON. Formerly Kirkby Kendale
= the Kentdale village with a church.]

Kendal is the second largest town in Cumbria, after Carlisle. Variously it is called 'The Auld Grey Town' because of its grey limestone buildings, and 'the Gateway to the Lakes' on account of its location a mile south of the Lake District National Park boundary, between the River Kent and Kendal Fell.

Historians surmise there may have been an Iron Age hill fort on Castle Howe.

Certainly, the Romans established a camp, Alauna, just south at Watercrook, protected on three sides by the River Kent, where it could be easily forded on the route to Hadrian's Wall.

Kendal's market charter, the earliest in Cumbria, dates from 1189. A Flea Market is held on Mondays and outdoor markets on Wednesdays and Saturdays.

In 1331, Edward III authorised John Kemp to encourage Flemish weavers to settle here, thus founding the great woollen industry. Its most famous product was the hardwearing Kendal green cloth, worn by foresters and bowmen. The green colouring was obtained by first dyeing the cloth yellow with dyers' broom and then blue with woad. Shakespeare mentioned it in *Henry IV Part I*, ' . . . *three misbegotten knaves in Kendal green came at my back and let drive at me,*' and Sir Walter Scott in *The Lay of the Last Minstrel.* The town's motto is, 'Pannus mihi panis' – 'wool is my bread.'

From the 13c to the 19c many mills operated by the River Kent. The earliest were saw mills and corn mills. There followed mills for the manufacture of bobbins, paper, gunpowder and iron. In the town, tobacco brought from Whitehaven by pack horse was crushed into snuff.

The Lancaster Canal opened in 1819. From the industrial zone at Canal Head, it gave access to the ports of Lancaster and Preston and to the Lancashire coalfield. The canal has now been filled in for two miles to make a cycleway.

Today, Kendal is perhaps best known for K shoes, Kendal Mint Cake and the Provincial Insurance.

A 'Gathering' is held in early September when the entertainments which include the County Show, end with a torchlight procession.

The Church of Holy Trinity, on the site of an Anglo-Saxon church, is 13c Gothic, the second widest in England, only seven feet narrower than York Minster. There are five aisles.

Of particular interest are:

Chapel with carved reredos dedicated to the Parrs of Kendal Castle.

Chapel dedicated to the Stricklands of Sizergh Castle.

Chapel dedicated to the King's Own Royal Border Regiment.

Several fine brasses to such landowners as the Bellinghams of Burneside. A former vicar, Ralph Tyrer (d. 1627) composed his own epitaph inscribed in a brass plate on the floor at the east end of the church. There is a memorial to George Romney, portrait painter.

A corona over the altar in memory of Bernard Gilpin, 'Apostle of the North'.

A sculpture, *The Family of Man* by Josephina de Vasconcellos.

The helmet and sword left behind by 'Robin the Devil', Robert Philipson of Belle Isle on Windermere. As a Royalist, he sought revenge on Parliamentarian Colonel Briggs who had besieged his house. Robin pursued his foe, on horseback, into Kendal church. The Colonel was not there, but the outraged congregation turned on Robin, who lost his sword and helmet in escaping.

The Ring of Bells pub, 1741, served as a refreshment place for church wardens, one of whose duties was to seek absentee church-goers, who faced a twelve-pence fine.

At one time there were as many as sixty inns in the town to serve the tradespeople and the travellers.

Abbot Hall Art Gallery derives its name from being built on the site of a monastic hall belonging to the Benedictines from St Mary's, York.

The present building is a Georgian mansion, reputedly the work of John Carr of York, built in 1759 for Colonel George Wilson at a cost of £8,000. In 1962 it was converted into an art gallery by a private trust and restored in 1992.

The period rooms are decorated in the 1760s style and display a variety of paintings and furniture which have local associations.

The paintings include works by George Romney (1734–1802), a Lancashire lad from Dalton-in-Furness and apprenticed in Kendal. He eloped with a servant girl from Kendal where she and the children remained when he left in 1762 to make his name as a portrait painter in London. At the age of 65 he returned to Kendal to be nursed by his wife in his old age.

Portraits by his pupil, Daniel Gardner (1750–1805) are also dis-played.

John Ruskin, who spent the last thirty years of his life at Coniston, is well represented by his water colours and J. M. W. Turner, whom he championed, has a painting.

The Scott Family Gallery shows many Lakeland landscapes painted by succeeding generations of artists from the 18c to the present day, together with prints and photographs.

Some of the elegant furniture was made by the local cabinet makers, Gillows of Lancaster.

The Abbot Hall Museum of Lakeland Life and Industry is housed partly in the Abbot Hall stable block and partly in a Jacobean Grammar School. It won the first Museum of the Year Award in 1973.

The museum brings to life Lakeland's social and economic history and seems to contain everything from tenter hooks to wrestler slates. Many items are displayed in reconstructed settings, such as a farmhouse parlour and barn, traditional trades' workshops and a Victorian pharmacy.

The Arthur Ransome room is laid out as the writer's study. Although he was born in Leeds, the son of a university lecturer, and worked in Russia as a journalist, he lived in the Lake District for many years to become best remembered as the author of books for children, such as *Swallows and Amazons*.

The John Cunliffe room features Postman Pat and Rosie and Jim, characters devised by this local author who was a teacher at Castle Park School in Kendal.

Take the riverside path. Cross over the River Kent. Ascend Parr Street.

Kendal Castle was built on a drumlin c. 1180 by Gilbert Fitz Reinfried and his wife Helewise de Lancaster. The castle now stands in ruins. From the 13c to the 16c, it was owned by the Parr family. Catherine Parr, the sixth and last wife of Henry VIII, was born here. On her marriage to Henry, which was her third out of four, she gave him a coat of Kendal cloth. During the border trouble the castle withstood attacks from the Scots, but even in 1586 William Camden described it as *'dropping with age'*.

Follow the footpath above the filled-in canal to Castle Road then to Castle Street and Wildman Street.

Castle Dairy, 14c. This is the oldest inhabited house in Kendal and is said to have the smallest window. It has become a restaurant.

The Museum of Natural History and Archaeology is housed in a former warehouse in Station Road. It claims to be one of the earliest museums in the country, originating from the private collection of Mr Todhunter, who set up an exhibition of 'curiosities' in 1796. In the 1830s, the Kendal Literary and Scientific Society, whose members included John Dalton (scientist), Adam Sedgwick (geologist), Richard Owen (socialist) and William Wordsworth (poet), acquired the collection and opened the museum. In 1986, it was the winner of the Judge's Special Prize in the Museum of the Year Awards.

There are three galleries:

The Kendal and Westmorland Gallery traces man's influence on Lakeland from the Stone Age to the development of Kendal as a wool town in the Middle Ages.

The Lake District Natural History Gallery provides an indoor nature trail.

The World Wildlife Gallery emphasises the conservation of rare species.

John Gough (1757–1825), Kendal's blind botanist, known to Wordsworth (*The Excursion VII*), is represented by his barometer, journals and plant collections. As a teacher of mathematics, he taught John Dalton who later became famous for his Atomic Theory. Wainwright in Lakeland is an exhibition of the life and work of Alfred Wainwright, 'A.W.', (1907–91), Kendal's Borough Treasurer, Curator of this museum for many years and renowned as author of the acclaimed *Pictorial Guides to the Lakeland Fells*.

Follow Stramongate over the river to the Market Place shopping area.

The Market Hall, 1886, was refurbished in 1988 and incorporated in the new Westmorland Shopping Centre.

The New Shambles were formerly the butchers' shops, built when the original meat market in the Old Shambles (off Stricklandgate, behind The Fleece Inn, 1656) was abandoned because the slope did not give sufficient drainage.

Lowther Street displays the Turk trade sign of Gawith Hogarth, snuff and tobacco manufacturers. Black Kendal twist, a notable pipe tobacco, is still a local speciality.

The Town Hall was rebuilt in 1825 in baroque style. The tall clock tower carries a carillon of bells which play folk tunes. On the pavement in front stands the Call Stone from which the proclamation of each new monarch was delivered. Two treasures of Catherine Parr's are her Prayer Book bound in silver and her Book of Devotions.

The Tourist Information Office occupies the room where A. Wainwright worked as Borough Treasurer, 1947–67, during the time that he was writing his seven *Pictorial Guides*, 1955–66.

Up Stricklandgate is The Westmorland Gazette shop of the oldest newspaper in Cumbria, once edited, 1818–19, by Thomas De

Quincey. Works by Wordsworth and Coleridge have been printed by the Gazette and, more recently, the books of A. Wainwright.

Shops 12–14 replaced the King's Arms coaching inn, which was used by Wordsworth, Coleridge and many others.

The Library was built on the site of Joseph Wiper's Kendal Mint Cake shop.

Opposite the Library, the trade sign of a hog with bristles along its back marks the site of a former brush factory.

Next to the YMCA is a building with a Civic Society plaque where Prince Charles Stuart, the Young Pretender, stayed on two occasions in 1745. On his way south, he was attempting to claim the English throne. On his way north, a few weeks later, after his defeat in the Battle of Derby, he was being pursued by 'Butcher' Cumberland, who is said to have slept in the same bed after Prince Charles's departure.

Kendal Yards. In medieval times, burgage plots existed on both sides of Stricklandgate and Highgate. As the cloth trade expanded more houses were needed. The crofts behind the roadside houses were built on but made accessible to the main street by narrow alleyways. These narrow passages, or 'ginnels', leading to the weavers' cottages grouped at the far end from the road, around a courtyard, provided protection. When danger threatened, the 'ginnels' could be sealed off by doors which were locked, barred and bolted.

Follow All Hallows Lane, opposite the Town Hall, Sepulchre Lane and the steps to Serpentine Road and High Tenterfell.

Kendal Fell was at one time common land providing grazing, building stone, and open space for stretching cloth to dry on tenter frames after the cloth had been dampened to improve the 'milling'.

Follow Bankfield Road and Captain French Lane.
Opposite gate no. 2, turn left along the 'ginnel'.

Castle Howe is the site of Kendal's original castle, a Norman motte and bailey construction, built in 1092 by Ketel de Tailbois, the third Baron of Kendal. This castle was burnt down in a Scottish raid in 1210 and abandoned. Its replacement was built on the opposite side of the river.

On top of the mound is a monument to William of Orange, commemorating the Glorious Revolution of 1688 when he invaded England and took over the throne from James II.

Continue to Beast Banks and All Hallows Lane. Turn right into Highgate. *After 30 yards, just before house no. 13a, turn right into* Collin Croft. This attractive yard won a Civic Trust Award. It was formerly occupied by a brass foundry, a tobacco factory and printing works.

Down Highgate to Kirkland. Note the period shop fronts of Ye Olde Highgate Pharmacy and Farrer's Tea and Coffee Shop.

There are several yards to explore.

Sandes Hospital. In 1659, Thomas Sandes, a cotton manufacturer, built almshouses for eight widows who were to work at carding and spinning. The present buildings are 19c, but the original gateway, with the arms and initials of Thomas Sandes, survives.

Brewery Arts Centre. This converted brewery has a theatre, a cinema, an exhibition gallery and a restaurant. Annual Folk and Jazz Festivals are held.

Turn right into Chapel Lane (under the arch) and left into Cross Lane.

Kendal Mint Cake Factory and shop. Joseph Wiper created this

Kendal

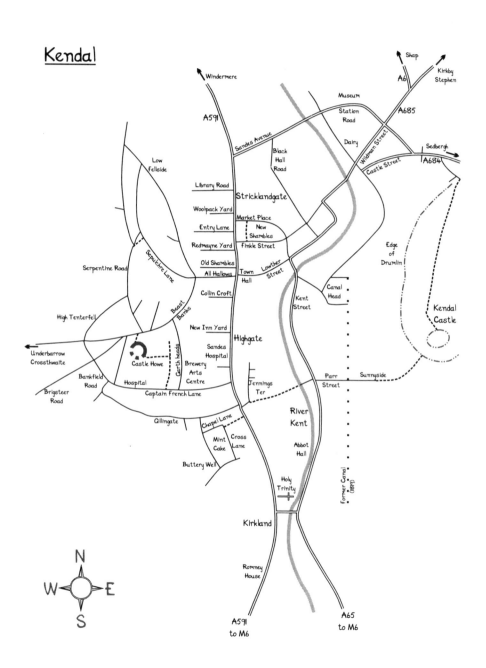

refreshing, energy packed mix of sugar, glucose syrup and oil of peppermint. The original recipe and the method of production have hardly changed since first used in 1869. The wrapping paper tells of the mint cakes' travels on expeditions by mountaineers, explorers and sailors.

The 'ginnel' back into Kirkland is one of the most ancient in town.

Romney House was the home of George Romney, the portrait painter. The plaque records his death here after a successful career in London.

Scout Scar OFOL 2

Kentdale

When climbing out of Kendal following the River Kent, the Drumlin scenery in the Kent basin is revealed.

The river, during the course of its 25 miles, drops 1,000 feet and is reputedly the swiftest flowing river in the country.

Prior to steam engines, 90 mills in this area were driven by water power. In terms of the numbers of industrial mills and the horse-power generated, Kentdale was more important than Birmingham. Kentdale had one industrial mill to 315 people; Birmingham one to 1380 people. Woollen, linen and cotton cloth was manufactured; bobbins, paper, snuff, carpets, rope and gunpowder.

To ensure a regular supply of water, Kentmere reservoir was constructed in 1848. But after 1850, the number of mills in Kentdale decreased as millowners were reluctant to change to steam.

Burneside [OE. Brunulf's hill.] High quality paper is still produced at James Cropper's paper mill, additional water coming by pipeline from Potter Fell.

Burneside Hall has a fine 14c pele tower, a walled enclosure for cattle, a remarkable gatehouse and a section of moat.

A 13c heiress, Elizabeth, married John Wessington from Durham, through whom the Washington family came to own land in these parts. Another notable family, the Bellinghams, were succeeded by the Braithwaites. It was Richard Braithwaite (1588–1673), known as

'Dapper Dick', who wrote poetry and doggerel verse under the name of 'Drunken Barnaby'.

In the 20c, another poet from the village, Margaret Cropper (1886–1980), vividly portrayed Westmorland life in her poems.

<u>Bowston Bridge</u>. In the 18c, Thomas Ashburner, printer and book-seller of Kendal, took over the mills for the manufacture of paper, using water from the River Kent supplied by a leat.

<u>Cowan Head Mill</u> was established in 1746 by Thomas Ashburner. He acquired a fulling mill from Dame Dorothy Fleming of Rydal Hall and converted it for the manufacture of paper, using water power from Cowan Head Falls. Linen backed registered envelopes became a speciality. In 1845, James Cropper took over the paper manu-facturing which continued until the 1970s when the business became uneconomical. The mill was finally closed in 1981 since when it has been converted into secluded luxury residential properties.

<u>Staveley</u> [OE. Wood where staves are cut] has a history of industrial activity based on the water power of the rivers Kent and Cowan. The cottage industries of spinning and hand-loom weaving produced a coarse woollen cloth. To clean and strengthen the cloth fulling mills were built close to running water. The earliest known fulling mill in Staveley was in 1328. By c. 1700, there were more than a dozen fulling mills on the local rivers. As demand changed, fulling mills were replaced by bob-bin or cotton mills in Staveley and wood turning continues to this day.

<u>St Margaret's Church</u> was begun in 1338 after William Thweng of Heslington had become Lord of the Manor of Staveley in 1328. The nave was demolished in 1865 and plaques have been placed on and near the tower to explain the history of the place.

Nearby in 1620, Lakeland farmers gathered to oppose successfully the plan of a later Lord of the Manor, supported by King James I, to abolish 'border tenure' whereby privileges were granted in return for helping to resist Scots raiding parties.

Staveley Wood Turning Company's factory manufactures tool handles. The mills started c. 1820 by tapping water from the River Kent – the weir and head race remain – and using local birch to manufacture bobbins for the Lancashire cotton mills on machinery, it is believed, invented by John Braithwaite of Ellerbeck Mill, Crook. The former drying sheds have been converted into several small workshops and retail outlets.

Manchester City Water Works pipes and iron grids at the water's edge are stamped 'MCWW'. The pipeline rises through Craggy Plantation and over the hill.

The Old Corn Mill, built c. 1790, was grinding local crops of oats until 1930. The head race which carried the water to the top of the water wheel is visible from Barley Bridge.

Hall Lane. The Hall, from which the Manor of Staveley was run, had fallen into ruin by 1690 and no trace remains.

Matthew Roddick's four-storey cotton mill was built at Barley Bridge 1785–9. The dam on the River Kent was necessary for water-power. By 1820, the mill had switched production to wool and to bobbin turning. Today, Kentmere Ltd manufacture coloured cartons and packaging whilst the adjacent new mill produces photographic paper.

St James' Church was built in 1865 to replace St Margaret's Church from where the 17c lectern came. The east window is a colourful example of the work of William Morris and Burne Jones.

The Working Men's Institute, 1874, was built with a newsroom and a billiard room, in keeping with the Victorian social improvement programme of benefits for the workers' leisure and of diverting the

16

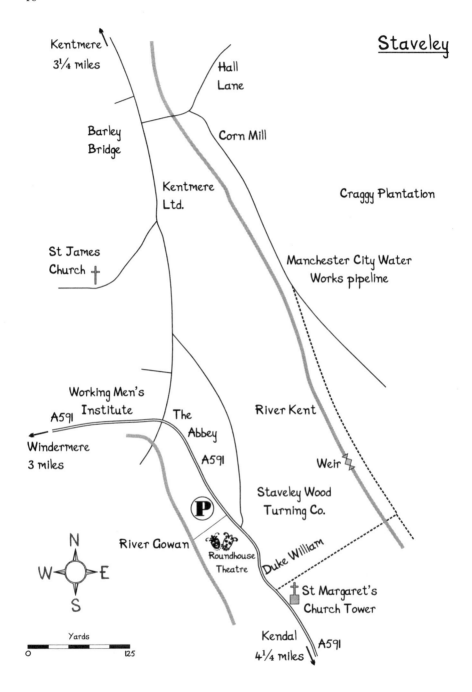

Staveley

Kentmere
3¼ miles

Hall
Lane

Barley
Bridge

Corn Mill

Kentmere
Ltd.

Craggy Plantation

St James
Church

Manchester City Water
Works pipeline

Working Men's
Institute
A591

The
Abbey

River Kent

Windermere
3 miles

A591

Weir

Staveley Wood
Turning Co.

P

River Gowan

Roundhouse
Theatre

Duke William

N
W   E
S

St Margaret's
Church Tower

Yards
0   125

Kendal
4¼ miles

A591

workmen from the pubs.

The Abbey, 1844, built as a hotel by J. H. Wilson, eventually became successively a gentlemen's residence, a children's home and an old people's home. The name originates from a field name, 'Abba Close'.

The Roundhouse Theatre took its name from its location at the gas-holder of the Staveley Near Kendal Gas Company, founded in 1867.

The Duke William stands on the site of hostelries which date back to the 15c.

In 1988, the Staveley By-pass cut off the inn – and the village – from the relentless flow of traffic on the A591.

Peter Hall and Son open their workshop for visitors to watch the process of manufacturing furniture and a range of domestic products fashioned by the traditional skills of wood turning.

| *Hugill Fell* | *OFOL 22* | *Reston Scar* | *OFOL 24* |
| *Potter Fell* | *OFOL 8* | *High Knott* | *OFOL 18* |

Kentmere [OE. Lake of River Kent] The narrow valley runs up into the High Street range with the parallel valleys of Troutbeck and Longsleddale on either side.

The lower valley has a Silurian landscape with relatively smooth green slopes and occasional rock outcrops. Further up, the valley follows a linear belt of rock strata weakened by faulting and shattering and also erosion.

Kentmere Tarn Glaciation created a hollow which later became a lake, 1 mile long and ¼ mile wide. The lake, which gave its name to the valley and village, had its water released in the 19c by blasting the bedrock. The tarn had intercepted the flow of water in the River Kent for the mills lower down in Kentdale. Some good agricultural land was exposed, but revealed also was a rich deposit, 20 feet deep, of diatomite. These minute vegetable organisms, with their external casing of silica, were quarried by the Cape Asbestos Company for use in the manufacture of insulating material capable of withstanding very high temperatures, such as heat insulated bricks. Diatomite was used also in the manufacture of sound-proofing materials, paper, rubber, plastic and floor covering. It provided the eggshell finish to paint.

In 1955 a 1,000-year-old canoe was dug out of the tarn.

The deposits have now been exhausted and the area has reverted to its original watery state with the river flowing alongside.

Millrigg. Here were the diatomite works which once processed the sediment of the former lake.

Kentmere's upper valley is divided into Quarters.

Kentmere Hall and Crag Quarter lie to the west of the village, where the softer Silurian landscape gives way to the crags and rock-scarred topography of the Borrowdale Volcanic Series. The surrounding fells are remote, bleak and harsh.

Nearly every building in the village is on a hill and all the lanes are rough and steep. The school, the shop, the pub and the blacksmith's no longer exist. A house near How Bridge was once the Kentmere Inn which made legal history as the first to lose its licence for allowing heavy drinking. Electricity only came in 1963.

St Cuthbert's Church has 16c roof beams. It was possibly built on the site of a church in which St Cuthbert's body rested on its way to Durham. There is a memorial plaque to the Rev. Bernard Gilpin (1517–83).

Just north of the church is a rock bar with its edges plucked and accentuated by ice, at the junction of soft, well-cleaved Browgill Slates and harder volcanic rocks, in an area of boulder moraine.

Kentmere Hall is a 16c farm with a 14c pele tower, which Turner sketched in 1816. The 30-foot long chimney beam above the kitchen fireplace was lifted into position single-handed by Hugh Herd, a giant of a man and a champion wrestler, who served King Edward VI in his Border battles and demonstrated his great strength to the King at court. Hugh, known as the Cork Lad, went to live at Troutbeck Park with his mother, a nun from Furness, who was deposed by the Dissolution of the Monasteries.

The Hall was the home of Richard Gilpin, whose claim to fame was for killing at Crook what was said to have been the last wild boar in England.

It was also the home of the Rev. Bernard Gilpin, who became Bishop of Durham. As an early Protestant reformer he ventured into remote areas, preaching and giving alms, earning for himself the title 'The Apostle of the North'. For attacking the Roman Catholic Church he was ordered to London to face charges which would have led to a trial and perhaps to burning at the stake for heresy. On his journey he fell and broke his leg. He was delayed by his convalescence during which time Queen Mary ('Bloody' Mary) died. Her successor, the Protestant Queen Elizabeth, restored him to favour.

<u>Garburn Pass</u> leads to Troutbeck
Old Roads of Eastern Lakeland:

Garburn Pass	4.2	Ill Bell	2.4
Sallows	2.2, 3	Sour Howes	2.2, 3
Yoke	2.5, 6		

<u>Kentmere Reservoir</u>. A gated road from the church leads to Hartrigg, the last farm in the valley. Beyond, a rough quarry road passes the towering cliffs of Rainsborrow Crag with an adit at its base. Across the valley, beneath Tongue Scar, are the remains of an ancient settlement. Disused quarries and spoil heaps make a desolate scene. On the opposite side of the river is a return path to the village.

Kentmere

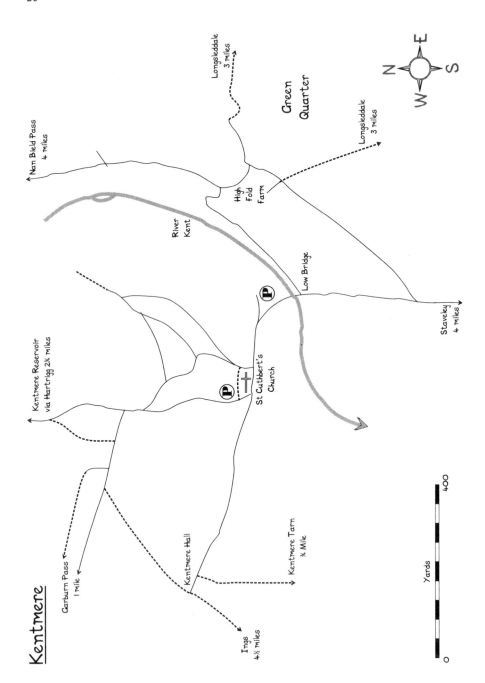

Nan Bield Pass
4 miles

Longsleddale
3 miles

Green
Quarter

Longsleddale
3 miles

High
Fold
Farm

River
Kent

Low Bridge

Staveley
4 miles

Kentmere Reservoir
via Hartrigg 2¼ miles

St Cuthbert's
Church

Garburn Pass
1 mile

Kentmere Hall

Kentmere Tarn
¾ Mile

Ings
4½ miles

N W E S

Yards

0   400

High Street   2.8
Mardale Ill Bell   2.6

The reservoir has a superb location overlooked by the peaks of High Street. The upper drainage basin receives the full effect of the rain-bearing south-westerly winds so the volume of water flow is considerable. The rock step and glacial features were masked when the dam was constructed in 1848 to regulate the variations in the flow of water in the River Kent for the benefit of the fifteen mill owners who were then in Kentdale, including James Cropper at his Burneside paper mill.

Ill Bell   2.5
Thornthwaite Crag   2.6

<u>Nan Bield Pass</u> leads to Mardale and Haweswater.

A return to Kentmere may be made via Gatescarth Pass, Longsleddale and Stile End.

Old Roads of East Lakeland:
Nan Bield Pass   49
Harter Fell   2.6
Kentmere Pike   2.5

<u>The Green Quarter</u> lies to the east of the village and is reached by a steep winding road.

Green Quarter Fell   OFOL 14
Shipman Knotts   2.2
Old Roads of Eastern Lakeland:
Kentmere to Longsleddale
     (Direct)   45
Kentmere to Longsleddale
     (Green Quarter)   47

Longsleddale

[OE.ON. Long Valley.]

Leave Kendal on the A6 towards Shap.

Skelsmergh area. [ON. Dairy farm of Skjaldmar] Drumlins abound on this glaciated lowland.

After four miles, turn left down a narrow road.
Almost immediately the whole of Longsleddale comes into view.
Garnett Bridge at the entrance to Longsleddale is on the River Sprint which once powered nine water mills along its course. The valley road, one lane only, is six miles long with a change of scene at each undulation. The old and original road up the valley lies to the west of the river.

Longsleddale. The River Sprint from its source at Wren Gill flows over Borrowdale Volcanic rocks to Silurian slate country. Features of a glaciated valley are visible as the river passes through a succession of former glacial lake basins with intervening breaks coinciding with rock bars or morainic ridges.

The valley is narrower than Kentmere and the fells on both sides rise to 2,000 feet giving protection to the scattered farms below.

The rural scene is totally unspoilt in spite of Manchester Corporation's aqueduct from Haweswater, built in the 1940s, and buried along the eastern side of the valley. Thirty years later, the

22

proposal for a second aqueduct alongside the first was successfully resisted. All would have changed, however, had not the motorway planners reconsidered when thinking of Longsleddale as the route for the M6.

Longsleddale became 'Greendale' in the *Postman Pat* series of children's books by John Cunliffe.

<u>Nether House Farm</u> is one of a series of 17c farms which occupy the valley and accommodate the sparse population. Behind it, the pastures are full of uncleared boulders, glacial erratics and bracken, typical of pre-medieval times.

The old farms of <u>Murthwaite</u> and <u>Bridge End</u> are located on a distinct bench on the old valley floor well above the eroded lower river level. The river flows over a rock bar in a small gorge.

Beyond Bridge End, where once was a lake basin, the open landscape, with hay fields on the valley floor, merges into deciduous woods on the slopes. This is the soft landscape of Silurian rock with relatively smooth, green slopes and only occasional rock outcrops.

<u>High House</u> has a mock pele tower.

<u>Kilnstones</u> was for centuries a wayside halt for drovers, packmen and traders who used the valley route to avoid paying tolls on the Shap turnpike. It was also the monastic route from Shap Abbey to Kendal and an abbey corn mill stood here. Some of the abbey stone remains in the garden wall.

<u>Yewbarrow Hall</u> (Ubarrow Hall) [*OE. Hill where ewes are pastured*], the oldest accommodation in the valley, is a fortified 'statesman' farm with a modified 15c pele tower built for protection against the Scots and the cattle raiders.

<u>St Mary's Chapel</u> half way up the valley, on a medieval site, was a

chapel of Kendal until 1712 when it was rebuilt and given parochial status. The present church dates from 1863. Amongst the treasures preserved from the earlier chapels are a silver chalice dated 1577, one of the oldest in England, and a carved oak door dated 1662, possibly off a spice or salt cupboard.

The chapel, like the old school, stands on a rock bar plastered with moraine extending across the valley floor. Upstream was once a large lake basin.

<u>Wad's Howe Farm</u> is situated on side moraine which crosses the valley floor restricting the former lake basin.

<u>High Swinklebank</u> has a massive byre and the remnants of an overhanging verandah.

<u>Stockdale</u>. A solitary farm occupies this side valley closed at its head by Grey Crag and watered by Stockdale Beck. Moraine covered the lower fell slopes. A small lime kiln in the farmyard made use of the nearby outcrop of Coniston limestone.

The softer Silurian landscape now begins to give way to the older Borrowdale Volcanic rocks, a wilderness of crags, rock buttresses and massive screes.

<u>Sadgill</u>. [*ON. Ravine where there are upland pastures.*] This is the highest settlement in the valley and the end of the macadam road.

The farms are built on moraine and screened by broad leaf woodlands. Two of the oak woods in the valley are classified as being of scientific interest. They are the remnants of the primeval mixed oak forest which once covered this area.

Traces of a small common field are discernible on the valley floor behind and above the moraine which is piled against the rock bar.

Old Roads of Eastern Lakeland:

Kentmere to Longsleddale

(Direct)   45

Kentmere to Longsleddale

(Green Quarter)   47

Grey Crag   2.4

Shipman Knotts   2.2

Tarn Crag   2.3, 4

Beyond Sadgill. The flat valley floor marks the site of another temporary glacial lake. Where the River Sprint has been artificially straightened to prevent flooding the rich alluvial soil can be cultivated. A wall built as a dam stopped debris brought down by the river from spilling over onto the fields. The reservoir planned for Longsleddale in 1845 to regulate the water supply to the mills proved too costly to build after the expense of Kentmere. Goat Scar and Buckbarrow Crag now dominate the valley.

Kentmere Pike   2.6

Valley Head. For 500 feet the track rises over a rock step, roughly paved against the slope on the steeper part to provide horses with a more secure footing. This is a wilderness area of rocks and fallen boulders.

Wren Gill, the source of the River Sprint, cascades as a waterfall from the slopes of Harter Fell into Wrengill Quarry.

Wrengill Quarry, an immense complex, produced roofing slate for two hundred years. Italian prisoners of war were the last to work in the quarry.

Surface features have collapsed but adits and tunnels are still visible in the cliff faces.

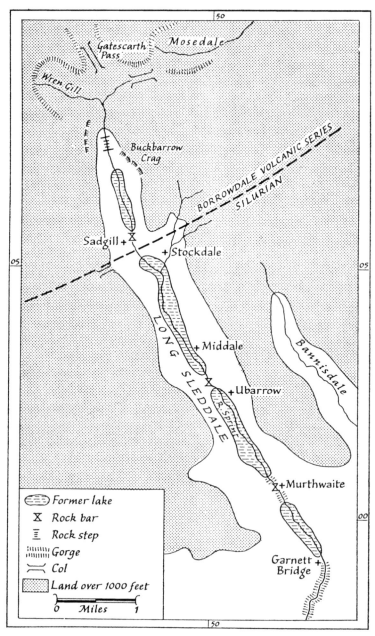

Landscape Features of Long Sleddale. Acknowledgement:
The Lake District, R. Millward & A.Robinson. Eyre & Spottiswoode

Col to Mosedale
Old Roads of Eastern Lakeland:
  Longsleddale to Wet Sleddale
    and Shap   57

Gatescarth Pass to Mardale and Haweswater.
Old Roads of Eastern Lakeland:
  Gatescarth Pass   54
  Branstree   2.5
  Harter Fell   2.7

The Valleys of Shap Fells

The Shap Fells of eastern Lakeland extend over a desolate, inhospitable area of forty square miles, crossed only by an old packhorse trail.

This lofty, silent, barren moorland is uninviting, uninhabited and unfrequented, except by creatures of the wild. Streams descend from the heights between the ridges which take shape as the central plateau declines eastwards. These become the valleys of Shap Fells accessible from the A6 Kendal to Shap highway.

Bannisdale

[ON. Bannandr's Valley – nickname meaning 'the man who curses'.]

Leave Kendal on the A6 towards Shap.
After five miles turn left into a narrow lane.

This narrow lane overlays the original road to Scotland. From Plough Farm, once a hostelry but now replaced by the Plough Inn on the A6, a grassy track continues to Bannisdale High Bridge and beyond. Nearby, Lowbridge House, in an attractive setting, was once the home of the Fothergill family, well known for their private coach and team of horses.

From Plough Farm, follow the vehicle road north to reach Bannisdale Beck at Dryhowe Bridge. The beck, originating from

Bannisdale Fell, eventually becomes a tributary of the River Mint, which in turn joins the River Kent before reaching Morecambe Bay.

Two ancient settlements stand above the valley floor. Below Lamb Pasture is a level platform with a parapet enclosing the remains of hut circles (OS 533020). At Dryhowe Pasture is further evidence of ancient habitation (OS 520028).

A farm access road continues up the valley for two miles through an empty and austere landscape to Bannisdale Head where a huge boulder, 'the Bannisdale Cobble', stands immovable by the farm door.

Manchester Corporation was deterred from building a dam and turning this secluded valley with but two farms into a reservoir.

Grey Crag   *2.5*
The Bannisdale Horseshoe   *OFOL 260*
Old Roads of Eastern Lakeland:
The Old Road over Shap
    Fells   *61*

Borrowdale
(Westmorland)

[ON. Valley of the fort.]
Access to Borrowdale by road is from the A6,
a mile south of Huck's Bridge.

In the vicinity was the Leyland clock, named after the advertisement it carried. It stood in isolation on an iron framework but its use-fulness declined when the M6 took traffic away. Now it enjoys a new life in the grounds of the Brewery Arts Centre in Kendal.

At <u>Huck's Bridge</u>, which spans Borrow Beck, the largest and the longest stream draining eastwards from Shap Fells, the A6 cuts

Borrowdale into two contrasting parts.

Grey Crag   2.6
The Crookdale Horseshoe   OFOL 254
Old Roads of Eastern Lakeland:
The Old Road Over
    Shap Fells   64

Upper Borrowdale

A little way upstream from Huck's Bridge is the confluence of Crookdale Beck with Borrow Beck.

High Borrow Bridge carried the old road to Shap summit. A section of this old road was surfaced to facilitate the construction of the second Haweswater aqueduct but has since been little used.

A farm access road up the valley leads to Borrowdale Head and High House Farm, beyond which is wild, desolate and marshy moorland, where Borrow Beck rises at 1,600 feet. Sheep roam the high fells and the occasional red deer strays over from Martindale.

Lower Borrowdale

The lower valley from Huck's Bridge is outside the National Park boundary. The landscape gradually changes from austere surroundings to a more gentle and, later, a more wooded terrain. The riverside track from Huck's Bridge passes High Borrowdale and Low Borrowdale to reach the Lune Gorge, with the incessant roar of motorway traffic. Borrow Beck is spanned by four bridges before it joins the River Lune.

Where Lower Borrowdale joins the Lune valley the Romans built a fort. Its name is unknown but Low Borrow Bridge is the site, between the old road and the railway, beneath Casterfell Hill, overlooking the Lune valley. The fort was on the route from Chester to Carlisle and a section of the line of the Roman road is well preserved south of Low Borrow Bridge on the eastern side of the Lune Valley.

Crookdale

[ON. Bend in the Dale.]

Access to Crookdale by road is from the A6 Borrowdale turn, a mile south of Huck's Bridge.

Cross High Borrow Bridge and follow Crookdale Beck for a further mile to Hause Foot. This is the only farmstead in Crookdale. Here, the second Haweswater aqueduct (from Wet Sleddale) emerges from its tunnel beneath Shap Fells and continues as a pipeline to the treatment plant at Watchgate.

Crookdale Bridge carries the old road up to the old road summit on Shap Fells at 1,460 feet. This is higher than the A6 summit at 1,397 feet.

Grey Crags	2.6	
The Wasdale Horseshoe	OFOL 248	
Old Roads of Eastern Lakeland:		
The Old Road Over		
Shap Fells	67	

Upstream is pathless, unfrequented and swampy. Although Crookdale Beck and Borrow Beck rise in the same lofty, wet wilderness, a dividing ridge keeps them apart until Crookdale beck lives up to its name and makes a wide southerly bend to meet its neighbour at High Borrow Bridge.

Wasdale
(Westmorland)
[ON. Valley with a lake.]

Upper Wasdale

Access to upper Wasdale is from the A6, a little more than a mile north of Shap summit.

Take the Shap Pink Quarry (Granite) road and continue further to the farm at Wasdale Head.

There are no tracks alongside Wasdale Beck across the desolate and deserted upland to its headwaters at Great Yarlside. On the summit, the Ordnance survey triangulation point is not the usual column but a circular metal plate sunk into the ground.

Lower Wasdale

Wasdale Beck leaves the National Park when it flows under the A6 at Wasdale Bridge on its way to Shap Wells and the Lune Valley.

Wasdale Old Bridge across Wasdale Beck carries the old road. To the south on the old road is Packhorse Hill, and a ruin, named Demmings on a map dated 1770. This may have been an inn or staging post after the long climb.

To the north, the old road continues through an afforested area only to become lost in the Shap Granite Works on the railway summit.

> The Wasdale Horseshoe   OFOL 248
> The Old Roads of Eastern Lakeland:
> The Old Road Over
>   Shap Fells   67

Lowther Valley

[ON. Foaming river.]

From the A6.

<u>Wet Sleddale</u> was acquired by the Manchester Water Authority to supplement the water supply from Haweswater. The dam is massive compared with the size of the reservoir.

After draining the upper reaches of the valley, the Sleddale Beck flows into the reservoir from which the River Lowther emerges. The river then continues its journey for fifteen miles in a northerly direction to Brougham and the River Eamont.

A unique Lakeland feature in the valley above the reservoir alongside Sleddale Beck, between Sherry Gill and Tonguerigg Gill, is the medieval deer trap. Although derelict, it is a grassy enclosure with walls ten to twelve feet high and only one entrance. It was used as a living larder by the early settlers, but there are no deer in this locality today.

> *The Wet Sleddale Horseshoe OFOL 242*
> *Old Roads of Eastern Lakeland:*
> *Longsleddale to Wet*
> *   Sleddale   57*

<u>Shap Neolithic Stone Circles</u>, c. 3000 BC.

<u>The First circle</u> (OS 567133) by the A6, a mile south of Shap, was originally 80 feet across. The granite stones which remain, 8 feet to 9 feet long, have fallen. This is the circle which some experts link with the avenue of stones extending north west to the <u>Thunder Stone</u> (OS 552157).

<u>The Second circle</u> (OS 568178) by the M6, north of Shap, consists of a mound incorporating a stone ring 52 feet across, of which one stone remains upright, and an outer ring of stones, 105 feet across, of which three are standing. A cist was found in the centre of the site.

<u>The Third circle</u> (OS 550184) two miles north of Shap, overlooking Shap Beck Quarry, has a diameter of 50 feet and 32 small stones.

Old Roads of Eastern Lakeland:
The Old Road Over
    Shap Fells   *61*

<u>The Shap Wells Hotel</u> was owned by the Earl of Lonsdale when it was requisitioned and transformed into a Prisoner of War Camp (No. 15) early in 1941. Security was naturally tight, but if officers gave their word of honour not to attempt to escape, walking on neighbouring fells was permitted. The ultimate destination of the 100–150 German officers was shipment from Glasgow to POW camps in Canada.

Two young Luftwaffe officers had ideas of their own. Oberleutnant Karl Wappler and Lt Heinz Schnabel painstakingly adapted their uniforms to resemble those of Dutch pilots. Skilfully they equipped themselves with identity papers, maps, meteorological charts and wind atlases. Their imaginative intention was to steal a plane and fly home.

After hiding in a stack of firewood to await nightfall, they jumped onto a slow moving freight train in Shap's deep railway cutting and alighted at Carlisle. They visited a cinema before heading for Kingstown airfield where the sentry was deceived by their 'Dutch' uniform and let them through.

The night was spent in hiding but next day the pair persuaded a young mechanic of their need to take up a Miles Magister trainer monoplane on a weather reconnaissance flight. They flew 325 miles before landing in a field near Great Yarmouth. It was vital to refuel for the North Sea crossing but too late in the day, it being November, to arrange an immediate take off. Luck ran out when they were received at RAF Horsham St Faith and were arrested whilst taking hot baths. Military Police returned them to Shap where they were sentenced to 28 days confinement.

Shap

[OE. Heap of stones (i.e. adjacent stone circles)]

This remote, 18c, moorland village, just below the summit of Shap Fell, 1,397 feet, grew to become a communications centre on the main north south route, from Scotland to England, for road and rail.

The wild and windswept fells have always proved difficult for travellers in bad weather and many lorry drivers have been stranded in snow drifts on the A6. The M6 motorway, opened in 1970, avoided as much of the higher ground as possible.

On the other hand, John Ruskin welcomed the bleak, exposed landscape: '*Ever since I passed Shap fells, when a child, I have an excessive love for this kind of desolation.*'

<u>Granite Quarries</u>. Shap is dominated by the quarry workings south of the village. The pink granite, flecked with white mica, glistens in

the sunshine and was used in such buildings as St Pancras Station and the Albert Memorial. Shap village is largely built of limestone because it is more easily worked.

The main street, on the busy A6 to Scotland, became much quieter when the M6 motorway was opened. The street is a mile long and flanked by several attractive 17c and 18c houses and inns.

Stuart House, 1671, in mid-village, near the Kings Arms, is a reminder of the 'Inne at Shape' where a very weary Charles Edward Stuart, 'Bonnie Prince Charlie', slept during his retreat from Derby to Scotland in 1745. He spent £4-7s. on 'ale, wine and other provisions and two guineas to the landlady – a sad wife – for imposing, for the Use of her House.' His pursuers were only a few hours behind.

The Market Hall, 1690, has semi-circular windows with diamond-shaped panes. It is now used as a library.

Shap's market charter, granted as late as 1687 permitted a weekly market (Wednesday) and three fairs a year.

The Parish Church of St Michael dates from the 13c and retains some of its Norman features in the structure of the south arcade.

This was the mother church of Mardale's chapel and the burial ground for those who died in Mardale prior to 1729. Before Mardale was submerged beneath Haweswater, St Michael's cemetery at Shap had to be extended to receive the exhumed remains of those buried in Mardale since 1729.

A churchyard memorial dated 1846, at the right of the main entrance gates, is dedicated to the men who died working on the Lancaster to Carlisle Railway, across the wilds of Shap Fell, and opened in the year of the memorial.

The minor road from Shap to Keld breaks through a line of stones which extends north-west from OS 562147 to the Thunder Stone, recumbent at OS 552157 and includes the Goggleby Stone at OS

559150. One theory suggests that the line of stones is the remains of an avenue leading to the first stone circle, OS 567133, alongside the A6, a mile south of Shap.

<u>Keld</u>. This riverside village has a common for the traditional rearing of ducks and geese.

<u>The 16c Chapel</u> (NT) was possibly built by the monks of Shap Abbey. The partition wall and fireplace are relics of the days when the Chapel was used as a cottage. With wooden benches and no electricity, the facilities are basic and plain for the one service held each year in August.

A field path leads to Shap Abbey.

<u>Shap Abbey of St Mary Magdalen</u>. The ruins stand in the wooded Lowther Valley one mile from Shap village.

The origins of the abbey date back to 1191 when Thomas Gospatrick founded a religious community of Premonstratensian (white) canons at Preston Patrick near Kendal. A move to Shap was made in 1201 and the construction of the abbey began.

The canons, seldom more than twelve in number, lived a life of prayer with the discipline of monks. They were followers of St Norbert and ruled from Prémontré in France to where the prior had to make an arduous annual journey to give a report. The economy of the order was based on wool which found favour with Italian cloth merchants.

In 1540, Henry VIII dissolved the organisation. The monks were granted a pension of £4 to £6 per annum. With neglect the buildings fell into disrepair and ruin. The only part of the abbey standing today is the impressive west tower commissioned by Abbot Richard Redman. The foundations of the other buildings convey an idea of their size and layout. When the abbey ruins became part of the Lowther estate, many of the abbey stones were removed for the building of Lowther Castle. In the walls of the farm alongside the remains of the abbey, carved fragments of stone are visible. Further decay was arrested when the Ministry of Works took over in 1948. English Heritage is the custodian today.

The abbey had several unique claims. It was the only abbey in the former county of Westmorland; the only abbey in a mountainous area of the National Park; the last abbey to be founded and the last to be dissolved. The delay in its dissolution may have been due to its usefulness as a refuge for travellers crossing the exposed fells.

Rosgill [*ON. Ravine where horses go.*] Following the Dissolution, abbey-lands at Hegdale were purchased by Richard Washington of the famous Washington family, kinsfolk of the American line.

Mary's Pillar, the obelisk on the heights above Rosgill, was erected in 1854 by a father in remembrance of his daughter who died at the age of twenty-four.

Swindale [*ON. Valley of the swine*] lies in the valley parallel with neighbouring Mardale, separated from it by a high ridge.

The only approach road over featureless moorland crosses the private waterworks road linking the reservoirs of Wet Sleddale and Haweswater. Water extracted from Swindale Beck unobtrusively passes through a tunnel to Haweswater.

Swindale Head is the terminus for vehicles, but parking is not always possible. Here, the Old Corpse Road from Mardale crosses on its way to Shap. This scenic and peaceful locality is unspoilt and unfrequented.

Further upstream, through an area of drumlins, a large, natural amphitheatre is revealed, where the beck from Mosedale cascades down a rocky ravine in a series of waterfalls. Mosedale Beck [ON. Valley of peat moss, or bog] on the descent changes its name to Swindale Beck in the valley.

Selside Pike   2.5
The Naddle Horseshoe   OFOL 224
Howes   OFOL 230
Seat Robert   OFOL 236
Old Roads of Eastern Lakeland:
Swindale to Mosedale
          Quarry   40

<u>Bampton Grange</u> [OE. farmstead by a tree on monastic land.] Cross the bridges which span the River Lowther, Haweswater Beck and Hawes Beck.

<u>St Patrick's Church</u>, 18c, is one of only two churches in Cumbria dedicated to this saint. (See: Patterdale). The first mention of a place of worship on this site was in 1170 when it was attached to Shap Abbey whose canons often took the service. By 1291, Bampton was already a parish in its own right.

The interior is remarkable for its double row of oak pillars.

An oil painting shows the Revd. John Bowstead (1754–1841) for 56 years master of Bampton Grammar School and 40 years minister of Mardale Church. He taught Latin and Greek which enabled him to direct as many as two hundred boys into the priesthood. Local people remarked, 'They drove the plough in Latin at Bampton'.

The water colour is of Mardale Church in winter. Before Mardale Church was submerged beneath the waters of Haweswater Reservoir, the fittings were dispersed for preservation. At Bampton are the altar candlesticks and the brass sconces above the choir stalls.

The former Grammar School, founded in 1623, stands next to the church and is now the Church Hall.

Bampton. When Mardale was engulfed by the waters of the reservoir, Bampton became host to Mardale's traditional events. St Patrick's Well Inn replaced Mardale's Dun Bull for such occasions as the Mardale Hunt Dinner and the Shepherds' Meet.

Loadpot Hill	*2.9*
Wether Hill	*2.8*
Knipescar Common	*OFOL 220*

Turn towards Haweswater Reservoir.

This is Carboniferous Limestone country, heavily covered with boulder clay. Grey stone walls and ash trees are a common feature.

Thornthwaite Hall was built as the family home of the Curwens in the 16c. It is thought to be Vavasor Hall in Anthony Trollope's novel, 'Can You Forgive Her?'

Thornthwaite Force, on Haweswater Beck, is reached from Naddle Bridge by a path to Park Bridge.

Haweswater

[ON. Hafr's Lake]

The U-shaped valley of Mardale, with an over-deepened lake, formed the largest reservoir in north-west England when a dam, 120 feet high and 1,550 feet long, was completed at its eastern end in 1940, by Manchester Corporation. It was the first hollow buttress dam to be built.

The enlargement of the lake from 2½ miles to 4 miles in length, ¾ mile to ½ mile in width, and 102 feet to 198 feet in depth, has the additional advantage of being 694 feet above sea-level. This altitude makes the supply of water to places 80 or 90 miles away much less difficult.

At the dam, the octagonal intake well was constructed using stone from the windows of Mardale Church. A tunnel connects with the aqueduct buried on the eastern side of Long Sleddale.

Before the flooding of the valley, Wordsworth described it as 'a *lesser Ullswater*'. After the flooding, Mardale was bitterly described as '*plunged up to the waist in cold water*'. The concrete edge around the shoreline aroused further disapproval.

Anglers still fish for brown trout and char; birdwatchers hope to spot a golden eagle.

Naddle Forest [*ON. Wedge-shaped valley*] is a relict native woodland consisting mostly of oak, sycamore and beech. The quiet valley of Naddle Beck is explored in *The Naddle Horseshoe, OFOL 224.*

Wallow Crag features in the local tale of Robert Lowther, a landowner and a rogue, who refused to stay in his coffin. He was banished by the priest to lie under the crag – the only stone big enough to keep him down!

Measand Beck, across the water, is a hanging valley with a water-fall, ending in a submerged torrent fan of gravel and boulders projecting far into the lake, almost severing it in two.

The Haweswater Hotel, built by Manchester Corporation to replace Mardale's Dun Bull, has an old, black pew from the demolished Mardale Church.

At Birks Crag across the water, below *High Raise (2.7, 8)* is an Iron Age hill fort. (500 BC.)

Hopgil Beck is the start of the Old Corpse Road to Swindale and Shap.

Old Roads of Eastern Lakeland:
The Corpse Road: Mardale

Green to Shap   30

At <u>Mardale Head</u> are the headwaters of High Street, Mardale Ill Bell [OE. ON. Bell-shaped hill] and Harter Fell [ON. Fell with deer.] Car park.

<u>Mountain Passes</u>

Detailed itineraries appear in *Old Roads of Eastern Lakeland*.

1.	*The Corpse Road: Mardale Green to Shap*	30
2.	*Gatescarth Pass to Longsleddale*	54
3.	*Nan Bield Pass to Kentmere*	49

<u>Mardale Head</u>

Branstree	*2.5*
Harter Fell	*2.8*
High Raise	*2.7*
High Street	*2.6*
Kidsty Pike	*2.3*
Mardale Ill Bell	*2.5*
Rampsgill Head	*2.6*

Gatescarth Pass (Harter Fell 2.8), Mosedale Beck, Swindale Head, Old Corpse Road, Mardale.

Mardale

[OE. Valley with a lake]

This remote and secluded valley supported a community of sheep and dairy farmers. As much as 3,000 lbs of butter were being sent each week from Mardale to Manchester using the newly established railways.

There was a 17c inn, the Dun Bull, a tiny church and a school.

The 'kings' of Mardale were self-appointed. The first was Hugh Holme, suspected of plotting against King John in 1209 and forced to take refuge in a cave above Riggindale. He remained an outlaw until after King John's death in 1216. Hugh then became a law unto himself and created a dynasty known as the 'Kings of Mardale', which lasted until 1885.

The Dun Bull, 17c, was once host to the Mardale Hunt and the Shepherds' Meet when lost sheep were rounded up in the autumn and returned to their owners. It was a time to make merry! The inn was demolished in 1936 before the village was flooded.

Mardale Holy Trinity Church occupied the site of a much older oratory founded by the monks of Shap Abbey. Mardale was the daughter chapel to the mother church at Shap. Originally, Mardale Church had no burial ground and coffins had to be transported by packhorses along the Old Corpse Road via Swindale and Keld for burial at Shap. A burial ground for Mardale was granted in 1729 and consequently over 100 corpses had to be exhumed and re-buried in an extended cemetery at Shap before Mardale Church was demolished and submerged.

The church held sixty people.

Buried in Mardale's churchyard was Thomas Holme, the deaf man Wordsworth wrote about in *The Excursion. Book VII.*

On one occasion, at the third reading of the marriage bans, a young bride-to-be and her father were the only people present and so the reading was not legal. The sympathetic vicar dashed out and ordered another person to attend the reading to enable the formalities to be completed correctly.

Relics from the Mardale Church were widely scattered, many into the safe keeping of other Cumbrian churches.

In the exceptionally dry summer of 1984, the water level dropped so low that the ruins of the drowned village of Mardale were revealed. Visitors flocked to see the eerie scene. Former inhabitants of the village were interviewed for radio and television. It became possible to walk over an old stone bridge and around ruined walls which had remained submerged for nearly half a century. There have been similar occasions more recently.

Burn Banks was the woodland base for the hundreds of workmen engaged in the construction of the Haweswater dam. The former valley road from Burn Banks to Mardale Green, and the large house and school it passed at Measand, are now submerged beneath the waters of the reservoir but, at a higher level, a footpath from the dam continues along the western shore to Mardale Head, a distance of four to five miles.

Wether Hill   2.8

Cawdale. Return to Bampton, where Cawdale Beck from the slopes of Wether Hill and Loadpot Hill joins the River Lowther.

Towtop Kirk (OS. 494179). The minor road uphill west from Bampton gives access to this Iron Age (500 BC) settlement overlooking Cawdale Beck. Surrounding the site is an oval wall enclosing an area 55 yards by 42 yards. At the centre is the outline of a U-shaped hut, with a second enclosure to the east. Obscured traces of a second hut are visible to the north-west, near the entrance to the enclosure.

> Wether Hill   2.8
> Continue along the Lowther Valley.

Whale. [ON. Isolated, rounded hill] On the opposite side of the river is the site of a former open field. Estate cottages indicate the presence of Lowther Park.

Helton [OE. Farmstead on the slope] is a linear settlement of stone cottages surrounded by dry-stone walled pastures.

Heltondale Beck supplies Haweswater reservoir by an aqueduct, the surplus water joining the River Lowther.

A minor road climbs out of the village to open country where cars may be parked on the grass verge.

Moor Divock [Br. OE. Dyfog's Moor] The fell track from the Helton road crosses Roman High Street at 1,050 feet, at the site of the chief Bronze Age settlement (1500 BC) in the region. This is an area of great antiquity.

Cop Stone (OS 495216) is thought to be all that remains of a former stone circle. It stands 5 feet tall.

Sink or swallow holes occur where the underlying limestone has fractured and collapsed, due to water action, resulting in small surface craters.

Tumuli indicate ancient burial sites.

'The Cockpit' (OS 483223) is thought to be the weathered ruin of a Romano-British upland settlement, the remains of a walled enclosure that once contained a compact settlement of huts. Its presence caused a diversion of the paved High Street.

Loadpot Hill   *2.3, 7, 8, 9, 10*
The Old Roads of Eastern Lakeland:
The Road Across Moor Divock 21

Continue north along the Lowther Valley.

Askham [ON. *Settlement among ash trees*] is a most attractive village on the hill slope between Askham Fell and the River Lowther.

The village was bought by the Lowther Estates in 1724 as part of an investment programme and a number of residents work for the Lowthers.

The mile long single street is lined on both sides by spacious grassy areas with a scattering of mature trees. The 17c and 18c limestone houses and cottages integrate into a pleasing scene. Two pubs serve the village: the Queens Head, dated 1682, and The Punch-bowl.

St Peter's Church, formerly St Columba's, by the river, is an 1838 replacement built on the foundations of a demolished 13c church. The original south transept was built by the Sandfords of Askham Hall as a family burial chapel. Its replacement is now the baptistry with a 1661 stone font.

Askham Hall was a 14c pele tower, enlarged into an Elizabethan mansion in 1574 by Thomas Sandford and castellated and turreted during later additions. The hall became a rectory in 1828. More recently, with the disrepair of Lowther Castle, Askham Hall became the Lowther family home for a time. Hackthorpe Hall is another Lowther residence. Huge trees screen Askham Hall which is within walking distance of Lowther Castle.

Askham Fell, above the village, has two deserted Romano-British village settlements enclosed by stone and earth banks and an exten-

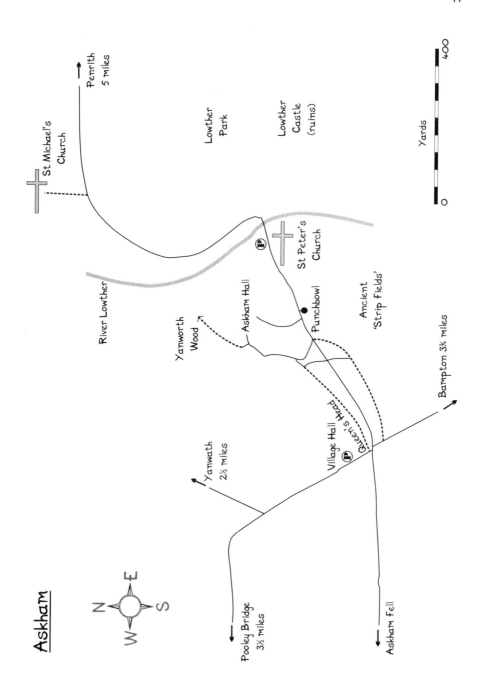

Askham

St Michael's Church

Pemrith 5 miles

River Lowther

Lowther Park

Lowther Castle (ruins)

St Peter's Church

Yanwath Wood

Askham Hall

Punchbowl

Ancient 'Strip Fields'

Yanwath 2¼ miles

Village Hall

Queen's Head

Bampton 3¾ miles

Pooley Bridge 3½ miles

Askham Fell

Yards

0   400

sive system of lynchets: OS 499234 and OS 497232.

Loadpot Hill	*2.8*
Heughscar Hill OFOL	*216*

Old Roads of Eastern Lakeland:
The Road Across Moor
            Divock.   *21*

Continue north from Askham towards Yanwath. [OE. Flat or level woodland.]

Castlesteads (OS 518252) is approached from Lowclose. This Iron Age (c. 500 BC) site in Yanwath Wood is a quarter of an acre in extent, bounded by three concentric banks and two ditches. The interior is divided into several small enclosures.

Yanwath Settlement (OS. 519260), to the north of Yanwath Wood, is of similar age. It is roughly D-shaped with a ditch and bank about 250 yards long forming the straight side. The north-western entrance is protected by two banks and a ditch. Inside the defence systems are several small enclosures.

The Lowther Estate

For a view of the Lowther Estate, return to Askham, cross the River Lowther and stop at St Michael's Church.

Across the parkland stands ruined Lowther Castle which prospered and declined according to the wealth and spending strategies of its owners. To the first pele tower in the 14c, was added a second tower in the 16c, followed by the replacement of the central section between the towers in the 17c, badly gutted by fire in the 18c and rebuilt in the 19c.

During the Lowther's most affluent era, Lowther Castle, a great castellated mansion, was built, 1804–14, to replace the fire damaged Lowther Hall. Shap Abbey stone was incorporated by the architect, Sir Robert Smirke, who was later to design the British Museum and King's College, London. The symmetrical, turreted north front was 420 feet long and the interior was equally palatial and luxurious.

A frequent visitor was Wordsworth, who wrote of the castle in 1833:

> 'Lowther! in thy majestic Pile are seen
> Cathedral pomp and grace, in apt accord
> With the baronial castle's sterner mien . . .'

With the decline in the Lowther family fortunes came the deterioration of the castle. It was finally abandoned in 1936 and partially demolished in 1958 after a fire. Today, the castle stands roofless and forlorn, a hollow shell set in a majestic landscape. It functions only as an impressive backdrop to the renowned Lowther Horse Trials and Country Fair held here each August.

Since the castle fell into ruin, heads of the Lowther family have lived at Askham Hall and Hackthorpe Hall, west and east of Lowther Park respectively.

Off the tree-lined avenue leading from near the church to the ruined castle, vague rectangular shapes of the foundations of demolished Lowther village cottages may be discerned.

The Parish Church of St Michael is the Lowther Estate Church. There is a theory that a dedication to St Michael, who overcame the forces of evil, indicates that the site was perhaps once a place of pagan worship.

In the porch, the pre-Norman remains include Norse hogback

stone coffins and the shaft of a Saxon cross.

Over the centuries, three churches have been superimposed, one upon the other.

The Norman church is revealed by the arcade of pillars and arches on the north side, together with the bases of pillars in the crossing and part of the chancel. Splendidly carved details on some capitals are in contrast with the rough finish on others. One pillar depicts the crushed face of a man at its base.

The 13c church is evident in the south arcade of pillars, the two transepts and the clerestory.

The 17c church was the work of Sir John Lowther IV c. 1686. The outer walls and windows were rebuilt creating a 17c shell around an ancient interior. The tower was raised and the reredos, Sanctuary panels, Communion rails, font and bell were added.

The Lowthers included the gallery in the 18c, followed in the 19c by the porch, the vestry and the raising of the tower by a further storey.

Something of the Lowther's family history is revealed by the many church memorials in contrasting styles.

The origin of the Lowther family in Westmorland is unknown. The name Lowther was first recorded in 1157 in reference to the river. There is documentary evidence that a Lowther lived in the village during the reign of Henry II (1154–1189) at the time (c. 1170) when the oldest part of the present church was being built.

South Transept

One of the sword crosses carved in the floor is possibly marking the grave slab of <u>Sir Hugh De Lowther</u> (c. 1250–1317), Attorney to Edward I in 1291. Since then, and continuing to the present day, every generation of Lowthers, with but two exceptions, has taken a significant part in county and national affairs.

It is believed that <u>Sir Hugh De Lowther III</u> (d.c. 1366) replaced the early family dwelling at Lowther by a pele tower, c. 1350, at the time of the campaigns against the Scots by Edward II (1307–1327) and Edward III (1327–1377) and the Scottish reprisals. Additional to these wars was the deadly plague of the Black Death in 1348 and again in 1361.

<u>Sir Robert Lowther</u> (c. 1365–1430) has a memorial brass in the floor, with an epitaph in Latin verse.

<u>Sir Richard Lowther</u> (1532–1608) is represented by an alabaster effigy dressed in armour and surmounted by his family tree. He lived through the reigns of five monarchs, from Henry VIII to James I. In 1565, he conducted Mary Queen of Scots to Carlisle Castle and on her next journey, to Bolton Castle, she spent a night at Lowther Hall. Twice Sir Richard was suspected of association with Catholic conspirators who wished to depose Elizabeth and put Mary on the throne. On each occasion he was imprisoned in the Tower of London and later released. During his second term, a new west tower was added to Lowther Hall c. 1572.

As Lord Warden of the Western Marches, his epitaph reveals '*he was thrice a Commissioner of ye great affraye between England and Scotland all in ye time of Queene Elizabeth.*' His epitaph also shows him to have been a great family man who had '*seene his children to the fourth degree, giving them vertuous education and meanes to live*'.

<u>Sir John Lowther I</u> (1582–1637). His bust rests on the left of the 17c monument on the west wall of the transept.

The low state of the family fortune, as explained in his autobiography, was rectified by choosing a wealthy bride, Ellinor Fleming of Rydal Hall. He was able to demolish the old central section between the twin towers of Lowther Hall and replace in 1630 with a new, central, three-storey structure, surmounted by an ogival dome.

Sir John Lowther II (1606–1675) shares the monument with his father, represented by the bust on the right.

In 1638 he was created a Baronet, the first of his family to receive a hereditary title.

During the Civil War, he commanded a Royalist regiment for the defence of Westmorland and was fined by the Parliamentarians for doing so.

His diaries report on the exploits of his 17 children and the matrimonial prospects for his daughters.

John Lowther IV (1655–1700). His semi-reclining effigy shows him proudly holding the coronet he received when becoming the first Viscount Lonsdale in 1696.

He supported the Protestant revolt against the Catholic ruler James II in the 'Glorious Revolution' of 1688, when William of Orange was invited to deliver the country from its unpopular king and rule jointly with his wife, Mary, daughter of James II. On one dramatic occasion, a shipment of arms at Workington, destined for the Jacobites opposed to William of Orange, was captured by Sir John and his yeomanry.

When William was proclaimed king in 1689, honours were heaped on Sir John for his support. Additional to positions of high office of state, he served in William III's cabinet.

Rather than repair Lowther Hall, he commissioned a substantial replacement sumptuously decorated. To make room, the village between the new mansion and the church was demolished and its replacement sited some distance away at Lowther Newtown, where his carpet factory later became Lowther College and is now the Estate Office. He also restored the old Norman church.

The Lowthers of Whitehaven, from Sir Christopher, the second son of Sir John Lowther I and Ellinor Fleming, followed by Sir John and ending with the unmarried Sir James, all became baronets and were instrumental in the town's foundation and development as a seaport. Their wealth came from the efficient exploitation of their coal resources.

North Transept

Richard (1692–1713) and Henry (1694 –1751) 'the two brothers', the second and third Viscounts, are commemorated by a stone memorial with a Latin inscription erected in 1802.

Henry, as Deputy Lieutenant of Cumberland and Westmorland, commanded the militia that was ineffectual in resisting the Jacobite uprising in 1715. The rebels crossed the counties before surrendering at Preston.

When the 'Forty-Five' Jacobite Rebellion, led by Bonnie Prince Charlie, advanced south and then retreated north through the same area, Henry, now as Lord Lieutenant, blamed illness for staying in Yorkshire, at Byram, from where he sent news bulletins to London.

During each rebellion, Lowther Hall was occupied overnight by the rebels. But the greatest disaster was the fire in 1718 which gutted the central section of Lowther Hall within 30 years of its construction.

Henry never married and the title Viscount died with him. Fire-damaged Lowther Hall, all the family estates and the baronetcy were inherited by his young cousin, James Lowther of Maulds Meaburn.

Sir James Lowther, First Earl of Lonsdale (1736–1802), known as 'Wicked Jimmy', is commemorated by a memorial with an epitaph in Latin.

The joint wealth and property of Lowther and Whitehaven was his inheritance, making him perhaps the richest young man in the kingdom.

His ambition was to control all public appointments in Cumberland and Westmorland by exploiting the corruption of 18c elections. Variously he was described as tyrannical, ruthless and violent.

He employed John Wordsworth, father of the poet, as his estate and law agent, but failed to pay him. On John Wordsworth's death in 1783, the outstanding debt remained unpaid and the Wordsworth children, William, sister Dorothy and their three brothers were left impoverished.

Thomas De Quincey told the story that the Earl persuaded Betsy Lewes, a farmer's daughter to live with him. On her death, he had her embalmed under glass as he could not bear to be parted from her.

Sir James was created Earl of Lonsdale in 1784. He died without children and all the estates of Lowther and Whitehaven passed to the Swillington branch of the family in Yorkshire, founded by Sir William, the youngest son of Sir John Lowther I and Ellinor Fleming.

Sir William Lowther (1757–1844), First Earl of Lonsdale (a new creation in 1807) KG, known as 'William the Good', shares the memorial of a large marble tomb chest with his wife. Inscribed are the words, '*He was the ardent and zealous patron of men of genius and was the early and confidential friend of William Pitt.*'

He not only repaid 'Wicked Jimmy's' debt of £5,000 (£8,500 with interest) to the Wordsworth family, but he also arranged for William to be appointed Distributor of Stamps for Westmorland.

The Earl became Wordsworth's patron to whom William dedicated *The Excursion* in 1814 and an interminable poem, *Lowther Park*. The poet regularly visited the Lowthers and in 1834 he completed '*Lines Written in the Album of the Countess of Lonsdale.*' Befriended also by the Earl was John Macadam (1756–1836), the Scottish engineer of road making fame.

Sir William continued to enlarge the family fortune derived from coal, iron and shipbuilding. He invested in more land and in building the third Lowther residence on the same site. This was the vast, Gothic Lowther Castle, completed in 1814.

East Window

<u>Hugh Cecil Lowther</u>, KG. GCVO, Fifth Earl of Lonsdale, known as 'the Yellow Earl', (1857–1944) is remembered, with his wife, Grace, in the stained glass window.

His epitaph, '*A great English sportsman*' is a summary of his life style. His brilliant horsemanship included circus performances in Switzerland, prairie ranching in the USA, fox hunting and horse shows in England. He is probably best remembered in boxing circles today by the Lonsdale Belts named after him.

Although he inherited one of the largest fortunes and one of the most extensive estates in England, he spent income extravagantly with little thought for re-investment. His entertaining was lavish and he mixed socially in the royal circles of the Prince of Wales, who later became Edward VII (1901–1910).

Through yacht racing, friendship was made with Kaiser Wilhelm of Germany, Queen Victoria's grandson. He was a guest at Lowther Castle for hunting and shooting in 1895 and 1902 and was persuaded to lay the foundation stone of the Emperor's Gate at Hackthorpe Hall. The Emperor's Drive is the main route through Lowther Park.

Sir Hugh's carriages were painted yellow and later, his motor cars, whilst his numerous servants were dressed in yellow livery, hence the sobriquet, '*The Yellow Earl*'. He became the first President of the Automobile Association whose chosen colour is yellow. To this

day, Cumbria Conservatives wear yellow favours and not the traditional blue of their colleagues elsewhere.

The Depression of the 1930s depleted the family income consid-
erably and Sir Hugh so neglected Lowther Castle that its deterioration became irreversible.

In the south aisle and the chancel are several more memorials to
members of the Lowther family.

Lowther Churchyard

The huge Gothic Mausoleum of 1857 is dedicated to the memory of Sir
William Lowther, the Second Earl of Lonsdale. His seated marble effigy is visible behind thick glass.

In the 20c, the Lowthers have been buried near the churchyard
entrance gate.

Lowther Newtown was the 17c estate village built to replace the
demolished medieval village near St Michael's Church c. 1682 when Sir
John Lowther wished to enlarge his house and to open up the view.
The present Estate Office, built in 1709 as the College, was used as
a carpet factory.

From the village, a footpath permits a closer view of the ruins of
Lowther Castle but there is no entry into the castle precincts.

Lowther Village was built from c. 1765 to a plan attributed to
Robert Adam. There are two closes of cottages and houses and a
crescent broken by the road in the middle, each half marked by square
pavilions with pyramid roofs.

Estate workers have replaced the Lowthers' private yeomanry who
once lived here.

Off the A6 at Hackthorpe:
<u>Lowther Leisure and Wildlife Park</u> is two miles south of ruined Lowther Castle. Visitors can enjoy around 150 acres of beautiful parkland which abounds with bird and animal life, including the historic red deer which have been in this area for centuries. Many popular fairground rides and attractions are included in the admission price.

Continue north along the A6.
<u>Clifton</u> [*OE. Farmstead on steep bank.*] This long, straggling village began as an Anglian settlement on the limestone scarp above Lowther.

<u>St Cuthbert's Church</u>, with its Norman nave, donated stained glass to Mardale Holy Trinity Church in the 17c and the glass was returned in the 20c when Mardale Church was demolished prior to being submerged beneath Haweswater.

<u>Clifton Hall</u>. All that remains is a three-storey pele tower dating from c. 1500, although the windows are 17c and 18c. The rest of the Hall was demolished in the early 19c and replaced by the present farm buildings.

<u>Battle of Clifton Moor</u>. In 1745, 'Bonnie Prince Charlie', called also 'the Young Pretender', and his Jacobite army advanced triumphantly from Scotland as far south as Derby in an attempt to claim the English throne. But the rebels were driven back from there and at Clifton Moor the Duke of Cumberland and his Hanoverian troops engaged them in an indecisive battle, the last military battle to be fought on English soil. Lowther troops were involved. The Jacobites withdrew and were finally routed in the half-hour battle at Culloden. Charles Edward Stuart escaped to France with the help of Flora Macdonald.

At <u>Lowther Bridge</u>, turn right onto the B6262.

<u>Brougham Hall</u>. This 19c residential castle, built around medieval, Tudor and 17c buildings on a site occupied since Roman times, was the former home of the Brougham family. Henry Peter Brougham (1778–1868), the first Baron of Brougham and a Lord Chancellor of England, gave his name to the Brougham carriage, a one-horse, four-wheeled, closed carriage with a raised driver's seat in front.

The hall became known as the Windsor of the North when King Edward VII (1901–1910) visited privately on a number of occasions.

The Carlton family bought the hall but it fell into disrepair in the 1930s. It was gutted by fire in 1956 and rescued from dereliction in 1985. Fragments of the hall have been built into the modern reconstruction containing small craft workshops.

<u>St Wilfrid's Chapel</u>, across the road from Brougham Hall, was rebuilt by Lady Anne Clifford, Countess of Pembroke, in 1658 during Cromwell's republic when a display of aristocratic wealth was viewed with suspicion. Little has changed in the long low exterior. The interior was altered considerably in the 1840s by Lord Brougham and Vaux, who installed masses of dark oak woodwork dating from the 16c and 17c, including a superb screen. The lectern carries the Brougham arms and the altar cloth is marked 'AP' – Anne of Pembroke.

Continue along the B6262. Turn right onto the A66(T) Penrith to Appleby road, of Roman origin, for 500 yards.

<u>Countess Pillar,</u> on the right hand side, decorated with sundials and family crests, has the following inscription:

'This pillar was erected in the year 1656 by Anne, Countess Dowager of Pembroke &c for a memorial of her last parting with her mother Margaret, Countess Dowager of Cumberland, on the 2nd

April 1616; in memory whereof she hath left an annuity of £4 to be distributed to the poor of the Parish of Brougham, every 2nd day of April for ever, upon the stone table placed hard by. Laus Deo!'

Wordsworth's sonnet 'Countess Pillar' celebrated Lady Anne's benevolence.

Continue along the A66(T) a distance four miles east of Penrith, to the signpost (northside) indicating a mile walk across the fields.

Ninekirks, St Ninian's Church, dedicated to the 5c Scottish saint, stands isolated beside the River Eamont on the site of a Roman civil settlement which no longer exists.

Lady Anne Clifford completely rebuilt the church, as recorded by the wreath on the east wall containing her initials 'AP' (Ann Pembroke) and the date 1660. The furnishings have hardly changed.

Nearby, on the river bank, is a hermit's cave.

Return along the A66(T) to the B6262. Take the first turn to the right off the B6262.

Brocavum Roman Fort was built at the confluence of the Rivers Lowther and Eamont. This was the crossing point of the Roman roads, from Carlisle in the north and from Chester in the south; from York by way of Stainmore in the east and from the coastal port of Ravenglass in the west.

The rectangular earthworks of the turf and timber fort are plainly visible and date from the time of its governor, Cnaeus Julius Agricola, commander of Legion XX, AD 78–84.

The confluence of the Rivers Lowther and Eamont was a place of strategic and significant importance to judge from the number of ancient, historical monuments which have survived in the vicinity: Brocavum Roman fort, Brougham Castle, King Arthur's Round Table and Mayburgh Henge. According to legend, it was also a meeting place in 926 of King Athelstane of Wessex, King Owain of Cumbria and King Constantine of Scotland, who came to resolve their differences.

<u>Brougham Castle</u> [*OE. Homestead near a fortification.*]

In the north-west corner of the Roman fort, on a grassy mound beside the River Eamont, this Norman castle was built as a defence against the Scots at the beginning of the 13c.

Towards the end of that century, the castle passed by marriage to Lord Robert Clifford, adviser to Edward I. Lord Clifford added the curtain wall and the inner and outer gatehouses (1290–1314) to make the castle the strongest in the Eden Valley. Later, Roger Clifford made further changes (1360–1389). James I and Charles I stayed at the castle but eventually it fell into disrepair.

After the Civil War, Lady Anne Clifford (1590–1676), the last of the Cliffords to live in the castle, set about its restoration as the inscription on the outer gatehouse records.

Although Lady Anne was more than sixty years of age, her strong family pride and sense of history impelled her to spend most of her time and money on the renovation of her many properties, between which she travelled by horse litter, like lesser royalty, having sent her state bed in advance. Cromwell felt no threat and said, '*Let her build what she will, she shall have no hindrance from me.*'

Lady Anne died at Brougham Castle in the room where her father had been born and was buried alongside her mother in Appleby Church.

Wordsworth wrote of Brougham Castle in *The Prelude, Book VI*. In the *Song of the Feast of Brougham Castle*, Wordsworth related the tradition concerning Lord Henry Clifford who took refuge as a shepherd on Caldbeck Fells for twenty-four years after defeat in the Wars of the Roses. He came safely out of hiding to reclaim his prop-

BROUGHAM CASTLE ∂B

11/98

erty on the accession of the Lancastrian Henry VII in 1485.

The ruins of Brougham Castle are cared for by English Heritage, which operates seasonal opening times.

Return to the B6262 towards Penrith. Cross Lowther Bridge on the A6 and turn left onto the B5320.

King Arthur's Round Table (OS 523284) c. 2000 BC, has no connection with King Arthur.

It is a circular henge, 300 feet in diameter, surrounded by a ditch and bank 5 feet high. One entrance survives in the south-east. The site was used for sports and games until the 19c and has been greatly disturbed. Excavations have revealed a cremation trench in the central plateau.

Mayburgh Henge [*OE. Maiden's Fort*] (OS 519285). This ancient monument is thought to be older than its neighbour. Stones taken from the Eamont river bed were used to construct a massive circular embankment 360 feet in diameter, 8 to 15 feet high, thus avoiding the need for a quarry ditch. A single entrance faces east. Near the centre stands a solitary 9 feet pillar but records show that more upright stones were here at one time. Bronze Age and Stone Age axes have been found.

Eamont Bridge [*OE. Confluence of steams*] on the A6, provides access to Penrith.

The bridge was partly paid for in medieval times by the sale of papal indulgences.

Kendal to Windermere

*The A591 to Windermere is the most direct route.
Staveley is by-passed. See: Kentdale.*

<u>Ings</u> [*ON. Outlying meadows*], situated on the old main road between Kendal and Windermere, was on the Kendal to Cockermouth turnpike from 1761.

<u>Robert Bateman's Almshouses</u> were endowed by this local benefactor, who, as a poor boy, travelled to London to seek his fortune. Wordsworth's poem, '*Michael*', tells the story:

> '*He was a parish boy. At the church door*
> *They made a gathering for him,*
> *Shillings, pence and halfpence*
> *Wherewith the neighbours bought a basket*
> *Which they filled with pedlars wares.*
> *With this basket the lad went up to London . . .*'

He found employment in a merchant's house and worked his way up to become the manager of the Italian office in Leghorne from where he exported Italian marble.

> '*Beyond the seas, where he grew wondrous rich*
> *And left estates and monies to the poor.*'

A partnership followed until eventually he became the sole

proprietor. He was to have retired to Reston House in the village in 1743. Whilst sailing home in one of his ships, he was said to have been poisoned and thrown overboard in the Straits of Gibraltar by the captain who turned the ship round and disappeared with its cargo. This story was disputed by Canon Trevor Jones in his book '*The Will of Robert Bateman*' in which he explained that Robert Bateman died in his bed at Leghorne, where a monument in the English cemetery stands to his memory.

<u>Reston House</u>, towards Staveley, is a long, white building with tall, sash windows and four cottages in a row near its gate.

   <u>St Anne's Church</u> in 1743 was rebuilt in the Renaissance style with Robert Bateman's bequest, using the Italian marble which he sent.

> '*And at his birth-place built a chapel floored*
> *With marble which he sent from foreign lands.*'

A portrait of Robert Bateman hangs on the chancel wall where a brass plate records Wordsworth's lines. It is known that boys from Hawkshead Grammar School visited to see the marble floor and that William and Dorothy Wordsworth saw it during a walking holiday in 1794.

   A plaque over the door commemorates '*Mr Robert Bateman. Merchant at Leghorne. Born in this hamlet.*' The three bells in the little tower are inscribed '*R.B. Merchant at Leghorne 1743.*'

   A local woodworker, Robert Fell, whose self-portrait is near the pulpit, carved the intricate panelling.

   <u>The School</u> also was endowed by Robert Bateman.

Sallows	2.3
Sour House	2.3

Hugill Iron Age Settlement OS. 437009
From Hill Farm on the A591, take the minor road. After one mile, at the crossroads, turn right to High Borrans.

A modern wall, constructed on the foundations of the original boundary bank, surrounds this two-acre site. There are three entrances. In the western sector is a group of circular hut-like enclosures, whilst a series of paddocks and terraces occupy the eastern area.

High Knott   OFOL 19

Bannerrigg offers the first glimpse of Lake Windermere from the crest of the hill.

Kendal to Windermere via Crook
At the northern roundabout of the Kendal bypass, turn left onto the B5284.

Crook. The Wild Boar Inn.

Less than ¾ mile further stands a church on the corner of Back Lane. South of here:

Crook Hall once belonged to the Royalist Philipson family who owned Belle Isle on Lake Windermere.

St Catherine's Church nearby, was built in the mid-17c, but today it stands in ruins.

Hollins Hall, just off the Crook road to Staveley, has a 15c pele tower.

Kendal to Windermere via Underbarrow Scar
Leave Kendal up All Hallows Lane, opposite the Town Hall.

Scout Scar   OFOL 2

Underbarrow Scar [*OE. Land under the hill.*] This 700 foot limestone ridge, with patches of limestone pavement, was, in geological time, the former coastline and, in the 8c, the frontier of Anglian settlement. Quarries provided Kendal with building material.

Cunswick Scar [*ON. conyng = kinglet; wick = dairy farm.*] lies to the north.

Cunswick Hall stands below the scar. This ancient dwelling became the Leyburn family's ancestral home, a partially fortified manor with a gatehouse over which are the royal arms. According to tradition, it was here that Henry VIII wooed young Catherine Parr.

A Leyburn ghost is said to haunt this locality. He stabbed a priest who was praying by his death-bed and consequently the church at Kendal would not accept his body for burial. The coffin bearers were compelled to return home with the corpse. Whilst they were crossing Cunswick Scar, a fierce storm arose, so they dropped the body and left it to be disposed of by the elements and the wild creatures. Only the ghost has remained.

Scout Scar lies to the south. A memorial shelter was erected to King George V. The dramatic western aspect from the escarpment edge reveals a broken Silurian landscape of confused rocky knolls where hard grit bands of Kirkby Moor Flags and glacial debris occur. Small walled fields with rough pasture in ill-drained hollows, rambling lanes and scattered white-washed farms are a feature.

Underbarrow is a scattered village, over a mile from Underbarrow Scar, centred around a triangle of roads connecting the pub, the church and High Gregg Hall. Of the original three inns only The Punch Bowl remains. All Saints Church beside Chapel Beck was built in 1869

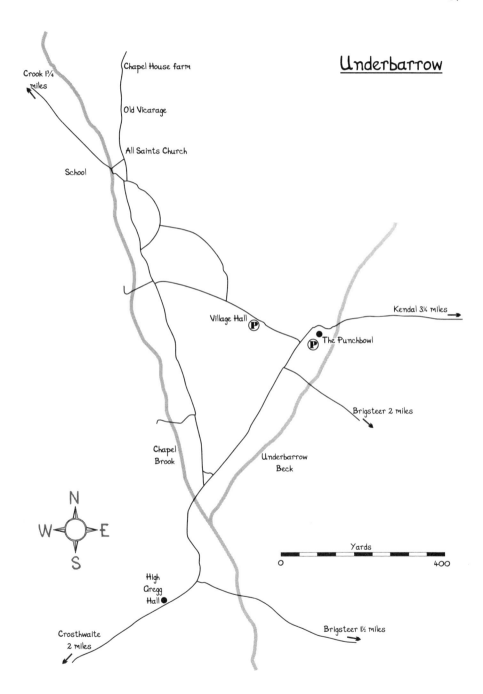

Underbarrow

Crook 1¼ miles

Chapel House farm

Old Vicarage

All Saints Church

School

Village Hall ℗

℗ The Punchbowl

Kendal 3¼ miles →

Brigsteer 2 miles

Chapel Brook

Underbarrow Beck

N
W · E
S

Yards
0   400

High Gregg Hall ●

Crosthwaite 2 miles

Brigsteer 1½ miles

on a site that has held a church for a thousand years or more.

Crosthwaite [ON. Clearing marked by a cross.]

A5074 to Bowness and Lake Windermere.

Windermere Town

The town of Windermere was originally a small village named Birthwaite, part of the medieval parish of Kendal. The plagues of 1348, 1361 and 1362 probably created the need for consecrating a local parochial churchyard and St Mary's, Applethwaite, was chosen.

It was the railway that transformed the village into a Victorian town and caused the name change to Windermere. A branch line from the main London to Scotland route was built from Oxenholme in 1847 against tremendous local opposition, led by William Wordsworth.

> *'Is then no nook of English ground secure*
> *From rash assault?'*

he asked in a sonnet.

It was intended originally to continue the railway line through Ambleside and Grasmere to Keswick, but the outcry caused the line to be terminated at Windermere station, which is more than a mile from the lake of the same name.

There followed an invasion of business men, called 'off-comers' by local residents, and, of course, tourists. To cater for tourists, an entrepreneur called Rigg opened the first hotel in 1847, The Windermere Hotel, close to the station, and arranged to carry the visitors around the lakes by horse-drawn carriage and charabanc.

Victorian gothic buildings with pinnacles and towers, mixed with Italianate residences and hotels, sprang up everywhere. Slate was greatly in evidence. The two separate communities of Windermere and Bowness on the lakeshore were integrated by massive housing developments to become one busy town.

Windermere Railway Station. Re-designing the original station, with financial help from a local pressure group, created space for a supermarket and a huge kitchenware shop, whose founder, Alan Rayner, was once a representative of a firm which supplied animal feed. During his visits to farmers he learned of their wish to sell poultry ready dressed for the oven. He offered to provide plastic bags in which to wrap the poultry and by 1959 had established the Lakeland Poultry Packing Company accommodated in the animal feed supplies warehouse at Windermere Railway Station. From the expanding business and diversification emerged Lakeland Plastics, now Lakeland Ltd., which includes John Tovey's Miller Howe Kaff.

A Tourist Information Centre stands at the station entrance.

The Terrace, above the station, was where Arthur Ransome's Great Aunt Susan lived. She provided him with a frequent refuge from the local preparatory school which he hated.

Orrest Head, indicated by a signpost across from the station roundabout, was once the residence of Josiah Brown, an eccentric who entertained beggars at his home for amusement and rode around on a bull. A plaque on the wall beside a kissing gate records that the family of Arthur Henry Heywood gave Orrest Head [ON. Hill where a battle took place] for public enjoyment. The views from the summit are a just reward for the climb.

Christopher North's Cottage, on a westerly path from the Orrest Head ascent, is painted white and identified by plaques. From 1807, it was the home of John Wilson, Professor of Moral Philosophy at the University of Edinburgh, and editor of 'Blackwood's Magazine' under the pen-name of Christopher North. Whilst living here, he built Elleray, a larger house further down the hill.

Elleray's lodge gates are a little way down the A591 from the station roundabout, opposite Elleray Road. During the construction of Elleray in 1808, John Wilson held a cock-fight on the turf covered floor of the drawing room. Sir Walter Scott stayed here in 1825 and celebrated his 54th birthday with friends watching a regatta on the lake. The house was demolished in the 1860s and St Anne's School occupied the large Victorian building which replaced it.

The Old College. In the next turning after Elleray Road, facing the Sports Ground in Phoenix Way, survives a row of residential buildings, all that remain of a former accommodation block of Arthur Ransome's preparatory school, 1893–97.

The Baddeley Memorial Clock marks the boundary between Windermere and Bowness on Lake Road. The dedication is the memory of M. J. B. Baddeley (1843–1906), author of a classic *Guide to the Lake District*. The headstone of his grave in Bowness cemetery is of rock from the summit of Sca Fell Pike, England's highest mountain (3,210 ft.)

Orrest Head	*OFOL 26*
School Knott	*OFOL 30*

Lakeside to Ambleside
Lake Windermere – East:
Lakeside to Bowness

Windermere [ON. OE. Vinandr's lake, a personal name]
In the past it was known also as Wynandremer.

This is England's largest natural lake, 10 miles long, ¼ to 1¼ miles wide and up to 219 feet deep.

More than 10,000 years ago, the last Ice Age ended in Britain. Combined ice-streams from Little Langdale, Great Langdale, Helvellyn and Troutbeck pushed southwards across lower Silurian country and etched out this great elongated hollow which became Lake Windermere. The retreating glacier ice left behind hillocks of boulder clay which jut out into the lake. The lake is fed by the waters of the Rothay, Brathay, Cunsey and Troutbeck. The southern outflow is the River Leven.

The lake shores were formerly pastures, open heath, scattered with gnarled oaks depleted by the 17c demand for charcoal. Clumps of holly were preserved for winter fodder. Today, rich woodlands screen the road from the lake and cloak the surrounding hills. The wave of Victorian settlers made this the most landscaped of all the lakes, especially along this eastern shore.

Windermere has also became the busiest of the lakes with

pleasure boats in profusion, including high-powered craft not permitted on other lakes, although this is under review.

According to William Wordsworth in his *Guide to the Lakes*, the best views are from the lake itself. *'None of the other lakes unfold so many fresh beauties to him who sails upon them. This is owing to its greater size, to the islands, and to its having two vales at the head, with their accompanying mountains of nearly equal dignity. Nor can the grandeur of these two terminations be seen at once from any other point except from the bosom of the lake.'*

Scattered around the lake are fourteen islands, many named 'Holme' [*OE. ON. Island*]. Only the largest, Belle Isle, is inhabited.

Lakeside, at the southern end of the lake, sprang into eminence with the growth in tourism.

The Lakeside Hotel was once a coaching inn on the road to Hawkshead.

The Lakeside and Haverthwaite Railway [*ON. Clearing where oats are grown*]. Steam trains run between these villages following the River Leven through woodland scenery and stopping at Newby Bridge. From Haverthwaite Railway Station at limited times a bus connects with Holker Hall and its many attractions.

The origins of this railway date back to the time when Henry Schneider and the seventh Duke of Devonshire financed four years of profitless exploration for haematite (iron ore) in the Furness limestone area before a rich vein was struck at Park, near Dalton-in-Furness.

Such was the increased demand for transporting escalating loads of iron ore that the traditional horse and cart was replaced by the Furness Railway. A passenger service followed later.

The first rail link with Lake Windermere had already taken place in 1847 with the opening of the branch line from Oxenholme to

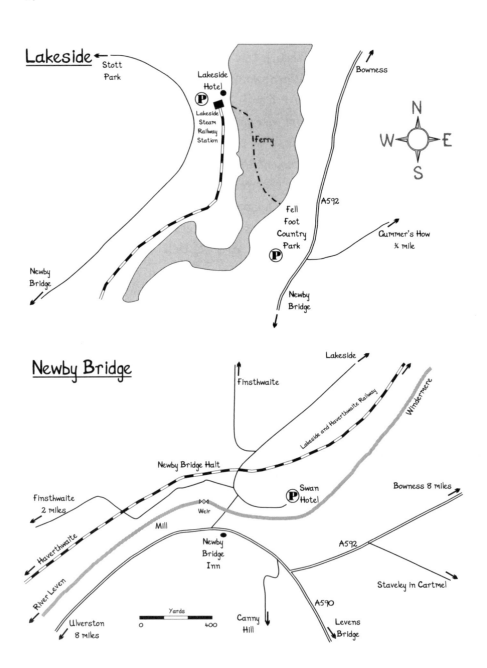

Lakeside

Stott Park

Lakeside Hotel

Lakeside Steam Railway Station

Ferry

Bowness

Fell Foot Country Park

A592

Gummer's How ¾ mile

Newby Bridge

Newby Bridge

N
W   E
S

Newby Bridge

Finsthwaite

Lakeside

Lakeside and Haverthwaite Railway

Windermere

Newby Bridge Halt

Swan Hotel

Bowness 8 miles

Finsthwaite 2 miles

Weir

Mill

Haverthwaite

Newby Bridge Inn

A592

Staveley in Cartmel

River Leven

A590

Ulverston 8 miles

Yards
0   400

Canny Hill

Levens Bridge

Windermere station. At the southern end of the lake, the Ulverston to Newby Bridge section of the Furness Railway was extended to Lakeside in 1869 and a deep-water jetty was built alongside the railway station. It was then possible for a large, powerful screw-propelled steam vessel, the 'Swan', to provide a service on the lake for the great influx of passengers. Previously, three small paddle steamers had served the public by operating from a jetty on the River Leven at Newby Bridge.

The development of the coal and iron industries had brought about the expansion of the railways. The decline of these heavy industries contributed greatly to the contraction of rail services. Park Mine closed in 1921 and Backbarrow Iron Works in 1967. British Rail closed Haverthwaite and Greenodd stations and then closed the Lakeside branch. Thus ended an era which had lasted for 99 years.

A group of enthusiasts preserved 3½ miles of track along the Leven Valley and re-opened this section in 1973 as the Lakeside and Haverthwaite Railway.

The Windermere Iron Steamboat Company, now trading as Windermere Lake Cruises, was founded in 1848 by the directors of the Kendal to Windermere railway and evolved into its present form by mergers with The Furness Railway Company, London Midland and Scottish Railway, British Rail, Sealink and Sea Containers of Orient Express fame. It operates lake 'steamers' today fuelled by diesel oil. They are named after water birds. 'Swan' and 'Teal', registered to carry 540 passengers each, were built by Vickers Armstrong at Barrow-in-Furness in 1936 and 1938 respectively and transported in sections by rail for re-assembly on the Lakeside slipway. 'Tern', the oldest, was built in 1891 by Forrest & Sons of Wyvenhoe, Essex, and is registered to carry 350 passengers. It was known as HMS Undine during World War II and served on Windermere as a mine-laying training ship and as a patrol boat guarding the Sunderland aircraft factory at White Cross Bay. The modern launches are named Miss Lakeland, Miss Westmorland and Miss Cumbria. Sailing the length of the lake calling at Bowness and Waterhead (Ambleside) takes 1½ hours at an average speed of 11 knots.

Newby Bridge is where road, rail and water squeeze through the narrow gorge of the Leven Valley. A helicopter pad behind the Swan Hotel adds to the transport systems.

Newby Bridge, which gives this settlement its name, was possibly called after its builder. The original wooden structure on stone pillars was replaced in 1652 by the present bridge with five, unequal, buttressed arches and recesses for pedestrians. It spans the River Leven at its outflow from Lake Windermere. Below the bridge a weir retains a head of water.

The river severs a complex series of end-moraines. With the deepening of channels for the coming of the first lake paddle steamer two fords were lost. The Upper Ford joined the lake shore at Fell Foot with Landing How, a distance of 55 yards, in less then 3 feet of water when a cheese-press marker stone was visible. The Lower Ford, half-a-mile above Newby Bridge, was 8 yards wide and 2 feet deep, except for an unfathomable Dry Hole.

Shallow draught barges once brought slates from the north end of the lake to be unloaded onto wagons here. The barges re-loaded with lime from kilns along the edge of Hampsfell in Cartmel. To mark the best passage between boulders in the shallow channel lumps of limestone were thrown overboard. When the steamer service began, the offending rocks were removed and deposited on shore just below Landing How.

The Corn Mill. Eel traps are set from August onwards to catch the eels swimming from the lake to the river on their way to their breeding grounds in the Saragossa Sea.

The Swan Hotel, 1622, one of the oldest coaching inns in Cumbria, is on the road to Ulverston and Barrow. Visitors have included Charlotte Brontë and Nathaniel Hawthorne. When Rowland Hill stayed here, it is said that he thought of the idea of cheap postage. He heard of a servant girl who had to refuse a letter from her sweetheart for lack of money at a time when the postage was paid by the recipient of a letter. By 1840, the penny post and adhesive postage stamps had been introduced.

Finsthwaite Heights	*OFOL 74*
Bigland Barrow	*OFOL 70*

Divert from the A592.

Staveley-in-Cartmel *[OE. Wood where staves are cut]*
   This was the village of William Robinson who died at the age of 28, but left several bequests which ensured his remembrance in later years. One of these was for the interest on £20 to be given annually to the 'Guide of Lancaster Sands'.

   Church. This replaced the older church where Priest Camelford angered George Fox the Quaker and then had him thrown out in 1652.

   School. Edmund Law, schoolmaster parson, walked 16 miles daily for nearly 50 years from his home at Buck Crag Farm, south-east of High Newton, to teach in the school and to serve his parishioners as their curate, earning for himself £20 per annum from 1693 to 1742. One of his sons became Master of Peterhouse, Cambridge, and later, Bishop of Carlisle. Of his other sons, John became Bishop of Elphin in the Highlands of Scotland, Edward was created Baron Ellenborough (Maryport) in Cumberland, (a son of his became Governor General of India) and George became Bishop of Bath and Wells.

Staveley Fell   OFOL 48

Return to the A592. Turn right up a minor road.
Gummer's How, 1,054 feet. [ON. *Gunnar's Hill, personal name.*]
The extensive views over the lake are replicated by Arthur Ransome
in the map he drew in *Swallows and Amazons.*

Gummer's How   OFOL 44

Return to the A592.
Fell Foot Country Park (NT) occupies the site of Fell Foot House.
The builder's wife, Mrs Dixon, was the daughter of the designer and
builder of the Eddystone lighthouse. She devoted herself to good works,
built a school and endowed it, helped the poor and the sick and provided a hearse for burials at Cartmel.

The Country Park, which can also be reached by ferry from Lakeside,
was opened in 1972 by the National Trust to provide a leisure and outdoor centre for boating, bathing, fishing and picnics. A large boathouse
had been converted into a cafe and there is chalet accommodation. The
restoration of the 18 acres park and garden is in the Victorian style.

Haws Wood shelters the Hill of Oaks Caravan Park.
Coppice wood was once grown and felled at regular intervals for
the making of charcoal to fuel the early primitive iron-smelting
bloomeries. The wood was used also to make swills, the plaited agricultural baskets of oak spales and hazel. Bobbins were made from
coppice wood and bark was used for tanning.

When the Lakes Flying Company was based here, the first entirely
successful flight of a British seaplane was achieved in 1911. Two seaplanes operated, the Watford and the Waterhen. The Northern Aircraft

Company made this their base. In World War I, the Royal Naval Air Service Sea Plane Flying School (RNAS Windermere) was stationed here.

Blake Holme, accessible from the Caravan Park, is a small, inshore island which can be reached by wading through shallow water. Arthur Ransome described it as '*the island most used as Wild Cat Island in* Swallows and Amazons.' As Blake Holme has no harbour, Wild Cat Island's secret harbour was based on Peel Island, Coniston.

Beech Hill Hotel. Adjacent is a viewpoint and picnic area.

Ghyll Head Road. On the OS map, Ghyll Head Education Centre is marked near the corner and, next door, is The Cottage where John Ruskin's secretary, W. G. Collingwood lived. His son, R. G. Collingwood, was born here in 1889. The family later moved to Lane Head, Coniston, to be nearer Ruskin at Brantwood.

Storrs Hall Hotel, built as a private mansion in 1790 by Sir John Legard, stands on a promontory close to where Constable was inspired to paint the scene.

Storrs Temple (NT), or the Temple of Heroes, at the end of the jetty, is an octagonal look-out built in 1804 in honour of the British admirals whose names are inscribed round the sides: Nelson, Howe, St Vincent and Duncan.

When Colonel Bolton, a wealthy slave trader, moved into Storrs Hall, it became a centre for the festivals and regattas on the lake. This is where William Wordsworth, Robert Southey, Sir Walter Scott, George Canning (the future Prime Minister) and Professor Wilson ('Christopher North') gathered in 1825 in celebration of Scott's 54th birthday. The highlight of the regatta which they watched was the spectacle of 50 barges being rowed down the lake.

Windermere Marina Village is an attractive mix of luxury self-catering and time-ownership cottages overlooking the boat moorings. The Spinnaker Club facilities include a leisure centre with a swimming pool.

The Windermere Ferry continues the 600 years old tradition of transporting foot passengers and vehicles across 500 yards of Lake Windermere.

Cockshott Point. It is difficult to visualise that an aircraft factory once stood on this site. From 1919 to 1920 it was the base of the Avro Seaplane Pleasure Flight Company which operated two Avro 504 seaplanes. A regular service was provided to deliver newspapers to the Isle of Man.

Bowness-on-Windermere

[OE. Bulness = headland or promontory shaped like a bull's head. The original settlement was named 'Undermillbeck'.]

Bowness was mentioned in documents as early as 1190. It remained a small fishing village for centuries and then grew to become the 'port' of Windermere for trade in the 19c. During the Victorian era, it was discovered by wealthy business men, many from industrial Lancashire. Wordsworth expressed lament at the coming of *'strangers not linked to the neighbourhood, but flitting to and fro between their fancy villas and their homes where their wealth was accumulated . . . by trade and manufactures'.*

Some of the 'fancy villas' have lakeside frontages and are still privately owned: others have become hotels.

The extension of the railway line to Windermere station in 1847 transformed Bowness into a very popular resort, especially for day visitors. At the same time it has developed residentially to become the largest conurbation in the National Park.

<u>Bowness Bay</u> is the centre for tourists wishing to enjoy the varied attractions of the lake and its surroundings. The first steam-driven paddle boats sailed from here in 1845, in spite of local opposition. Wordsworth recommended a boat trip in his *Guide to the Lakes*, which had gone through five editions by 1835. The popularity continues of sailing on a lake 'steamer' or of hiring a small boat.

Bowness is 'Rio Grande' in Arthur Ransome's *Swallows and*

Amazons. The Victorian wooden sheds he described in 'Rio Bay', where 'Swallow' was repaired in *Swallowdale*, used to provide dry storage for pleasure boat seat cushions. The sheds were demolished in 1973 and replicas were built a short distance away.

Sepulchre Hill was the site of a mass grave unearthed by roadmen in 1912.

St Martin's Church. Martin was the Roman officer who split his cloak in half to help a beggar. A 17c wooden sculpture of him stands inside the church.

The present church was built in 1483 to replace a much older structure first recorded in 1203. Enlargement and alterations occurred 1869–73. The old floor is believed to be 5 feet below the nave.

The East window of medieval glass from an earlier building possibly came from Cartmel Priory after the Dissolution, especially the three lights in the centre depicting the Crucifixion. In the third light from the right, in the top right hand corner, is the coat of arms of John Washington, twelfth ancestor of George Washington. The 'mullet and bars', 1403, were the foundation of the 'stars and stripes' of the flag of the U.S.A.

In the North aisle, a small piece of glass has the mark of a packhorse carrier who, in the 1600s, carried lead, free of charge, over Wrynose Pass for the roof of the church.

In the South aisle, under an arch, is a Latin inscription put up by the Philipsons of Belle Isle, rejoicing at the failure of the Gunpowder Plot.

References can be found to Robert Philipson (1631) of Long Holme, later named Belle Isle, and to Bishop Watson (1816) who, although he was Bishop of Llandaff, resided at Calgarth Hall, just outside Bowness, and is said to have visited his Welsh congregation every three years.

A poignant grave in the churchyard marks the mortal remains of 47 people who were returning from a wedding in Hawkshead and were drowned when the ferry capsized in 1635. There is a memorial dated 1822 to Rasselas Belfield, an Abyssinian slave, who found freedom here.

The Old England Hotel was first built in 1869 on the site of Captain Elm's house. At the base of the wall which comes uphill from the lake, are stone blocks set at intervals to protect the wall from damage by horse-drawn vehicles.

The Stag's Head Inn displays, high up on the wall, the ancient words 'Post Horses for Hire'.

The Royal Windermere Yacht Club received its Royal Warrant in 1887.

Lowside, or Old Bowness. This network of streets and cottages, nestling in a depression and so protected from cold winds, is the original village.

Sawpit Hill is a reminder of the ancient system of cutting logs.

New Hall Inn is the oldest tavern in Bowness. Its alternative name 'The Hole Int' Wall' derives from the window through which ale could be passed to the adjacent smithy.

A sign claims that Charles Dickens stayed here as a guest during his walking tour of the lakes in 1857. The sign above the doorway commemorates Thomas Longmire, a former landlord and wrestling champion called the 'Hero of a Hundred Rings'. Longmire won more than 200 bouts in 20 years.

The Royal Hotel, so named after the visit in 1840 of Queen Adelaide, widow of William IV. It had previously been called Ullock's Hotel and the White Lion. Wordsworth, in *The Prelude II*, describes it as 'a splendid place'.

In Queen's Square stands the remaining tree of two planted

c. 1900 called Mary and Martha.

<u>Crag Brow</u> is the principal shopping area where many buildings have retained their original Victorian architectural features.

<u>The Old Bath House</u> is situated on Lake Road, near the corner of Craig Walk, just past the Police Station. Remedial bathing was fashionable in Victorian times and visitors who were not patronising the Windermere Hydropathic Hotel facilities were encouraged to take the waters at the Old Bath House.

Return to –

<u>The Windermere Hydropathic Hotel</u>, Helm Road, was built as a private house in 1875 and began offering remedial baths to guests in 1881. Previously, guests stayed at Thornburrow House (Hall) and took the waters in the Old Bath House.

Ascend Helm Road to reach the viewpoint of <u>Biskey Howe</u>.

<u>Ash Street</u> took its name from a tree, the Deborah Ash, which traditionally was a meeting point for gossip. For a small fee, notices pinned to the tree would be read to the illiterate.

<u>Brantfell Road</u> is where <u>Laurel Cottage</u> stands. It was built in 1613 as the village school. John Bolton of Storrs Hall replaced it in 1836 with a Grammar School (demolished in 1963) for which William Wordsworth laid the foundation stone.

Ascend Brantfell Road to reach the viewpoints of <u>Post Knott</u> and <u>Brant Fell</u>.

<u>The Belsfield Hotel</u>. The Baroness Sternberg had this Italianate-style mansion built in 1845. In 1869, it became the residence of the industrial magnate, Henry William Schneider, the chairman of Barrow Steelworks and Shipyard, who travelled to and from work in grand style. He would leave his lakeside mansion in the morning preceded by his butler, Mr Pittaway, who carried a silver breakfast tray. Schneider would eat his breakfast on board his private steam boat,

Bowness- on- Windermere

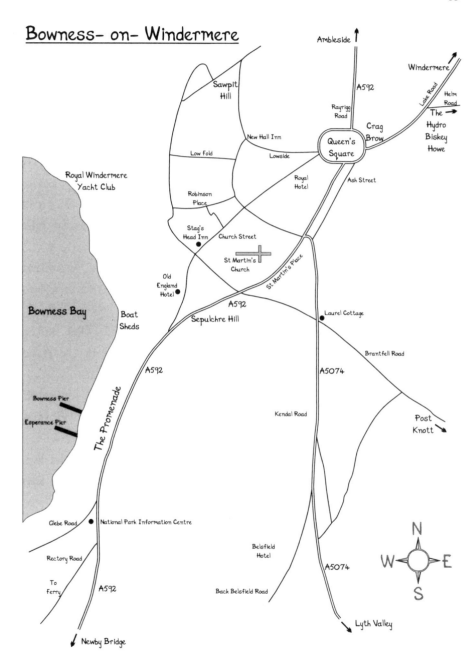

'Esperance', as it cruised down Windermere to Lake Side. Here, a train awaited to convey him to his office in Barrow. The procedure was reversed in the evening, returning the great man home again in time for dinner.

Rectory Road leads to Parson Wyke House, formerly Bowness Rectory, and to Ferry Nab beyond.

Ferry Nab. There has been a ferry here since the 15c. The early ferries were man-powered by oars, but large enough to carry a horse and cart. The first steam-powered ferry was introduced in 1869 and could carry a coach and four, with passengers, saving a ten mile journey round the lake.

Today, the 'Drake', which came into operation in 1954, has been converted to diesel power to pull itself across 700 yards to Ferry House on two chains strung under the water.

Return to Bowness Bay via Cockshott Point *(N.T.).* This is the site of an old aircraft factory and the former base of the Avro Seaplane Pleasure Flight Company.

Belle Isle is Lake Windermere's only inhabited island, covering 38 acres of landscaped gardens. This is 'Long Island' in Arthur Ransome's novels.

The De Lindesays were the first recorded occupiers in the 14c. Until the late 18c, it was the property of the Philipson family who also owned Calgarth Hall on Windermere's eastern shore.

During the Civil War, the Royalist, Major Philipson, nicknamed 'Robin the Devil', was besieged on the island for eight months. His brother raised the siege and Robin pursued his enemy the Parliamentarian, Colonel Briggs, to Kendal Holy Trinity Church with the consequences previously described. Sir Walter Scott incorporated this story in his narrative poem, *Rokeby*, (1813).

Thomas English became the owner of the island in 1776 when he commissioned the architect, John Plaw, to construct the first completely round house in England at a cost of £5,000. It was built, we are told, on the site of a Roman villa over the original well. Outspoken critics ridiculed the house calling it a 'pepper pot'. Unable to bear the censure, English sold his property in 1781 for a mere £1,700. The new owners were the Curwen family whose fortune had come from the Workington coal mines. The island had previously been known as Long Holme or Great Holme, but was now re-named Belle Isle after Isabella Curwen, who later married Wordsworth's son, John.

The island contains two of Thomas West's 'stations' listed in his 'Guide' (1778) for viewing the lake and its surroundings, but he disapproved of the formal gardens as '*An unpleasing contrast to the natural simplicity and insular beauty of the place*'. Both William and Dorothy Wordsworth commented unfavourably.

The Curwens have continued in ownership and in 1988 they turned the house into a conference and special interest centre.

The Glebe is a recreation area with boatyards along the water's edge.

The National Park Information Centre, near the boat landings, has a Countryside Theatre which is used as a lecture hall.

Brant Fell   *OFOL 34*

Vale of Winster

Travel south from Bowness-on-Windermere on the A5074.

<u>Winster</u>. This scattered village stands at the head of an attractive, wide, undulating valley, sheltered between the limestone mass of Whitbarrow Scar, screened by Witherslack Woods, and the slate country of Cartmel Fell.

The River Winster once marked the eastern boundary of the land of Cartmel Priory and defined the former boundary between Lancashire and Westmorland.

The valley was saved from becoming a reservoir by the action of the Winster Protection Society.

<u>Holy Trinity Church</u> was built of local stone in 1875. Inside are some curious texts on wooden tablets and an impressive east window.

The old school room is across the road.

<u>Bryan House Farm</u> was once the home of Jonas Barber, a reputable, 17c, maker of grandfather clocks.

A later occupant was William Pearson who, in his capacity as a naturalist, showed William Wordsworth around Winster Valley.

<u>Birket Houses</u>, now a country house hotel, is a secluded medieval manor house in spacious ornamental gardens.

<u>Winster House</u> has Georgian origins.

<u>Brown Horse Inn</u>.

Turn onto the minor road at the inn and travel south keeping to the east of the river.

Barkbooth. Arthur Ransome's fishing friend, Colonel Kelsall, once lived here. To arrange fishing trips, these fishermen devised a system of signalling by hoisting wooden shapes, as neither of them had a telephone. This signalling device was incorporated in Arthur Ransome's novel, *Winter Holiday.*

Borderside. Wordsworth's Quaker friend, William Pearson, (1780–1856) built this house when he married. After twenty years in banking, he became a farmer and established a reputation as a naturalist. His great knowledge of local life and traditions was gathered together in his 'Notes on the Natural History of Crosthwaite and Lyth, and the Valley of the Winster.'

Cowmire Hall. This medieval pele tower had Elizabethan additions built on by the Fleming family.

Pool Bank Farm was built by the Hartley family. The porch door lintel is dated 1693 and an old gallery remains over the kitchen door. A traditional tale tells of a housewife who was walled up alive in the house.

Witherslack [ON. Wooded Valley] The Church, with its fine 17c woodwork, the Village Hall and the Master's House were all endowed and built by the Rev. John Barwick (1618–69), a local boy who became Dean of St Paul's. He also left money as dowries for poor maids and for a new burial ground.

John Barwick was educated at Sedbergh and St John's College, Oxford where he became a Fellow in 1636. During the Civil War he gave the College plate to support the King. Cromwell turned him out but he continued to support the Royalists and consequently was imprisoned in the Tower of London. At the Restoration he re-covered his freedom and his fortune. His initials, JB, can be seen on the

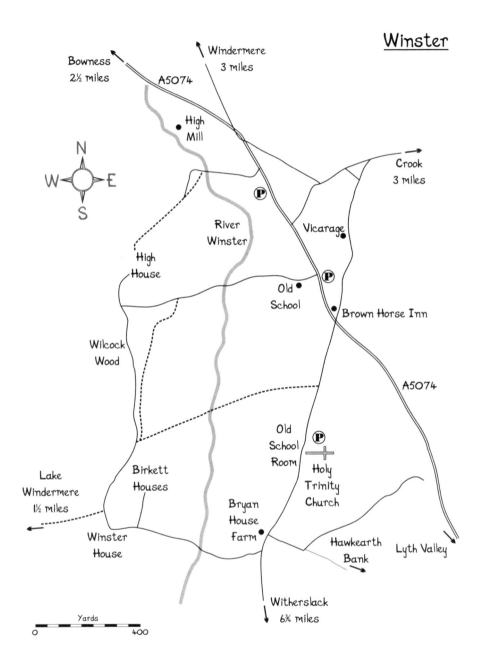

Winster

sundial in the churchyard.

John Barwick had a younger brother, Peter, who was a physician to Charles II and courageously stayed on in London during the Great Plague of 1665 ministering to the sick.

Past Witherslack Church, take the first turn right towards High Newton. At ¼ mile from High Newton, turn right on the high fell road.

The Height is a former Friends' Meeting House with a porch tablet dated 1677, the year when George Fox visited. Above the porch is a look-out window. The burial ground is across the road.

Return as far as the Winster Valley at the foot of Tow Top. Turn left and travel north, keeping to the west of the river.

Tow Top with a gradient of 1:4, was on the route that Fletcher Rigge of Cark Hall brought his young bride when travelling home in 1782. She was so scared that she refused to stay in such a dreadful place and they both turned back to live at Northallerton instead.

Low Tarn Green. John Wilkinson, a forgemaster of Wilson House at nearby Lindale, had a canal cut in the River Winster to transport peat for fuel to smelt the haematite ore. At his forge, he made the first iron ship and tested it on Helton Tarn.

Thorphinsty Hall [ON. *Thorphin's sty. Sty = steep path.*] This Tudor house was begun by the Cartwrights and developed by the Huttons. Richard Hutton left money for the poor of Cartmel Fell.

Hodge Hill is of Elizabethan origin, 1560, with a wooden balcony. It was built by the Philipsons of Belle Isle on Windermere and had been carefully restored to become a hotel. The barn has retained its wooden threshing floor and oak-pegged doors.

Turn left uphill and then right, continuing north.

Cartmel Fell. To save having to walk the seven miles to Cartmel Priory Church, St Anthony's Church was built here by local farmers

In 1504, on the site of a hospice for the swineherds who worked for the priory of Cartmel. St Anthony is the patron saint of herdsmen, as well as of basket makers and charcoal burners. A corruption of his name – Tyson – is a common surname in Lakeland.

Marks on the stonework in the entrance porch are said to have been caused by sharpening arrows. Of interest are the box pews, the 17c three-decked pulpit and the 16c east window – a rare example of a seven sacrament window – possibly from Cartmel Priory. St Anthony and his pig are depicted.

A unique pre-Reformation carved wooden figure of Christ from a vanished rood screen, and once used as a poker is now displayed in the Kendal Museum.

Cartmel Fell   *OFOL 42*

<u>Great Hartbarrow</u>. In 1924, Arthur Ransome married Trotsky's secretary, Evgenia Petrovna Shelepina, and a year later the married couple lodged here whilst waiting to move into Low Ludderburn.

<u>Low Ludderburn</u> was the Ransomes' home from 1925 to 1935. The upper storey of the barn became Arthur's workroom where he wrote articles for the *Manchester Guardian*, including the angling column.

Here, the Ransomes entertained Dr Ernest Altounyan, his wife, Dora, daughter of W. G. Collingwood, and their five children whose holiday home was Bank Ground Farm, near Tarn Hows. The adventures of the children learning to sail the dinghies 'Swallow' and 'Mavis' on Coniston Water became models for the fictional characters in *Swallows and Amazons* (1930).

Also written at Low Ludderburn were *Swallowdale* (1931), *Winter Holiday* (1933), *Coot Club* (1936), and most of *Pigeon Post* (1936).

Return to Bowness-on-Windermere via Winster or along Windermere's shore.

Lyth Valley

[ON. Hill slope.]

This is the valley of the River Gilpin, named after the family to which the Rev. Bernard Gilpin, 'The Apostle of the North' of Kentmere Hall, and the Rev. William Gilpin of Scaleby Castle, Carlisle, both belonged. It was the writings of William in 1772, *Observations on . . . Cumberland and Westmorland*, which led to tourists visiting the Lakes.

This is damson country, particularly in the lower valley sheltered between the heights of Underbarrow Scar and Whitbarrow Scar. There is a belief that the first damsons were grown by the monks of Cartmel Priory who grafted wild sloe and wild plum. The white damson blossom is a feature in May and the fruit is picked in September.

Leave Bowness-on-Windermere on the B5284 towards Crook.

After 2½ miles turn right towards Winster and then first left past Gilpin Mill.

Turn south and follow the east side of the River Gilpin to Crosthwaite and the A5074.

Low Yews Cottages are on the A5074, ⅓ mile west of the Crosthwaite road junction.

At The Yews, which formerly stood near the cottages, William

Pearson, who became a banker, a naturalist and an author, was born in 1780.

Continue south on the A5074, following the west side of the River Gilpin, under the limestone ridge of Whitbarrow, to Sampool Bridge, known also as Gilpin Bridge, and the Derby Arms on the A590.

Whitbarrow   OFOL 36

Lakeside to Ambleside
Lake Windermere – East:
Bowness to Ambleside

<u>Bowness-on-Windermere.</u> *Leave Queen's Square on the A592 Rayrigg Road.*

<u>Mill Beck Bridge</u>, a former sand and gravel site, is now <u>The Windermere Steam Boat Museum</u>, opened in 1979 by HRH the Prince of Wales.

All the craft have associations with the Lake District and several have been rescued from the bottom of a lake or tarn. Amongst the exhibits are:

Beatrix Potter's flat-bottomed rowing boat, salvaged in 1976 from Moss Eccles Tarn.

The original dinghy, 'Amazon', retains its battered red sail, as featured in Arthur Ransome's novel.

Ferry boat 'Ann', an example of an old wherry, was raised from the bed of Lake Windermere near Belle Isle. The boat was built to carry a coach with horses, as well as foot passengers and livestock.

The steam launch 'Esperance', once owned by H. W. Schneider, was raised from the bottom of Lake Windermere in 1940. It is the oldest boat on Lloyd's Register of Yachts. Arthur Ransome used the boat as a model for Captain Flint's houseboat in *Swallows and Amazons*.

'Dolly' is claimed to be the oldest mechanically propelled boat in the world. It was built in 1850 and lay submerged in Ullswater for 67 years.

The steam launch 'S. L. Osprey' continues to take up to 12 passengers for a cruise.

Lady Holme (NT) and the Hen Holme islands lie offshore from the Steam Boat Museum.

On Lady Holme, no traces remain of the hospital founded in 1256 by Walter De Lindesay, Lord of the Manor of Windermere, nor of the later chantry dedicated to the Virgin Mary in the reign of Henry VIII.

Rayrigg Hall was the summer residence from 1780 to 1787 of William Wilberforce. As an MP, he devoted himself wholeheartedly to the cause of abolishing the slave trade and slavery.

Queen Adelaide's Hill (NT) was called Rayrigg Bank until re-named when Queen Adelaide, widow of William IV, visited in 1840. She landed at Millerground and walked up the hill to the viewpoint – Thomas West's 'fifth station'.

There is a car park and a picnic area.

Low Millerground on Wynlass Beck is a Sailing Centre.

Low Millerground House is claimed to be the oldest inhabited house on Windermere. The bell in the old bell tower at the end of the barn was used to summon the ferry that formerly crossed the lake from Belle Grange.

A footpath follows Wynlass Beck to the lake shore and continues south past the foot of Queen Adelaide's Hill and the public jetties to Rayrigg Meadow (NT).

Miller Howe had a long established reputation for '*the ultimate in elegance*' and for John Tovey's unique style of cooking and presentation. It is now under new ownership.

Hammarbank Viewpoint has a few car parking spaces.

At the roundabout, turn left onto the A591.

<u>Troutbeck Bridge</u>. In this locality, Julius Caesar Ibbetson (1750–1817), a landscape painter of the Lakeland scene, lived for a while after fleeing from London to escape from his creditors.

<u>The Sun Inn</u> is reputedly where Hartley Coleridge first met Alfred Lord Tennyson and wrote a sonnet about the event.

Walk past Lakes School and the Indoor Swimming Pool, which is open to the public at certain times.

<u>Calgarth Hall</u> *[ON. Kale Yard]* According to a 17c legend, this vegetable plot belonged to Kraster Cook and his wife. The land was coveted by Robert Philipson of Belle Isle, 'Robin-the-Devil'. He invited the Cooks to dine, accused them of stealing a silver cup, arranged for it to be found in their home and caused them to be hanged as thieves. Hauntings and cursings are said to have followed and no matter where the two skulls of the wronged people were buried, they made repeated re-appearances at Calgarth Hall. The skulls were finally exorcised by Dr Watson, Bishop of Landaff, Cardiff.

The Hall was later taken over by the Ethel Hedley Orthopaedic Hospital.

Cross the footbridge over Trout Beck.

<u>Calgarth Park</u> was the residence built by the remarkable Dr Richard Watson, Bishop of Llandaff (1737–1816). He held the Oxford chairs of Divinity and Chemistry simultaneously. In 1787, he improved the method of making charcoal for gunpowder by using cylindrical retorts. This discovery, he claimed, saved the Government at least a hundred thousands pounds a year in the wars that followed shortly after the French Revolution.

<u>White Cross Bay</u>. The white cross commemorates the death by drowning of two local men in 1853. The cross is inscribed, *'Watch*

therefore for you know neither the day nor the hour.'

At the lake side and at Ecclerigg Crag, a constable from Ambleside, John Longmire, is reported to have spent six years in the 1830s chiselling to engrave the rocks with such slogans as, *'National Debt £800,000,000. O save my country George and William Pitt* [followed by a list of 16 names]. *The Liberty of the Press.'* Some inscriptions remain: other were removed when stone was quarried for building Wray Castle on the opposite shore.

During World War II, White Cross Bay was a Short Brothers Aircraft Factory where Sunderland Flying Boats were assembled and a housing estate was built for the workers. The first Sunderland flew from here to Pembroke Dock in 1942. Twice the weight of a Sunderland was the Short Shetland prototype which landed here in 1945. The concrete areas, which were once the factory floor, have become a hard standing for caravans.

This is also the site of one of Manchester's underground pumping stations.

Cragwood House, on the A591, was the home of Norman Buckley, MBE, a friend of Donald Campbell, and the holder of water speed records in his hydroplane 'Miss Windermere'. The garden was designed by Thomas H. Mawson, whose work brought him fame throughout Britain and as far afield as Denmark, Greece and Canada. His lecture tours were worldwide.

Brockhole became The Lake District National Park Visitor Centre in 1969 when it was converted from the country house built in 1900 for William Henry Gaddum, a wealthy Manchester textile merchant who lived here until his death in 1945. The house and the 30 acres of terraced gardens and grounds, which extend down to the lake shore, were planned by Thomas Mawson. A jetty provides for boats bringing tourists. There are exhibitions, audio-visual presentations, a Visitor Information Service, a gift and book shop, special events throughout the holiday season and refreshments.

The Langdale Chase Hotel, built as a private house, was the first residence on Windermere to be lit by electricity. Thomas Mawson designed the grounds.

Briery Close, off Holbeck Lane to the right, was the former home of Sir James Kay-Shuttleworth, the industrialist and educationalist. His guests, Elizabeth Gaskell and Charlotte Brontë met here and, years later, Mrs Gaskell wrote the first biography of Charlotte.

The Lowood Hotel, built in 1850, replaced an older coaching inn. Among many distinguished visitors was Thomas West who praised the view and the echo which resulted from firing a small cannon. William Wordsworth, Thomas Arnold, and Professor Wilson met here in 1847 to oppose the extension of the railway from Windermere.

A Water Sports Centre operates from the lake shore.

Dove Nest, half way up the fell side, was built in the late 18c by John Benson, who also owned Dove Cottage. For a short time, Felicia Hemans (1793–1835) lived here. Her best known poem, 'Casablanca' (1829) has familiar opening lines:

> *'The boy stood on the burning deck*
> *Whence all but he had fled.'*

From 1853, Dove Nest was the home of the great-uncle of the poet Robert Graves, the Rev. Robert Perceval Graves.

Stagshaw Garden (NT) created by Cubby Acland, Regional Agent for the National Trust, is a woodland garden with azaleas and rhododendrons planted on the hillside.

Waterhead Marina, jetties and Lake Windermere 'Steamer' Pier, combine to make this a busy tourist area.

Ambleside

*[ON. A melyr saetr = summer shieling or
pasture by a river sand bank]*

Waterhead

This is the 'port' of the town of Ambleside, which is a mile away, and
the terminus for the Lake Windermere 'steamers' since regular services began in 1845. Smaller launches also ply their trade and small
boats may be hired.

Many of the buildings were constructed for the Victorian visitors.
On the promenade is one of the largest Youth Hostels.

Borrans Park [*ON. Heap of stones*] is a lakeside recreation area. The
adjacent Roman Fort of Galava was protected on two sides by water.
Originally it was built of wood and turf on the delta flat at the confluence of two rivers, the Brathay and the Rothay, by Julius Agricola
in AD 79. Hadrian, by building with stone, replaced the original structure in AD 122. To avoid the flooding which had beset the earlier fort,
the rectangular replacement with four corner towers was built on a
raised platform superimposed on the original site. The main gateway
in the eastern wall and the location of such buildings as the Principia
(HQ), the Commandant's House and two granaries have been identified.

Hadrian's fort, with a garrison of 500 men, protected the
Roman road which extended from the coast at Ravenglass

(Glannaventa) and on to High Street and Penrith (Brocavum), giving access to routes north and south and to York (Eboracum).

The fort was attacked at least once during its 150 years existence, as testified by a Roman gravestone, now in the Museum of Natural History and Archaeology at Kendal. Inscribed are the words, *'To the Good God of the Underworld: Flavius Romanus, Record Clerk. Lived for 35 years. Killed in the fort by the enemy.'*

The stones have long been plundered.

The layout of the fort is best seen from Todd Crag on Loughrigg, described in 1607 by William Camden as the *'carcass as it were, of an ancient city'*.

The confluence of the Rivers Brathay and Rothay provides a breeding place for char and trout. The parent fish swim together upstream from the lake before separating towards their spawning grounds, the char taking the Brathay and the trout the Rothay. Char, an Arctic fish, prefers the cold depths of the lake and fishermen must sink a long, heavily weighted line, holding bright metal spinners, and pull the line slowly behind a rowing boat to prevent the hooks becoming entangled. At one time, char was popular at court in London, but before fast transport and refrigeration, the fish was baked in a pie to withstand the journey.

Lake Road

Hayes Garden World, on the A591 to Ambleside, is acclaimed as a gardener's paradise. It has been chosen Garden Centre of the Year in the past.

The Wooden Cabin, nearer the town, was imported from Norway in 1911 by the artist father of the Grasmere painter, W. Heaton Cooper, for use as a studio. There have been several changes of use since then.

Ambleside Town

This popular, south-facing town in the Rothay Valley, sheltered on three sides by fells, is one mile north of Waterhead.

The town still retains the character and architectural interest of Victorian times and contains many 'listed' buildings. In 1980, the town centre was designated the Lake District National Park's first Conservation Area.

Although railway building stopped at Windermere in 1847, tourists travelled on by steam launch, carriage and charabanc. In 1855, the Ambleside Turnpike Trust recorded over 21,480 carriages crossing Troutbeck Bridge, and a further 15,240 paid the turnpike toll on the Grasmere to Keswick section of the road. Yet fifty years earlier, a single carriage passing Dove Cottage merited an entry in Dorothy Wordsworth's diary. The growing numbers of tourists present difficult problems for the authorities to solve.

Kelsick Road

Turn downhill. Pass the Library, which, for many years, stored the Armitt Collection in very congested upstairs rooms. These items are now in the Museum and Library of the Armitt Trust.

Market Square. The Wednesday market is held on the small car park.

St Mary's Church, with its distinctive 180 feet spire, was designed by Sir George Gilbert Scott, grandfather of Sir Giles who built Liverpool's Anglican Cathedral.

Wordsworth took a great interest in the plans but he died before work started. His widow, Mary, attended the consecration in 1854.

The Wordsworth Memorial Chapel contains stained glass windows in memory of the four women in Wordsworth's life: Mary, his wife (Jacob and Rachel at the well); Dora, his daughter (Ruth and Naomi); Dorothy, his sister and Sarah Hutchinson, his sister-in-law (Martha and Mary).

The south chancel window shows Christ blessing the children ('*of such is the Kingdom of Heaven*') and Peter ('*Feed my lambs*'), in memory of John Kelsick, who left property and wealth for the education of the children of Ambleside.

In the centre of the south aisle, Saints Anne and Mary are the patron saints of Ambleside's old church and its replacement. The window was the work of Dean Walmsley and his wife, stained glass artists from St Anne's in Langdale.

West of the south porch, the 'Children's Window' commemorates Matthew Arnold, poet, critic and HM Inspector of Schools, and the Forster Education Act of 1870, which provided for the election of school boards, empowered to levy rates to supplement Government grants and to compel children over five and under thirteen to attend school.

On the west wall is the large Rush-bearing Mural designed and painted by Gordon Ransome in 1944 when the Royal College of Art was in war-time residence in Ambleside. The rush-bearing ceremony dates back to medieval times when rushes, strewn as a floor covering on earth floors, were renewed in the summer. The common rush (juncus effusus) was used and the clearing out of old rushes (juncus) may have led to the word 'junk' for rubbish. Ambleside commemorates this ceremony on a Saturday early in July.

Charlotte Maria Shaw Mason, who founded the College of Education in Ambleside in 1892, is remembered by a slate plaque in the north-west corner.

Two pieces of sculpture are the work of Josephina de Vasconcellos: the 'Nativity' and the 'Virgin and Child'.

In the churchyard is the grave of Kurt Schwitters (1887–1948).

He was driven out of Nazi Germany as a 'degenerate artist', one of the founders of 'Merz', an abstract art form developed in Hanover between the wars. In 1945 he resided in Ambleside at No. 2 Gale Crescent and moved to No. 4 Milland Park in 1946. His studio was a barn at Elterwater. In poor health and nursed by his English friend, Edith Thomas, he died of asthma in Kendal.

<u>Church Street,</u> formerly Ratten Row.

<u>The Old Court House</u>. The Police Station moved here in 1882 to bring together within one building the 'station', the cells, the court-room, the magistrates's retiring room and the police house. In 1964, a modern Police Station was built in Rydal Road.

<u>The National Park Information Centre</u> now occupies part of the Old Court House.

<u>Kelsick Buildings</u>. The Kelsicks were merchants and their grocery business served customers for more than 300 years before closing. John Kelsick founded Kelsick Grammar School in Ambleside during the reign of George I (1714–1727), replaced now by the Lakes School at Troutbeck Bridge.

<u>The Old Stamp House</u>. William Wordsworth, whilst living at Rydal Mount, worked from here as the Stamp and Excise Collector for Westmorland on an annual salary of £200. All legal documents required stamps and it was Wordsworth's duty to distribute official stamps and later to collect the money.

Market Place.

<u>Post Office</u>. The present building occupies the site of the home of William Green (1761–1823), the Ambleside landscape artist whose etchings are greatly prized.

<u>The Office of Brown's Luxury Coaches</u>, one of the earliest com-

panies offering tours of the Lake District, was formerly the Old Post Office. Here, in 1835, Owen Lloyd, curate of Ambleside, wrote the Ambleside Rushbearing Hymn:

> *'Our fathers to the house of God*
> *As yet a building rude,*
> *Bore offerings from the flowery sod*
> *And fragrant rushes strewed . . .'*

The annual Rushbearing procession to the church pauses here whilst this hymn is sung.

The Town Hall and Mechanics Institute date from 1858. Harriet Martineau, journalist and novelist, held winter lecture courses here.

At the side, above the modern shop window level, are visible the remains of the old entrance to the Council Chamber.

The Market Hall (Cross House). The present building dates from 1863. In front, the Market Cross previously stood, dated 1651.

The Queen's Hotel. On this site once stood the earliest inn in Ambleside – the Cock, or the Black Cock. More recently it was the Commercial Hotel and also a Youth Hostel.

The Slack, a narrow alleyway from the side of the hotel, passes Sheila's Cottage on the way to Zeffirelli's cinema.

The Salutation is a former coaching inn where the yard and outbuildings can still be identified. Wordsworth in his *Guide to the Lakes* anticipated that visitors would start to explore Lakeland from here. Eminent visitors have included Keats (1818), John Stuart Mill (1831) and Tennyson (1835).

The Market Cross was moved to its present site in 1885, probably to ease traffic flow. Ambleside's market charter was granted in 1650 when there was a thriving wool trade.

Across the road, the former bus station, now a shopping centre,

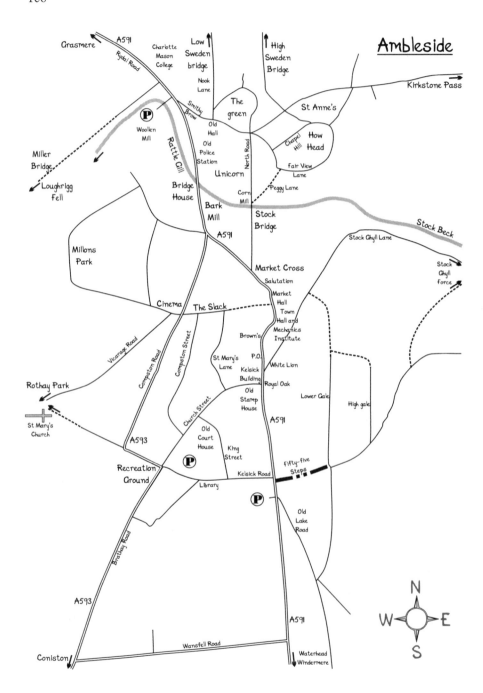

Ambleside

was built on the old 'tenterfield' where newly woven cloth from the riverside mills was stretched out to dry.

North Road

<u>Stock Bridge</u> The River Stock, which rises two miles away on the Kirkstone Pass, plunges nearly 90 feet at Stock Ghyll before tumbling through the town where it used to power a succession of mills. Upstream was a fulling mill which became the bobbin mill of Messrs. Horrax before being converted into holiday flats. Below Stock Bridge was a corn mill which now has a replica overshot water wheel (1973). It has become a studio of art and craft. Opposite, on the south bank, a bark-crushing mill once produced tannin for the leather

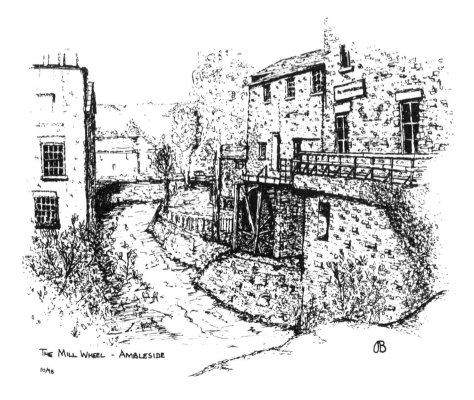

THE MILL WHEEL - AMBLESIDE
10/98

trade. Just below Bridge House was a woollen mill, which became a saw mill and a carriage works before conversion into a restaurant with a water wheel.

The River Stock has always divided the town in two. To the north of the river, 'above Stock', was the original settlement, an area of narrow streets, cobbled alleyways and houses built with dark blue-grey Silurian flagstones and slates.

Stock Bridge was the original river crossing for packhorses and later, in 1763, the turnpike followed the same route through Ambleside. Along this route stand six inns: the Golden Rule, the Unicorn, the Salutation (1656), the Queen's Hotel, the White Lion (1740) and the Royal Oak.

Descend Rattle Gill. The name originated from the noise of the mills, the water wheels and the turbulent waters of Stock Ghyll.

Rydal Road

Bridge House (NT), on a bridge over Stock Ghyll, has existed since the early 16c, with two rooms and an outside staircase to reach the upper floor. It was probably a summer house and an apple store for Ambleside Hall, the former home of the Braithwaite family in the area of Smithy Brow. Their estate extended down to Stock Ghyll and across the bridge to the other side. The Rydal Road, which now intervenes was only constructed in 1883.

At various times, Bridge House had been used as a cottage — the Rigg family reputedly raised six children in it — a tea-room, a weaver's, a cobbler's, an antiques and a gift shop. This unique building, which retains its 'wrestler' slates interlocking along the roof ridge, was opened in 1956 as the first National Trust Information and Recruitment Centre.

The Old Police Station can be recognised by its heavy, studded

'Wrestler' or 'Wrostler' slates on roof ridge

door. At the time of the Napoleonic Wars, local business men united as 'Bondsmen' to encourage a respect for the law within 15 miles of the Market Cross.

The Police Station moved to Church Street in 1882 and to Rydal Road again in 1964.

Charlotte Mason College was once a large Victorian private house, Scale How, where F. W. Faber worked as a tutor, 1840–42. The College was founded in 1892 '*for the education of earnest, well-bred young gentlewomen*'. Charlotte Mason remained as Principal until her death in 1923 at the age of 81. Governesses were trained here and now teachers. Since being privately owned, the property has passed to the Council (1961), the University of Lancaster and now the University of St Martin.

In August, the Lake District Summer Music programme is based at the College.

The Armitt Museum and Library opened in 1997. This collection of rare and interesting books and artefacts was the bequest of Mary

Armitt (1851–1911), reflecting her particular interest in local history and the Lake District. Roman relics from Ambleside Fort, fungi watercolours by Beatrix Potter, drawings and prints by Ambleside artist William Green, documents and manuscripts relating to Lakeland poets and authors, paintings and photographs are amongst many of the items featured.

<u>Ambleside Sports</u> are held in Rydal Park, further along Rydal Road.

Smithy Brow

This road is known locally as 'The Struggle' on account of the difficulty with which horse-drawn traffic ascended the steep gradient leading to the Kirkstone Pass.

<u>Old House</u>. In this area, between Smithy Brow and North Road, Ambleside Hall was probably built. It was the early 16c home of the prosperous Braithwaite family of yeomen farmers. Ancient pinkish stones from the Roman Fort in Borrans Park, once owned by the Braithwaites, were said to have been incorporated into the walls of the family home.

Many of the old properties up the hill date from the 17c.

Chapel Hill

<u>How Head</u> is a modified 'statesman's' residence, which appeals by virtue of its cobblestone walls with wooden lintels, large roofing flagstones lessening in size towards the ridge, 'wrestler' slates along the ridge and tall cylindrical slate chimneys. 'Crow-stepped' gables are another distinguishing feature of such properties.

<u>St Anne's</u> was for 42 years the former parish church, built in 1812 on the site of a chapel whose earthen floor brought about the origin of the Rushbearing Ceremony. The church was deconsecrated and divided into apartments when St Mary's Church was completed.

<u>Fair View Lane and Peggy Lane</u>. There are many old properties, several of them modified 'statesman's' residences in this uphill area 'above Stock'.

<u>Josephina de Vasconcellos,</u> the English born daughter of a Brazilian diplomat at the London Embassy, became a sculptress and established her home and studio in this part of Ambleside. Many of her works, of a religious nature, may be seen in numerous Lakeland churches and in St Paul's Cathedral.

Descend North Road to the town centre.

Dove Crag	1.5	Fairfield Horseshoe	1.3
High Pike	1.3	Low Pike	1.2
Little Hart Crag	1.4	Nab Scar	1.2
Red Screes	1.5	Wansfell	2.4, 5

Loughrigg Fell	3.6

Rydal

[OE. ON. Rydale = Valley of the rye.]

Leave Ambleside on the A591, which passes through a landscape of Borrowdale Volcanic rock, following a major geological fault line, enlarged and deepened by glacial action.

This has always offered the best route for communication. By the end of the Middle Ages it was used by pack animals engaged in the wool trade. Carters and waggoners became involved in quarrying and mining. The turnpike brought road improvements in the 1720s and Thomas West's *A Guide to the Lakes in Cumberland, Westmorland and Lancashire* (1778) encouraged the development of tourism. The pace of change quickened when, in 1811, the 'Good Intent' coach, holding four passengers travelled this way three times a week from Kendal to Whitehaven. Those early travellers could never have remotely imagined what the volume of road traffic has become today.

<u>The Knoll</u>. Harriet Martineau, writer and lecturer, built this house in 1846 and lived here for thirty years, during which time she wrote *The Complete Guide to the English Lakes* (1854). Locally, she was well known for her atheism, her interest in mesmerism and her small, model dairy farm. Wordsworth, one of her many literary visitors, planted two pine trees in her garden.

<u>Scandale Bridge</u> crosses Scandale Beck.

<u>Old Hall Hill</u> is a low knoll with trees near the path leading to step-

ping stones across the River Rothay. This was the site of the Manor House of le Flemings, great landowners since the Conquest. A replacement Rydal Hall was built in the 16c in Rydal village.

Alternatively, leave Ambleside on the A593 Coniston/Langdale Road. Cross the Bridge over the River Rothay and turn sharp right onto the minor, Under Loughrigg Road, which follows the River Rothay to Rydal.

<u>Miller Bridge House</u>. When this was a school, run by Parson Dawes in the early 19c, amongst the pupils were Owen Lloyd; Hartley and Derwent Coleridge; and Wordsworth's sons, Willie and John.

<u>Fox How</u> was built as a holiday residence in 1833 by Dr Thomas Arnold (1795–1842), Headmaster of Rugby School, 1828–1842. He had ten children, five of whom, together with Mrs Arnold, were buried in Ambleside churchyard. Dr Arnold was buried in Rugby School Chapel. Fox How was inherited by his son, Matthew Arnold (1822–1888), poet, critic and inspector of schools.

<u>Fox Ghyll</u>. Thomas De Quincey (1785–1859) made this his home from 1820 to 1825 during which time he wrote *Confessions of an English Opium Eater.*

<u>Loughrigg Holme</u> formerly belonged to Edward Quillinan, widower, who married Wordsworth's daughter, Dora, in 1841. Wordsworth initially opposed the marriage, but eventually there was a tentative reconciliation with Quillinan.

<u>Stepping Stones</u>, originally 'Lanty Fleming's Cottage', was the home of Edward Quillinan during his first marriage. Later, the house belonged to Wordsworth's son, William, and then to the poet's grandson, Gordon, who arranged and annotated Wordsworth's manuscripts. The house faces the stepping stones across the River Rothay.

Pelter Bridge, a packhorse bridge, crosses the River Rothay, and provides access to the A591.

Rydal Hall. The le Fleming family of Coniston Old Hall, who were first mentioned in the Charter of Furness Abbey, 1126, acquired land at Rydal by marriage to the de Lancasters in 1408. In 1652, Sir Daniel le Fleming commissioned probably the first Lakeland landscape paintings of the Hall and its grounds. In 1671, he wrote the first history of the county, *Description of the County of Westmoreland* and one of the earliest topographical reviews, *Survey of Westmoreland and Cumberland* in 1671. The Hall was enlarged in 1799 and remains largely 18c.

In 1963, Rydal Hall became the Carlisle Diocesan Conference and Retreat Centre.

Rydal Cascades comprise a series of waterfalls in the grounds, greatly admired by artists and writers. A Grotto, or summer house, frames the view of the lower falls.

The gardens are open to the public.

Rydal Park is crossed by a public footpath which passes the site where the Ambleside Sports are held on the Thursday before the first Monday in August. The Sports include hound trailing where the dogs follow an aniseed trail and are encouraged to the winning post by the frantic shouts and whistles of their owners; and Cumberland and Westmorland style wrestling where the competitors lock their arms behind each other's back and attempt to throw their opponent to the ground.

Rydal Mount originally was a farmhouse built by John Keene in 1570 and enlarged by subsequent owners.

In 1813, at the age of 43, William Wordsworth, his wife Mary, their three remaining children, William's sister Dorothy and sister-in-law

Sarah Hutchinson moved into Rydal Mount from their third home in Grasmere, the Old Rectory.

This was their fourth and last home, and the most comfortable. It was rented from Lady Diana le Fleming of Rydal Hall. Until then, Wordsworth's income had been modest, but his appointment as Distributor of Stamps for the County of Westmorland (1813–1842) remunerated him substantially whilst making relatively few demands on his time. He was able to afford a clerk, two maids and later, a gardener.

Wordsworth's reputation as a poet was already established, but his fame continued to grow with the publication of *The Excursion* and *The River Duddon Sonnets*. Rydal Mount became a place of pilgrimage whose visitors included some of the most notable literary people of the day.

A state pension was awarded to Wordsworth in 1842 and he became Poet Laureate in the following year on the death of Robert Southey. This coincided with Wordsworth virtually ceasing to write poetry. He directed his energies, in speeches and writing letters to 'The Times', protesting against the railway line to Windermere and succeeded in preventing the proposed extension to Keswick. He lavished his creative talents on landscaping the 4½ acres of garden until his death in 1850 at the age of 80.

Wordsworth was outlived until 1855 by his sister Dorothy who declined into senility, and by his wife Mary who died in 1859. His children, John, Dora and William grew up here and Dora died here.

The Wordsworth Trust purchased the property in 1970 and opened it to the public, preserving it much as Wordsworth knew it.

'<u>Coffin Track</u>'. Behind Rydal Mount is the old packhorse route along which coffins were carried for burial at Grasmere before Rydal became a parish in its own right in 1824.

Rydal

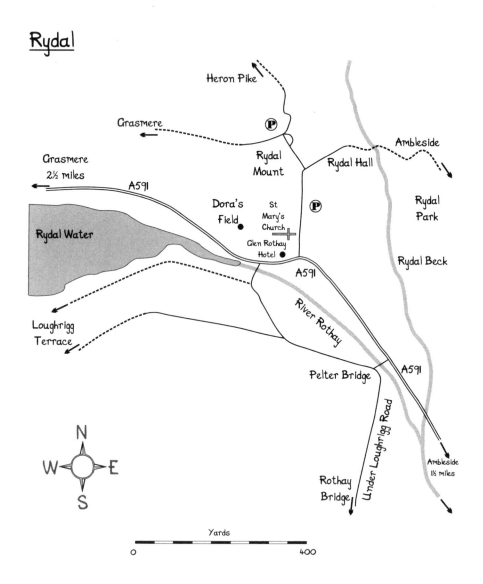

<u>Dora's Field</u> (NT), or Rashfield, is reached by a gate from the churchyard. It was bought in 1826 for a building site by Wordsworth as a safeguard against having to move from rented Rydal Mount. The field was given to Dora, Wordsworth's daughter, but she died before her father.

Daffodils are a spectacular feature in the spring.

<u>St Mary's Church</u> was built in Rydal Hall's orchard by Lady le Fleming in 1824 and enlarged in 1884. The Wordsworth family pew was in front of the pulpit. In front of the lectern was the pew of Dr Arnold and family. In the south wall, a window commemorates Dr Arnold, his wife and their ten children. The step daughters of Dora Wordsworth, Jemima and Rotha Quillinan, are remembered in the next window.

The Fairfield Horseshoe	*1.3*	*Loughrigg Fell*	*3.7*
Hart Crag	*1.5*		
Heron Pike	*1.3*		
Low Pike	*1.2*		
Nab Scar	*1.3*		

<u>Glen Rothay Hotel</u> was once known as Ivy Cottage, the home of Edward Quillinan and his first wife, Jemima, who died here tragically in a fire in 1822.

<u>Rydal Water,</u> once known as Rothaymere after the river which flows through it from Grasmere to Ambleside, is the smallest of the lakes, ¾ mile by ¼ mile, maximum depth 60 feet, average depth 25 feet. It lies in the glaciated valley between Wordsworth's favourite walk along the foot of Nab Scar and the path along Loughrigg Terrace opposite. In the early 18c, Sir William le Fleming began, and then abandoned, the building of a 'pleasure house' on one of the islands.

<u>Nab Cottage,</u> formerly Nab farm dated 1702, was the home of John

Simpson. His daughter Margaret was courted by Thomas De Quincey and bore him a son in 1816. They married a year later. When John Simpson fell on hard times, De Quincey helped him financially and lived in the house from time to time. But De Quincey had to sell the house in 1833. It was the subsequent residence of Hartley Coleridge who died here in 1849. He was the son of Samuel Taylor Coleridge.

White Moss Quarry, at the head of Rydal Water, has a car park near the River Rothay, which links the two lakes of Grasmere and Rydal Water.

The A591 continues on the level, around the base of White Moss Common *above, using a causeway built about 1831.* The road cuts through Bainriggs Wood and by the roadsign 'Grasmere', through Brothers' Wood, so-called because Wordsworth composed *The Brothers* here whilst walking in 1799.

The old road rises over the 'craggy hill' of White Moss Common, where Benjamin in *The Waggoner* (1806) expertly drove his heavy wagon and team of eight horses, without the use of a whip, on the journey from Ambleside to Keswick.

The Glow Worm Rock, near the start of the rise, features in several of Wordsworth's poems. The whole area inspired both William and Dorothy to write about their impressions.

Ladywood, at the highest point on the road, was built by Ernest De Selincourt (1870–1943), editor of the Standard Edition of Wordsworth's poems.

There is parking space in the disused quarry nearby.

The wooden Wishing Gate, beloved by Sarah Hutchinson, Wordsworth's sister-in-law, was sometimes known as Sarah's gate.

John's Grove, entered at one end through an iron gate, was named after Wordsworth's brother John, a naval captain, who loved this place.

How Top, opposite the duck pond, is where the old carriageway meets with the 'coffin track' bridleway from Rydal. The track beneath Nab Scar and past heron-frequented White Moss Tarn was a favourite walk and a source of inspiration for the Wordsworths who, for fifty years, lived at one end or other of it. Paths from the tarn lead up to the viewpoint at 460 feet on top of White Moss Common.

How Top farm buildings have retained much of their typical white-washed fellside character of the kind Wordsworth described '*like separated stars with clouds between*'. The bank barn is a traditional structure.

How Foot was the holiday house of the Rev. William Spooner, Warden of New College, Oxford (1844–1930) from whom 'Spoonerisms' emanated when he transposed the initial sounds of two words, e.g. blushing crow, for crushing blow.

Grasmere

[ON. Gris-mere = lake of the pigs. OE. Lake with grassy shore.]

Wordsworth described Grasmere as *'the loveliest spot that man hath ever found.'*

<u>Grasmere Lake</u> (NT) is glaciated, 1 mile long, ½ mile wide, maximum depth 75 feet. The central island of moraine was a favourite destination of the Wordsworths who used to row across taking a picnic. The barn on the island became the subject of Wordsworth's poem, *'Written with a pencil upon a stone'* (1800).

The setting is dominated by Helm Crag to the north where the summit rocks seem to assume the shape of the 'Lion and the Lamb', or 'The Old Woman playing the Organ' according to one's imagination. The steep sided fells of Silver How to the west and of Heron Pike to the east enclose the valley.

The classic view of the lake is from Loughrigg Terrace to the south, but Wordsworth preferred to admire the scenery from a boat on *'the bosom of the Lake.'*

Town End

This hamlet, which retains its 18c character, was declared a Conservation Area in 1984. The old packhorse route over White Moss Common descends through the settlement along How Head Lane.

<u>Dove Cottage</u>, formerly an inn, 'The Dove and Olive Branch', was

built before 1617. From 1799 to 1808, it was the first and probably the happiest home of William Wordsworth and his sister Dorothy, who rented the property for £5 per annum. Previously they had always lived with friends or relatives.

In 1802, William brought his bride, Mary Hutchinson, to live at the cottage where three of his five children were born: John in 1803, Dora in 1804 and Thomas in 1806.

'*Plain living and high thinking*' epitomised the Wordsworths' life style.

'*Plain living*' involved a spartan domestic routine with William tending the garden and chopping wood, whilst Dorothy and Mary were engaged in housework. Wild flowers gathered from the fells were planted in the garden where William built the flight of steps with the help of his neighbour, John Fisher.

'*Plain living*' included the children's bedroom which was so damp that William papered the walls with newspaper to offset the effect.

Plain breakfasts were too basic for the visiting Sir Walter Scott who, according to reports, blocked his bedroom door with a chair, climbed out of the window and walked to the Swan Hotel for something more to his liking before returning undetected to his bedroom.

The '*high thinking*' is represented by some of Wordsworth's most inspired poetry written whilst living at the cottage: '*The Green Linnet*', '*The Cuckoo*', '*The Rainbow*', '*Daffodils*', '*Michael*', '*The Ode on the Intimations of Immortality*', the completion of '*The Prelude*' and the beginnings of '*The Excursion*'. During the same years, Dorothy compiled her famous journal, recording almost daily events and observations.

'*High thinking*' emanated from the intellectual stimulus of conversing with visitors to the cottage, including such literary notables as Samuel Taylor Coleridge, his brother-in-law Robert Southey,

Thomas De Quincey and Sir Walter Scott.

The Wordsworths only left Dove Cottage when short of space as their family increased.

Thomas De Quincey had made several attempts to visit the Wordsworths at Dove Cottage but his nerve failed him and he returned to Oxford. Finally he arrived in 1807 and perhaps more than anyone he was instrumental in introducing Wordsworth's work to a wider public.

When the Wordsworths moved to Allan Bank in 1808, De Quincey took over the lease of Dove Cottage. Dorothy was pleased and made him some curtains. But the Wordsworths were most upset when he knocked down the moss bower they had built in the garden and cut back the orchard to let more light into the cottage. The Wordsworths further disapproved when he married the farmer's daughter from Nab Cottage in 1817.

Although De Quincey moved out of Dove Cottage in 1820, he retained the tenancy for a total of 27 years in order to store all his books.

De Quincey became the second editor of *the Westmorland Gazette*, 1818–19, but was sacked for not going to the office. His memories of the Lake Poets are gathered in *Recollections of the Lakes and the Lake Poets*, but he is most remembered for the book based upon his drug addiction, *Confessions of an English Opium Eater*. His opium balance is displayed in Dove Cottage. De Quincey died in Edinburgh in 1859.

The Wordsworth Trust acquired Dove Cottage and opened it to visitors in 1890, furnished in the style of the Wordsworths' era.

The Wordsworth Museum, adjacent to Dove Cottage, exhibits paintings of early Lakeland scenes, together with pictures and manuscripts of the life and work of Wordsworth, other Lake Poets and some of their associates.

The Rock of Names, at the rear of the Museum, was transported here from Thirlmere, where it marked the former meeting place of Wordsworth and Coleridge halfway between their respective homes at Grasmere and Keswick.

Sykeside Farm was once the home of John and Agnes Fisher. John occasionally helped Wordsworth in the garden of Dove Cottage, and John's sister, Molly, assisted domestically.

In the former barn at the back of Sykeside is The Wordsworth Library.

Ashburner's Cottage belonged to Thomas and Agnes Ashburner. Thomas sometimes helped Wordsworth with odd jobs whilst Agnes's story of the family's financial misfortune was the theme of Wordsworth's poem 'Repentance'.

Rose Cottage. Hartley Coleridge lived here from 1829 to 1840 during which time he frequently wandered off around the country, drinking and sleeping rough, leaving Wordsworth to pay the bills.

The Prince of Wales Hotel was built in 1855. The Wordsworths were irritated by the earlier obtrusive structure of a boat house on the lake shore. The present boat house, with the inscription 'WP 1843', refers to one of Wordsworth's school fellows at Hawkshead, William Pearson, who became an eminent mathematician.

Grasmere Village

The Wordsworth Memorial Drinking Fountain at the road junction to Grasmere village, B5287, has separate drinking troughs for man and beast. When the turnpike road was built in 1770, now the A591, this was a refreshing watering place before the struggle up Dunmail Raise.

The Sports Field is the venue for Grasmere Sports held on the third Thursday after the first Monday in August. It is the biggest traditional sports event in the Lake District and, like the Ambleside Sports, includes Cumberland and Westmorland wrestling, the Guides Race to the summit of Butter Crag and back, and hound trailing.

St Oswald's Church, by the River Rothay, dates from the 14c and is thought to be the third church on this site. Tradition claims that St Oswald preached here in the 7c. Oswald was King of Northumbria, classed by the Venerable Bede as one of the seven greatest Anglo-Saxon kings. Opposite Grasmere's Garden Centre, in a field, is St Oswald's Well.

The north aisle of the church, constructed c.1500, was called the Langdale Aisle because the congregation came from the Langdale Valley. The well of the nave was modified to carry a new roof in the 17c.

> Not raised in nice proportions was the pile,
> But large and massy; for duration built;
> With pillars crowded, and the roof upheld
> By naked rafters intricately crossed.
>   *The Excursion V.*

Before the floor was paved in 1841, rushes provided a covering. A Rush-bearing Ceremony is still held on the Saturday nearest to 5th August, St Oswald's Day, to commemorate the occasion when fresh rushes were brought into the church and the bearers were rewarded with gingerbread and ale.

Until 1861, men and women sat apart in church – the men's door is at the west end.

Wordsworth's memorial tablet has an inscription by John Keble, the Oxford theologian. Wordsworth's prayer book is preserved in a glass case.

An epitaph to Jemima Quillinan, first wife of Edward Quillinan, records her tragic death, and there are chancel memorials to the le Flemings of Rydal Hall.

The churchyard once served three parishes, each of which has its own entrance: a lych gate for Grasmere, an arch for Rydal and Ambleside, and a small gate for Langdale. In the churchyard are the graves of William Wordsworth (d. 1850), his wife Mary (d. 1859) and his sister Dorothy (d. 1855). Nearby is the grave of Mary's sister, Sarah Hutchinson (d. 1835). Buried here also are Catharine ('Kate') and Thomas, the poet's children who died in 1812, and Dora Quillinan, the poet's daughter.

There are graves also of Hartley Coleridge; Sarah Nelson of Gingerbread fame; Sir John Richardson, the Arctic explorer; William Green, the Lakeland artist and, by the path from the lych gate, the grave of John and Sarah Green, who perished in a snowstorm between Langdale and Easedale whilst their family of small children waited in vain for their return.

The churchyard yew trees were planted by Wordsworth.

Church Stile, opposite the church, now a National Trust shop, was formerly an inn with a cockpit. In 1799, William Wordsworth and Samuel Taylor Coleridge stayed here whilst on a walking holiday. Wordsworth wrote to his sister that he had found, '*a small house in Grasmere empty which perhaps we will take*'. This turned out to be Dove Cottage.

The Old Rectory, opposite the church, became the Wordsworths' third home in Grasmere, 1811–1813, after leaving Allan Bank. Wordsworth completed *The Excursion* here in 1812.

The Old Rectory stood on undrained land, '*a hateful house*' according to Sarah Hutchinson. The damp and poor sanitation may have contributed to the deaths in 1812 of two of Wordsworth's chil-

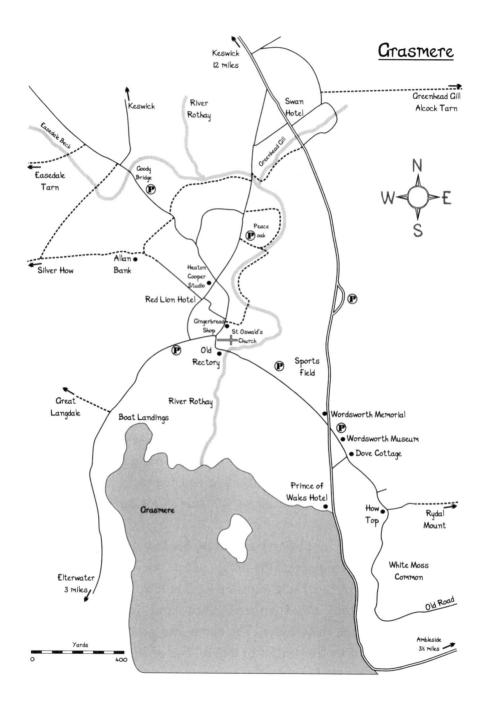

Grasmere

dren within six months of each other. Catharine ('Kate') died, age 3, in June while both parents were away and was buried before they knew of her death. Thomas, age 6, died in December to the utter despair of the family. The urgent desire to leave The Old Rectory drove the family to seek sanctuary at Rydal Mount.

The <u>Gingerbread Shop</u> is housed in the tiny schoolroom, built in 1660, where William Wordsworth briefly taught and where his children had lessons. William claimed that universal education was the key to eliminate ignorance and poverty.

In 1854, the schoolroom was let as a home to a former cook of Patterdale, Sarah Nelson. She first made the gingerbread which was bestowed on the rushbearers. Grasmere gingerbread continues to be sold from the premises.

The <u>Red Lion</u> dates from the early 18c with subsequent modern additions. Adjoining are the former stables and coach house. At the rear, <u>Moss Side</u> cottages derived their name from the land created by the medieval drainage of the marsh.

The <u>Heaton Cooper Studio</u> is named after a local water colour artist. Contemporary Lake District landscape pictures and prints are on sale.

<u>Allan Bank</u> was built in 1805 by a Liverpool merchant, John Crump. Whilst it was being built, the Wordsworths considered it to be *'a temple of abomination'*. But this house was the only one available in Grasmere large enough to hold a growing family when the time came to move out of Dove Cottage. Allan Bank became the Wordsworths' second Grasmere home from 1808 to 1811. Catharine and William were born here.

Contributing to an uncomfortable stay were the disputes with the landlord and the smoking chimneys. The household became congested with five adults and five children and long-staying visitors, such as

De Quincey and Samuel Taylor Coleridge and his two sons.

Wordsworth wrote several of his prose works here, including the earliest parts of his *Guide to the Lakes* in which he presaged a National Park by remarking that persons of taste 'deem the district a sort of national property in which every person has a right and an interest'.

When the friendship between Wordsworth and Coleridge grew increasingly strained and living at Allan Bank became too expensive to maintain, the move took place to The Old Rectory.

Subsequently, Allan Bank became the home of Canon Rawnsley, founder, with Octavia Hill, of the National Trust, which now owns the house, although it is not open to the public.

The Peace Oak stands in Broadgate Meadow. It was planted by Canon Rawnsley, on 19 July 1919, to mark a Day of Peace on the anniversary of the start of World War I.

The Swan Hotel. *'Who does not know the famous Swan?'* asked Wordsworth, when Benjamin, *The Waggoner*, resisted the urge to call for a drink. This is the old coaching inn where, it is said, Sir Walter Scott 'escaped' secretly to enjoy the kind of refreshment which was not available from his teetotal hosts at Dove Cottage.

Greenhead Gill, behind the hotel, is the setting for Wordsworth's poem 'Michael.

Dollywaggon Pike	1.5	Blea Rigg	3.6
Fairfield	1.6	Calf Crag	3.3, 4
Great Rigg	1.4	Gibson Knott	3.2
Helvellyn	1.17	Harrison Stickle	3.11
Heron Pike	1.2	Helm Crag	3.4
Nab Scar	1.3	High Raise	3.5
St Sunday Crag	1.6	Loughrigg Fell	3.5

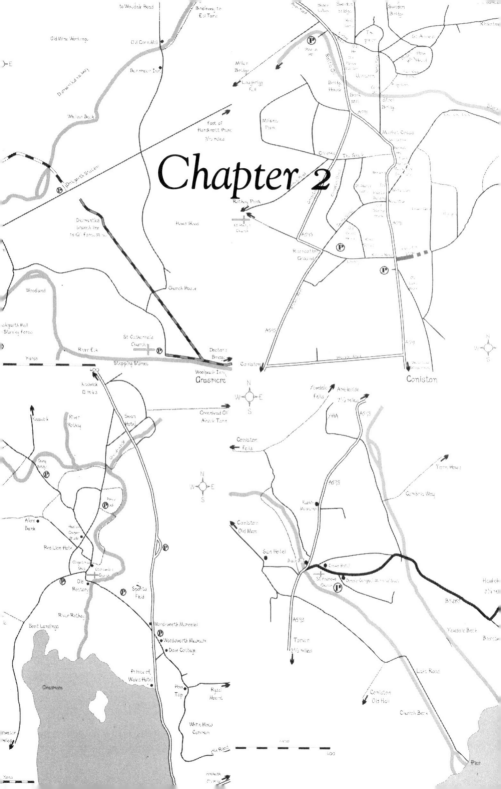

Chapter 2

Ambleside to Lakeside
Lake Windermere – West

On leaving Ambleside, the A593 Coniston road crosses the narrow Rothay Bridge and then follows the valley of the River Brathay. [ON. Broad River.]

<u>White Craggs</u> is a sheltered, south-west facing garden containing exotic plants, shrubs and rock gardens developed by the Hough family since 1904. Some of the plants were sent from the Far East by Reginald Farrer, the Yorkshireman who became known as the 'father' of modern rock gardening.

<u>Clappersgate</u>. [ON. road over a rough bridge.] This was an 18c port for loading Langdale slate onto barges that sailed down Lake Windermere.

> Loughrigg Fell   3.9

Turn left, across Brathay Bridge, onto the B5286 Hawkshead road.

<u>Low Brathay</u> is reputed to have been occupied c. 1780 by two gentlemen, the brothers Gilbert, who were highwaymen. A later occupant was Charles Lloyd, a minor poet and friend of Wordsworth, Coleridge and De Quincey. B.E.G. Explorations now operate from here.

<u>Brathay Hall</u> was bought by a Jamaican merchant, George Law, c. 1784, rebuilt and painted white. In the early 19c, it was the home

of John Harden, an amateur landscape painter, with whom John Constable sometimes stayed. It is now a Management Training Centre.

<u>Skelwith Fold Caravan Park</u> occupies the former estate of a member of the wealthy Marshall family, where his cousin, A. C. Benson, essayist and critic, frequently stayed. Benson had the habit of hiding small objects, which he called 'fetishes', under stones, or in tree crevices when he went for a walk. The house was demolished in the 1960s, but the site can be identified and the swimming pool.

Turn left along a minor road to <u>Low Ray</u>.

<u>Wray Castle</u> (NT) is a castellated, Gothic mansion, built in 1848 for a Liverpool surgeon, James Dawson, who used his wife's inheritance from a gin fortune. She refused to live in the castle, her husband ended up bankrupt and the architect drank himself to death.

Beatrix Potter spent an idyllic summer at Wray Castle when her family rented it for an extensive holiday in 1882. It was here that the family became friends with Canon H. D. Rawnsley, who was the vicar of the nearby church. He it was who suggested that Beatrix should submit *The Tale of Peter Rabbit* to Frederick Warne & Co., who eventually published all her books.

The castle is now a Marine Telecommunications College known as 'RMS Wray Castle'. Only the grounds are open to the public.

<u>St Margaret's Church,</u> besides the Castle gates, was the incumbency of the Rev. H. D. Rawnsley from 1878 to 1883. He became a Canon and a co-founder of the National Trust. To him is attributed the sonnet on the plaque in the church to Richard Fletcher Broadrick, *'Drowned when crossing Windermere on the ice January 31, 1879.'*

<u>The Dower House</u> has become a hotel.

Access: Along the west shore of Windermere – north to Wray Crag; – south to Red Nab car park and beyond to the ferry landing.

Blelham Bog, fed by the outflow from Blelham Tarn, sustains habitats of fen, bog and wet woodland, the nesting place of the great crested grebe.

High Wray provides access to Red Nab car park on the lake shore. Just south of Red Nab is Belle Grange, a remote, tree-sheltered house overlooking that part of the lake associated with Sir Henry Seagrave. He created a land speed record of 231 m.p.h. and, on Windermere, a world water speed record of 98.76 m.p.h. in 'Miss England II'. Tragically in 1930, whilst attempting to increase his water speed record, his speedboat 'flipped' opposite Belle Grange and both he and his engineer were killed.

Colthouse. Whilst attending Hawkshead Grammar School, Wordsworth lodged here with Ann Tyson after her move from Hawkshead. Wordsworth wrote in *The Prelude II*,

My morning walks
Were early; oft before the hours of school
I travell'd round our little lake, five miles
Of pleasant wandering, happy time.

It is thought that Wordsworth was referring to Esthwaite Water, a detour when walking to school in Hawkshead. Ann Tyson's cottage has been identified as Greenend Cottage (NT). On the other hand, Beatrix Potter, drawing on local tradition, identified a different site for Wordsworth's lodgings. The building no longer stands at the corner where the road forks, opposite the post box and the sign to the Friends' Meeting House.

The Friends' Meeting House was built on a plot of land called Benson's Orchard, purchased in 1688. This was the nearest available site to the Friends' burial ground which, by that time, had been in use for thirty years.

The ground floor is divided by movable panels into two rooms; the meeting room with the minister's gallery and the original women's meeting room, now called the school room. When the panelling is slid back, the whole of the ground floor can be used to seat over 100 people.

Latterbarrow (NT).   OFOL 84.

Priest Pot is an oval shaped tarn which was one connected to Esthwaite Water until silting separated them. Folklore claims it is supposed to hold enough water to satisfy a priest's thirst, but more realistically, it was possibly a fish pond for Furness Abbey. A floating island with trees is mentioned in Wordsworth's *Guide to the Lakes*.

Between the Pot and Esthwaite Water, a study has been made of how fenlands have evolved from shallow lakes; from water to woodland; from reed swamp to regenerated alder, willow and oak.

Esthwaite Water [*ON. Lake by a clearing of ash trees*] is an irregular-shaped lake, 1½ miles long, ¼ mile wide and 80 feet deep. Green drumlins and intervening hollows make a pattern of peninsulars and bays. It is Beatrix Potter country with a small lake surrounded by undulating fields and low wooded hills. When water-lilies bloom in early summer, it is not difficult to conjure up Beatrix Potter's watery character, Jeremy Fisher.

The lake is privately owned but a public road runs all round it. On the west side, a promontory at the north end called the Nab, near the site of Hawkshead's common field, provides the best view.

Esthwaite Lodge was the home of novelist Francis Brett Young from 1928 to 1932, before he moved to Worcestershire because, he explained, '*rainfall is twenty-three inches against eighty.*' The fine

Regency house is now Hawkshead Youth Hostel.

<u>Strickland Ees</u> (or Ears) was probably where Wordsworth, age nine in his first week at Grammar School, saw a heap of clothing left by a drowned schoolmaster. He witnessed the body being lifted out of the lake and recorded this event in *'The Prelude V'.*

<u>Esthwaite Hall,</u> a white-rendered farmhouse, was the birthplace of Archbishop Edwin Sandys (1516–1588) who founded Hawkshead Grammar School in 1585. The Sandys family moved about two miles south to Graythwaite Hall.

<u>From the car park</u> at the south-west end of the lake there is access to the shore.

The outflow from the lake is Cunsey Beck, which flows through Outer Dubs Tarn into Lake Windermere.

<u>Near Sawrey</u> [*'Near' refers to its location relative to Hawkshead, the old administrative centre.*]

At the age of 30, Beatrix Potter wrote, *'It is as nearly perfect a little place as I ever lived in and such nice old-fashioned people in the village.'* Years later, following her marriage in 1913 at the age of 47, Near Sawrey became her permanent home.

<u>Hill Top Farm</u> (NT). Beatrix Potter's farm house contains her collection of furniture, china – and her clogs – and will forever be associated with her illustrated story books for children. *'I can't invent, I only copy,'* she once wrote to a friend. This 17c farm house – the dresser, the fireplace and the stairs – provided much material to 'copy' as Beatrix always preferred to draw and paint by 'copying' from real life rather than from memory.

At least six of her books are set in and around the farm. The interior of Hill Top appears in *The Tale of Tom Kitten, The Tale of Samuel Whiskers* and *The Roly Poly Pudding.* The latter book was

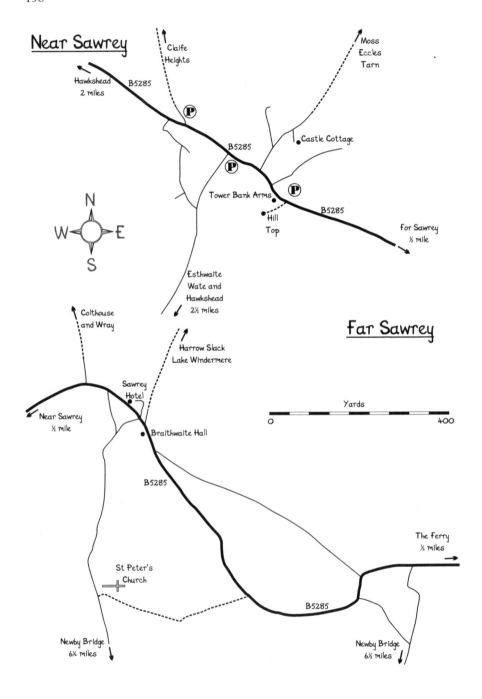

inspired by rats which over-ran the house when first she bought it. 'Mrs Cannon has seen a rat sitting up eating its dinner under the kitchen table in the middle of the afternoon.' The dolls' house contains some of the dolls' things that appear in *The Tale of Two Bad Mice*. It is Hunca Munca who steals the bird cage.

The exterior of the farm is shown in *The Tale of Jemima Puddle-Duck*. Jemima's egg is still hidden in the rhubarb patch. The cottage garden became Tabitha Twitchit's garden in *The Tale of Tom Kitten*. The Cannons, the tenant farmers, make an appearance. An experiment with pig-farming inspired *The Tale of Pigling Bland*. 'I spent a very wet hour inside the pig-sty drawing the pig. It tries to nibble my boots which is interrupting.' Scenes of the farm and village cottages can still be recognised in *The Tale of the Pie and the Patty Pan*.

The Tale of Ginger and Pickles is set in the village shop. Mr Tod lived in the hills around Sawrey and Beatrix depicted the wider Lakeland scene when Pigling Bland encountered difficulties crossing from Lancashire into Westmorland, when Squirrel Nutkin sailed across Derwentwater on a raft, and when Mrs Tiggy-Winkle was visited by Lucie on Cat Bells.

Beatrix Potter (1866–1943) was born in London to wealthy parents. Her father was a non-practising barrister and her mother had connections with the Lancashire cotton trade. Beatrix received the formal and restrictive upbringing of life in the nursery, seldom seeing her parents. She was educated at home whilst her younger brother, Bertram, was sent away to school. Keeping pets gave her great pleasure and provided models for her drawings and paintings. At the age of 15 she started a secret diary, using a code, and wrote in it until she was 30 years old.

Beatrix first came to the Lake District at the age of 16 to spend a family holiday lasting three months at Wray Castle (Lake Windermere). She fell passionately in love with Lakeland. Subsequent family holidays at Lingholm (Derwentwater), Fawe Park (Derwentwater) and Lakefield, now Ees-Wyke Hotel (Near Sawrey) reinforced her love of Lakeland's countryside and inspired her to record her impressions avidly in sketches and paintings.

The idea for *The Tale of Peter Rabbit* was born in a letter to the 5 year old son of a former governess in 1893. '*My dear Noel, I don't know what to write to you, so I shall you a story about four little rabbits whose names were Flopsy, Mopsy, Cotton-tail and Peter.*' She fully illustrated the letter. Encouraged by Canon Rawnsley, Beatrix tried to have the story published, but to no avail. In the end, she published 250 copies at her own expense in 1901 and never looked back. From October 1902 Frederick Warne and Sons became her life-long publisher, although Beatrix had *The Tailor of Gloucestershire* printed privately at first, in December 1902, as she did not know if Frederick Warne would want it. By the end of that year, 28,000 copies of *The Tale of Peter Rabbit* were in print.

The books of illustrated animal stories were so popular that from the royalties, supplemented by a legacy, she was able to buy Hill Top Farm in 1905 as an investment and as a retreat. In the same year, at the age of 39 and still living with her parents, she became engaged to Norman Warne, the son of her publisher. Her parents were most reluctant to accept this but, sadly, within one month, Norman had died. Beatrix was devastated. For the next eight years she devoted all her energy to producing children's books and to travelling as frequently as possible to the Lake District to look after her property.

Beatrix never lived at Hill Top Farm. In 1906, she built an extension to the house for the tenant farmer, John Cannon, so that he could continue as farm manager, and kept the original 17c building for her own use. She used Hill Top as a retreat – somewhere to write and illustrate children's stories. During the summers, when her parents continued to rent a large house in the Lake District, Beatrix would travel over to Hill Top four days in the week.

In 1909, Beatrix bought another, larger farm in Near Sawrey, Castle Farm, which became her main Lakeland base. Then, in 1913, at the age of 47, she married the local solicitor, William Heelis, and moved into the farm cottage, Castle Cottage. With this move, her creative period of writing all but ended. Only five more books were written to bring the total to twenty-three.

As Mrs Heelis, she became a reputable farmer, respected for her flock of Herdwick sheep and becoming President of the Herdwick Sheepbreeders' Association. Increasingly, she used her money to buy up land, seeing ownership as the only way to protect the Lake District from harmful development.

At her death, age 77, she left 16 farms with their Herdwick flocks, many cottages and 4,000 acres of land to the National Trust. She stipulated that Herdwicks should continue to be bred, although they don't grow fat, have coarse wool and provide few lambs – but they can survive up to 2,000 feet. She insisted that the farms and cottages should have local and reliable tenants. Her special affection for Hill Top Farm caused her to make clear in her will that it was not to be lived in, nor altered.

Tower Bank Arms (NT) is the village inn portrayed in *The Tale of Jemima Puddle-Duck.*

Village cottages, such as Buckle Yeat; the cottage with the gilded weather vane – formerly the village shop; Low Green Gate with its classical doorway – formerly The Old Post Office; and High Green

Gate, can be identified from pictures in *The Tale of the Pie and the Patty Pan*, *The Tale of Ginger and Pickles*, and *The Take of Samuel Whiskers*.

Village scenes appear in *The Tale of Tom Kitten* and *The Tale of Pigling Bland*, Hawkshead was the setting for *The Tale of Johnny Town-Mouse* and *The Fairy Caravan*.

Castle Cottage, a white-rendered cottage, was bought by Beatrix Potter in 1909 and enlarged. It was her home from her marriage to William Heelis in 1913 until her death in 1943, during which time she was mainly occupied with farming and with conservation. Her published writings amounted only to five books.

Access: Oatmeal Crag, and Bull Banks on its lower slopes, provided the setting for *The Tale of Mr Tod*.

Moss Eccles Tarn, with its water lilies, was a location for *The Tale of Mr Jeremy Fisher*.

Continue along the B5285 to Far Sawrey. It was along this road that Wordsworth encountered a discharged soldier making his way home. '*The Prelude IV*'.

Far Sawrey is only half-a-mile from 'Near' Sawrey but attracts fewer tourists.

St Peter's Church, 1869, stands somewhat isolated in open fields. It has an unusual stained glass window of the Good Samaritan.

Sawrey Hotel commemorates in its Claife Crier Bar the local legend of the Windermere ferry man who rowed out during a stormy night to answer pitiful cries coming from across the lake. He returned next morning, alone, speechless and horror-stricken. A few days later he was dead, never having spoken a word. The desperate cries continued to terrify people until the monks of Furness

Abbey finally laid the ghost to rest in a Claife Heights quarry.

Claife Heights   *OFOL 80*

<u>Windermere Ferry</u>. The landing point is beside Ferry House, the head-quarters of the Freshwater Biological Association, which moved here in 1950 to foster research into biological freshwater environments. It occupies the former Ferry Hotel, built in 1879, which, in turn, was converted from the Ferry Inn, where the annual wrestling competition developed into a sports day and transferred to Grasmere in the 1860s to become Grasmere Sports.

There has been a ferry here for at least 500 years.

The diesel ferry carries up to 18 cars, takes 7 minutes for the crossing and saves a 10 mile journey round the lake.

<u>Claife Heights</u> (NT) [*ON. Steep hillside with path.*] This long wooded fell stretches northwards from the ferry landing, parallel with the lake shore. It was planted with 30,000 larches in 1798 by the Curwens of Belle Isle.

<u>Claife 'Station'</u> is just above the ferry landing, on the footpath to Claife Heights. This ruined octagonal tower was built in the 1790s on the site of the first 'station' for viewing Windermere established by Thomas West in his *Guide to the Lakes* published in 1784.

Beyond, and directly below the TV mast, is the area marked on the OS map, the 'Crier of Claife'. (See: Sawrey Hotel).

Access: It is possible to walk north along the largely uninhabited lake shore as far as Wray Castle and Wray Crag.

Half-a-mile from the ferry landing, turn south. Follow the minor road through much woodland along the west shore of Lake Windermere towards Newby Bridge.

<u>High Cunsey</u>. A lakeside path starts just east of here and rounds

Rawlinson Nab to Holme Well Wood.

Rawlinson Nab was Thomas West's fourth viewing 'station' for Windermere.

<u>Cunsey Bridge</u> – <u>The Forge</u>. See: Grizedale Industrial Trail.

<u>Boat House Wood</u>. An unfrequented path leads to the shore and follows it for nearly a mile, opposite Silver Holme island, the 'Cormorant Island' of Arthur Ransome's *Swallows and Amazons*.

<u>Graythwaite Hall</u> is the present home of the Sandys family, one of whose ancestors was Archbishop Sandys, founder of Hawkshead Grammar School. The grounds are open to the public, especially in May when the azaleas and rhododendrons are in bloom. The gardens were landscaped by Thomas Mawson who wrote *The Life and Work of an English Landscape Architect*.

<u>Low Graythwaite Hall</u>, or 'Graythwaite Old Hall', is a 17c house which the family outgrew in the 18c. Its topiary is a feature.

<u>Finsthwaite</u> [*ON. finn's clearing*] <u>The church</u> contains a cross made from a plank cut from a pontoon bridge over the River Piave in northern Italy and a communion cup made from a shell casing. These were brought from Italy by the vicar who had been an army padre in World War I.

Buried in the churchyard is the Polish Princess, Clementina Johannes Sobieska Douglas. According to tradition, she was the daughter of Bonnie Prince Charlie.

<u>Finsthwaite House</u>, a Georgian mansion with yew hedges, was the former home of Barbara Sneyd, who wrote of her eventful youth but spent the last fifty years of her life in nursing homes following a breakdown caused possibly by the death of her fiancé in the Boer War.

<u>Finsthwaite Tower</u> carries the inscription, '*Erected to honor the*

officers, seamen and marines of the Royal Navy, whose matchless conduct and irresistible valour decisively defeated the fleets of France, Spain and Holland and preserved and protected liberty and commerce. 1799.'

<u>Stott Park Bobbin Mill</u> See: Grizedale Industrial Trail.

<u>Lakeside/Newby Bridge</u>

Hawkshead

[ON. Haukr's saeter = Haukr's dairy farm.]
Take the B5286 Ambleside to Hawkshead road.

At <u>Outgate</u> is a landscape of hummocky drumlins. The farms date from the close of the monastic period. Slate fences line the roadside.

<u>Hawkshead Hall</u>, 16c, was the monastic grange, or manor farm, of Furness Abbey, from which stewards managed the large estate between Lake Windermere and Coniston Water. The estate thrived on the medieval wool trade which was well suited to this Silurian landscape of Bannisdale Flags.

The outlying farms, created by enclosures for sheep rearing, may be recognised by the place-name 'park'. [Old French Enclosed piece of ground for pasture or arable farming.]

The Scandinavian settlers, identified by the place-name 'thwaite' [ON. a clearing] occupied the valley floor.

In the 16c, the Abbey made formal agreements with tenants on the monastic land allowing the enclosure of not more than 1½ acres and the building of a farmstead. Each farmstead had the name 'ground' attached to it, usually coupled with the surname of the family who created the new farm.

Ruin threatened when Henry VIII dissolved Furness Abbey in 1537, but permission was given by James I for Hawkshead to hold its own markets and fairs. It grew to become the regional market centre, especially for wool. The surrounding woods supplied material for many trades, including charcoal production for iron smelting. The yeomen farmers, known locally as 'statesmen', who acquired their own land after the Dissolution, became wealthy from the trade in locally produced woollen cloth.

By the 19c, however, Hawkshead had become a small town stranded by the changes in manufacturing, economy and society.

The Old Courthouse (NT), 15c, is all that remains of Hawkshead Hall. Rents were payable here and wrong-doers were tried and sentenced. The gallows on a nearby hill awaited extreme cases.

Local records report the occasion when William Sawrey, the Vicar of Urswick, stayed here in 1548. For two days he was besieged by a '*tumult of insurrection*', men armed to the teeth with swords, clubs and daggers. They demanded that he should come out '*for they would have one of his arms or legs before going away*.' Eventually, the mob was dispersed by neighbours. There is no explanation of what it was all about.

Hawkshead in the rolling countryside near the head of Esthwaite Water, and formerly in Lancashire, is one of the most attractive small towns in the Lake District – apart from the crowds. It has two squares linked by passing under archways, numerous courtyards and narrow alleyways, flower bedecked in summer. Cobbled streets are overhung by timber-framed 17c houses, some with outside staircases. 'Bump and Bend' Cottage in the Main Street aptly identifies the difficulty lorries and buses once had avoiding overhanging upper storeys, such as Thimble Hall. Thankfully today, only residents' cars are allowed in the village.

The Grammar School was founded in 1585 by Edwin Sandys of Esthwaite Hall. He later became Archbishop of York. A tablet over the front door, beneath the sundial, records the school's origins.

William Wordsworth was a scholar here from 1779 to 1787 when he went to St John's College, Cambridge. As many of the hundred scholars were not local they had to be boarded out. The school's boarding house held fifty boys and others stayed in the village. Wordsworth lodged with Ann Tyson, a childless married lady who provided a mother's care, 'my old dame, so motherly and good'.

These were happy times for Wordsworth, according to his accounts in *The Prelude, I, II and IV*. He took advantage of the freedom he was given to roam the countryside. His first poems were written whilst he was a pupil at the school.

The two-storey Grammar School, last used as a school in 1909, has now become a museum.

Downstairs, the main room is set out as it was in Wordsworth's time with a large open fireplace, oak desks and long wooden benches.

Wordsworth's desk has his name carved on it. A list of the schoolmasters hangs on the wall. In Wordsworth's poem 'Matthew', memories of his schoolmaster, William Taylor, are recollected.

> the 'village schoolmaster
> With hair of glittering grey'.

The upper schoolroom, where the older boys were taught, contains exhibits illustrating the history of the school, including Ann Tyson's account book. The school library contains Archbishop Sandys' copy of the *Bishop's Bible*, which he helped to translate.

Opposite the Grammar School, the cottages were formerly the Gymnasium.

Parish Church of St Michael's and All Angels. The church is built on a knoll where the original Norse settlement was established. In the 12c there was a Norman chapel on the site, but the present church dates from the 15c. The Sandys Chapel was added by Edwin Sandys who founded and endowed Hawkshead Grammar School.

In 1788, Wordsworth, on a visit from Cambridge – '*saw the snow-white Church upon its hill*'. (1805 *The Prelude IV*)

The whitewash was scraped off in 1875 to reveal the grey Silurian stone, with red sandstone around the doors and windows.

One of Wordsworth's school fellows, John Tyson, was buried in the churchyard in 1782,

> *A full half hour together have I stood*
> *Mute – looking at the grave in which he lies.*

Ann Tyson, with whom Wordsworth lodged for eight years, was buried here in 1796. A gravestone against the church wall praises Thomas Cowperthwaite (d. 1782), an ironmonger and local wit, who featured in Wordsworth's poem '*The Fountain*'. The Anglo-Saxon style cross is a 1919 War Memorial designed by historian W. G. Collingwood.

Inside the church, the huge columns without bases or capitals are rounded on one side and squarish on the other. Painted texts on the walls date from c. 1680. Monuments to the Rawlinson family include Daniel, a former scholar at the Grammar School, who founded its library in 1675. Another memorial is dedicated to Wordsworth's schoolmaster at the Grammar School from 1786, Thomas Bowman.

A framed 'Buried in Woollen' certificate, dated 1696, is one of more than two hundred. It records that an Act of Parliament in 1666 made the burial of corpses in wool compulsory in order to boost the declining home trade in woollen cloth. Witnesses had to testify that '*the corps was nott put in wrapt or wound up or buried in any shirt, sheet or shroud made or mingled with flax, hempe, silke, haire, gold or silver or other than what is made of sheeps wool onely.*'

A showcase exhibits an ornamental processional halberd and some measures connected with trading at the weekly market and the two annual fairs.

150

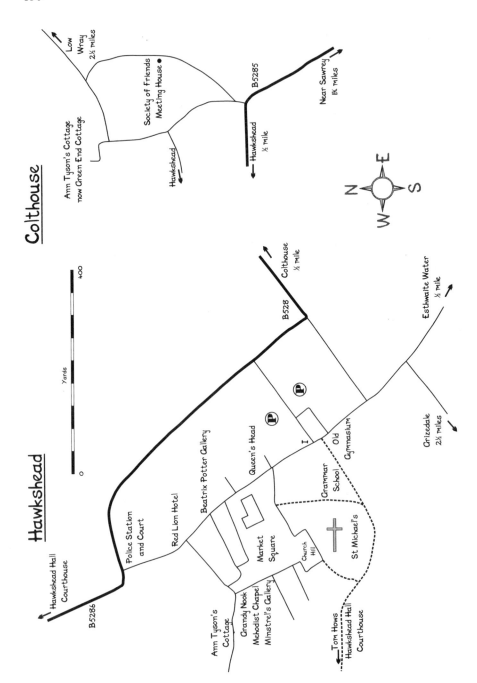

Colthouse

Low Wray
2½ miles

Ann Tyson's Cottage
now Green End Cottage

Society of Friends
Meeting House

Hawkshead

Hawkshead
½ mile

B5285

Near Sawrey
1¾ miles

N E S W

Hawkshead

Yards

0   400

Hawkshead Hall
Courthouse

B5286

Police Station
and Court

Red Lion Hotel

Beatrix Potter Gallery

Ann Tyson's Cottage

Grandy Nook
Methodist Chapel
Minstrel's Gallery

Market
Square

Queen's Head

P

P

Church Hill

St Michael's

Grammar
School

Old
Gymnasium

Colthouse
½ mile

B528

Esthwaite Water
½ mile

Grizedale
2½ miles

Tom Hows
Hawkshead Hall
Courthouse

The church also possesses Elizabethan copies of earlier parish records, so local family histories are very well documented.

Church Hill. Pillar Cottage is so named because of the column which supports the overhanging first floor, the entrance to which is by a flight of stone steps. Nearby is the only remaining spinning gallery, a relic of Hawkshead's once flourishing wool trade.

In the small side street, The Spout House continuously gushes an undiminished supply of water even in times of severe drought.

The Market Square is dominated by The Town Hall. A Market House has stood here since c. 1650. The 1790 building included open-arched bays for the parish butchers on the ground floor and a 'smart Assembly-room' above. Wordsworth recorded his disgust that in the building process Nanny Holme's stone slab, from which she had sold her wares for sixty years, had been destroyed. (*The Prelude II*). The present structure resulted from the 1887 commemoration of Queen Victoria's Golden Jubilee. As a Town Hall it ceased to function when Hawkshead was no longer the administrative centre for local affairs.

The Kings Arms Hotel, on the opposite corner of the Market Square, is one of the four inns remaining from the original seven.

Flag Street is so named because the flagstones cover the stream from which householders used to draw water. The stream joins Poole Beck before entering Esthwaite Water.

The adjacent smaller square was at one time named Berkeley Square.

The Minstrel's Gallery, a 15c building that was once the Crown and Mitre Hotel, is now a restaurant.

The Methodist Chapel, formerly a cottage, was originally called the 'Union Chapel' to encourage all denominations to worship here. Stained glass windows commemorate Mrs Satterthwaite, one of the

Society of Friends from Colthouse, who founded the Chapel and provided for its upkeep.

Grandy Nook is a restaurant with an archway link to neighbouring cottages.

Ann Tyson's Cottage, at the junction of Vicarage Lane and Wordsworth Street, has an outside staircase. Note the Sun Insurance Company fire mark. A plaque indicates the link with Wordsworth. He lodged here from 1779 to 1783, aged nine to twelve, whilst attending Hawkshead Grammar School following the death of his father and a brief period boarding with guardians in Penrith. Part of the cottage was used by Ann as a small shop selling groceries and haberdashery. Her husband, Hugh, was a joiner. When the Tyson's moved to Colthouse, Wordsworth continued to lodge with them from 1783 to 1787.

On Main Street, at the north end, the Police Station and Court were built together in 1883.

The Red Lion Hotel has a Victorian frontage which belies its age as one of the oldest buildings in Hawkshead. It was a 15c coaching inn for the Morecambe Bay, Cartmel, Coniston coach. The yard at the rear housed the stables and a blacksmith's shop. A small figure below the eves shows a farmer taking a pig to market. Another figure is of a man with a whistle. A whistle used to be blown to start the market sales.

The Beatrix Potter Gallery (NT) was once the office of her husband, the solicitor William Heelis. The interior remains largely unaltered since his day.

Exhibited is a splendid selection of Beatrix Potter's original drawings and illustrations which were printed in her animal story books for children. Many of the drawings and paintings were previously displayed at Hill Top Farm (NT) which became overcrowded. There is also an exhibition telling her life story as an author, artist, farmer and preserver of her beloved Lake District.

The <u>Queen's Head Hotel</u>, timber framed, is named after Elizabeth I who was the monarch when the inn was built.

<u>Hawkshead Hill</u>, above the valley, on the B5285 Coniston road, has a small <u>Baptist Chapel</u> which dates back to 1678 when it was a cottage. The house on the south side of the Chapel was once an inn.

The 'Bobbin Mill' in the deep rocky gorge of Thurs Gill, where the water supply was plentiful, turned wood into *'cuppes and dishes'* barrels, baskets, swills and hoops.

<u>Tarn Hows</u> (NT). This famous beauty spot, featuring a tarn half-a-mile long, was artificially formed by the Victorian owners of the <u>Monk Coniston Estate</u>, who built a dam to raise the water level of three smaller tarns in an attempt to create an ideal Arcadian landscape.

A Nature Trail around the tarn takes in the delightful scene of wooded islands and shores, with distant views of high fells.

OB TARN HOWS, CUMBRIA - ON THE MONK CONISTON ESTATE (NATIONAL TRUST)

Walking from Hawkshead is feasible, but the most attractive approach starts from near Yew Tree Tarn on the A593 Coniston road. This route passes close by <u>Lane Head,</u> the former home of W. G. Collingwood, the distinguished historian of Lakeland.

Grizedale Industrial Trail

<u>Grizedale Forest</u> [ON. Valley where young pigs are reared.]

In 1120, Stephen of Blois granted the monks of Furness Abbey this huge area of land between the lakes of Windermere and Coniston. The monks developed sheep farming on the hills and woodland management on the valley floor.

With the Dissolution of the Monasteries, the monks were replaced by a succession of individuals.

<u>Industrial Past.</u> In addition to house and ship timbers, the forest supplied wainwrights, wheelwrights, turners, coopers, cloggers, barkers, tanners, ashburners and basket makers. Most of these trades survive in surname only.

But the destruction of the woodland gained momentum as more and more coppice wood for charcoal was required for the smelting of iron in bloomery furnaces.

<u>Coppicing</u> [*French. couper = to cut*]. Most often when our native broadleaved trees are felled, they sprout again from dormant buds in the tree stump. These shoots grow up into poles which, in Grizedale ,were cut down every fifteen years or so to supply many trades.

This is 'coppicing'.

A few oak seedlings would be left to grow into large timber trees, or standards, to produce house and ship timbers.

This is 'coppice with standards'.

Coppicing largely ceased a hundred years ago and the coppice woods have grown up into tall forest trees — the home of red deer, red squirrel and red fox.

<u>Charcoal Burning</u>. The greatest users of coppice wood were the charcoal burners. To produce charcoal, coppice wood of ash or hazel was cut into short lengths which were then arranged upright in a circular stack in a hollow hearth or pitstead. This arrangement was then covered with charcoal dust from previous firings, turf and earth. A few air vents around the stack assisted even burning. After two or three days of firing and the smoke having reached a certain colour, these vents were blocked up and the fire died out. When cool, the stacks were broken open and the charcoal sent to the furnaces and powder mills.

<u>Bloomeries</u>. Iron ore was first smelted in these primitive medieval furnaces which were basically a small depression lined with stones and clay. Charcoal was the fuel and greater heat was generated by hand-operated bellows. The impurities were run off as liquid slag and the iron removed as a soft mass which could be shaped by hammering.

The larger furnaces in the 18c required 200 acres of coppice annually, which the forest could no longer supply. Consequently the ironmasters started to leave the district. Only the largest furnace at Backbarrow remained. It continued to use charcoal until 1920.

<u>Wooden Bobbins</u>. In the 19c and 20c, the cotton spinning and weaving industry of Lancashire created an insatiable demand for bobbins manufactured from coppiced poles of wood. Today, bobbins are made more cheaply in plastic.

The forest also supported:

Chop wood kilns, where wood was dried for the smelting of lead and copper; and

Potash pits, where bracken was burned to make soap for the woollen industry.

<u>Grizedale Hall</u> was built in 1905 by a Liverpool shipping merchant, Harold Brocklebank.

In 1937, the Grizedale Hall Estate was bought by the Forestry Commission which today operates the twin policy of afforestation and amenity provision. The uplands are still disfigured by spruce and fir, but areas of larch have encouraged herds of deer. Highly commended is the re-establishment of the ancient mixed oak forest.

During World War II, a prisoner of war camp was established here. Its most notorious occupant was a Luftwaffe fighter pilot, Oberleutnant Franz von Werra, who had been shot down over Kent during the Battle of Britain in September 1940. Although he was convinced that the war would soon end in a German victory, he organised his escape within twelve days of arrival at Grizedale. Whilst on exercise with fellow prisoners, marching beyond Satterthwaite Village, he slid over the stone wall at Bowkerstead Corner and remained at large for five days before he was recaptured on Hesk Fell. A second escape from Swanwick POW Camp near Derby ended when he was arrested as he was about to take off in a Hurricane fighter aircraft from RAF Hucknall. On his way to a POW Camp in Eastern Canada, he escaped from a train and crossed the St Lawrence River to reach the USA, which was then in a state of 'armed neutrality'. By jumping bail, he reached Rio de Janerio from where he was flown, via Spain, to Germany. He was given a hero's welcome and was able to import invaluable information about British interrogation procedures and the security systems in British POW camps.

(See: *The One that Got Away*. Kendal Burt and James Leasor. Collins/Michael Joseph.

Also: Film of that title with Michael Goodliffe, directed by Roy Baker. 1957 b/w.)

Although Grizedale Hall was demolished in 1957, some of the remaining buildings now house the administrative centre of the Forestry Commission and the facilities for visitors, which include an Information Centre, a Wildlife Exhibition, a Sculpture Trail, refreshments and a shop. Forest Trails have been provided to extend the viewing of wildlife and to lead to traces of the industrial past.

In 1970, the stable block was converted into The Theatre-in-the-Forest with a seating capacity of 229. Plays, concerts and films are presented. The future of the theatre is uncertain.

The ornamental grounds of the Hall are now used as a caravan and camping site. Stone balustrades and steps grace the area which has become a car park.

Carron Crag   *OFOL 88.*

Satterthwaite. [ON. Summer farm in a clearing.]

The village lies on a three mile long area of fields, watered by Grizedale Beck, enclosed to the east and west by forested fells.

All Saints Church, with its squat tower, replaced from 1840 the old chapel spared by Henry VIII at the Dissolution of the Monasteries. The history of the church and village has been written by local schoolchildren whose pictures hang round the walls.

The old schoolroom, 1848, across the road, is now used as a village hall.

Two magnificent barns remain, one used as a store for the

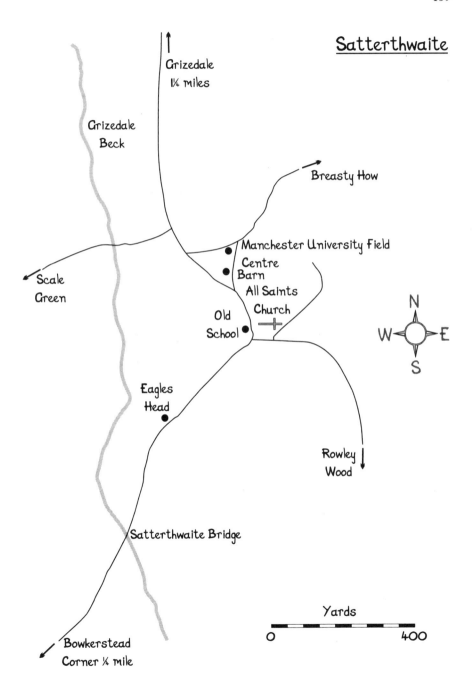

Satterthwaite

Grizedale
1¼ miles

Grizedale
Beck

Breasty How

Scale
Green

Manchester University Field
Centre
Barn

All Saints
Church

Old
School

N
W E
S

Eagles
Head

Rowley
Wood

Satterthwaite Bridge

Yards

0   400

Bowkerstead
Corner ¼ mile

Manchester University Field Centre.

At High Bowkerstead Corner, to the south of the village, Oberleutnant Franz von Werra made his escape from the German prisoner of war group which had halted during the exercise of a route march.

Force Mills

The early bloomeries in the forest smelted iron ore with the help of hand or foot operated bellows. A greater source of power for working bellows and trip hammers came with the invention of the water wheel. From then onwards, the iron makers sited their furnaces and forges besides the becks. The water of Force Beck powered a number of industrial sites.

An iron forge was located across the beck from Force Mills Farm. According to records, iron was made here for almost 500 years, only ceasing in 1822. The ironmaster's house and mill race outlet can still be seen. Later, a bobbin mill was built on the site but was burned down in 1923. The columns of the coppice barn remain.

Further down stream were situated another three forges.

Rusland Woods

These broadleaved woodlands have been acquired by the Lake District Special Planning Board to preserve the amenity value and to protect wildlife.

Rusland Tannery obtained its supplies of bark from the Grizedale Forest. The sale of bark account for half the income from a coppice wood 150 years ago.

The remains of the old Rusland Tannery are now owned by the National Park Authority. In the bow-fronted mill, a pony walked round in a circle to turn the millstone which ground the oak bark.

Tanning. To loosen the hairs, the hides were first put into

limepits and then hung in a smoke house. They were often then draped over a wooden beam, or scraping stone, and the hair was removed with a curved knife. After further cleaning, the hides were soaked in pits of tannin (an infusion of ground bark and water) before being placed in a 'scouring' pit, which contained an acid solution. This soaking process was repeated several times, sometimes over a period of two years. The hides were finally dried, compressed and beaten smooth using 'beetles' (wooden hammers) before being sold.

Rusland Hall. This early Georgian mansion stands in attractive landscaped gardens where peacocks stroll. The house contains period panelling, paintings and furniture.

Haverthwaite [*ON. Clearing with oats.*] This was the limit of the estuary of the River Leven in the post glacial period. Roudsea Wood above the tidal Leven estuary is a mixed woodland inhabited by roe deer and red squirrels. It has been designated a National Nature Reserve.

Haverthwaite is the terminus of the Lakeside and Haverthwaite Railway which runs steam trains along 3½ miles of track.

At Haverthwaite crossroads (A590), take the B5278 Cark road. Immediately after crossing the River Leven, turn left into Low Wood.

Low Wood Gunpowder Mill

The remains of this gunpowder mill, one of seven in the Lake District, lie between the River Leven and the bridleway to Backbarrow.

Beside the leat is the old steam engine house, where steam was generated for the drying sheds, and a tall tower.

Explosives were needed by the slate quarries and copper and lead mines, and the location of Lakeland's gunpowder works was influenced by the presence of charcoal and water power. For 150 years, gunpowder was made by mixing locally produced charcoal with imported saltpetre and sulphur.

When the gunpowder works closed in 1937, Board of Trade regulations ensured that the mills and sheds were dismantled, but the ex-workers' cottages now house a craft centre.

Backbarrow (A590)

Backbarrow Iron Works, which once stood on the side of the River Leven, opened in 1711. Isaac Wilson, the father of John who became known as 'the father of the iron industry', helped it to prosper. (An obelisk to John dominates the village of Lindale.) Supplies of charcoal came from the Grizedale Forest and were transported down Lake Windermere to Newby Bridge. So successful was this ferrying system that Backbarrow's iron furnace only changed from charcoal to coke in 1920 and was still producing iron until the 1960s.

Reckitts 'Dolly Blue' Works was another riverside industry. Industrial 'blue' was manufactured for laundering purposes – the first 'whiter than white' additive. The dust from its tall chimney, now demolished, used to stain everything – including the ducks on the river – until the works closed in 1981.

Now, the five-storey building, which commanded the riverside setting for 400 years, has been converted into the luxury Whitewater Hotel, named after the 'whitewater' effect produced by the River Leven negotiating the narrow stone bridge. The hotel is part of The Lakeland Village time-share complex which also includes riverside cottages and a Health and Leisure Club.

Stott Park Bobbin Mill [ME. Enclosure for bullocks.]

This bobbin mill was built in 1835 to supply the insatiable demands of the cotton spinning and weaving industry of Lancashire. The sheer quantity of wood to produce enough bobbins to satisfy the massive demands of the cotton mills meant that the bobbins had to be made where the raw material was most easily obtained.

Originally the machines which shaped the bobbins out of long, thin poles of birch were turned by a water wheel, superseded by steam turbines. Electric motors were introduced in 1941. By 1971, however, all its products could be made more cheaply in plastic and the Coward family, who had owned the mill since 1855, had to close it.

Saved from demolition, the mill has been preserved as a working reminder of a bygone age at Low Stott Park.

Cunsey Bridge – The Forge

The footpath alongside Cunsey Beck, on the edge of Cunsey Wood, leads to The Forge, a medieval bloomery hearth, or smelting site. The slag heaps and the water leat remain.

The site was favoured by the swift-flowing stream for water power, by the woodland which served as a source of fuel and by the proximity of rich haematite deposits at Low Furness. Lake Windermere was available for transport.

At The Forge, a furnace was installed in 1711 and the slag heaps and water leat remain.

Ambleside to Coniston

The A593 from Ambleside, via Clappersgate, follows the River Brathay [ON. Broad River] to Skelwith Bridge.

Skelwith Bridge [*ON. Ford near the noisy one (i.e. waterfall)*]

At 526 feet, this is a watershed between the drainage towards Lake Windermere and the drainage towards Coniston Water – a narrow, ice-shaped corridor across a rough, hummocky col. The lower, milder scenery of Silurian rocks to the east contrasts with the scarred, hummocky topography of the Borrowdale Volcanic Series to the west in the massif of Coniston Old Man and the Coniston Fells.

The two-arched Skelwith Bridge spans the River Brathay, which has cut a deep narrow gorge through a rock bar of toughened volcanic ash.

The water, conveyed in a leat from near Skelwith Force, once powered a corn mill and, later, a bobbin mill, which was in turn replaced by the present slate-dressing centre using Kirkstone green slate. Slate products, gifts and refreshments are on sale at the adjacent Kirkstone Galleries.

A riverside path on the north bank of the River Brathay leads to Skelwith Force, a 16 foot fall of water over the rocky ledge, with a volume of water said to be greater than any other Lakeland waterfall. Close growing coppice woods give occasional views of the Langdale Fells.

SPY HILL

10/98

BANK BARN - HIGH OXENFELL FARM

12/98

- BARN BUILT INTO THE SLOPE ('BANK') OF A HILL
HIGH ENTRANCE UP RAMP FOR UPPER STOREY. LOW ENTRANCE FOR CATTLE

<u>The Skelwith Bridge Hotel</u> was originally a 17c inn called the Hare and Hounds. A small farm was attached. During World War II an outbuilding, which is now a cottage, became the guard room of the local Home Guard charged with the task of protecting Skelwith Bridge. Since then, considerable extensions to the hostelry include <u>The Talbot</u> which provides food and drink.

Loughrigg Fell	*3.10*	*Black Fell*	*4.2*
		(Borwick Lodge)	

<u>Colwith Brow</u>
  Turn right for Little Langdale and the Wrynose Pass.

<u>Tongue Intake Plantation</u>
  Turn right for Low and High Oxen Fell.

<u>Oxen Fell High Cross</u> is where the Cumbria Way crosses the A593 from Tarn Hows and the Langdale Valleys.

<u>Yew Tree Tarn</u> (NT) is an artificial lake with a small dam.

<u>Glen Mary Bridge</u> is where a footpath leads to Tarn Hows.

<u>High Yewdale</u>
  Turn right for Shepherd's Bridge.

  Holme Fell   *4.2*

<u>Great Intake</u>
  Turn right for the Tilberthwaite Valley between Holme Fell and Wetherlam with its 'hundred holes' – caves, shafts and quarries.

<u>Low Tilberthwaite</u>. Adjacent to Tilberthwaite Gill car park are the remains of Penny Rigg Slate Quarry and Penny Rigg Copper Mill – the models for *Slater Bob's Mine* in Arthur Ransome's *Pigeon Post*. There was formerly a connection with Tilberthwaite Mine by a thousand-yard-long tunnel.

On the slopes of Wetherlam are the mining relics of Tilberthwaite, Hawk Riggs, Hellen's, Borlase, Birk Fell Hause, Wetherlam and Man Arm.

Wetherlam   4.7, 8, 10.

The A593 follows the attractive valley of Yewdale Beck, which Ruskin used to illustrate his geological lecture 'Yewdale and its Streamlets' (1877).

<u>Low Yewdale</u>. Arthur Ransome spent the summer of 1908 working in the adjacent cottage in bad weather and in a tent 'on a small mound close to Yewdale Beck' in good weather. In his novel, *Winter Holiday*, he used the farmhouse as a model for Dixon's Farm.

<u>Holly How</u>, now a Youth Hostel, became *Bank Ground Farm* in *Swallows and Amazons*.

Coniston Water

[Formerly Thurston's Mere]

*The name of the lake changed to that of
the village of Coniston c. 1800.*

Coniston Water extends from the dramatic volcanic rock of the Old Man of Coniston range to the gentler, low rounded hills of Silurian slate in the south. The lake is long and narrow: 5¼ miles long, ½ mile wide, an average depth of 79 feet and a maximum depth of 184 feet. At the head of the lake, Yewdale Beck, Church Beck and Black Beck are the main feeder streams. The outflow is the River Crake which reaches the sea in Morecambe Bay.

The three small islands belong to the National Trust.

In the Middle Ages, the lake was a busy commercial highway, frequently used for carrying iron ore from Low Furness to the lakeside bloomeries in the forests for smelting. The woods on the eastern shore still have traces of iron smelting bloomeries and pitsteads which produced the charcoal. Years later, copper ore was transported in the opposite direction, from the mines of Coniston to the port of Greenodd, for onward shipping to South Wales.

The lake will forever be associated with the water speed record attempts of the Campbell family. It was Sir Malcolm Campbell who first set up the world water speed record of 141.76 m.p.h. on Coniston Water in his speedboat 'Bluebird', in 1939. Following the

168

tradition started by his father, Donald Campbell established a higher water speed record of 260.35 m.p.h. He advanced this record to 276.33 m.p.h., but in 1967, while attempting to reach 300 m.p.h., his jet-propelled 'Bluebird' back-flipped and sank. Donald Campbell was killed, but his body and most of the wreckage have never been recovered.

A more sedate craft to ply Coniston Water is the steam yacht 'Gondola', which was built in 1856 by the Furness Railway Company and launched from Coniston Hall in 1859. The *Illustrated London News* at the time described the 'Gondola' as *a perfect combination of the Venetian Gondola and the English Steam Yacht, having the elegance, comfort and speed of the latter and the graceful lightness and quiet gliding motion of the former.* Arthur Ransome, as a small child, was allowed by the captain to steer the 'Gondola', a recollection transformed into Captain Flint's houseboat in *Swallows and Amazons.*

The 'Gondola' regularly sailed the length of Coniston Water until the service ceased in 1937. The engine was then sold to power a saw mill and the hull became a houseboat. The boat was blown ashore during a storm in 1963 and there it remained, derelict, until it was sold in 1966.

A lengthy period of restoration began, with the National Trust eventually becoming involved and raising £250,000 towards a complete renovation. The hull was transported in sections for renewal at the Vickers Shipbuilding Yard at Barrow. By 1980, the 'Gondola' was back on Coniston Water and re-launched by Mrs Howell, the great grand-daughter of Captain Hammill, master of the 'Gondola' 1863–1913.

During the holiday season, the 'Gondola' carries up to 86 passengers in luxury up and down the lake from Coniston Pier to

Park-a-Moor, stopping at Brantwood, the former home of John Ruskin.

East Shore

Coniston Water, is best seen from the east shore, where the road runs through woodlands close to the lake, with glorious views across to Coniston Old Man.

Waterhead Hotel. Distinguished visitors have included Lewis Carroll in 1857, Charles Darwin in 1879 and John Ruskin in 1887, when domestic upheaval, attributed to his mental instability, drove him from Brantwood temporarily.

Sir Malcolm Campbell stayed here in 1939 when he established the world water speed record. Friendship between the Campbells and the hotel's proprietors, the Robinson family, continued when the Robinsons' grandchildren became licensees of The Black Bull and then The Sun Hotel in Coniston village.

Thwaite Court was the home of Ruskin's friend, the author John Deever and his botanist sisters.

The Labyrinth, a circular clump of trees, was once a maze which has become neglected and overgrown.

Coniston Boating Centre, controlled by the National Park Authority, has a variety of boats for hire.

Tent Lodge derived its name from the tent where Elizabeth Smith, a young scholar and translator, died from tuberculosis in 1806. Fresh air was a recommended method of treatment. Among many visitors to Tent Lodge were the Tennysons, who spent part of their honeymoon here in 1850.

Lanehead was built on the site of the Halfpenny Alehouse where the artist Turner is said to have stayed in 1797 when preparing sketches for his first Royal Academy exhibition.

The present house was the home of John Ruskin's secretary, W. G. Collingwood who became a close friend of Arthur Ransome. Lanehead became the inspiration for 'Beckfoot', the home of the Blackett girls in Arthur Ransome's *Swallows and Amazons*.

Bank Ground Farm was the model for 'Holly House' where the Walker family spent their summer holiday in *Swallows and Amazons*. W. G. Collingwood's grandchildren took holidays here and the exploits of these youngsters on Coniston Water, in their dinghy named 'Swallow', gave Arthur Ransome ideas for his novel.

Lawson Park, a lonely farm on the edge of pine woods above Brantwood, is reached by a bridleway. Richard Adams based his Animal Research Station on this farm in his novel *The Plague Dogs*. The bridleway continues to Low Parkamoor and High Nibthwaite.

Brantwood was the home of John Ruskin from 1872 to 1900.

He was born in London in 1819, the son of a successful wine merchant, a partner of Domecq, the sherry family. In 1869, Ruskin was appointed the first Professor of Fine Art at Oxford. He worked so hard that his health suffered and in 1871 he bought Brantwood, unseen, from William Linton for £1,500, on the basis that '*Any place opposite Coniston Old Man must be beautiful.*' As it happened, the house was '*a mere shed of rotten timbers and loose stones*', but Ruskin transformed it into a attractive house. He enhanced the magnificent views from his bedroom overlooking the lake by adding a six-sided turret.

John Ruskin was a supremely gifted artist, art critic, writer, philosopher and social reformer. He influenced many of his contemporaries, amongst whom were such diverse people as the Pre-Raphaelite painters, Marcel Proust (French novelist), Octavia Hill (co-founder of the National Trust), Frank Lloyd Wright (American architect who designed New York's Guggenheim Museum) and Mahatma Ghandi (Indian political and spiritual leader). Leo Tolstoy, the Russian novelist and social reformer, wrote, 'Ruskin was one of the most remarkable of men, not only of England and our time, but of all countries and all times. He was one of those rare men who think with their hearts, and so he thought and said not only what he himself has seen and felt, but what everyone will think and say in the future.' Indeed, as a pioneering conservationist, Ruskin forewarned of the 'greenhouse effect' more than a century ago.

On the domestic scene, however, Ruskin's wife, Effie Gray, claimed that he made her life a misery. After years of non-consummated marriage, she divorced him to marry the artist Millais.

The house is now owned by the Brantwood Trust and is open to the public. In each room, Ruskin's possessions remain as they were in his lifetime, even to the Ruskin designed wallpaper in the downstairs rooms. On display are many of Ruskin's drawings and water colours and those of his friends. A video explains Ruskin's life and works.

The Old Printing Room was built by William Linton to house the press for printing a magazine called *The English Republic*, which he edited. It is now used as an exhibition gallery.

Jumping Jenny, the name of Ruskin's boat, is on display, in a tea room in the converted stables, where stands the double Brougham carriage designed by Ruskin for his 1875 tour. Upstairs is a craft gallery.

A nature trail extends up to three miles round the Brantwood estate.

The Heald, below Heald Brow, was Arthur Ransome's home, 1940–45.

Park-a-Moor is the southern terminus for the steam yacht

'Gondola', on its sail from Coniston.

<u>Peel Island</u> (NT) is named after the pele tower that once stood here. The island, with its 'secret' rocky harbour, was a favourite picnic spot for the Collingwood family and Arthur Ransome. It featured as '*Wildcat Island*' in *Swallows and Amazons*.

When Arthur Ransome went to Russia as a foreign correspondent in 1913, he took a sprig of heather from the island and kept it with him throughout the Russian Revolution.

<u>High Nibthwaite</u>. Moraines and a rock-bar are visible. An old forge oven once operated here, but the present mill on the River Crake is a later rebuilding.

Laurel House is where Arthur Ransome spent boyhood summer holidays. The farm features as '*Swainson's Farm*' in his novels.

> *Top o' Selside*   *OFOL 92*

<u>Spark Bridge</u> spans the River Crake [*Br. Rocky river*], where once there was an early charcoal-iron industrial site, followed later by a bobbin mill. Patches of coppice wood remain, but the mill closed in 1983.

The Farmers' Arms has retained its spinning gallery.

<u>Greenodd</u> is located at the confluence of the River Crake flowing out of Coniston Water, and the River Leven [*Br. Smoothly flowing river*], which drains Lake Windermere.

It was once a busy port handling the ores and slates which had been transported down Coniston Water from Coniston's mines and quarries. The rotting stumps of the uprights at the side of the estuary once supported the 'staithes' or wooden jetties. Because of silting, the port closed towards the end of the 18c.

The most notable example of Greenodd's shipbuilding days was an experimental sailing boat shaped like a square box, with identical bow and stern, and a removable bowsprit which could be attached to either end. Aptly, it was named the 'Elephant'.

The Haybridge Nature Reserve is a refuge for red deer and other wild life.

West Shore

Complete the circuit of Coniston Water by returning to Coniston along the A 5092 and A 5084 on the west shore.

Lowick Bridge [*ON. Leafy hollow*] A water mill from 1776–1906 powered a spade forge, which became a saw mill and then a swill basket workshop before conversion into a residence.

Blawith [*ON. Dark wood*] also had a water mill at one time.

The 16c church, which stands in ruins, has been replaced by the Victorian church of St John the Baptist.

In 1792, a local bishop is said to have ordered the parishioners to sell a piece of common grazing land to pay for the enlargement of the church and to buy a bell:

> *Blawith poor people/An auld church and new steeple,*
> *As poor as hell/They had to sell*
> *A bit of fell/To buy a bell*
> *Blawith poor people.*

Blawith Fells. The Lake District Special Planning Board acquired 1,600 acres in 1971 to link its northern boundary with Torver High Common, already owned by the Board, which protects moorlands and wildlife habitats whilst retaining areas for walking and picnics. Scattered remains of settlements, stone circles and ancient cairns are visible.

Beacon Tarn is '*Trout Tarn*' and Beacon is the '*Watch Tower*' in Arthur Ransome's *Swallowdale*.

> *Beacon Fell*   *OFOL 98*
> *(from Brown Howe)*

Sunny Bank. Nearby, The Cumbria Way, after descending from Blawith Fells, follows the shoreline of Coniston Water to the village of Coniston.

Sunny Bank Mill on Torver Beck manufactured bobbins until c.1934.

At Mill Bridge, less than a mile upstream, Torver High Mill operated on a medieval site until 1907.

Torver [*ON. Shieling with peat*] This small village, at the junction of the A5084 and the A593, was once served by the Coniston branch of the Furness Railway. The single track has been dismantled but the station remains as a private dwelling.

The 19c church has replaced the chapel, which was consecrated by Archbishop Cranmer in 1538. Previously, corpses from Torver had to be carried to Ulverston for burial although Torver had been a place of Christian worship since the 12c.

> *Coniston Old Man*   4.9
> *Dow Crag*   4.7

The A593 passes Torver Common which, with Blawith Fells, forms the second largest single area of land, after Caldbeck Fells, owned and managed by the Lake District Special Planning Board.

It passes between Bleathwaite Coppice and Park Coppice whose coppice woods once served the local bloomeries and the early iron industry of Furness.

Coniston

[ON. King's tun or settlement.]

The name possibly preserves the memory of a small Scandinavian mountain kingdom.

Over many centuries, the industrial life of Coniston has changed from mining to tourism.

Copper Mining. It is conjectured that the Romans mined for copper here, followed by the monks of Furness Abbey. As a copper-mining centre, Coniston was established from Elizabethan times when, in 1599, The Society of Mines Royal, which was already operating in the Newlands Valley, engaged Daniel Höchstetter and his German miners to exploit the copper ore in two veins on Coniston Old Man. These were the Bonsor and the Thriddle, which crossed the valley of the Red Dell Beck to the south-east of Levers Water. The copper ore was carried by pack horse trains to the Brigham Smelter at Keswick.

In 1619, a dispute arose between the local farmers, represented by John Fleming, and the miners represented by Daniel Höchstetter. The town fields on flat land by the lake shore, south of Church Beck, had become flooded and polluted as a result of the mining activities. To alleviate this and to resolve the dispute, the course of Church Beck was straightened below Coniston village.

Mining continued until the Civil War when, in 1650, the Brigham Smelter at Keswick was destroyed. Copper ore then had to be ferried down the lake and through the port of Greenodd to South Wales. Thereafter, mining became more sporadic as companies which had hoped to find gold and silver, as well as copper, pulled out.

The decline was followed by an upturn, which reached a peak in 1860 when 900 men and boys were employed. Mining depths of more than 1200 feet were reached with improved technology. To meet the renewed demand for transport, a branch railway line was opened in 1859, in spite of John Ruskin's protest, to link the mines at Coniston with the main coastal railway at Foxfield, south of Broughton-in-Furness.

There followed the final decline c. 1875 caused by the increasing cost of pumping from deep levels and by the availability of cheap supplies of copper from abroad. Mining virtually ended shortly after World War I but lingered on intermittently until the 1950s. The railway struggled to continue until it closed in 1958. The old railway station, in its elevated position beyond the Sun Hotel, still commands outstanding views across the lake.

The area between Miners Bridge on Church Beck and Levers Water on the slopes of Coniston Old Man is still known as Coppermines Valley. The adits, spoil heaps, mill races and 19c processing plant site for sorting, crushing and washing the ore, remain as evidence of this once flourishing copper mining industry. The locality around the former mine office, Coppermines House, now a Youth Hostel, has been declared an Area of Historical and Scientific Interest.

Coniston Copper Mines, a Field Guide,
Eric G. Holland. Cicerone Press 1981.
Brim Fell   4.3
Coniston Old Man   4.10, 11, 12

<u>Iron smelting</u> flourished for nearly a century using iron ore from Low Furness to be smelted in the many lakeside bloomeries.

<u>Slate quarries</u> were opened on Coniston Old Man and at Tilberthwaite, attracting more workers to the village. Pack horses carried the slate to Waterhead on Coniston Water for transport by barge to the foot of the lake.

Opposite the car park and the Tourist Information Centre, a memorial plaque and stone seat on the village green commemorate <u>Donald Campbell</u>, who was killed on Coniston Water in 1967 whilst attempting to break the world's water speed record.

<u>St Andrew's Church</u> was built in 1819 on the site of a chapel that William Fleming of Coniston Hall had built in 1586. Restorations with additions took place in 1891.

John Ruskin, who died at Brantwood in 1900, was buried in the churchyard rather than in Westminster Abbey. His grave is marked by a Celtic-type cross designed by his secretary, W. G. Collingwood, carved from local Tilberthwaite green slate, and standing on a rock from Elterwater. The designs on the cross are symbolic of Ruskin's interest and writings.

Nearby is the Collingwood family grave.

<u>The Black Bull</u> was once a coaching inn where the artist Turner stayed in 1797, Coleridge in 1802 and the young De Quincey in 1805 and 1806 when, on both occasions, he set off to visit Wordsworth in Grasmere only to lose his nerve and turn back.

Younger members of the Robinson family were the proprietors when Sir Malcolm Campbell's son, Donald, continued the family friendship and tradition by staying here whilst attempting water speed records in 1949, 1950 and 1951. On the last occasion, 'Bluebird' hit a log and sank. Photographs in the bar lounge commemorate these

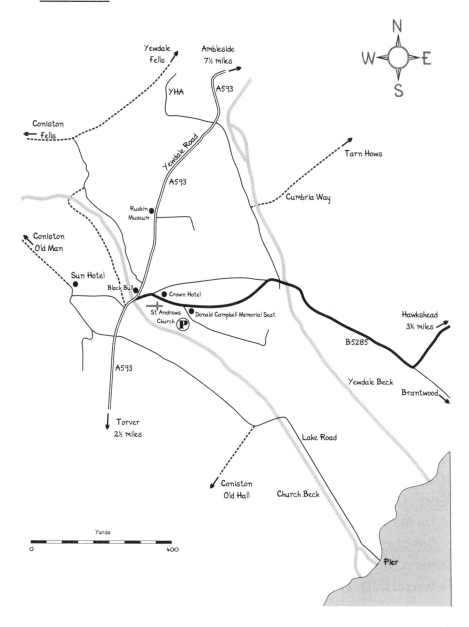

Coniston

Yewdale
Fells

Ambleside
7½ miles

YHA

A593

Coniston
Fells

Yewdale Road

Tarn Hows

A593

Cumbria Way

Ruskin
Museum

Coniston
Old Man

Sun Hotel

Black Bull

Crown Hotel

St Andrews
Church

Donald Campbell Memorial Seat

Hawkshead
3¾ miles

B5285

A593

Yewdale Beck

Brantwood

Torver
2½ miles

Lake Road

Coniston
Old Hall

Church Beck

Pier

Yards

0   400

events.

The Victorian buildings in Yewdale Road and the miners' cottages of local blue-grey, nearly black, Silurian slates and flagstones present a rather dour facade.

The Ruskin Museum opened in part of the Village Institute by admirers of John Ruskin in 1901, the year after his death. The museum contains a collection of Ruskin's personal belongings, such as his paintbox, his billhook and his set of musical stones. Ruskin's interests and activities are reflected by exhibits of pictures, 'Ruskin Lace' and 'Ruskin Rose Queens'.

The Sun Hotel, 16c stands in an elevated position up a steep hill, near the old railway station.

After eleven years at The Black Bull, the Robinsons became licensees here and again Donald Campbell returned to stay with them on four occasions before his fatal accident on his fifth visit. Memorabilia and pictures record these occasions.

From here begins one of the main routes up Coniston Old Man and to the Duddon Valley along the Walna Scar Road formerly used by quarrymen and packhorses.

Dixon Ground Farm is reached by an alley next to the Sun Hotel. The number of 'grounds' in these parts mark the pioneering efforts of settlers breaking in new land, dating from the 1530s, when the Abbot of Furness Abbey made the first agreements with the tenants of the Manor of Hawkshead.

Coniston Old Hall (NT) on the lake shore, with access along the Cumbria Way, was originally a pele tower built by Sir Richard le Fleming c. 1250. It remained the Flemings' main residence until 1408 when Sir Thomas Fleming married Isabel, heiress of Sir John de Lancaster of Rydal. Rydal Hall then became part of the Flemings' vast estate. For the next three centuries, the family moved between the two residences until finally settling at Rydal.

By the 15c, the pele tower had been converted into a cruck-framed building with four enormous chimneys. It became a farmhouse in 1815 and the Great Hall was used like a barn to store corn. In 1972, the National Trust saved the building from total ruin and has restored it.

Brim Fell	4.3
Coniston Old Man	4.7, 8
Dow Crag	4.8
Swirl How	4.4
Wetherlam	4.11
Walna Scar	OFOL 114

Torver to Broughton-in-Furness

A593 One mile south of Torver,
turn right up Old Rake onto Hummer Lane.

This narrow lane, along the length of the lower slopes of the Dunnerdale Fells, offers fine views south-east across the Silurian fell country of High Furness and north-west across a dissected 900–1,000 feet platform of extensive Bronze Age settlements and cremation burials.

The Forestry Commission has supplied a series of parking and picnic sites in an area where it has absorbed abandoned farms into its plantations.

At The Scissors cross-roads, turn acutely right to enter –
  The Lickle Valley [ON. River with loops and meanders.]
  Cross Appletreeworth Beck, a tributary of the River Lickle, at the pack-horse bridge, Hawk Bridge. On the afforested heights above, are the remains of an enclosure and hut walls, probably of late Bronze Age, known as The Hawk.

  Continue up the valley towards the distinctive cone of Caw, 1,735 feet. At Water Yeat, cross the River Lickle by the pack-horse bridge.
  Stephenson Ground. On the hillside are the remains of a stone-built kiln where bracken and birch twigs were once roasted to produce potash. Lime was added and boiled with tallow to make a soft soap ('lye') used for washing the cloth in a fulling mill.

From the farmhouse, a sledgait heads northwards. This track was used for bringing slate by sledge from the quarries on the slopes of Walna Scar. At Stephenson Scale, the track passes the remains of a huge walled enclosure surrounding the ruins of Bronze Age dwellings.

<u>Jackson Ground and Carter Ground</u> are passed on the western side of the river. These and other 'grounds', perpetuate in name the pioneering efforts of the first settlers, who developed new land c. 1509 when the Abbot of Furness Abbey made the first agreements with his tenants in the Furness Fells. There are more than 36 'grounds' in High Furness.

Join the minor road, from Hall Dunnerdale in the Duddon Valley, at Dunnerdale Beck, a tributary of the River Lickle.

<u>Broughton Mills.</u> [*OE. Settlement by the brook.*]

The church, built in 1887, replaced the previous venue for worship – a barn.

Hesketh Hall, rebuilt from a 16c farm, overlooks the River Lickle.

The Blacksmith's Arms is dated 1748.

This tiny hamlet, astride the River Lickle, where the ancient pack-horse bridge has been widened, was once an industrial complex. Mill-races remain which channelled water to turn the water wheels in a bark mill and a corn mill. Above the Blacksmith's Arms was a 'walk' mill, or fulling mill, where woven cloth was soaked and then trodden on to increase its thickness. The mills have been converted into private dwellings.

Stickle Pike (The Dunnerdale Horseshoe)   OFOL 126.

At <u>Lane End,</u> in the Lickle Valley, south of the road between Hartley Ground and Croglinhurst, is <u>Tenants' Meadow,</u> which survived into the 20c as a 'common' field, shared under communal management. Several farmers jointly worked the land, each farming a number of 'dales' (strips of meadow). 'Mere' stones marked the farmers' plots. Generally, this 'open' field system became extinct between 1550 and the late 18c with the rise of 'statesman' farms under single tenancy of ownership.

South of Broughton-in-Furness

Foxfield overlooks the Duddon Estuary where merchant ships sailed at one time to load with coppice wood cut from the fell sides.

The railway came just to the north of Foxfield in 1850 when the Furness Railway established a trailing connection with the Whitehaven and Furness Junction Railway. A connecting curve between the two lines was opened in 1858 and a joint railway station was built at Foxfield. The link with the London and North Western main line route was made in 1862.

The names of railway companies change and today Foxfield station is on Cumbria's Coastal Railway route. The branch line from Foxfield to Coniston closed in 1962.

There are walks from Foxfield to observe the bird life on Angerton Moss using the ancient trackways of the peat cutters, who have enjoyed rights of turbary for centuries.

Woodland and Adjacent Fells from Broughton-in-Furness.

    Burney   OFOL 112

Take the A595/A5092 Newby Bridge road. 1¼ miles beyond Grizebeck, turn left onto Woodland Fell Road, the so-called 'Burma Road'. Park 350 yards from the A5092.

    Blawith Knott   OFOL 108

Along Woodland Fell Road, 2 miles from the A5092. Start 20 yards north of where a cart track leaves for Tottlebank.

Heathwaite Fell Settlement

SD 251883, just south of the Woodland Fell Road junction.

There is evidence of the footings of a complex of seven conjoined

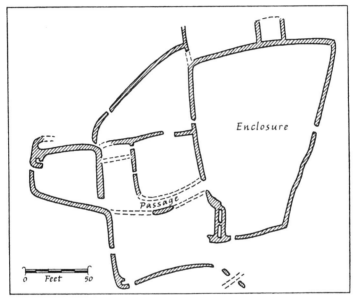

The prehistoric features known as the Homesteads on Heathwaite Fell.
Acknowledgement:
The Lake District, R. Millward & A.Robinson. Eyre & Spottiswoode

stone huts, irregular in shape, and the remains of the enclosing dry stone walls, 3 to 7 feet thick. This Bronze Age settlement, with the entrance to the south, is known as Homesteads.

Woodland Fell   OFOL 102
Start ¼ mile north of Woodland Church.

Broughton-in-Furness

[OE. The settlement by the stream.]

Broughton grew from a 12c settlement into an 18c hillside market town, where markets have been held since 1593. The traditional sheep market has survived, interrupted only by the Russian Chernobyl nuclear disaster in 1986 when contamination from the fall-out seriously restricted the movement of stock in Cumbria.

Local trades in the past have included spun wool sold to the mills in Yorkshire, coppice wood transported by merchant ships from Foxfield on the Duddon Estuary and swill basket making.

In Victorian times, the growth of heavy industry caused venture capital to be invested in the neighbouring iron and steel towns of Millom and Barrow, bypassing Broughton and the local Duddon Furnace.

Changes in the town have hardly altered its appearance and it has been designated a Conservation Area.

<u>The Georgian Market Square</u> is the focus of the town. The developer, John Gilpin Sawrey of Broughton Tower, based the design on the squares he had seen in London, c. 1760.

Chestnut trees shade the square and the three-storeyed terraced houses, built largely of dark grey Coniston granite, define the boundaries. The King's Head, formerly the Manor Arms Hotel, occupies the south-east corner. It was here that Digby Driver met

Mr Powell in Richard Adams' *The Plague Dogs*.

The Obelisk, erected in 1810 to commemorate the 50th year of the reign of George III, was the gift of Mrs Gilpin. Adjacent are the old stocks and the stone slabs from which fish used to be sold.

The Charter, granted c. 1575 by Queen Elizabeth I for holding a thrice-yearly fair, is proclaimed in the square each year on August 1st, by a representative of the Lord of the Manor (currently Cumbria County Council). Pennies are then thrown to the local children and the dignitaries retire to a local hostelry for refreshment.

An annual fair is held at Whitsuntide during the Spring Bank Holiday weekend.

The Old Town Hall or Market Hall, with its turret and weather vane, faces the square, but it existed before the square was developed. The clock was added in 1766, about the time of the building of the square. The arches were shop fronts in its Market Hall days.

The building was handed over as a gift to the people of Broughton in 1947 when Sir Robert Rankin relinquished the Lordship of the Manor in favour of the County Council. At various times these premises have housed a Reading Room, a Social Club and Jack Hadwin's Motor Cycle Museum. The present occupants include a Snooker Hall and a Tourist Information Centre.

Broughton Tower, off the north-west corner of the square, originated as a 14c pele tower, built as a defence against the marauding Scots, commanded by Robert Bruce, who, in the Great Raid of 1322 had pillaged and ravaged the country as far south as Preston.

There may have been an earlier stronghold built by the first known Lord of the Manor, Ailward de Broctuna, c. 1130.

Since 1658, when Roger Sawrey acquired the manor, additions constructed around the tower, in 1744 and in the 1880s, have resulted in a spacious mansion featuring a mixture of architectural designs.

The Sawrey family supported Cromwell in the Civil War, unlike other local gentry.

More recently, whilst the Lordship of the Manor belonged to the County Council, a special school occupied the premises but the future use is uncertain.

New Street came into being following a public meeting in 1792 at which John Gilpin Sawrey, Lord of the Manor, was thanked for his gift of land.

Gable Mount, 1884, became a cottage hospital in the early 20c where Dr Fawcitt took a lead in the north of England by treating diabetes with insulin and by his use of radiography.

Broom Hill, at the beginning of the 19c, belonged to Martin Gilpin, whose successful career was with the East India Company. The occupier c. 1870 was Nathaniel Caine, an iron merchant from Liverpool. In partnership with John Barrat of Coniston, he established the haematite mines at Hodbarrow, where the houses for the miners and their families contributed to the creation of the town of Millom, which grew further when the iron and steel works opened in 1865.

Return to the square.

Griffin Street. The Griffin was one of a number of inns in Broughton which have ceased to exist. It is now a private house, Griffin House.

More reminders of a bygone era are premises named Tailor's Cottage or Cobbler's Cottage.

Church Street was formerly Old Street. On the corner stands Broughton House, built in 1780. In 1840, it was the home of Robert Postlethwaite, Deputy Lieutenant of Cumberland, whose sons were tutored by Branwell Brontë. Dr Fawcitt lived here and added a wing where his patients were treated. He later moved to Gable Mount. John Betjeman, in the 1920s, sometimes visited friends here.

The large front windows of some of the houses indicate that these were once shops.

The Old School, at the approach to the church, has been converted into a group of four houses.

The Church of St Mary Magdalene is said to have Saxon foundations. Its Norman south doorway has been retained. The sanctuary was added in 1547 when the burial ground was consecrated to eliminate the journey for burial at Kirkby. Further extensions and rebuilding have resulted in a largely Victorian interior and a ring of ten bells, an unusual feature in such a small church. An interesting churchyard headstone is that of the son and grandson of Peter Litherland, inventor of the lever watch.

Syke is reached from the north-west corner of the churchyard, across the field to the west, through the stile and then by turning right onto Church Street.

Syke is Norse for a brook originating in swampy ground and drying out in summer. The brook flows from a field near the Coniston road and gives its name to many of the houses hereabout. This is possibly the oldest part of Broughton.

Low Syke House, 1780, belonged to William Tyson, a skinner. Middle Syke, 1879, became the home of Jill Crossland, a landscape artist. High Syke House, 1753, is believed to be where Branwell Brontë lodged during his stay in 1840 with Mr Edward Fish, a surgeon. Syke House, at the top of the hill, displays a 1655 date stone.

Return down Church Street.

On the left was once the workshop of a swillmaker, the stable yard of a carter at the rear and a tannery beside the stream.

Peel House has two basement cells from the days when it was a

Broughton- in- Furness

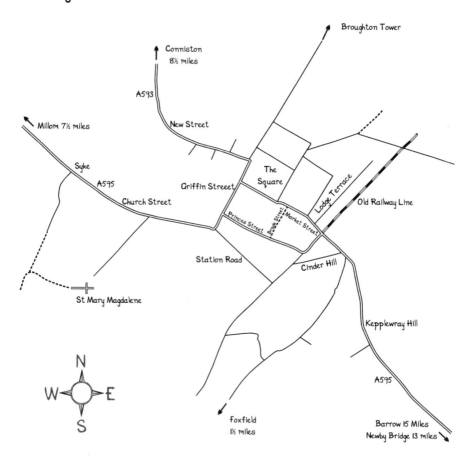

Broughton Tower

Conniston
8½ miles

A593

New Street

Millom 7½ miles

Syke

A595

Church Street

Griffin Streeet

The
Square

Princes Street

Brook Street

Market Street

Lodge Terrace

Old Railway Line

Station Road

Cinder Hill

St Mary Magdalene

Kepplewray Hill

N
W E
S

A595

Foxfield
1½ miles

Barrow 15 Miles
Newby Bridge 13 miles

Yards

0   400

police station.

Station Road. The Old King's Head was known as Church House when first it was built on church land to provide for travellers connected with Furness Abbey. It later became the King's Head. The adjective 'Old' was added when the inn in the square was re-named the King's Head.

Victory Hall, built in 1930 to commemorate victory in World War I, was the gift of Robert Rankin, (later Sir Robert), the Lord of the Manor.

Round the corner, the Cattle Market has served the local farmers for centuries. Tuesday is market day.

Across the road are the remnants of the railway era. From the station building, two houses have been constructed. The goods yard has been built over, but a row of railway cottages remain at Cinder Hill.

Broughton was reached in 1848 by the extension northwards of the Furness Railway (FR) from Barrow, via the slate wharf at Kirkby. The Whitehaven and Furness Junction Railway (W & FJR) extended southwards and avoided the cost of crossing the Duddon Estuary by taking a route to link with the Furness Railway at Broughton, making Broughton a joint station in 1850. By 1857, the Ulverston and Lancaster Railway (U & LR) provided access at Carnforth with the country's main line system.

The installation of a curve at Foxfield in 1858 linked the FR and the W & FJR without the need for through trains to run into Broughton. The interchange was transferred to a new station at Foxfield.

But Broughton regained its interchange function with the opening of the Coniston Railway in 1859 in recognition of the tourist potential and the launching of the lake steamer 'Gondola' on Coniston Water. Freight traffic followed a year later enabling ore from Coniston's copper mines and slate from its quarries to be transported more economically in cost and time.

Mining at Coniston clung on fitfully until the 1950s, but Coniston Railway became less and less viable. The line closed for passengers in 1958 and Broughton station closed in the same year. By 1962, Coniston Railway had closed down completely.

Princes Street. The former Smithy ceased trading in 1978.

Nathaniel Caine built the Methodist Chapel in 1875.

Next to the Black Cock, the cottage was once the King George Inn. It became the Brown Cow Institute, a social club which closed in 1950.

Market Street is reached from the Square.

Brade Street is the location of Kiln House. It was once a malt kiln. The perforated tiles remain through which hot air rose from the furnace to roast the malt.

Lodge Terrace was built for the local members of the Oddfellows Friendly Society in 1886.

At the end of Market Street, go over the former level crossing which was on the old railway line to Coniston.

The drive on the left leads to the Vicarage.

Further on, Glebelands was formerly the Old Parsonage.

Opposite Glebelands, a complex of buildings used to be the workshops of Broughton's swill-making traders. These shallow, oval baskets, about 2 feet long, were made from hazel and woven strips of oak.

'Kepplewray', at the top of the hill, was built in 1900 by William Isaac Barratt, who became managing director of the Hodbarrow Mining Company following Nathaniel Caine. In 1981, the primary school moved here from its Church Street premises which it had outgrown.

Loughrigg

Loughrigg was once a distinct administrative area with its own lordship of the manor. From the 14c, it was included with Langdale, but from 1838, for the purpose of the tithe apportionment, it was combined with Rydal. Historically, however, it is more closely associated with Langdale.

From Skelwith Bridge, take the minor road signposted Grasmere via Red Bank.

<u>Loughrigg Fold and Crag Head</u>. Tenters' Pond is on top of Little Loughrigg hill, beneath which, overlooking Loughrigg Tarn, was once an attractive group of cottages called The Fold. Only Loughrigg Fold and Crag Head cottages remain. Ruins are visible of the demolished cottages near the road and of the former blacksmith's shop, traditionally 'neath the spreading chestnut tree'.

From the 16c, the Benson family of wool merchants and clothiers lived in this Quaker hamlet. In 1663, Francis Benson, his wife and others were charged at the Quarter Sessions with illegally holding Quaker meetings here. Although the Quaker register records the death of Francis Benson in 1672, his burial place is unknown. There is a tradition of a Quaker burial ground in the vicinity of this former hamlet.

High Close, *on the back road to Elterwater*, has records dating back to 1621. In 1857, the farm was bought by Edward Wheatley-Balme who extended the farmhouse but did not farm the land. He later bought the greater part of Loughrigg. Today, High Close is a Youth Hostel.

Scroggs was a smallholding bought by Mr Balme for one of his gardeners.

The Oaks took over the use of High Close farm land together with the sheep. It ceased to be a farm in 1968 on the death of Frank Jones-Balme when the National Trust became the owner in lieu of the payment of death duties. The land was then apportioned to farms in Langdale.

The How, on the Drive, a gated road north of Loughrigg Tarn, consists today of two small cottages with a barn attached. In times past, they were smallholdings. The views from this sunny spot, across Loughrigg Tarn and up to the Langdale Pikes, are magnificent.

Tarn Foot, further along the Drive, continues as a working farm.

The Ellers has a datestone inscribed ECR 1849. In 1961 it ceased to be a farm and the farm buildings, across the road from the farmhouse, have been converted into holiday cottages.

Mill Brow. The mill, which once stood here, was powered by the water flowing from Loughrigg Tarn.

Mere Syke, another small mill, is believed to have stood nearby. The occupant of Mere Syke in 1855 was the artist, Edward Tucker.

Neaum Crag, the former residence of Albert Fleming, who revived the crafts of spinning and weaving in Langdale, was built into the rock face with its only entrance at the top. The views from here are superb.

Great Langdale

B5343 from Ambleside and Skelwith Bridge. From Skelwith Bridge, walk into Great Langdale alongside the River Brathay, via Elter Water, Elterwater Village and Chapel Stile.

Elter Water [ON. Lake of the swans.]

Elter Water is more a series of lakes, the shrunken remnants of a larger lake which was gouged out of the valley floor by a glacier. The Great Langdale Beck and the River Brathay enter the lake bringing considerable amounts of silt. Although this small lake is only half-a-mile long it can double in size after continuous heavy rain and has been known to rise 5 feet in a night. It is drained by the River Brathay. The lake is deeply indented with a reedy margin, indicative of infilling and set in a pastoral landscape of lush green drumlins, some covered with tiny spinneys, the result of extensive reclamation over a century ago. The lake is privately owned, but a public fieldpath along the northern shore opens up magnificent views of the Langdale Pikes.

Whooper swans regularly winter here after migrating from Siberia.

Elterwater Village

Elterwater Common is attractive, bracken-covered, common land, with high fells in the background.

Elterwater

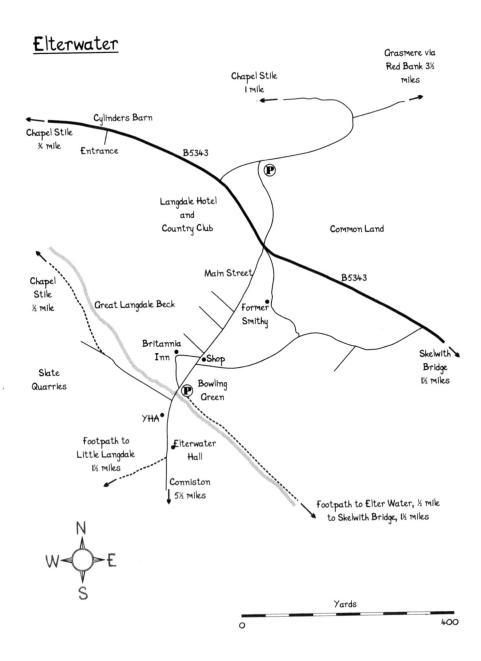

Grasmere via
Red Bank 3½
miles

Chapel Stile
1 mile

Cylinders Barn

Chapel Stile
¾ mile

Entrance

B5343

Langdale Hotel
and
Country Club

Common Land

Main Street

B5343

Chapel
Stile
½ mile

Great Langdale Beck

Former
Smithy

Skelwith
Bridge
1½ miles

Britannia
Inn

Shop

Slate
Quarries

Bowling
Green

YHA

Footpath to
Little Langdale
1½ miles

Elterwater
Hall

Conniston
5½ miles

Footpath to Elter Water, ½ mile
to Skelwith Bridge, 1½ miles

N
W   E
S

Yards

0   400

Much of the surrounding area was swamp until John Harden bought it in 1820, then deepened the lake and drained the marshes before selling the reclaimed land back to the local farmers in the 1830s.

The field by the car park was once used as a firing range to test the efficiency of the gunpowder manufactured locally.

<u>Gunpowder Mill</u>. In the 19c, the village expanded into an industrial community with the opening of the slate quarries and a gunpowder mill.

Water power for the mill came from the Great Langdale Beck, conveyed along a sluice from a dam opposite Weir Cottages. Supplies of water were supplemented in dry weather from a dam at Stickle Tarn.

Availability of local wood facilitated the manufacture of storage barrels and charcoal. The charcoal was mixed with saltpetre (potassium nitrate) and sulphur in the proportion 15:75:10 to make gunpowder, the strong smell of which clung to the workers' clothing. When ignited by a spark, the black granular powder produced large quantities of gases which exerted enormous pressure when released in a confined space. To contain the blast in the event of an accidental explosion the site was thickly wooded.

Sulphur and saltpetre had to be collected by horse and cart from Windermere railway station and gunpowder was then carted back to Windermere for onward transport by rail.

Local supplies of ash or hazel were converted into charcoal by using cylindrical retorts, a manufacturing process invented by Richard Watson, Bishop of Llandaff (1737–1816). The 'cylinders site' is commemorated by place name only. A remnant of Cylinders Farm is the stone barn, once used by Kurt Schwitters, in the woods opposite the entrance to the Langdale Hotel and Country Club.

Kurt Schwitters (1887–1948), a German refugee and one of the founders of abstract art, Merzbau (collage), designing with scrap material — tickets, wire, cork, etc. To conserve some of his work, one wall of the barn was transported to the Hatton Gallery at Newcastle University in 1965. Examples of his work may be seen at the Abbot Hall Art gallery in Kendal. He is buried in Ambleside church-yard.

Elterwater Gunpowder Mill opened in 1824, operated by local quarry owners, the Robinsons of Elterwater Hall. Eleven water wheels provided the power and up to 90 people were employed. The mill was eventually taken over by Nobel Ltd. and later by **ICI**. With the introduction of dynamite in the First World War, the use of gun-powder in the quarries became obsolete. The demand dwindled in the 1920s and complete closure followed around 1929.

Although many buildings were demolished for safety reasons, the drying sheds were converted into a variety of uses during the next 60 years, including a hotel and restaurant. The site also became a holiday caravan park.

In 1981, the Langdale Partnership acquired the site and began a sophisticated scheme of reclamation. This 'timeshare' enterprise retained many of the old ponds, waterwheels and grinding wheels of the former gunpowder mill in a complex of Scandinavian-style chalets, de-luxe hotel, restaurant, pub and leisure centre. Completely transformed are the sites of the original Carpenter's Shop (Beckside rooms), the Drying or Stove House (Country Club) the Coppice Barn (Langdale Hotel) and the Nightwatchman's Rooms (Fellside).

The Village Green, with its maple tree, is flanked by the 17c Britannia Inn, the bowling green and the village corner shop.

Former village trades are perpetuated in name only by cottages such as Wheelwrights, Saw Pit Flat, built in 1875 and reached by a flight of outdoor stone steps, and The Woodshed a converted wood drying loft. Burnhowe, a Spinning Studio, stands on the site of the old blacksmith's shop which closed in the 1920s. To supply water, Smiddy Dub by the roadside was dammed.

<u>Across the bridge</u>. Old Hall Farm was a dairy farm until the Elterwater Estate was sold in 1936. The farm buildings were then converted into a Youth Hostel.

The farmhouse next door, built in 1692, now known at St Martin's, became the centre of the linen industry, started by John Ruskin in the 19c. The revived craft was continued here by Albert Fleming of Neaum Crag, Marian Twelves and Elizabeth Pepper.

Although Elterwater grew as an industrial community, it is now largely dependent on tourism.

Silver How	3.5
Lingmoor Fell	4.7

Chapel Stile

The B5343 continues along the zone of faulted and shattered rock, coinciding with a series of joint planes in the Borrowdale Volcanic Series. As at Skelwith Bridge, there is a rock bar and a river gorge. Glacial drift is in evidence on the upper side of the Great Langdale Beck.

The dominant feature of this slate built village is the backdrop of a steep and rocky fellside with Thrang Crag particularly prominent. Slate quarrying, especially at Thrang Quarry, provided local employment, but quarrying in this area has almost ceased.

<u>Wainwright's Inn</u> was formerly a small farmstead called The Grassings. In the early 1930s, it was converted into the Langdales

Chapel Stile

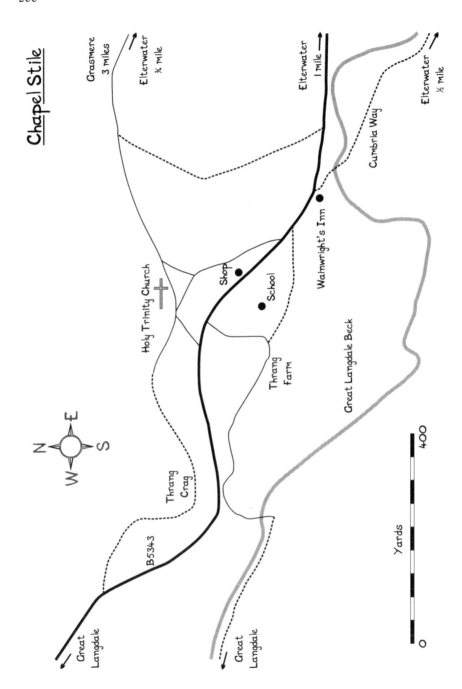

Hotel with a licence transferred from the White Lion which was closing down in the village. Following extensive refurbishment in the 1980s, the Langdales Hotel became Wainwright's Inn with landscaped gardens extending down to the Great Langdale Beck.

Holy Trinity Church is perched high above the slate grey cottages, on a wide hillside ledge supported by a tall slate wall. It was built in 1857 by the two squires of Elterwater Hall and High Close to replace a chapel of 1754. Before 1828, Langdale folk were carried along the difficult 'corpse road' over Hunting Stile for burial at Grasmere.

The St Francis of Assisi window was created by the Walmsleys in 1937–38, delightfully illustrating local wildlife and including Jimmy, the Walmsley's dog. The fell side of the church has no windows.

From the churchyard there is a splendid view across the village towards Lingmoor Fell. The headstone to George Macaulay Trevelyan (1876–1962) is engraved '*Historian of England*'. The epitaph to Owen Lloyd, vicar from 1829 to 1841, is by William Wordsworth. It was the Rev. Lloyd who wrote the rushbearing hymn which is still sung in Ambleside and Grasmere at their rushbearing services.

The White Lion Inn, 1843, once stood to the west of the church. It used to be the house of the parson who sold ale to supplement his income.

An 1887 Water Fountain on the street below the church commemorates Queen Victoria's Golden Jubilee.

Walthwaite How, on the back road to Elterwater, was where, according to legend, a murder took place years ago. W. G. Collingwood's book, *The Bondswoman* is based on this old farm.

Walthwaite House, on the south side of the road, stands in a sheltered position, protected further by yew trees.

The land to the south-east, called Cylinders, was once owned by the Elterwater Gunpowder Company.

Thrang Farm ['*Thrang*' *is Cumbrian dialect for* '*busy*'] is situated south of the B5343 on the site once occupied by two small farmsteads, the records for which date back to 1590.

St Anne's was the stained glass studio built by Bernard Dean Walmsley and his wife, Beatrice, in 1931, to meet a country-wide demand for their craftwork. Bernard was the expert in making stained glass. Beatrice was a gifted artist, embroiderer and maker of jewellery.

From here is a classical view of the Langdale Pikes.

Silver How   3.6, 9 Lingmoor Fell   4.7

The B5343 continues to follow the line of faulted and shattered rock, alongside Great Langdale Beck, as far as the Dungeon Ghyll New Hotel. Here there is a change of direction in the valley floor to Stool End and Oxendale where erosion has taken place along the anticlinal axis.

Great Langdale [OE. *Long Valley*] is a glaciated valley. It is estimated that it was probably affected by glacial action on at least three occasions and that the last remnants of glacial ice disappeared about 8200 BC. A landscape of dramatic beauty has resulted.

Farming. There is a succession of statesman's farms in the valley, most of them on the north side where they receive longer periods of sun and generally higher temperatures. The farms were carved out of the medieval woods along the south-facing slopes and sheep pastures were developed. The farmsteads stand on rocky knolls above the level of the valley floor that was once a glacier-gouged lake and is still subject to flooding. The annual rainfall for Mickleden at the head of the valley is 130 inches, but this decreases eastwards to 75 inches at Ambleside only ten miles away. A devastating 4 to 5 inches of rain fell each hour throughout the night of 13 August 1966. Farms were only connected to the telephone in 1923 and to the electricity supply in 1956.

<u>Baysbrown</u> [*ON. Bruni's cowshed*] on the north-facing, sunless side of the valley, is surrounded by woodland which shows evidence of coppicing. Behind, on the slopes of Lingmoor, are several slate quarries, most of them disused. The farm, one of the oldest in Langdale, was probably settled in the 10c. In the 12c it belonged to William of Lancaster, Baron of Kendal, who endowed it to Conishead Priory, near Ulverston. After the Reformation, the farm came into the ownership of a succession of private families.

The present house, built in traditional style with tall rounded chimneys, is dated 1687. The farm has extended to incorporate land from neighbouring Oak Howe.

Baysbrown was the venue for the annual Whit Friday games and sports held on Gala Field. After a lapse during World War II, the Langdale Gala was revised in Jubilee Year 1978 and has continued to the present day.

<u>Oak Howe</u>, another ancient holding, is associated by tradition with the plague victims who were buried here in the 16c.

<u>Side House Farm</u>, on the Cumbria Way, was given to the National Trust as a memorial to Professor G. M. Trevelyan, the eminent historian. A plaque on the wall commemorates his great love of the Langdale Valley.

<u>Harry Place</u>, on the south-facing side of the valley, was named in the 1600s after the local Harrison family. The farmhouse has distinctively tall, rounded chimneys and pointed windows. Gone is the gate across the road to stop the sheep from wandering, but the old square water trough remains on the roadside. The views of the Langdale Pikes are spectacular. Professor G. M. Trevelyan bought

Harry Place and left it to the National Trust in 1944.

Harrison Place, now Robin Ghyll. In 1692, this was Anthony Harrison's home, where he worked as a cordwainer (shoemaker). Professor G. M. Trevelyan spent many summers here writing his histories. He acquired the property in 1911 and the National Trust became the owners in 1979, thanks to his grandchildren.

Robinson Place has the initials TFA (Thomas and Agnes Fearon) and the date 1693 on the front of the house. Through the garden runs Robin Ghyll Beck. The farm was sold to the National Trust in 1974.

Below Robinson Place on the roadside are the remains of a stone seat called Nick Stick Seat. The first of the Nick Stick annual meetings connected with the common rights of pasture was held on Holy Thursday, 1888.

Ellers is the local name for alder tree. Here, once stood a small farm with a blacksmith's shop and a joiner's shop in an adjacent field called Shop Field. These buildings were demolished to provide the stone to build the new house of Ellergarth in the early 1900s.

Pye Howe [ON. *Hill of the Magpie*] was the birthplace of Tom Buntin, author of *Life in Langdale*, published in 1993. Into the wall to the west of the farmhouse was built a bee house to protect the straw 'skeps' in which the bees lived.

Above Pye Howe is Pye Howe sled gate (*gate = track, way*) used by shepherds, peat diggers and weavers who would travel with their cloth to the fulling mill at Grasmere. On this track in 1808 George and Sarah Green perished in a snowstorm whilst returning to Easedale from a sale at a Langdale farm. At their home at Blind Tarn they had left six children, the eldest eleven years old.

Long House. A path from the main road gives access to the fells above Long House intakes and Pye Howe.

Raw Head derives its name from being the head of the row of

houses in Raw Lane, as the road was once called. Scale Gill supplies unlimited water. The farm house was bought in 1946 by the Fell and Rock Club and the old barn next door became an annexe.

A neighbouring barn has been converted into a Roman Catholic climbers hostel called 'Bishop's Scale'. A chapel was built by the roadside.

Across the road, derelict Raw Head Cottage has been restored and renamed Robertson Lamb Hut, in memory of a keen fellwalker.

<u>Low Millbeck</u> was named after the corn mill which stood at the bottom of Mill Ghyll, known also as Stickle Ghyll. From 1621 to 1884, the farm was owned by the Benson family, one of the oldest families in the district. The owner from 1932 was Professor G. M. Trevelyan who gave it to the National Trust in 1944.

<u>High Millbeck,</u> higher up the valley than its namesake, has been known as Stickle Cottage since 1980, but its history dates back to 1666. Before the Dungeon Ghyll New Hotel was built in 1862, the farm-house was an ale house. The barn is now Stickle Barn, 'a Tavern and Eating-House'. The coach house, which was built when the farm functioned in conjunction with the hotel, has been converted into a bunk house called 'Long Tram'.

<u>Dungeon Ghyll New Hotel.</u> (*Dungeon = a fissure in the valley side*) Dungeon Ghyll Force is a series of waterfalls one of which has a drop of 60 feet. Wordsworth was inspired by it to write his poem, '*The Idle Shepherd Boys, or Dungeon Ghyll Force*'.

The datestone, in the hotel's front entrance paving, is marked 1862. In recent years Quest Adventure Holidays leased the hotel but it has reverted to being a Country House Hotel. On the field in front, in the early 1900s, the Langdale Football Club played its games.

This is where the valley floor changes direction.

Blea Rigg	3.7, 8
Harrison Stickle	3.7–10

High Raise	3.4
Loft Crag	3.5
Pavey Ark	3.3–10
Sergeant Man	3.4
Thunacar Knott	3.2

The Langdale Pikes [ON. *Sharp summit*], which rise almost sheer from the valley floor, consist of Harrison Stickle and Pike o' Stickle, including Loft Crag and Gimmer Crag.

Rossett dates back to c. 1650, but the cruck-beamed barn attached at the rear is even older.

Pack horse ponies rested here after a journey over Rossett Ghyll Pass, which was named after this farm.

Dungeon Ghyll Old Hotel, was originally a farm and an inn named Middlefell Inn. The centre section of the hotel building is the original farmhouse, but the present dining room was made out of the stables and the bar out of the shippon. During the days when horse-drawn 'charas' brought visitors to the valley, both the Old and the New Dungeon Ghyll Hotels were under the same management. The Old Hotel became the first property owned by the National Trust in Langdale when Professor G. M. Trevelyan bought it and promptly gave it to the Trust. It became a popular rock climbers' base and many of Britain's best climbers, who took part in Himalayan expeditions, including Everest, stayed at the hotel.

The bus terminal is at the car park.

Bowfell	4.5, 6	Loft Crag	3.5
Crinkle Crags	4.5–7, 11–18	Pike o' Stickle	
3.3–5			
Esk Pike	4.10		
Great End	4.10–14		

Lingmoor Fell	4.5
Pike o' Blisco	4.5, 6
Rossett Pike	4.6
Scafell Pike	4.19

<u>Middlefell Farm</u> stands at the head of Great Langdale where two valleys, Mickleden and Oxendale, provide access to the highest peaks. The farm is reached across an old, widened pack horse bridge.

North-west, by the ash trees and the river, are the remains of Ash Busk Farm, for which records date back to 1690.

<u>Mickleden</u> [*OE. Large valley*] follows the line of a weakened shatter belt as far as the huge cluster of moraines at the foot of Rossett Gill. Some of these steep-sided mounds rise up to 40 feet high. The valley is on the Cumbria Way following Mickleden Beck.

| Pike o' Stickle | 3.5 |

<u>An Axe Factory</u> of Neolithic (3000 BC) age was found in 1947 on Pike o' Stickle at a height of 2,000 feet. Along side a rock shelter, the screes and ledges are littered with roughly shaped axes made from the hardened and compressed volcanic ash (tuffs) of the Borrowdale Volcanic Series. No finished, polished specimens have been found at the site. After being roughly shaped using granite hammers, the axes were brought to the valley floor, or transported to the coast for shaping and polishing with the help of rubbing stones, e.g. St Bees Sandstone. These axes have been found in the Isle of Man, the Yorkshire Dales, Gloucester and Bournemouth, implying long distance trade by land and sea. The site may have remained in production until c. 1400 BC. Other axe factories have been located at Scafell Pike, Great End and Glaramara.

Pike o' Stickle   3.3

At the head of Mickleden are two exit routes: Stake Pass and Rossett Gill.

Stake Pass is on the Cumbria Way to Borrowdale.

Pike o' Stickle   3.6

Rossett Gill is the old packhorse route ascending to Angle Tarn, past Sprinkling Tarn to Sty Head and down into Wasdale. On a map of 1777 this was marked as a major road.

This route was also an old smugglers' path linking with Ravenglass on the coast.

On the slopes of Hanging Knotts, near the path, not easily seen, is a sheepfold where animals could be safely hidden in the days of border raids. There is also a secret grave of a packwoman who perished nearby in a winter storm two centuries ago. She had regularly crossed the fells from valley to valley selling household wares.

Bowfell   4.7
Rossett Pike   4.3, 4
Scafell Pike   4.19

Oxendale is the more southerly valley along the anticlinal axis at the head of Great Langdale. In the wide boulder-strewn course of Oxendale Beck, deep-cut ravines testify to its power in times of heavy rain.

Stool End is situated at the foot of The Band, which separates Mickleden from Oxendale, and is approached across Oxendale Beck where the bridge was washed away in the floods of 1966.

Bowfell   4.5
Crinkle Crags   4.5, 6, 7, 11, 13

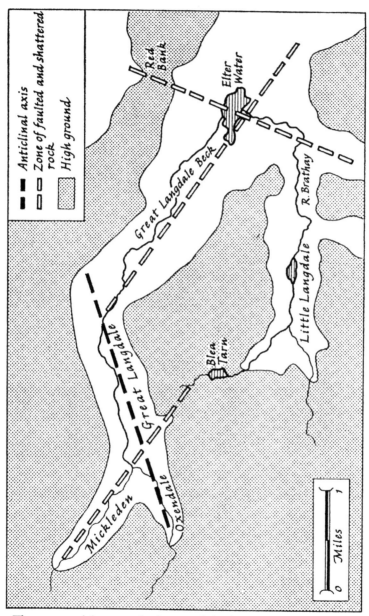

The structural features which control the form of Great Langdale.
Acknowledgement:
The Lake District, R. Millward & A.Robinson. Eyre & Spottiswoode

Pike o' Blisco   4.6

A minor road climbs from the valley floor at the head of Great Langdale to Blea Tarn Pass and Little Langdale.

Wall End. From this farm at the foot of Blea Tarn Pass, glacial drift is plastered against the valley side as far as Side House, opposite Dungeon Ghyll New Hotel.

No sun reaches Wall End in the depths of winter and the yew trees in front accentuate the cheerlessness. In the front wall of the house the twin peephole windows are a unique feature. Kettle Ghyll falling past the house has caused flooding. The farm was bought in 1929 by Professor G. M. Trevelyan and given to the National Trust.

Pike o' Blisco   4.5

Blea Tarn Pass [*ON. Dark tarn*] This was one of the main routes for ice flowing out of Great Langdale into Little Langdale, lowering the col about 300 feet.

The Pass is a continuation of the Mickleden shatter belt line in the Borrowdale Volcanic Series, the fault line being clearly etched out by a narrow wooded gully running up the slopes of Lingmoor Fell above Blea Tarn House.

Blea Tarn House was the farmstead immortalised by Wordsworth in *The Excursion, Book II*: 'one bare dwelling, one abode, no more!' Wordsworth's Solitary lived here where the Poet and the old Wanderer spent the night.

In 1972, the farmland was added to Fell Foot Farm, at the bottom of Wrynose Pass, when the farm was given to the National Trust. A climbers' hut stands nearby.

Blea Tarn is set in a hanging valley beneath pine trees. An investigation of pollen preserved in the mud and silt indicated evidence that forests once grew as high as the 2,000 ft contour. In about 3000 BC, the Neolithic settlers gathered elm leaves and young green shoots for fodder, so opening up the virgin forest. Erosion on the bared hill slopes inevitably followed.

Lingmoor Fell   4.3

Beyond Blea Tarn, the minor road descends steeply into Little Langdale.

Little Langdale

From Skelwith Bridge, follow the A 593 Coniston road to Colwith Brow, approximately one mile.

Turn sharp right downhill, crossing the River Brathay at <u>Colwith Bridge</u>, over which Pigling Bland and Pig-wig escaped, as illustrated by Beatrix Potter in *The Tales of Pigling Bland* (1913).

<u>Low Colwith</u> is somewhat secluded.

<u>High Colwith</u> alongside the road, was the farm of the guide to Colwith Force in 1885 when an entrance fee was charged to visit the waterfalls.

<u>Colwith Force</u> is almost hidden in a tree-filled gill in the dark woods of the Tongue Intake Plantation. The River Brathay cascades in two distinctive falls, the combined drop of water being about 90 feet.

At the junction with the minor road to Elterwater, turn left into Little Langdale, which is roughly parallel with Great Langdale.

The road then follows the north side of the valley of the River Brathay throughout its length. The river formerly marked the old boundary between Lancashire and Westmorland.

At the top of the hill, turn right up a winding old road.

<u>Low Hacket</u> was one of several properties once owned by Langdale Church. 'Hacket' is probably derived from 'Hacaat Water', the old name for the River Brathay.

<u>High Hacket</u> was the home of Betty Yewdale and her husband Jonathan *'in childless solitude'*. Betty looked after the *'poor abode'* and smallholding whilst Jonathan worked in the quarries of Little Langdale and was guided home on dark evenings by his wife carrying a lantern. Writers were fascinated by Betty's lonesome lifestyle and her Westmorland dialect.

William Wordsworth stayed here in 1810 and wrote of the cottage and its situation in his *Epistle to Sir George Beaumont* (1811) and more romantically of the humble heroine in *The Excursion, Book V,* (*'The Pastor'*).

Robert Southey revealed her as a sterner, dominant character in *The Doctor* (1837) where he included a sample of her story-telling in *The Terrible Knitters i' Dent.*

The views from amongst the craggy knolls and sheltering trees are magnificent.

<u>Hacket Forge</u> on the Little Langdale roadside, dates back to 1608. A bloomery for smelting iron was built near the river. Charcoal for fuel was produced locally and the presence of pitsteads can still be found.

The iron originated from Red Tarn near the summit of Wrynose Pass and also from the top of Rossett Ghyll. The track up Rossett Ghyll was constructed by forge owners between 1690 and 1720 to facilitate the transportation of the ore.

The earliest reference to the forge is dated 1623. A few years later, it was recorded that two fulling mills had been converted into a forge. By 1710, smelting in a bloomery forge had been replaced by the refining of pig iron into bars at Backbarrow and Hacket Forge. This work closed down c. 1720.

<u>Iving Howe, or Ivy Howe</u> is one of several houses from which Lanty

Lee is said to have operated his illicit whisky distilling business. (See: *Wetherlam 4.9, 14*).

Greenbank. According to tradition, Lanty Lee, from the profits of his illicit trade, bought a small farm called Greenbanks where he died in 1878 at the age of 76.

Wilson Place is one of the few farms in the area not owned by the National Trust. It used to belong to the Elterwater Estate which was sold in 1936 after the death of Mr Robinson. The purchaser then was Norman Birkett, later Lord Justice Birkett.

Relatives of the original Wilson family developed Wilson's Kendal Mint Cake.

The few scattered buildings in Little Langdale are hard to recognise as a village.

The Three Shires Inn was built in 1872, in the early days of tourism, near the meeting point of the three old county shires of Cumberland, Westmorland and Lancashire. Its name is historical now that Cumbria is the one and only county.

The Chapel of Ease, where Anglicans meet, is part of a block of four units – church, school, school teacher's house and a cottage.

The Old Post Office was once an inn named Birch House. An iron ring beside the front door is a reminder of where customers of the inn secured their horses.

Travelling north:

The Brow lies off the old Ullets [*Owlets*] Nest road to Elterwater and has tremendous views across Little Langdale Tarn and up to Wetherlam.

Dale End alongside Ullets Nest road, is owned by the National Trust. Grazing rights extend to Lingmoor Fell.

Lingmoor Fell   4.8

Travelling south:

<u>High Birk Howe</u> [*Birk = birch; howe = hill.*] This 17c farmstead in the middle of the valley is crossed by the public footpath leading to Slater Bridge. The National Trust bought the farm in 1947.

<u>Little Langdale Tarn</u> in an idyllic setting was a welcome watering place for the packhorse trains crossing the mountain passes.

SLATERS BRIDGE - LITTLE LANGDALE   JB

<u>Slaters Bridge</u>, a much photographed packhorse bridge over the River Brathay, was built and used by quarrymen who worked in the Tilberthwaite quarries. Evidence of the once important quarrying

industry is very plain to see.

Great Carrs	4.5
Swirl How	4.5
Wetherlam	4.9

Across the River Brathay:

Low Hallgarth was too small to be viable as a farm unless the living was supplemented by outside work. One building has become a climbers' hut.

High Hallgarth, perched on the edge of slate quarry debris, has been converted by the National Trust into holiday accommodation.

Bridge End dates back to 1578 and is now a holiday cottage owned by the National Trust.

Travelling west:

The Bield or Low Bield [*Bield = a safe shelter for man or fox*] This old farmhouse in a lovely setting was once the studio home of Delman Banner, artist, and his wife Josephina de Vasconcellos, sculptress.

High Bield is a smaller property higher up the slopes of Lingmoor Fell.

Chapelmire, the field opposite the entrance to The Bield, was the site of the old chapel which dated back to the 1600s. No trace of the chapel remains.

Busk House, by the roadside, has views across Little Langdale Tarn and up to Wetherlam.

At the bottom of Horse Brow, is the junction with the minor road to Great Langdale.

Fell Foot Farm, with its slated porch on stilts, stands at the foot of Wrynose Pass, the last farmhouse in the valley before the ascent. High above the main door, Fletcher Fleming placed his coat of arms in

1707. The farm remained in the same family until it was sold to the National Trust in 1957. Grazing rights were then extended to include those of Bridge End and Blea Tarn farms.

At one time, the farmhouse served as an inn, the last stopping place for the packhorsemen and their animals before climbing up the pass.

The River Brathay flowing into Little Langdale, has etched its valley into the lip of a glacial rock step above the farm.

Behind the farmhouse is a curious flat-topped, rectangular terraced platform, with steep sides shaped into a flight of grassy steps. It has been described as an ancient 'Thing' mount, a meeting place of the Viking Council for Little Langdale, and has been compared with Tunwald Hill, the Norse-Irish assembly point in the Isle of Man, where new laws were proclaimed.

From Fell Foot the road begins to climb steadily towards the Wrynose Pass.

Pike o' Blisco   4.7

The Pedder Stone is a flat-topped boulder of a convenient height to take the weight of a backpack off the shoulders of the pedlars who rested here.

Wrynose Bridge crosses Wrynose Beck, a tributary of the River Brathay.

The gradient becomes steeper and there are glimpses of the old Roman road alongside. For long stretches the Roman road is overlaid by the modern tarmac surface, but is easily seen on the right when descending to Cockley Beck. This, with Hardknott Pass beyond, was the Roman route through the mountain barrier from the port of Ravenglass to the camp at Ambleside and beyond.

<u>Wrynose Pass</u>, 1,281 feet. [*OE. Twisted headland*]. The headwaters of the River Brathay and the River Duddon rise at the summit where the <u>Three Shires Stone</u> was erected in 1816 to mark the meeting point of the former boundaries of Cumberland, Westmorland and Lancashire. In 1974, this area became Cumbria and Lancashire totally lost its foothold in the Lake District.

Cold Pike	4.2	Crinkle Crags	4.10, 11
Great Carrs	4.3	Grey Friar	4.7
Pike o' Blisco	4.8		

Duddon Valley

[OE. Black; or a personal name, Dudd.]

<u>Wrynose Bottom</u>. *[OE. Twisted headland]* The Roman Tenth highway is closely followed along this mountainous section of the route between the Roman fort at Ambleside (Galava) and the harbour at Ravenglass (Glannaventa). The Roman road was probably constructed in AD 79–80 during the campaign of Agricola against the northern tribes. It was sufficiently important to be included in the Antonine Itinerary, an official list of Roman roads compiled during the third century.

Although Roman roads were generally built in a straight line, there were exceptions, particularly in mountainous regions. Evidence of this is in the twisting and turning of the road over Wrynose Pass and Hardknott Pass where the greatest need was to provide easy gradients.

As the modern road descends to Wrynose Bottom, it diverges from the Roman road, which can be discerned a few yards away to the right.

The descent follows the infant River Duddon which rises in the vicinity of the Three Shires Stone at the summit of Wrynose Pass.

<u>Gaitscale</u>, on the descent, is a ruined farm, evidence of depopulation.

The roads throughout the moraine-filled, rock-strewn area of Wrynose Bottom were unsurfaced until 1939. There were seven

219

water splashes. This was tank training ground in the Second World War when so much damage was done that the roads had to be completely remade.

Cockley Beck Bridge, featured in *The Plague Dogs* by Richard Adams, is at the junction of two routeways.

The Roman road continues westwards over Hardknott Pass to Eskdale. The remains of that road can be recognised between Cockley Beck Bridge and Black Hall as a broad track following a beck, with the faint linear mound of its 'agger' (the raised central portion) beyond the track.

The second route follows the River Duddon from the '*lofty waste*' southwards into the Duddon Valley.

Bowfell	4.15
Crinkle Crags	4.9

The Duddon Valley is a valley without a lake, where the River Duddon was once the boundary between the old counties of Lancashire and Cumberland. Below Ulpha Bridge, the valley becomes known as Dunnerdale.

The remote and secret qualities of the valley were greatly praised by Wordsworth. His 34 Duddon Sonnets were the work of fourteen years collected together in *The River Duddon: A Series of Sonnets* (1820). Quotations are taken from these sonnets.

Dunnerdale Forest. At one time, the Forestry Commission had designs on the whole of Upper Eskdale and Dunnerdale, but a public outcry halted the planting and most of the land was eventually sold to the National Trust. The plantation dates from the 1930s and Wordsworth's principles of laying out plantations have been followed, i.e. avoiding massive straight lines of a single species.

Stepping Stones is where, in times of flood wrote Wordsworth, children test their courage and the elderly 'note the sly/And sure encroachments of infirmity.'

Froth Pot has a Forestry Commission car park.

There is a riverside footpath, after crossing the bridge, to Birks Bridge, Wallowbarrow Gorge and the hamlet of Seathwaite.

Birks Bridge This packhorse bridge spans the River Duddon where it flows through a deep, narrow, rocky gorge, a 'Fairy Chasm'. After rain, the water has been known to rise up to the parapet. The flow-through holes are there to protect the bridge from damage by flooding.

On the west bank, *the riverside footpath continues through coniferous woods,* passing Fickle Crag Stepping Stones, where a steel cable serves as a handrail, to Wallowbarrow Gorge. Here the river flows in a 'deep chasm, where quivering sunbeams play'. This huge rock step occurs where the river cuts through a shatter belt between Wallowbarrow Crag and Hollin House Tongue, which has the summit vantage point of Pen for the view over Seathwaite. Cross Seathwaite Footbridge, its parapets set with engraved stones to reach Seathwaite village. Seathwaite Stepping Stones, in a curving line, are a little further downstream.

On the east bank, the winding road crosses Seathwaite Bridge over Tarn Beck, that 'torrent white', a tributary of the Duddon, from the reservoir at Seathwaite Tarn. Terminating at the Bridge is the Walna Scar Road (a footpath) from Coniston. Under Crag was the birthplace of the Rev. Robert Walker (1709–1802) the youngest of twelve children, who became known as 'Wonderful' Walker, the curate-in-charge of Seathwaite parish for 66 years.

Seathwaite. [*ON. Clearing amid the sedge.*]

<u>Holy Trinity Church</u>, built in 1874, is on the site of a previous chapel whose curate was Robert Walker, renowned in Wordsworth's *The Excursion VII*.

Robert, or 'Wonderful' Walker, *'whose good deeds formed an endless retinue'*, married a local maidservant and raised eight children on a yearly stipend that began at £5. Thereafter, he increased his income to £20 by renting a few acres of land and carrying the produce grown over Wrynose Pass to Ambleside market – on foot. He taught the village children in the unheated chapel sending them in groups in winter to warm themselves by his own fire at home or to run up the fells. To parishioners poorer than himself he gave hot soup on Sundays and dispensed an excellent home-brewed beer to his congregation on Sunday afternoons. He acted free of charge as physician, lawyer and letter writer. He spun wool, made his own clothing and worked for wages as an extra farmhand at lambing, shearing and harvest time, raising his annual income to £50, or more. He was honest, industrious, humane and thrifty. When he died at the age of 92, he left a fortune of £2,000.

Robert Walker's gravestone, to the south of the chapel, came from the Vale of Festiniog and was donated by a grandson. Near the porch, a brass plate on top of the 'clipper' stone explains that the stone was used by the Rev. Walker as a stool when shearing sheep. Inside the chapel, a brass plaque commemorates Robert Walker and his wife.

On Tarn Beck, just below the chapel, was a yarn spinning mill in the 1820s, but no trace remains. Oak coppice woods hereabouts doubtless supplied the iron furnace at Duddon Bridge.

<u>Walker House</u>, opposite Holy Trinity, was once the parsonage.

<u>Newfield Inn</u> was a farmhouse which served as an inn in Wordsworth's era.

Dow Crag	4.9	Caw	OFOL 120
Grey Friar	4.6		
Harter Fell			
[ON. Fell with deer]	4.5		

Hall Dunnerdale Bridge. *A road to* Broughton Mills *rises over the shoulder of Stickle Pike and crosses Dunnerdale Fells before descending to follow Dunnerdale Beck to its confluence with the River Lickle at Broughton Mills.*

Stickle Pike   OFOL 126

Ulpha *[ON. Wolf Hill, or, derivation of Ulph, son of Evard, who was granted a manor and lands shortly after the Norman Conquest.]*
Tall, close-growing coppice woods grow nearby.

Joining the Dunnerdale road is the Birker Fell road to Eskdale Green. From the Birker Fell road:
The Traveller's Rest Inn *was once the name of the house on the first corner after the junction, where the inn signpost still stands. Hugh Walpole in* The Bright Pavilions *has Philip Irvine rest here and plot his final confrontation with Nicolas Herries. Journeying on through a blizzard, a quarrel developed at* Crosbythwaite Farm *and ended with the murder of the farmer and his wife.*

Woodend Bridge

| Great Worm Crag | OFOL 136 |
| Hesk Fell | OFOL 140 |

The Viewpoint, *a mile beyond, is spectacular northwards across the heavily glaciated 'lunar landscape' of the Borrowdale Volcanic Series around Harter Fell and towards Scafell.*

High Ground and Birkerthwaite [*ON. clearing in the birches*], to the east of the road, were farms which marked the limits of medieval colonisation.

Devoke Water is 1 mile long and ½ mile wide. On the fell side are the high level channels of the main escape route for waters from the former Lake Eskdale, trapped between the valley glacier at Eskdale and the ice sheet over the Irish Sea which impinged on the Cumbrian coast. Devoke Water, noted for its red trout, spills over into Eskdale via Linbeck Gill.

Hugh Walpole's villain in *The Bright Pavilions* was pursued here by local people in a blizzard and killed beside the lake.

Woodend Farm, to the south, was a former Quaker settlement.

Devoke Water   OFOL 144

Barnscar, a Bronze/Iron Age settlement on Birkby Fell, is 1½ miles SW of Devoke Water. About 350 cairns follow the ridge for 800 yards. The cairns are 5ft to 25ft across and 1ft to 2ft high. On the west side, six ruined hut sites cover ¾ acre. One circular hut site was cleared to reveal a central hearth. A 1957 excavation dug 12 cairns which all proved sterile.

Barnscar (Stainton Pike)   OFOL 155

Return to the Duddon Valley.

Ulpha Church of St John the Baptist appears on a map of Lancashire in 1577, but is much older. In Wordsworth's sonnet:

The Kirk of Ulpha to the pilgrim's eye
Is welcome as a star, that doth present
Its shining forehead through the peaceful rent
Of a black cloud diffused o'er half the sky.

From the pleasant interior, it is sometimes possible to hear the waters of the River Duddon, *'soothed by the unseen river's gentle roar'*. Of interest are a set of wall paintings, uncovered in 1934, an altar made from a fruit tree and a pair of handcuffs, used when the sexton was ex-officio the constable.

Harriet Martineau, in 1854, told of the officiating blind clergyman who heard the late arrival at church of the stoutest farmer in the neighbourhood *'thunnerin down the aisle'*. *'Wha's comin now?'* asked the blind priest. On being told, the priest inquired further, *'a-foot or a-horse-back?'*

In the *'wave-washed Church-yard'*, a grave commemorates the man who, *'perished on Birker Moor during the pelting of the pitiless storm on the 1st January 1826'*. Opposite the church door is the headstone of Robert Jenkinson of Hole House. He was the Parish Constable who followed his own occupation and, in addition, carried out instructions of the Church Wardens and Vestry-meeting of ratepayers. Robert was once sent for by the local innkeeper, who suspected a lodger of being a robber. The thief, hearing footsteps approaching his bedroom, believed he had been found out and swallowed the stolen banknotes. After much searching and questioning, the Constable discovered the truth. Undismayed, he dosed the thief with a potion of water, salt and mustard. This caused the thief to vomit what he had swallowed. The Constable then washed and dried the notes and later escorted the prisoner, with the evidence, by coach to Whitehaven for trial.

<u>From Ulpha Bridge</u>:

<u>Long Dub</u> is a semi-circular *'hidden pool'*, overlooked by a *'steep rock'*, reached along the east side of the river, turning off at the gate at *Birks Wood*. Wordsworth associated this setting with a

traditional tale of a '*love-lorn Maid*' who drowned whilst attempting to reach a primrose, which was there only in reflection.

The Sepulchre, beyond Birks Wood and east of New Close, was a Quaker burial ground, unused since 1755. The stone enclosure very much overgrown, contains a group of pine trees and the unmarked graves of '*the loyal and the brave*'.

The route along Dunnerdale now divides to pass on one side or other of Ulpha Park, which is a relict fragment of a medieval deer park. Within the park, Frith Hall was built as a hunting lodge.

The Easterly Route crosses Ulpha Bridge and follows the River Duddon.

A 'Bloomery', near Cinderhill Beck on Dunnerdale Fells, is recognisable by the hummocky mounds on the rocky hillside. Car park.

Stonestar. The cairn clusters on the fell mark a Bronze Age upland settlement.

Dunnerdale Fells.   OFOL 132

The Westerly Route crosses Bobbin Mill Bridge, past the house that was the bobbin mill until c. 1910. The water to power the water wheel was conducted along a pipeline, the remains of which can still be seen. Timber was dried in the square tower.

Holehouse Gill, a wooded gorge, has a pool at the foot of the waterfall. According to legend, this is Lady's Dub where a woman was drowned whilst fleeing from a wolf.

Old Hall Ruin. At the west end of Old Hall Farm are the ruins of a 16c pele tower, '*that embattled house*'. Wordsworth's sonnet tells of the inhabitants who were driven out by a haunting, a legend he borrowed from Rydal Hall.

Beckfoot is named after Logan Beck, a tributary of the River Duddon.

Here is the junction with Thwaites Fell road, which crosses open moorland in the direction of Ravenglass.

From Thwaites Fell road:

Swinside Bronze Age Stone Circle. From Crag Hall, a signposted bridleway leads to the stone circle, which is known locally as Sunkenkirk. Its diameter is 90ft and there are 55 stones, each bedded on a foundation of small, packed pebbles. Two outlying stones suggest an entrance.

It was a favourite place of Wordsworth's, *'that mystic round of Druid frame'*, the destination of horse rides during his schooldays at Hawkshead.

Black Combe	OFOL 170
Whit Fell	OFOL 156
Stainton Pike	OFOL 154

Duddon Bridge *is the meeting point of the easterly and westerly routes round Ulpha Park with the A595.*

This is the last crossing point of the River Duddon before it reaches the sea.

The Site of an Old Iron Furnace, built in 1736, is conserved at Duddon Bridge. Iron ore was locally available and fuel in the form of charcoal came from the neighbouring coppice woods. The River Duddon powered a water-wheel enabling the very high temperatures to be generated to make molten iron.

By the 19c, coke had replaced charcoal as the main fuel and rural furnaces closed down. When new blast furnaces were built on industrial sites, Duddon closed. From 1867, the site gradually deteriorated. All that remained were such buildings as the furnace, the huge iron ore and charcoal stores and the workers' derelict cottages.

Archaeological excavations on the site, which began in 1981, have been completed. The furnace has been 'consolidated as found' rather than being rebuilt or restored.

<u>Duddon Estuary</u> offers less charm than the upper reaches of the river. It is best seen from Foxfield. Wordsworth should have the last word,

> *In radiant progress toward the Deep*
> *... now expands*
> *Majestic Duddon, over smooth flat sands*
> *Gliding in silence with unfettered sweep!*

Eskdale

[ON. Valley of the Esk (eski = ash). OE River name Isca.]

<u>Cockley Beck Bridge</u>. The Roman highway from Ambleside meets with the road which follows the River Duddon southwards into the Duddon Valley.

The Roman road itself crosses over Cockley Beck Bridge before continuing westwards, via Hardknott Pass, into Eskdale.

<u>Hardknott Pass</u> 1,291'. *[ON. Craggyhill.]* This mountain road is flanked to the north by Hard Knott and to the south by Harter Fell. The tremendously steep climb is achieved by a series of hairpin bends with a gradient of 1 in 3. The summit of the pass offers a superb view of the whole of Eskdale.

This is an area of orographic fault where blocks of rock have been thrown up by the grinding of the earth's plates beneath the crust.

Hard Knott	4.5
Harter Fell	4.6

<u>Roman Fort</u>. *[Mediobogdum = the fort in the middle of the curve.]*

Wordsworth wrote of '*that lone Camp on Hardknott's height*'.

This square-shaped, three acre, auxiliary fort, with an external bathhouse and a parade ground overlooked by an inspection platform, stands on the lower slopes of Hard Knott fell, at a height of 800 ft, and halfway along the route from Ambleside (Galava) to Ravenglass (Glannaventa).

The fort had a turret at each corner and a double-portalled gate-

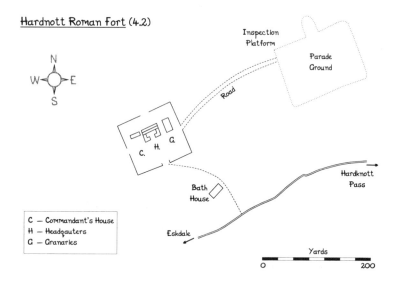

Hardknott Roman Fort (4.2)

C — Commandant's House
H — Headqauters
G — Granaries

way in each side, except to the north where the gateway was single. Along the main street (Via Principalis) were the Commandant's House (Praetorium), the Headquarters Building (Principia) and the Granaries. Behind and in front were the barrack blocks for the soldiers. Slate insets in the walls indicate where new additions to the walls have been made during restoration.

The fortress, one of a chain across Cumbria, was built during the administration of Trajan in the first century AD to command the inland route from the Roman port at Ravenglass. It was garrisoned by the Fourth Cohort of Dalmatians (Yugoslavians), 500 strong. These auxiliary troops were not Romans but were recruited from tribes friendly to Rome. On discharge at the end of their service, or following some meritorious action, they would be made Roman citizens. It was normal to man forts and frontiers using auxiliaries, keeping the legions back in reserve at strategic centres. The fort was later used by Agricola, in AD 158, to put down the unrest in the upland parts of Brigantia.

Upper Eskdale

The upper one-third of Eskdale can only be reached on foot.
Car Park at the cattle grid at the foot of Hardknott Pass.

Bowfell	4.8
Crinkle Crags	4.8
Harter Fell	4.6

Brotherilkeld [*ON. Ulfkell's booth; or summer farm belonging to Ulfkell.*] Since the 13c this has been a sheep farm, which once belonged to Furness Abbey. It is now a 'statesman's' farm. The menfolk living here, and at Black Hall at the other end of Hardknott Pass, were once responsible for the maintenance of the road.

Taw House. Coleridge stayed here after climbing Scafell in 1802. Next morning, his host guided him on a tour of Upper Eskdale.

Upper Eskdale is a glaciated U-shaped valley. The well-marked series of terraces were former lake beds which are now being cut into by the River Esk. The main terrace is 30 to 40 feet above the present river bed and cut into it is a very distinct old river channel 400 yards upstream from Brotherilkeld Farm. Above this is another, older, more dissected terrace. This gradually merges with the apron of boulder scree from Yew Crags – a misnomer today, as the landscape has long since been denuded by grazing animals and other influences.

Throstle Garth [*ON. Enclosure of the thrust.*] A packhorse bridge of slate over Lingcove Beck leads to a medieval sheep fold. The remains of a medieval boundary wall in the bracken once defined the extent of the sheep pasture.

Esk House, 2,490 ft, is where the River Esk rises. This is the Lake District's highest pass, the meeting point of tracks from Langdale, Borrowdale, Wasdale and, of course, Eskdale.

The River Esk flows 17 miles from these wild and rocky heights to the sands of Ravenglass and the sea, dropping 1,000 ft in a single mile in its early stages.

Lower Eskdale

The lower two-thirds of Eskdale are accessible by road.

Whahouse Bridge [*Wha = wath or ford*] Eskdale granite, similar to Shap granite, but with smaller crystals of felspar, underpins a landscape of scattered farms, tiny verdant fields and a patchwork of oak, ash and sycamore woods.

Esk Pike	4.7
Scafell	4.11, 12
Scafell Pike	4.21, 22
Slight Side	4.2

The Woolpack Inn provided refreshment for pack horse trains and their menfolk when loads of wool were being carried across the fells. Sheep farmers gathered here each autumn for the annual renting of Herdwick tups.

Green Crag	4.3
Harter Fell	4.6

The road now runs through the former river valley of the Esk whilst the river itself has diverted south, round a rocky how, in a shallow wooded gorge, where it has cut down through a succession of bare rock outcrops.

Doctor's Bridge is a 17c packhorse bridge across the river. It was widened in 1734 by a local doctor, Dr Edward Tyson, to enable him to cross in his horse and trap.

Boot . . . Eskdale

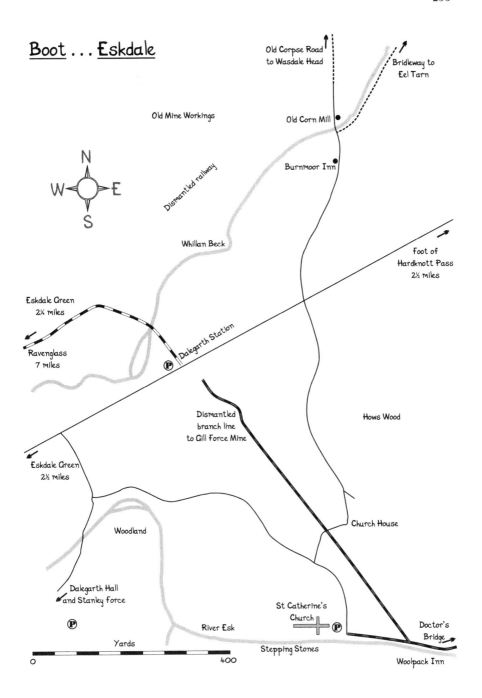

Old Corpse Road
to Wasdale Head

Bridleway to
Eel Tarn

Old Mine Workings

Old Corn Mill

Burnmoor Inn

N
W E
S

Dismantled railway

Whillan Beck

Foot of
Hardknott Pass
2½ miles

Eskdale Green
2¼ miles

Ravenglass
7 miles

Dalegarth Station

Dismantled
branch line
to Gill Force Mine

Hows Wood

Eskdale Green
2½ miles

Woodland

Church House

Dalegarth Hall
and Stanley Force

St Catherine's
Church

Doctor's
Bridge

Yards

River Esk

Stepping Stones

Woolpack Inn

0   400

<u>Boot</u>. [M.E. *Bend in the valley*.] This tiny unspoilt village in the sparsely populated valley is clustered around Whillan Beck. Walls of granite boulders, up to 5 feet thick, have been built to deposit the stones which littered the valley floor before field clearance.

<u>Eskdale Corn Mill</u> on Whillan Beck, is reached by a 17c packhorse bridge. The mill was established in 1578 and had long been disused when it was restored in 1975 and opened as a working tourist attraction.

ESKDALE CORN MILL
12/98

At the bridge, former packhorse trails meet the old corpse road used until 1901 for the conveyance of coffins from Wasdale, via Burnmoor Tarn, for burial at Boot.

<u>Mining</u>. In the 19c, during the Industrial Revolution, there was an iron ore mining boom. Valuable deposits of haematite were discovered in the Eskdale granite on both sides of the valley.

<u>Nab Gill Mine</u> was opened in 1872 and cottages for the miners and families were built at Boot. By 1875, a 3 foot gauge light railway had been completed to carry the iron ore down the valley to the main line at Drigg, just north of Ravenglass.

<u>Gill Force Mine</u>, on the opposite side of the valley, was served by a branch line from Boot. The remains of the railway bridge across the River Esk can still be seen. After eleven years, the price of iron ore collapsed and the Whitehaven Iron Mines Ltd. experienced financial difficulties. Other mines closed, but Nab Gill Mine struggled on until 1912.

In the following year, the Eskdale railway line also closed.

<u>Ravenglass and Eskdale Railway</u>. In 1915, the Eskdale railway was leased to a new company, Narrow Gauge Railways Ltd., which converted the 3 foot railway track to a 15 inch gauge. The famous model engineer, W. J. Bassett-Lowke, tested his model steam locomotives on this narrow gauge track. Extra revenue for the line came with the opening of <u>Beckfoot Granite Quarry</u> near Dalegarth in 1922. The granite was transported for crushing to Murthwaite and from there to the main line at Ravenglass.

Following the closure of the quarry, the railway was sold by auction in 1960 for £14,000 to the Ravenglass and Eskdale Railway Preservation Society and re-opened as a tourist attraction. It now provides a delightful forty minutes ride along the scenic track from Dalegarth to the coast at Ravenglass, a distance of seven miles. On one of these trains, Snitter and Rowf escaped in *The Plague Dogs* by Richard Adams.

The origin of the local name for the railway, 'La'al Ratty', is thought to have been derived from Ratcliffe, the name of the contractor who built the original line in 1875.

<u>St Catherine's Chapel</u>, the parish church of Eskdale, stands isolated by the stepping stones over the River Esk, a quarter of a mile south of the village. It is a typical dale chapel, built on a 12c foundation, with a combined nave and chancel beneath a black and white roof, dating from the 17c.

In the churchyard is the ornate headstone for Tommy Dobson, (d.1910) who, in his day, rivalled the reputation of John Peel. The headstone is sculptured with his portrait, a fox, a hound, a horn and a hunting crop — an appropriate memorial to the founder, and master of the Eskdale and Ennerdale foxhounds.

Illgill Head	4.5, 6
Boat How	OFOL 178

<u>Dalegarth Station</u> [*ON. clearing in the valley.*] This is the eastern terminus of 'La'al Ratty', the Ravenglass and Eskdale miniature steam railway. Refreshments. Car Park.

Burnmoor Tarn.	WFR 5.
Eel Tarn.	WFR 6.
Dalegarth Force.	WFR 7.
A Riverside Walk.	WFR 8.
Hardknott Roman Fort.	WFR 9.
Harter Fell.	WFR 10.

<u>Dalegarth Hall</u> is a 16c fortified farmhouse with splendid round chimneys. The Hall belonged to the Stanley family whose name is

given to the waterfall nearby.

<u>Stanley Force</u> is an unimpeded 60 foot fall of water into a wooded glen. During the Ice Age, a huge glacier gouged out Eskdale into a characteristic U-shaped valley. With the retreat of the melting glacier, a hanging valley was formed with a waterfall where the drop into the main valley occurred. The deep ravine has resulted from considerable river erosion.

<u>Beckfoot</u>, a request stop on the Ravenglass and Eskdale Railway, is situated at the confluence of Whillan Beck, which flows out of Burnmoor Tarn, with the River Esk.

Blea Tarn.   WFR 4.

<u>Spout House Farm</u>. The rocky crags of Eskdale granite are clearly visible.

Eskdale Green

The valley widens and several routeways meet.

From the east, the Birker Fell road from Ulpha in Dunnerdale passing Devoke Water, joins the Eskdale Valley road.

To the west, a minor road leads to Santon Bridge and Wasdale.

Travelling towards Ravenglass offers a choice of two roads, one on each side of the granite ridge of Muncaster Fell.

The scattered village has inns of character at both ends. <u>King George IV Inn</u> dates from the 16c, but has an even older cellar and the remains of a Roman bath house. It was once called 'Tatty Garth' after the adjacent potato field. Until World War I, it was called 'The King of Prussia', but the general attitude towards things German at that time prompted the change of name. <u>Bower House Inn</u> stands at the other end of the village.

Between the inns are two stations on the Ravenglass and Eskdale Railway. <u>The Green</u> station was built and paid for by a group of preservation enthusiasts from Yorkshire in 1968. Half a mile away, at the other end of the village, is <u>Irton Road</u> station.

<u>St Begas Church</u> is quite modern. Eskdale granite is in evidence as a building material, beautifully coloured and sparkling with shades of pink.

<u>The Outward Bound School</u> occupies two large country houses in extensive grounds, with woods and a private lake. A Mountain Rescue Centre is based here.

Whin Rigg	4.3, 4, 6
Irton Fell.	WFR 2
Miterdale.	WFR 3
Irton Pike	OFOL 182

<u>Miterdale</u>, the valley of the River Mite, remains little known and unfrequented although only four miles in length and accessible by car to the half-way point. It is not signposted.

Home Farm was formerly a bobbin mill.

One of the ruined farmhouses is said to be haunted. The story is told of a gypsy women who called at the farm to request lodgings for the night whilst the farmer was away. The farmer's wife agreed to provide accommodation, but later was horrified to notice that the gypsy 'woman' was wearing man-sized boots. Fearing the worst, she waited until the gypsy was asleep. She then poured boiling tallow down the gypsy's open mouth. It is said that even to this day his horrible gurglings can still be heard on moonlit nights.

Miterdale: Whin Rigg 4.3, 4   WFR 3.

From Eskdale Green the River Esk meanders through woods and

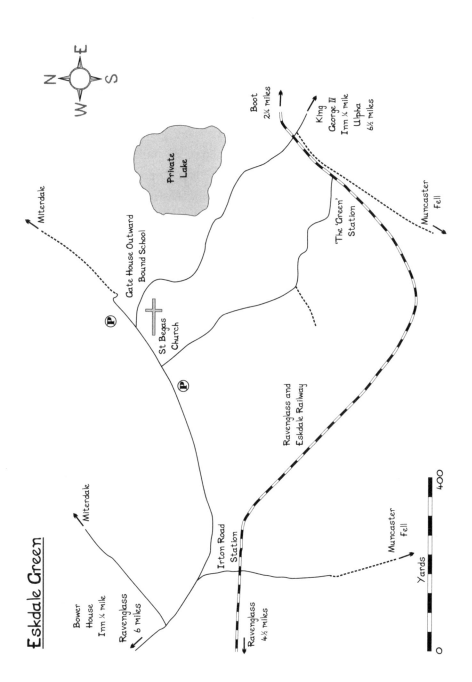

Eskdale Green

239

Miterdale

Miterdale

Bower House 1m ¼ mile
Ravenglass 6 miles

Irton Road Station

St Bees Church

Gate House Outward Bound School

Private Lake

Boot 2¼ miles

King George IV 1m ¼ mile
Ulpha 6½ miles

'The 'Green' Station

Muncaster Fell

Ravenglass and Eskdale Railway

Ravenglass 4½ miles

Muncaster Fell

N W E S

Yards

0   400

pastures, overlooked by Muncaster Fell. Above the flood meadows of the Esk in this pastoral landscape is a line of farms, such as Field Head, Linbeck, Knott End and Cropple How.

Along the northern base of Muncaster Fell runs the River Mite from Miterdale and the Ravenglass and Eskdale Railway.

Muncaster Fell is a granite ridge, about 3½ miles in length, with panoramic views. Notches cut in the ridge top at each end once functioned as lake overflow channels from the former Lake Miterdale to the north. At Chapel Hill, 500 feet, an artificial dam across the flat floor of the channel has created Muncaster Tarn.

As the ice margin oscillated so the level of the former Lake Miterdale moved up and down. As the lake level dropped, other over-flow channels functioned at Ross's Camp, 425 feet, and Branken Wall, 270 feet.

The 19c Tower, near Chapel Hill, commemorates the spot where the deposed Henry VI was found wandering by a shepherd after his defeat at the Battle of Hexham in 1464. The shepherd took him to Muncaster Castle for shelter.

Muncaster Fell   OFOL 186   WFR 1.

Turn left onto the A595, through Broad Oak to Millgate, the junction with the Thwaites Fell road to the Duddon Valley.

Continue along the A595 for ¼ mile and turn right to –
Hall Waberthwaite [*Wath = ford; thwaite = forest clearing.*] The old ford crossed the wide, curving, tidal estuary of the River Esk.

The church, where box pews were installed in 1807, served as the chapel for Muncaster Castle on the opposite side of the river. Services were timed according to the tides to enable the ford to be used.

In the churchyard are fragments of a carved cross.

The church and the Manor Farm mark the centre of one of the primary parishes of Cumbria.

At Waberthwaite, traditional Cumberland sausages are made – produced in one continuous strip rather than in links.

The River Esk flows between the sand hills at Newbiggin and under the railway viaduct at Eskmeals, before turning north for a mile to Ravenglass. Here it is joined by the River Irt and the River Mite to form an estuary and swings back in a loop to find its way through the sand dunes to the sea.

Ravenglass

[OI. Glass's lot, or shore – Irish personal name.]

Three rivers, the Esk, the Mite and the Irt form an estuary almost landlocked by the sand dunes that block the mouth.

The Romans made Ravenglass their port for all their operations in north-west England and built a large fort, 'Glannaventa' [= *the town on the bank*] on the sea shore. From here, the Roman Tenth Highway was constructed up Eskdale, over Hardknott Pass and Wrynose Pass to Ambleside ('Galava') then along High Street to Penrith ('Brocavum') and beyond. Little remains of the fort that held 1,000 men. The bathhouse, known as Walls Castle, survives. It is the highest standing remains of a Roman domestic building in this country. The red sandstone walls are 12 feet high in this barn-like structure.

The village was granted a Market Charter in 1208. In the main street, which ends abruptly on the stony shore a cross was erected. Fairs were held until c.1800.

Ravenglass never developed as a port. The last shipment of iron ore left the rapidly silting harbour in the 1880s. Today, small pleasure craft are the sole occupants of the harbour.

According to legend, there was once a pearl fishery here.

Tradition would have us believe that the famous Herdwick sheep first came ashore here from the wreck of a Spanish galleon.

Hugh Walpole placed Harcourt House in Ravenglass in his novel

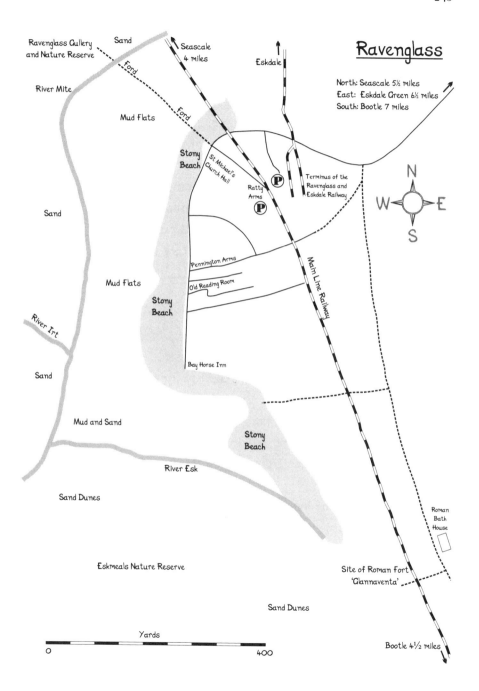

Ravenglass Gullery
and Nature Reserve

Sand

Seascale
4 miles

Eskdale

Ravenglass

North: Seascale 5½ miles
East: Eskdale Green 6½ miles
South: Bootle 7 miles

River Mite

Mud Flats

Ford

Ford

Stony
Beach

St. Michael's
Church Hall

Ratty
Arms

Terminus of the
Ravenglass and
Eskdale Railway

N

W   E

S

Sand

Mud Flats

Stony
Beach

Pennington Arms

Old Reading Room

Main Line Railway

River Irt

Sand

Bay Horse Inn

Mud and Sand

Stony
Beach

River Esk

Sand Dunes

Roman
Bath
House

Eskmeals Nature Reserve

Site of Roman Fort
'Glannaventa'

Sand Dunes

Yards

0   400

Bootle 4½ miles

Rogue Herries.

The village was once notorious for smugglers. Today, it caters for nature lovers and tourists. To the north, across the sand dunes, is Ravenglass Gullery and Nature Reserve, which contains the largest colony of black-headed gulls in Europe. To the south is Eskmeals Nature Reserve and the firing range of the Ministry of Defence experimental establishment.

The Ravenglass and Eskdale Railway brings the tourists. Here is the terminus of the oldest narrow gauge railway in the country connected with the main line railway by a footbridge.

In the Railway Museum the history is told of this miniature line operated mainly by volunteers. The pub is inevitably called by the railway's nick name – 'The Ratty Arms'.

Muncaster Castle [*OE, ON. Personal name joined to OE 'caester', a Roman fort, i.e. 'Glannaventa' at Ravenglass.*]

A defensive pele tower built in 1325 on Roman foundations has been incorporated into this Victorian mansion constructed of Eskdale granite. A second tower, at the opposite end of the castle, was built in 1862 by Anthony Salvin, an architect who specialised in modernising castles. Since 1208, the castle has been the home of the Pennington family.

Seven centuries of history unfold during a guided 'Walkman' tour. On display are paintings by Gainsborough and Sir Joshua Reynolds and family portraits of several interesting characters. One portrait is of the 17c Muncaster fool who, it is claimed, gave the word 'tomfool' to our language as his name was Thomas Skelton.

The panelling in the billiard room came from the famous battleship, 'The Fighting Temeraire', which had been the subject of one of Turner's paintings.

The right of shipwreck is owned by the family and exotic cups have been made from gourds mounted with silver buttons, all salvaged from wreckage washed ashore at Drigg in 1648.

But the family's special treasure is 'The Luck of Muncaster' a glass drinking bowl decorated with gold and enamel, which is said to have been given to the family by Henry VI when he stayed in the care of the Penningtons following his defeat at the Battle of Hexham during the Wars of the Roses in 1464. The king was found wandering on Muncaster Fell (a tower now marks the spot) by shepherds who took him to the castle where he was sheltered for nine days. Assurance was given that '*the family shall prosper so long as they preserve the cup unbroken.*'

Good fortune held in 1513 when Sir John Pennington led his men to Flodden Field in Northumberland where the English defeated the Scottish army and James IV of Scotland was killed.

Perhaps the particular 'luck' which the bowl has brought is that the castle has never lacked a male heir. The 'cup' has been the subject of paintings and poems illustrating the evil of those who tried to destroy the cup and the Pennington's family fortune.

Muncaster Park. Overflow water from the former Lake Miterdale, on the north side of Muncaster Fell, flowed into the former Lake Eskdale on the south side, carrying great quantities of debris which were deposited as a lake delta. When Lake Eskdale finally disappeared, the delta remained as a terrace on the hillside, now incorporated into the landscaping of the estate. From the terrace, the view towards Eskdale was described by John Ruskin as '*Heaven's Gate*'. The ornamental gardens of the castle enjoy the highest reputation for azaleas and rhododendrons.

Muncaster is also the headquarters of the British Owl Breeding and Release Scheme (BOBARS). All British and many foreign owl species are studied here, with the object of helping wild populations to prosper.

<u>Muncaster Water Mill</u>, on the River Mite, is one mile upstream from Ravenglass harbour and located at the first stop on the Ravenglass and Eskdale Railway.

A mill has occupied this site since 1455 when it was a manorial mill for the Manor of Muncaster, the Pennington family being the Lords of the Manor. The present structure dates from c. 1700.

Wholemeal flour was ground here until World War I. Afterwards, animal feed was largely produced until the mill ceased to function in 1961.

A period of restoration followed and the mill with its 12½ foot 'overshot' waterwheel became operational again in 1978, producing a range of stoneground products for the benefit of visitors.

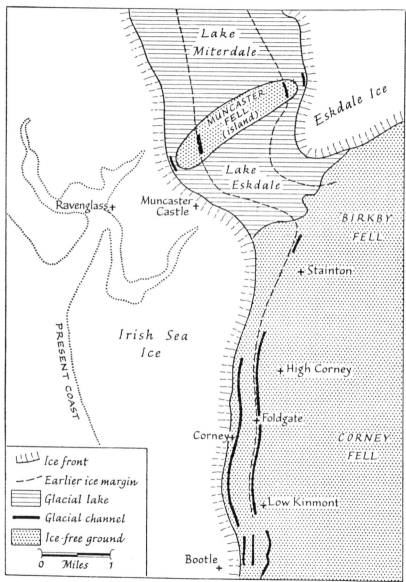

The ice marginal and overflow channels associated with the
former lakes of Eskdale and Miterdale.
Acknowledgement:
The Lake District, R. Millward & A.Robinson. Eyre & Spottiswoode

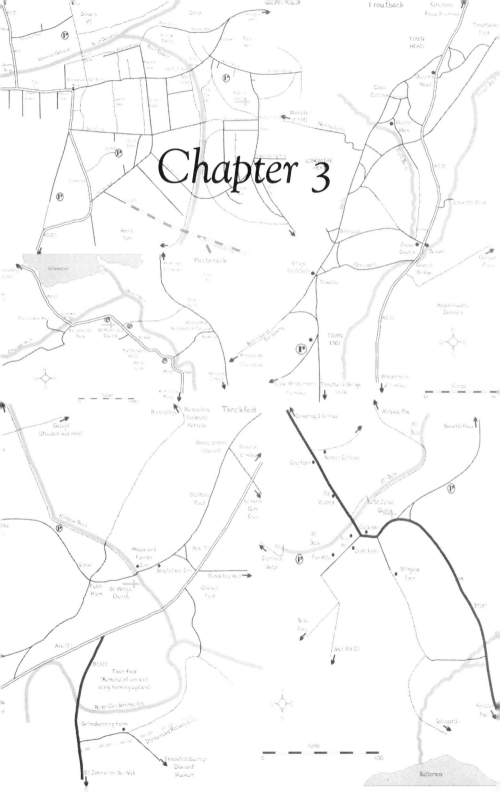

Chapter 3

Thirlmere

[OE. The lake with the hollow.]

Continue along the A591

The <u>Travellers' Rest Inn</u> is aptly named for those journeying wearily up the long steep incline of Dunmail Raise.

<u>High Broadrayne</u> was the home of the Rev. Joseph Sympson, Vicar of Wythburn, Wordsworth's fishing friend. The house is described in *The Excursion VII* and the sad story told of the deaths of all his family within the short period of two years.

<u>The lay-by</u> provides a stopping place to view the summit rocks of Helm Crag. Their shapes were variously described in *The Waggoner* as the Astrologer and the Ancient Woman. Locals refer to the same rocks as The Old Woman playing the Organ and The Lion and the Lamb.

<u>Dunmail Raise,</u> at 781 feet, has a tumulus or cairn in the middle of the A 591 dual carriageway, marking the spot where the Norse King Dunmail, the last King of Cumberland, was defeated in battle by Edmund, the Anglo-Saxon King of Northumbria in AD 945.

King Dunmail is said to have been slain and buried under a mound of stones, but it is also said that he survived another thirty years and either died in Rome or on a pilgrimage to Rome.

The cairn, at the highest point of the pass, marked the ancient border between England and Scotland and, later, the old boundary between Cumberland and Westmorland.

Irish navvies were said to have dug into the cairn whilst working on the Thirlmere aqueduct under the road but no treasure was reported.

Here, Benjamin in *The Waggoner* gave a lift to a mother and child whilst her husband, a sailor, followed with his ass.

Dolywaggon Pike	1.6	Steel Fell	3.6
St Sunday Crag	1.6		
Seat Sandal	1.5		

<u>Thirlmere</u>, now a reservoir, lies in the geological fault which runs north-south through central Lakeland.

It was once two natural lakes spanned at the narrowest point by a wooden footbridge. Horses had to cross a ford. One lake was called Wythburn Water and the other Leathes Water after the local landowner at Dale Head Hall.

In spite of intense local and national opposition, Parliament approved this first of Manchester's Lakeland reservoirs in 1879.

A dam was constructed at the north end of the valley: 800 feet long and 100 feet high; 50 feet wide at the base and 20 feet wide at the top. It took ten years to build and was completed in 1892.

As a result, the original water level was raised by 54 feet. Two villages, Wythburn and Armboth, several farms and 463 acres of farmland were submerged. The two lakes became one and expanded to create Thirlmere Reservoir, 3 ⅝ miles long, ½ mile wide and 160 feet deep. In 1894, the water supply began to flow through the aqueducts connecting the reservoir with Manchester 95 miles away.

Although the campaign to prevent this transformation was unsuccessful, out of the fierce opposition by such worthies as John Ruskin, William Morris, Thomas Carlyle and many others, was born the National Trust in 1895, co-founded by Octavia Hill, Canon Rawnsley and Sir Robert Hunter.

New roads were constructed around Thirlmere, but the promised uninterrupted views of the water were obscured when two thousand acres of Sitka spruce were planted in 1908 and grew to maturity. At that time, deciduous trees were thought to be harmful to the purity of the water. People, sheep and deer were excluded from the reservoir by a shoreline wall and fence.

With the passing of time, changes in policies have created a more appealing approach to encourage public interest. These changes include: modifying the monoculture afforestation to allow mixed woodlands; attaching nesting boxes to conifers; making the reservoir more accessible to the public and establishing Forest Trails from car parks.

Thirlmere – West

This lakeside road was offered to counter the objection to the construction of the reservoir.

Dobgill Bridge. A lakeside path extends from here to Armboth, a distance of 1½ miles. Another path is signposted Harrop Tarn and Watendlath.

Hause Point is reached by metal steps to view the reservoir against the backdrop of the Helvellyn range.

The 'Steading Stone', now under water, was a grey stone with a sloping flat top, a meeting place, or moot, where the Wythburn Parish business was transacted and the Manorial Court was held. Fines and penalties were exacted for breaking such by-laws as grazing too many sheep on the fells, allowing horses and cattle to stray, or polluting the becks.

The 'Web Stone' is also submerged. Here webs of homespun cloth were sold to merchants at the time of the Great Plague of 1665 as a precaution against importing the plague. Money was disinfected in vinegar.

Launchy Gill. When the great oak trees of this last surviving corner of the original forest were cut down by the developers, Canon Rawnsley described the action as '*inexcusable spoilation of a fascinating feature of the Lake District*'.

A Forest Trail climbs up the Gill for a view of the waterfalls.

Armboth Hall belonged to the Jackson family when it was submerged with the rest of Armboth. A monkey puzzle tree is the only reminder of its existence. When the palatial mansion was owned by Countess Ossalinsky, it was featured in Sir Hall Cain's novel, *The Shadow of a Crime* (1885).

The Hall was renowned for tales of hauntings, particularly by the Calgarth Skulls. These were the skulls of the falsely accused married couple who were executed for theft. To their accuser, who had thus wrongfully acquired Calgarth Hall, the skulls appeared and defied all attempts to remove them. At night, two headless skeletons would come and fit the skulls onto their shoulders before setting off to Armboth Hall to join others in ghostly celebrations. By daybreak, they would return from whence they had come.

Armboth Fell	3.2
High Seat	3.7
High Tove	3.3
Thirlmere Dam	
Raven Crag	3.3

Thirlmere – East

Continue on the A591 from the junction with the west road.

Wythburn All that remains of the submerged village is the chapel and three cottages at Steel End.

Wythburn Chapel dates from 1640, although an earlier chapel

stood here in 1554. The chapel is isolated now that the homes of its former congregation lie drowned beneath the waters of Thirlmere.

From Wythburn, Wordsworth climbed Helvellyn in 1805 with Sir Walter Scott and Humphrey Davy, the scientist. This ascent was recommended in Wordsworth's *Guide to the Lakes*.

Helvellyn	1.12	Calf Crag	3.5
Nethermost Pike	1.5	High Raise	3.6
		Sergeant Man	3.7
		Steel Fell	3.5
		Ullscarf	3.6

<u>The Old Nag's Head Inn</u>, opposite Wythburn Chapel, was used as a cottage for waterworks staff until it was demolished in 1972.

<u>The Cherry Tree Inn</u>, just north, and now no more, was the scene of the '*Merry Night*' in Wordsworth's *The Waggoner*. The lights, the music and the sailor's persuasion proved too much for Benjamin, and

. . . soon, of all the happy there
Our Travellers are the happiest pair.

Two hours later, and very drunk, their journey continued.

<u>OS. 'Cairn'</u>, opposite Hause Point, marks the former meeting point of Wordsworth and Coleridge, halfway from their respective homes at Grasmere and Keswick. They carved their initials into a '<u>Rock of Names</u>' which was damaged during the construction of Thirlmere Reservoir. The shattered fragments were collected by Canon Rawnsley and cemented together. Following a landslip in 1984, the 'Rock of Names' was removed to the garden behind Dove Cottage. A plaque now marks the original site.

<u>Clarke's Leap</u>, below the plaque, is where a hen-pecked husband, following the advice and guidance of his wife, drowned himself.

<u>Station Coppice</u> Car Park and Picnic Site is the starting point

for the Swirls Forest Trail.

<u>Thirlspot</u>. The King's Head Hotel, an old coaching inn, was known as John Stanley's old hostelry in Wordsworth's days.

The landlord has the wayside stones whitewashed to mark a footpath down from Helvellyn to his pub where old photographs of Wythburn village are on view.

Helvellyn	1.11
Raise	1.5
White Side	1.5

<u>Dale Head: Fisher Place</u> is a terrace of white cottages. To no. 3 in 1881 came Dante Gabriel Rossetti, the Pre-Raphaelite poet and painter. He was seriously ill and addicted to chloral, but hoped for a beneficial holiday. The following year he died in London. Rossetti's secretary, Hall Caine, who had accompanied him on holiday, based his novel *The Shadow of a Crime* on this locality.

From the road junction, the B5322 traverses <u>St John's-in-the Vale</u>.

<u>Dale Bottom</u>. Approximately ¾ mile past Dale Bottom Farm, a single farmhouse has become <u>Stone Cottage</u> and <u>Piper House</u>. The latter is said to have been named after a Scottish piper who was snowed in here and played his bagpipes for amusement until the weather cleared.

John Richardson (1817–86) dialect poet and stonemason was born here.

Bleaberry Fell	3.6
High Seat	3.6

<u>Shoulthwaite</u>. Above Raven Crag, an Iron Age hill fort on <u>Castle</u>

Crag covers ½ acre. One main bank, roughly circular, is reinforced on the east side by a second, smaller rampart.

The ascent of <u>Nest Brow</u> to <u>Castlerigg</u> suddenly reveals <u>Keswick</u> and <u>Derwentwater</u> amid the encircling fells.

At 'Castlerigg's naked steep', Benjamin in *The Waggoner*, the worse for drink, is met by his master. Poor Benjamin!

> *When duty of that day was o'er,*
> *Laid down his whip – and served no more.*

St John's-in-the-Vale

*The B5322 follows St John's Beck from
the A591 to the A66, avoiding Keswick.*

Reputedly the valley takes its name from the Knights Hospitallers of St John who were said to have founded a hospice here in the 13c.

<u>Castle Rock</u> was known as Green Crag until early writers described it as looking like a castle.

This location, '*with airy turrets crowned*', was used by Sir Walter Scott whilst he was staying at the Royal Oak in Keswick, when he wrote his poem '*The Bridal of Triermain*' (1805) about the sorceress who caused the destruction of King Arthur.

The Knights of King Arthur had been fighting so fiercely at a tournament in Carlisle for the hand of the beautiful Gwyneth that the Order of the Round Table was in danger of disintegration. To prevent this, Gwyneth was spirited away by Merlin and put to sleep in the enchanted castle. Five hundred years later, Sir Roland de Vaux, Baron of Triermain, rode up and broke the magic spell by hurling his axe at the rock face.

<u>Legburthwaite's</u> tiny mission church, originally founded in 1881, serves a community of foresters. '*Lying under the range of mighty Helvellyn, speaking of stability and eternity, is a witness of God's unchanging and eternal love in this world of everchanging values.*'

Great Dodd	1.8
Stybarrow Dodd	1.3, 5

258

Watson's Dodd   1.3

<u>Fornside</u>
Great Dodd   1.7

<u>Wanthwaite</u>. Across the bridge, and up a long, steep road is <u>The Church of St John's-in-the-Vale</u> in an isolated and dramatic location on the saddle of the pass between the Vale of St John and the Naddle Valley.

The present church, nestling among yew trees, dates from 1845 according to the plaque over the door, but a place of worship is thought to have been built in the 13c by the Knights Hospitallers of St John who founded a hospice here.

The Church of St John eventually became one of the five chapels of St Kentigern's Church at Crosthwaite, Keswick, before separating into its own parish in 1865.

The altar and the panelling to pew height came from Crosthwaite Church. The east window commemorates Thomas Leathes Stanger-Leathes of Dale Head, Thirlmere.

The ruins of the village inn disappeared when the site was taken for a churchyard extension. In the churchyard, opposite the east window of the church, a headstone commemorates <u>John Richardson.</u> He was born at 'Piper House', Naddle, the son of a builder, and spent half of his working life in the building trade. Amongst his many contracts in Keswick and elsewhere, he restored St John's Church and built the adjacent village school. After twenty-five years as a builder, he changed his career and became a schoolmaster in the school which he had built. He was then living at Bridge House, at the foot of the hill, with his wife, Grace, and eight children. In later life, his talent flourished as a successful writer of dialect poems and stories. He was the author of *Cumberland Talk 1871–6* and his knowledge of the Cumbrian dialect made him an authority consulted by other writers.

The school building has been enlarged and converted into the Carlisle Diocesan Youth Centre, with residential facilities.

High Rigg   3.3

<u>The British Village</u>. *From Wanthwaite take the old coach road towards Dockray in Matterdale. North of the road at OS327240 is this Dark Age (Celtic) Settlement in a grassy hollow.*

The remains of five or more roughly rectangular enclosures and the foundations of four or five hut circles are visible. The largest had walls 5 feet thick and an internal diameter of 20 feet with a south-east entrance.

To the north and east are at least thirty small cairns averaging 20 feet to 25 feet across. Traces of charcoal found in several suggest that these may have been burial structures.

The site is divided now by a high stone wall built at the time of the 19c enclosure.

As this site is north facing it would have been less sheltered than the Norse settlement at Threlkeld across the valley. But it is possible that the Celtic and Norse communities lived side by side until the 10c.

Clough Head   1.5

Keswick

EC. W. Mkt.S. [OE. cesewic = cheese farm.]

The town is dominated by the Northern Fells of Skiddaw and Blencathra (Saddleback) in the background whilst looking out over Derwentwater in the foreground.

The Moot Hall was a ruined courthouse in 1571 when it was converted into a Receiving House where copper from the nearby Brigham smelter received the Queen's mark. It was rebuilt in 1695 with materials from a ruined mansion on Lord's Island, Derwentwater, and again restored in 1813. During its long history, the Moot Hall has functioned also as a courthouse, a market — when the ground floor arches were left open to shelter the trades people — a prison, a museum and a town hall.

Today, the Tourist Information Centre is on the ground floor. Upstairs slide shows and exhibitions are held.

The bell was brought from the Redcliffe family's ancestral home on Lord's Island and served as a curfew bell in the 17c. The clock has only one hand.

The Saturday market around the Moot Hall originated when Thomas de Derwentwater obtained a market charter from Edward I (1272–1307).

The Packhorse Yard is an example of how 'back land' can be greatly altered to provide a modern shopping precinct.

The yards on both sides of the Market Place are a relic of medieval times. Behind a street front of timber-framed houses, narrow strips of land were cultivated as gardens or orchards. These plots were known as 'burgages'. By the 18c, timber as a building material was more frequently replaced by stone and, on the land at the rear of the houses, workshops were built and cottage industries developed.

<u>Home of Sir John Bankes,</u> next to John Young's antique shop. Sir John Bankes provided a Charitable Trust and a Poorhouse in the town. He was born in 1589 at nearby Castlerigg and educated at Crosthwaite School and Queen's College, Oxford. By 1641, he had become Lord Chief Justice of the Common Pleas and, in the following year, a Privy Councillor. He died in Oxford in 1644 and was buried in the chapel of Christ's Church College.

Panelling from his house has been incorporated into the antique shop next door.

<u>King's Head Court</u> leads up steps on the left to the cottage of <u>Jonathan Otley</u> (1766–1856), who was born near Grasmere and came to Keswick in 1791. He worked as a watch and clock repairer, but had a special interest in geology and meteorology. He published a Lakeland geology text in 1820 and a guide book to the Lake District in 1823.

<u>The Queen's Hotel</u> accommodated John Hatfield, the imposter and fraudster, who bigamously married the 'Maid of Buttermere'. The exposure of his crimes began when Samuel Taylor Coleridge of Greta Hall reported to London's *Morning Post*.

<u>The Post Office</u> stands on the site of the Poorhouse. Sir John Bankes left £200 for the building and funds *'to raise a stock of Wool, Flax, Hemp, Thread, Iron and other necessary wear and stuff to set the poor on work who were born in the parish of Crosthwaite'.*

<u>The Council Offices</u> were originally built in 1864 as the Cumberland Union Bank, which gave the name to Bank Street.

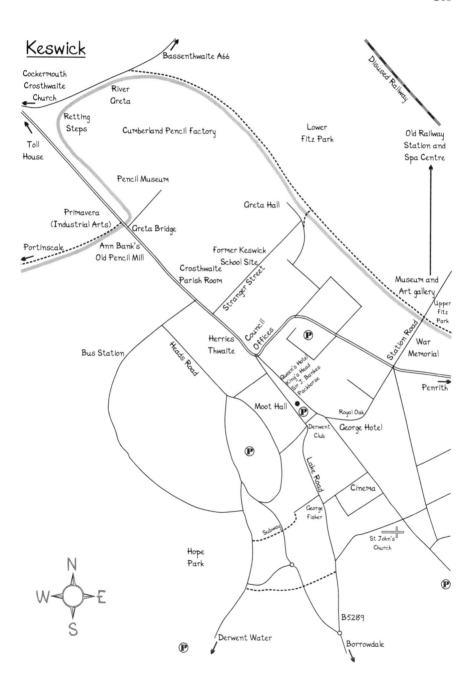

Keswick

Cockermouth
Crosthwaite
Church

River Greta

Bassenthwaite A66

Disused Railway

Retting Steps

Toll House

Cumberland Pencil Factory

Lower Fitz Park

Old Railway Station and Spa Centre

Pencil Museum

Greta Hall

Primavera (Industrial Arts)

Greta Bridge

Portinscale

Ann Bank's Old Pencil Mill

Former Keswick School Site

Museum and Art gallery

Crosthwaite Parish Room

Stranger Street

Upper Fitz Park

Bus Station

Heads Road

Herries Thwaite

Council Offices

P

Station Road

War Memorial

Queen's Hotel
King's Head
Sir J. Bankes
Packhorse

Penrith

Moot Hall

P

Royal Oak

George Hotel

Derwent Club

P

Lake Road

Cinema

George Fisher

Subway

St John's Church

Hope Park

N
W   E
S

B5289

P

Derwent Water

Borrowdale

P

<u>Herries Thwaite Shopping Centre</u>. A plaque in the pavement indicates that this was formerly Museum Square. The museum belonged to Peter Crosthwaite (1736–1808) who was born near Keswick. He served in the East India Company as a Customs Officer at Blyth before settling in Keswick in 1780 to exhibit his large collection of strange objects.

<u>The Crosthwaite Parish Room</u> is recognisable by the bell on the gable end. The room was opened in 1879 as a memorial to the Rev. G. G. Goodwin, vicar of Crosthwaite, and is used for religious and secular meetings.

<u>Keswick School</u> opened for day and boarding pupils in 1898 with financial help from the Hewetson family. In 1980, it merged with Lairthwaite Secondary Modern School to become a comprehensive unit which has retained the Keswick School name.

<u>Greta Hall</u> is a Georgian building on the hill behind the former Keswick School buildings.

From 1800 to 1803, Greta Hall was the home of Samuel Taylor Coleridge (1772–1834), his wife and very young son. Coleridge wanted to be within visiting distance of the Wordsworths at Grasmere and frequently he would walk over to Dove Cottage or to meet Wordsworth half way. At Greta hall Coleridge wrote, '*I question if there be a room in England which commands a view of mountains and lakes and woods superior to that in which I am sitting.*' But when Coleridge's opium-addicted health began to fail, he left his family for the warmth of Malta before eventually moving to London where he died.

In 1803, the deserted Sarah Coleridge and her young children were joined for support at Greta Hall by her sister and her husband, Robert Southey (1774–1843) and family. Southey, who was made Poet Laureate in 1813, lived at Greta Hall for forty years and helped to make Keswick a place of literary pilgrimage, as Wordsworth had made

Grasmere. Unlike Wordsworth, Southey wrote hardly any verse connected with Lakeland. One exception was his onomatopaeic poem written for his children about '*The Cataract of Lodore*'. Southey was mainly engaged in writing epic verse, essays and historical works. His prose writing included the original version of *The Three Bears*, a biography of Nelson and the first official history of Brazil. With Coleridge's family and his own wife and seven children to support, he was still able to build up a library of 14,000 books.

Since 1872, Greta Hall has been a girls' school, a boarding school for most of the time. It was once part of Keswick School.

<u>Ann Bank's Pencil Mill</u>, formerly a woollen mill alongside the River Greta [ON, rock stream], was taken over c. 1886 by the widow of Joseph Banks, the principal pencil manufacturer in Keswick.

Today, the mill has become a Youth Centre.

<u>The Cumberland Pencil Company Works</u>, built in 1934, owned by Rexel, is the only survivor of a traditional industry in Keswick.

The discovery at Seathwaite, Borrowdale, of plumbago, or graphite, known locally as 'wad', gave rise to the manufacture of the first lead pencils in 1566 when Forge Mill at Braithwaite began production. The wood for the pencils was ultimately chosen to be Florida cedar.

Manufacture from 1868 was halted by a fire and production was moved to Keswick in 1898. Since then, several companies have been engaged in the manufacture of pencils, but Seathwaite graphite became exhausted resulting in imports from Sri Lanka, Korea and Mexico.

<u>The Museum</u> traces the development of the pencil from the earliest to the latest, including a wartime pencil containing a map of Germany and a compass. Early production machinery is featured.

See: *Cumberland Heritage*. Molly Lefebure. Gollancz (1970).

<u>The Keswick School of Industrial Art</u> was founded 1894 by Edith, the wife of Canon Rawnsley, to secure employment for local men when they were out of work in the winter. Woodcarving and metalwork predominated. The income from sales helped to build the school. Across the front of the building are the words,

The Loving Eye and Patient Hand
Shall Join Together and Bless This Land.

Primavera, an Italian Restaurant has occupied the building since 1984.

<u>Porch Cottage and Ruskin Cottage</u> were the centre of the flourishing Ruskin Linen Industry from 1894. Miss Marian Twelves, inspired by John Ruskin, who had realised that spinning was a dying skill, started the industry in Langdale in 1883, and brought it to Keswick in 1889.

<u>The Retting Steps</u> are where flax was soaked in the River Greta to break down the cellulose coating and expose the fibres.

The drinking fountain was one of several erected in the town by Samuel Ladyman in the 1870s.

<u>Toll Bar Cottage</u>. An Act of Parliament in 1761 set up Turnpike Trusts responsible for the road from Kendal to Cockermouth via Keswick. Each route in and out of Keswick had its own Toll House.

<u>Crosthwaite C of E First School</u> was financed by James Stanger in 1833. A contemporary newspaper described it as *'one of the most splendid schools in this part of the kingdom as regards architectural beauty.'* Girls were taught reading, sewing, knitting and cooking.

<u>Quaker Cottage</u>. Hugh Tickell bought a house and orchard in 1685 for use by the local Society of Friends. Subsequent replacement and alterations have resulted in the present Quaker Cottage.

The Meeting House in use today opened in Church Street in 1919.

The Catholic Church of Our Lady and St Charles was built in 1926 on a plot of land bought by Father Stephen Dawes, a monk from Ampleforth. The church was opened in 1928, but not completed until 1965, and consecrated in 1972.

Keswick School, Lairthwaite, up Vicarage Hill, began in 1951 as a Secondary Modern day and boarding school, built around the former home of the Stanger family, after whom one of Keswick's streets is named.

Crosthwaite Old School. Possibly founded in the 14c by Sir Thomas de Eskhead, this school was known to be in existence in 1571. A decree of 1616 stated that 'there hath been a Grammar School within the parish of Crosthwaite time whereof the memory of man knoweth not the contrary.' The school closed in 1976 and the building was put to use by Keswick School.

Crosthwaite Parish Church is dedicated to St Kentigern, a 6c saint, who fled from his pagan persecutors in Glasgow, where he was known as St Mungo, first to Carlisle and then to north Cumbria, where eight parish churches are dedicated to him.

St Kentigern reputedly preached here in 553 AD. In 1181, Alice de Rumelli, granddaughter of the first Norman overlord, built a stone church on the site. This was incorporated in the 1523 building, which was restored in 1844 by James Stanger. Uniquely preserved is a full set of 16c consecration crosses carved to mark the points of the new building blessed by the bishop.

Church archives in the 16c record that 176 children were born to German miners at the time when copper and other rich minerals in Newlands and Borrowdale, copper in particular, were being extracted.

Within the church is an altar tomb to Sir John Radcliffe and his wife, whose family founded Keswick. They were the ancestors of the

Earls of Derwent whose property was forfeited for supporting the 1715 Jacobite Rebellion.

The effigy of Robert Southey has an inscription by William Wordsworth.

In the baptistry, Canon Hardwicke Drummond Rawnsley (1851–1920) and his wife are commemorated for their work in campaigning for the preservation of the Lakeland scenery, which resulted in the foundation of the National Trust in 1895. Canon Rawnsley was the vicar of Crosthwaite (1883–1917), Canon of Carlisle (1893) and chaplain to King George V (1912–1920). He was also an author, an educationalist and a favourite of the young Beatrix Potter. He encouraged her to publish her writings and paintings. The Rawnsley graves are at the north end of the churchyard.

The grave of Robert Southey in the churchyard was restored in 1961 by the Brazilian government, for whom Southey had written the first published history of that country without ever visiting it.

Also buried here are Sir Edmund Harrison, founder of London's CID; William Jackson (1797–1809), who built Greta Hall; and Jonathan Otley, the Keswick 'clocker', who fathered Lakeland geology and investigated the phenomena of the floating islands of Derwentwater, plotting their appearances for more than thirty years.

The church stands in a magnificent position in Crosthwaite [*ON. The clearing marked by a cross*], with the surrounding fells indicated on the viewfinder in the churchyard.

Return towards Keswick, following the River Greta into Crosthwaite Road and then through Lower Fitz Park to the bridge on Station Road.

<u>Station Road Bridge</u>. Downstream, several small blocks of flats

have been converted from riverside mills.

<u>The Museum and Art Gallery</u>. The Museum was built in 1897 and the Art Gallery was added in 1905.

Original manuscripts include *Herries* novels by Sir Hugh Walpole, letters associated with Robert Southey including his children's story, *The Three Bears*, the Cumbrian hunting song *John Peel*, and documents originating from Wordsworth and Ruskin.

On display are a portrait of Jonathan Otley, a painting of the 'Beauty of Buttermere' and water colours by J.M.W. Turner.

Flintoff's 1834 scale model of the Lake District took seventeen years to build.

Amongst the collection of fossils, minerals and stones are the Richardson family's Musical Stones gathered from Skiddaw during the first half of the 19c. They are played like a xylophone. The weirdest exhibit is the 500 years old cat.

<u>Keswick Spa Leisure Complex</u> opened in 1987 and boasts a wave-effect swimming pool.

<u>The Old Railway Station</u>. The Cockermouth, Keswick and Penrith Railway was built in 1864 to transport iron and iron ore to the steelworks of Durham and to bring coal and coke from the Durham coalfield into West Cumberland. By 1865, passengers were being carried and Keswick station was built, together with a covered walkway to the new Station Hotel, which opened in 1869.

The line closed in 1972. *The Old Railway Station is now the start of the Railway Walk which follows the trackway through the wooded gorge of the River Greta.*

<u>Old Windebrowe</u>, off Brundholme Road, was where William and Dorothy Wordsworth stayed in 1794 whilst nursing their sick friend, Raisley Calvert. He was the son of a wealthy landowner who lived nearby in what is now the Brundholme Country House Hotel. When

Raisley died of consumption in 1795 (See: Penrith, The Robin Hood Inn), he left William £900 to further his career as a poet.

Old Windebrowe now belongs to the Calvert Trust, which operates a Riding Centre for the Disabled.

Upper Fitz Park was bought as '*a pleasure ground and place of recreation*' from the Hewetson family's generous gift in the 1880s.

Jenkinson's Gates, facing the Museum, were erected in memory of Henry Irwin Jenkinson, a writer of popular guide books and a local philanthropist, who was influential in the creation of Fitz Park.

In the park, near Jenkinson's Gates, is a memorial bust to Sir John Bankes.

Station Street contains memorial plaques and a drinking fountain.

The War Memorial has a copper tablet on the back in memory of the employees of the Cockermouth, Keswick and Penrith Railway.

The Royal Oak Hotel was formerly a coaching and a posting inn. The innkeeper was also the postmaster who, when he retired, called his house 'The Acorn'.

A plaque by the door commemorates the visits of Scott, Tennyson, Southey and Wordsworth. John Ruskin spent his honeymoon here. Stained glass windows, which were once part of the hotel, depict the Lake Poets — William and Dorothy Wordsworth, Samuel Taylor and Hartley Coleridge, Robert Southey and Thomas de Quincey.

Part of the hotel has become an arcade giving access to Pack Horse Yard.

The George Inn, formerly a 16c coaching inn, claims to be the oldest in Keswick. It was originally the George and Dragon, but the name Dragon was dropped on the accession of King George I in 1714.

A plaque by the entrance states, '*Here German miners of lead and silver, whose smelting house was at the forge, paid their dues to the officers of Queen Elizabeth I, and here also many unscrupulous traders bought the plumbago ore stolen from the mines in Borrowdale.*

It was here that the Earl of Derwentwater called the last time he was in Keswick to quaff a tankard of ale from the saddle, after which he road off to join the 1715 Rebellion. The end result was death on the scaffold on Tower Hill, London.'

The local hostelries embody much of Keswick's history. Such inns as <u>The Woolpack</u> and <u>The Pack Horse</u> are reminders of early local trade and transport, whilst <u>The Dog and Gun</u> reflects country pursuits.

<u>The Derwent Club</u> replaced the 'Governor's House', built in the 1730s by Edward Stephenson (1691–1768). He was employed by the East India Company and was appointed Governor of Bengal for less than two days in 1728. He retired a wealthy men and is buried in Crosthwaite Church, beneath the altar steps.

<u>The Alhambra Cinema</u> opened in 1913. As a red-brick building it is somewhat unique in the centre of Keswick.

<u>St John's Library</u> was built in 1849 when the Reverend Frederick Myers was the incumbent of St John's Church (1833–1851).

It was used as a library until 1973, but is now a school building.

<u>St John's School</u> opened in 1840 as a Sunday School and for the teaching of infants during the week. Today it is a First School.

<u>St John's Church,</u> built of sandstone, opened in 1838, financed by John Marshall, a member of a wealthy Lake District property owning family. He was Lord of the Manor and a former MP for Leeds.

This was the favourite church of Sir Hugh Walpole (1884–1941), author of the *Herries Chronicles*, who lived at Brackenburn on the shores of Derwentwater from where he could see the church. He is buried in the churchyard overlooking Derwentwater, in a grave marked by a replica Celtic cross.

By the gate on the east side of the churchyard is the grave of

F.W.H. Myers, founder of the Society for Psychical Research.

The vicar of St John's, the Rev. Canon Harford Battersby, assisted by Robert Wilson of Broughton, near Cockermouth, founded the <u>Keswick Convention</u> in 1875. The annual assembly of Christians of all denominations is held in July.

<u>Derwentwater Place</u>, now the Cumbria Hotel, was built by John Richardson of St John's-in-the-Vale, the stonemason who became a writer and an expert in Cumberland dialect.

<u>The Plosh</u> is a cottage with outside steps.

<u>George Fisher's Mountain Equipment Shop</u> has a long tradition of supplying the needs of mountaineers.

Above the shop was once the photographic studio of the Abraham brothers, whose superb monochrome studies of Lakeland people and places have become collectors' items.

<u>Maysons</u> were renowned pioneers of early Lakeland photography also. The premises were restored in 1984 to become a gift shop and bistro.

<u>Hope Park</u> was donated to the town in 1974 by a local architect, Sir Percy Hope.

A miniature golf course adjoins.

<u>The Century Theatre</u>, also named the <u>Blue Box Theatre</u>, was, for nearly twenty years, a touring organisation which took live entertainment to the more rural areas by using ex-army trailers, which unfolded into an auditorium seating 230 people. A combination of rust and the cost of transport caused a settled residence to be established here in 1976. Funds have been raised to finance purpose-built, permanent accommodation, on the same site. This 'Theatre by the Lake' will accommodate an audience of 400 people.

<u>The National Trust Information Centre</u> is opposite the boat landing stages.

<u>Boat Landing Stages</u>. Keswick launches start from here on a clockwise or anticlockwise circuit of Derwentwater, taking about 50 minutes. Passengers may leave or join the launch at any of the other six landing stages.

Brigham [*ON. The 'holme', or patch of meadow by the bridge.*]

North-east of Keswick, near to where the A66 crosses the River Greta, is the site of the former Brigham smelter, although the only evidence is the artificial channel which carried water from the river, through a hole in the rock.

The smelter was constructed in the 16c by the Company of Mines Royal promoted by Thomas Thurland (d. 1574) and managed by Daniel Hochstetter (d. 1581). The principal mineral was copper, which was brought by pack horse and boat from mines in the Newlands Valley, such as Goldscope, Castle Nook and Dale Head, from Ellers Mine in Borrowdale and from Coniston.

During the Civil War in 1650, all the buildings were destroyed by Cromwell's troops, including the smelt house, the stamping sheds and the storehouses for copper ore and fuel. Some of the miners were enlisted into the Parliamentary army.

Bleaberry Fell	3.5	Latrigg	5.5
Walla Crag	3.3, 4	Lonscale Fell	5.4
		Skiddaw	5.11, 12
		Skiddaw Little Man	5.10, 12

Around Derwentwater

Derwentwater claims to be the '*Queen of the English Lakes*'. It is 3 miles long, half that in width, oval in shape, and 60 feet deep, fed and drained by the River Derwent, [*OB. Abounding in oaks.*]

The vast water catchment of the lake makes a difference of 9 feet between low and high water. During August Bank Holiday in 1938, the water level rose 6 feet 8 inches in 24 hours.

To the north and west of the lake, the fells are of Skiddaw Slate, a fairly uniform rock composition, mainly shales with occasional grit bands, which tend to weather evenly and produce relatively smooth, uniform slopes, well grassed with shaly debris.

There are four main islands, all owned by the National Trust.

<u>Derwent Island</u> is the largest. It was owned by Fountains Abbey until the Dissolution and later became the headquarters of the German miners, the Ritselers and Steinbergers, who established a colony here, growing their own vegetables and brewing their own beer, until they were better accepted by local people. They had come over to work for the Society for Mines Royal in 1564 as part of Lord Burghley's policy for Queen Elizabeth to exploit local resources. Copper, silver and lead were mined from the fells to the west of the lake.

Whilst the island was still called Victor's Island, it was bought in 1778 by Joseph Pocklington, an eccentric retired banker, who constructed a variety of buildings on it, including a house, a church and a number of follies such as a mock Druid Circle and a miniature fort. On the lake he staged extravagant regattas using decorated boats and mock naval battles with cannon fire.

The Marshall family became owners in 1884 and the National Trust in 1951.

<u>Lord's Island</u> was the site of the manor house of the Radcliffe family who founded Keswick. With materials from the ruins of the manor house, including the bell, the Moot Hall at Keswick was built in 1813.

<u>Rampsholme Island</u>. Charcoal-fuelled furnaces on the island once smelted iron ore from the local mines. In 1735, the island was given to the Commissioners of Greenwich Hospital after Lord Derwentwater was beheaded for his part in the Jacobite uprising of 1715.

<u>St Herbert's Island</u> has the ruined sanctuary of a 7c hermit, a disciple of St Cuthbert of Holy Island. A chapel was built in 1374 for pilgrims who possibly embarked from Friar's Crag. After celebrating an annual mass, they were granted an indulgence of 40 days and bought little crucifixes as souvenirs. The mould for these is in the Keswick Museum. This was Owl Island in Beatrix Potter's *The Tale of Squirrel Nutkin.*

<u>The Floating Island,</u> in the south-east corner, prompted Wordsworth's comment, 'with more propriety might be named the *Buoyant Island*'. The phenomena was investigated by Jonathan Otley who plotted its appearance for more than thirty years. Several scientific papers have been published describing and explaining the conditions which cause its appearance. During prolonged hot weather, marsh gas generated by decaying vegetable matter permeates layers of sunken vegetation causing them and the mud on top to float to the surface. When the temperature cools, the island sinks.

A circular walk round Derwentwater covers a distance of 10 miles.

<u>Crow Park</u> (NT), opposite Lake Road car park, slopes down to the

lake shore. The oak trees were cut down and sold in 1751 by the Commissioners of Greenwich Hospital. Thomas West in his '*Guide*' of 1784 named this as one of his Derwentwater viewing 'stations'.

Keswick Launch Terminal. The 50-minutes circular tour of the lake operating from March to November, stops at various landing stages.

Cockshot Wood (NT) reaches to the boat landing stages.

Castle Head (NT) is a wooded volcanic outcrop at 529 feet, over-looking the whole of Derwentwater. The direction finder indicates Skiddaw to the north and the Jaws of Barrowdale to the south. West commended this 'station'.

Friar's Crag (NT), another volcanic outcrop, is said to have been named after the Lindisfarne pilgrims who once embarked from here for St Herbert's Island to receive a blessing from the solitary 7c hermit.

West acclaimed this beauty spot and John Ruskin wrote this is '*one of the three or four most beautiful views in Europe*'. Ruskin's memorial plaque set up in 1900 reads:

> *The first thing which I remember*
> *As an event in my life was being*
> *taken by my nurse to the brow of*
> *Friar's Crag on Derwentwater.*

In his diary he goes on to write of ' . . . *the intense joy, mingled with awe, that I had in looking through the hollows in the mossy roots, over the Crag, into the dark lake*'.

There is a memorial tablet also to Canon Rawnsley, vicar of Crosthwaite, co-founder of the National Trust and its Honorary Secretary until his death in 1920.

Arthur Ransome based Darien on this locality in *Swallows and Amazons*'.

On the water line, plaques mark the lowest levels, the latest in 1983.

<u>Ings Wood</u> (NT). A bridge spans Brockle Beck.
<u>Stable Hills Farm</u>. <u>Broomhill Point</u>.
<u>Calfclose Bay</u> is another of West's 'stations'. The
'Hundred Year Stone' on the lake shore was commissioned
by the National Trust for its centenary Commemoration.
Peter Randall-Pope was the sculptor.
<u>Great Wood</u> has car parking facilities.

N.T. 'HUNDRED YEAR STONE' DERWENTWATER   DERWENTWATER BETWEEN CALF CLOSE & BROOMHILL POINT
11/98   1995   SCULPTOR PETER RANDALL-PAGE CUMBRIA PUBLIC ART BOULDER

<u>Walla Crag</u>. Here the Skiddaw Slates dip beneath the Borrowdale
Volcanic Series of rocks with Walla Scar marking the northern limit
of a line running diagonally to Grange and on to Narrow Moor and
Pillar. The main characteristic is a succession of toughened lava
beds interspersed with softer tuffs of fine-grained rocks formed of
volcanic ash. This succession of hard and soft beds has the visual

effect of a gigantic staircase where the treads coincide with the more resistant beds. Where tuffs have been altered by igneous activity, they too stand out as sheer rock walls.

Cat Gill and its waterfall provide access to the top of Walla Crag, from where a return to Keswick can be made via Rakefoot.

Lady's Rake, a great rift, is named after the tradition that Lady Derwentwater fled from Lord's Island up this ravine after her husband's involvement in the 1715 Jacobite Rebellion for which he forfeited his life and property.

Walla Crag   3.4, 3

Ashness Gate Launch Landing is where the unclassified road leads to Ashness Bridge and Watendlath.

Bleaberry Fell   3.3, 4
High Seat   3.4
Walla Crag   3.4

Barrow House, the Derwentwater Youth Hostel since 1961, was originally called Cascade Hall. It was built in 1787 by Joseph Pocklington, the eccentric who moved here from Derwent Island.

Barrow Falls, in the grounds, cascade 108 feet in two falls, the second highest in Lakeland. To improve the waterfall, dynamite was used to blast the rock in the 19c.

Barrow Bay promontory has the remains of a World War II lake defence emplacement.

Lodore Launch Landing.

The Lodore Hotel, in 1789, was only a small inn, which has grown into a huge Victorian hotel with 20c additions.

The cannon which for a fee used to be fired from the lakeshore to set off the resounding echoes no longer exists.

<u>The Falls of Lodore,</u> behind the hotel, are accessible to the public. The Watendlath Beck, in a wooded chasm, plunges 150 feet between the towering perpendicular rocks of Gowder Crag and Shepherd's Crag. Robert Southey in 1809 wrote a highly alliterative onomatopoeic poem about it for his children. He took 200 lines to answer the question, 'How Does the Water Come Down at Lodore?'

> *Rushing and lushing and brushing and gushing*
> *And flapping and rapping and clapping and slapping*
> *And curling and whirling and purling and twirling*
> *And thumping and plumping and bumping and jumping*
> *And dashing and flashing and splashing and clashing*
> *And so never-ending, but always descending*
> *Sounds and motions for ever and ever are blending,*
> *All at one and all o'er, with a mighty uproar,*
> *And in this way the water comes down at Lodore.*

The increasing length of the lines imitates the shape of the falls.

Cross the flat flood plain of the River Derwent to wooded Manesty Park, using the board walk. Classic views unfold of the 'Jaws of Borrowdale'.

On <u>Brandelhow Point</u> is Abbot's Bay House, former home of Percy Withers, biographer of A.E. Housman.

<u>Brandelhow Bay</u>, with its boathouse, is littered with the old lead mine spoil heaps jutting out into the bay and overgrown with trees. This was one of the most extensive mines in the Skiddaw Slates. Its age was unknown, but old workings had been cut with stope and feather before the introduction of gunpowder. The water in the mine was heavily impregnated with salt. Employment was given to 70 to 80 men and boys.

Flooding was always a problem. In 1848 the Keswick Mining

Company erected a thirty-foot water wheel to drain the mine. When the supply of water to power the wheel was found to be inadequate, a steam engine had to be used at greater expense. Costly repairs to the engine could not be afforded and the mine was abandoned in 1864.

Twenty years later, the Brandley Mining Company re-opened the mine by installing a more powerful steam engine to pump out the water and to extend into new depths. In 1888 a powerful beam engine was introduced for pumping.

High Brandelhow Launch Landing.

Brackenburn was the former home of the author Sir Hugh Walpole, who was born in Auckland, New Zealand in 1884, the son of an Anglican clergyman. On his father's appointment as Principal of Bede College, Durham, Hugh came to England to be educated at King's School, Canterbury and Cambridge University. He became a preparatory school teacher, but soon abandoned this for writing and journalism. In 1923, he bought Brackenburn '*a little paradise on Cat Bells*' and shared it with his friend, Harold Cheevers.

The small stone house built in 1909 was enlarged and the room above the detached garage was converted into a library and study. Another storey was added later to house his library of 30,00 books and collection of paintings. This is now Brackenburn Lodge.

Although Walpole frequently split his time between Brackenburn and London, the splendour and variety of the Lakeland landscape viewed from his study inspired the setting of many of his novels. Cumberland life in the 18c was vividly created in his *Herries Chronicles: Rogue Herries* (1930), *Judith Paris* (1931), *The Fortress* (1932), and *Vanessa* (1933). Keswick life in Tudor Times was equally well portrayed: *The Far Pavilions* (1940) and *Katherine Christian* (1944, unfinished.) He wrote forty novels in addition to short stories and a long sequence of diaries.

Sir Hugh Walpole died in 1941 at the age of 57 and was buried in St John's churchyard, Keswick.

Walpole's Seat, above the house, on the fellside, was placed there by Harold Cheevers to mark Walpole's favourite viewpoint.

Brandelhow Park was the first piece of land in the Lake District bought by the National Trust. In 1902 four oak trees were planted at the ceremony by Princess Louise, Octavia Hill, Sir Robert Hunter and Canon Rawnsley. The purchase was almost entirely due to the campaigning by Canon Rawnsley and, as a memorial to him, the National Trust bought Friar's Crag on the opposite shore in 1922.

Low Brandelhow Launch Landing.

Hawes End Launch Landing is a starting point for Cat Bells, 1,148 feet, and the Newlands Valley.

The onward way now coincides with the Cumbria Way and the Allerdale Ramble.

Catbells   6.4, 5

Lingholme Gardens, open to the public, feature azaleas and rhododendrons in the acid, peaty soil.

When the house was available for summer lettings, Beatrix Potter's family stayed on several occasions. Backgrounds for *The Tale of Benjamin Bunny* and for *The Tale of Squirrel Nutkin* were painted here by Beatrix.

Lingholm is now the property of Viscount Rochdale.

Fawe Park was another Potter family holiday home. Mr MacGregor's vegetable garden in *The Tale of Peter Rabbit* and Old Brown's Oak in *The Tale of Squirrel Nutkin* were based on features here. It was here also in 1901 that Beatrix met Lucie Carr of Newlands and included her in *The Tale of Mrs Tiggy-Winkle*.

<u>Nicholas End Marine Launch Landing</u>. Sailing boats, windsurfing equipment and chandlery are available.

Follow the metalled road.

<u>Portinscale</u> [*ON. Prostitute's hut!*] Divert towards the village to see the two wells: *Dorothy Well*, and the well with the inscription:

> Whoever drinketh of this water shall thirst again
> But whosoever drinketh of the water that
> I shall give him shall never thirst.

Cross the suspension bridge over the River Derwent to reach Keswick.

Watendlath

[ON. Vatns Endi = End of the lake.]

Approach from the Keswick-Borrowdale road, behind Barrow House.

The tributary, side valley of Watendlath, was fashioned when glacial ice gouged out the main valley of Borrowdale. The melting ice left the valley of Watendlath suspended at a higher level, creating a typical hanging valley with the waterfalls of Watendlath Beck dropping 600 feet before reaching Derwentwater, the final descent being the Lodore Falls.

Only in the 1930s was the single track road built along the valley. Mains electricity and the telephone (1984) followed later.

Historically, Alice de Rumelli gave this land to Fountains Abbey in 1195. Watendlath today is owned by the National Trust.

Kettlewell Car Park, on the shore of Derwentwater.

Ashness Bridge, a packhorse bridge over Ashness Gill (OS. Barrow Beck) offers a very popular viewpoint over Derwentwater, with Skiddaw in the background to the north and Catbells to the west.

High Seat   3.4

Ashness Wood. Just beyond the second gateway after crossing a tiny rill, 250 yards from the road, is Surprise View, a superb vantage point from which to admire Borrowdale and Derwentwater.

Upper Lodore Falls. These are best seen between Gowder Crag and Shepherds Crag where the Watendlath Beck plunges into the gorge.

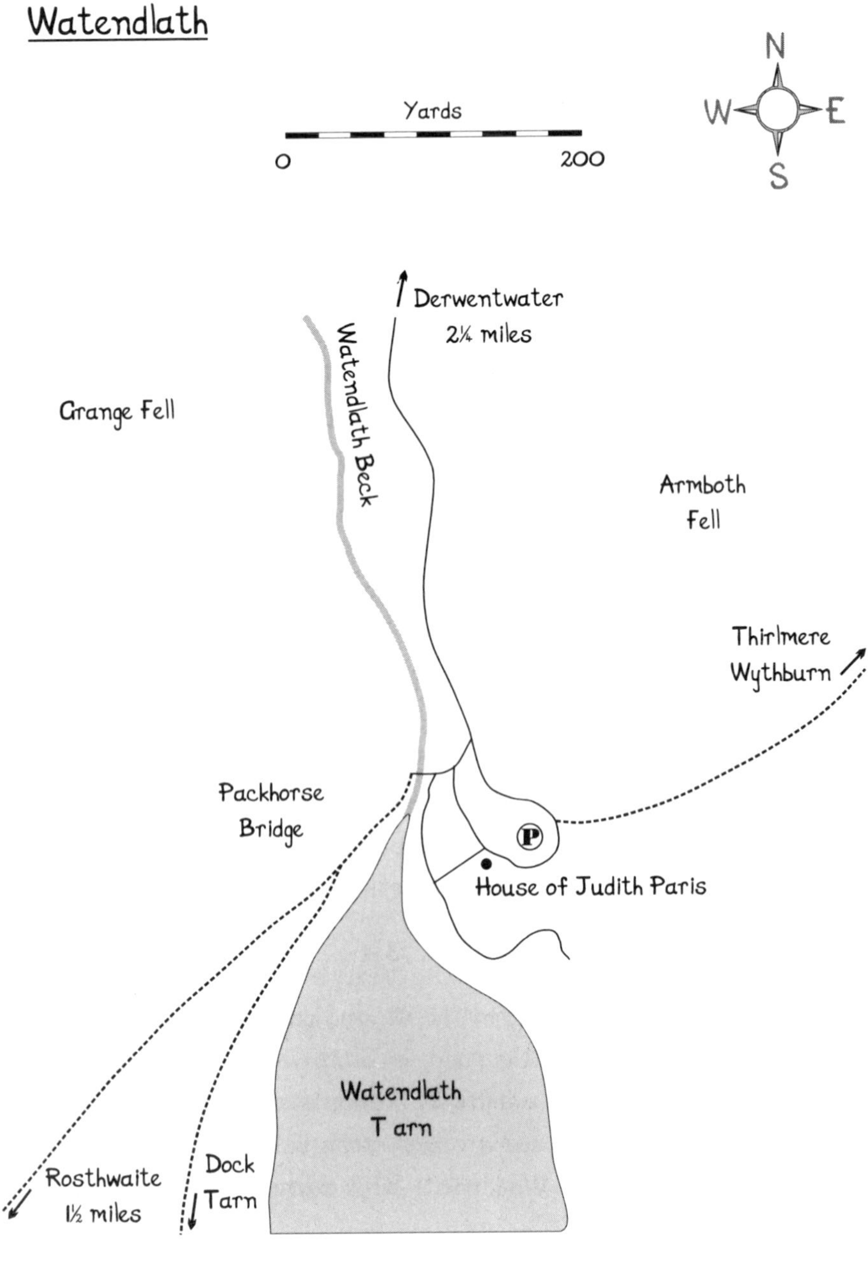

Watendlath

Yards

0   200

N
W · E
S

Derwentwater
2¼ miles

Grange Fell

Watendlath Beck

Armboth
Fell

Thirlmere
Wythburn

Packhorse
Bridge

House of Judith Paris

Watendlath
Tarn

Rosthwaite
1½ miles

Dock
Tarn

Thwaite House. Nearby, on the Watendlath side, are the sites of former tiny lakes in the valley floor.

Reecastle Crag. This is the site of a ¼-acre Iron Age hillfort, defended by triple banks on the steep slopes to the west and by a single rampart to the east.

The Churn, or Devil's Punchbowl, about 100 yards short of Watendlath hamlet, is a hollow with a hole in the bottom scraped out by the Watendlath Beck.

Watendlath. This isolated hamlet, nestling midst moorland fells, consists of a cluster of cottages and 'statesman's' farmhouses alongside a tarn well stocked with trout. A packhorse bridge crosses the beck.

Before the days of motor vehicles, this was the meeting place for ancient trackways coming from Keswick in the north, Great Langdale in the south, Wythburn in the east and Rosthwaite in the west. The pony track from Rosthwaite is known as Bowdergate [*ON. Road by the booth, dairy farm, or temporary summer settlement.*]

The hamlet was described by Dorothy Wordsworth in her Journal of 1800 as '*Wattenlath, a heavenly scene*'.

Watendlath was featured by Sir Hugh Walpole in the second of *The Herries Chronicles, Judith Paris*, and in his last novel *Katherine Christian*. Judith Paris came to live here for a time with her smuggler husband, George Paris. This 'hidden' valley provided the remoteness and the secrecy George needed for carrying out his nefarious exploits. The exact location of the house of Judith Paris is claimed by a plaque on the wall of Fold Head Farm. But in 1937, Walpole denied that he had a particular house in mind. Since the publication of *Judith Paris* the farmhouse has been a popular place of pilgrimage, reinforcing the mistaken idea that Walpole's characters actually existed in this location, or that this was a specially chosen model for inclusion in his story.

The tarn is the source of the Watendlath Beck. Still visible on the southern side are the rectangular enclosures of strips of the former common field, once shared by the farmers of the hamlet. It was to the side of this tarn that Nicholas Herries was brought by his servant Gilbert, to witness a witches' sabbath in Walpole's *The Bright Pavilions*.

Grange Fell	*3.5, 6*
Great Crag	*3.4*
High Seat	*3.5*
High Tove	*3.3*
Ullscarf	*3.7*

Borrowdale

[ON. Borgardlr. Borgar = fortress (i.e. Castle Crag). dalr = dale.]

The origin of the dramatic scenery is attributed to the Borrowdale Volcanic rock in a glaciated valley – the twin action of fire and ice.

The volcanic eruptions date back four hundred and fifty million years, but the Ice Age began a mere two million years ago and ended ten thousand years ago, with intermittent periods of warmer climates.

The ice flowed from the region of Scafell and Great Gable, down Styhead Gill, Grains Gill and Longstrath. When the ice melted, it deposited its load of stones as scattered boulders or as moraines. Two moraines near Borrowdale church mark where the Seathwaite and Stonethwaite glaciers met. Moraines occurred also in the hanging valleys of Watendlath, Gillercomb (Sourmilk Gill) and Combe Gill. Hollows, or rock barriers damming the valley floor, caused water to collect and lakes to be formed. Former lakes were located between Seathwaite and Seatoller and around Stonethwaite and Rosthwaite. Gradually, the lakes silted up, but these areas are still prone to flooding at times of heaviest rainfall in this wetter part of Lakeland.

The earliest evidence of habitation in Borrowdale is the Iron Age hill fort on Castle Crag from which the valley probably takes its name.

In the 10c, the main settlers were the Norsemen who came via Ireland and the Isle of Man. They left a legacy of Old Norse place names and a dialect.

When the Normans invaded, Cumbria was excluded from the Domesday Survey, c. 1086, as it was part of Strathclyde, Scotland. Loyal Norman barons were rewarded by their king with gifts of land. Borrowdale was awarded to the de Rumelli's, Lords of Allerdale. The granddaughter of the first Norman overlord, Lady Alice de Rumelli, inherited the barony and sold the Manor of Borrowdale as a sheep run to the monks of Furness Abbey for the sum of £156 : 13s : 4d. Previously, she had gifted the eastern side of Borrowdale, including Watendlath and Stonethwaite, to Yorkshire's Fountains Abbey.

Following the Dissolution of the Monasteries, 1536–39, Borrowdale became Crown property and Henry VIII's bailiffs leased the farms for rents amounting in total to £29 : 14s : 0d. Not until 1615, when James I sold off Crown land, were wealthy farmers able to buy their farmsteads and establish the 'statesman' era of single farm ownership.

The B5289, past the Lodore Hotel, follows the River Derwent between the wooded slopes of the fells. The trees are mostly hardwoods which were planted to replace the natural forests almost totally cleared to supply the 16c copper smelting furnaces operated by the Company of Mines Royal and the German miners.

Only in 1842 was the road through this part of the valley made suitable for wheeled vehicles. Horse-drawn coaches then came into service. Tourists now add greatly to the valley residents who use this one through road.

<u>Newton Place,</u> opposite the Borrowdale Hotel, was built, it is claimed, by Mary Barker, Dorothy Wordsworth's climbing and painting friend, who took refuge in Boulogne in 1818 because of financial difficulties. An opposing claim for Mary Barker's house was the forerunner of the Scafell Hotel at Rosthwaite.

<u>Troutdale,</u> on the left, is named after its ancient fish ponds

Grange

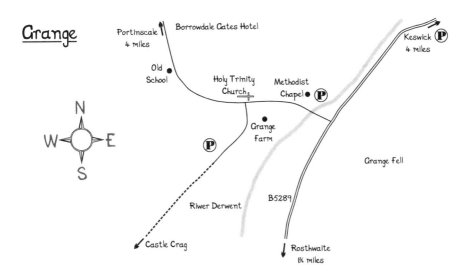

N W E S (compass)

- Portinscale 4 miles
- Borrowdale Gates Hotel
- Old School
- Holy Trinity Church
- Methodist Chapel
- Keswick 4 miles
- Grange Farm
- Grange Fell
- River Derwent
- B5289
- Castle Crag
- Rosthwaite 1¾ miles

Rosthwaite

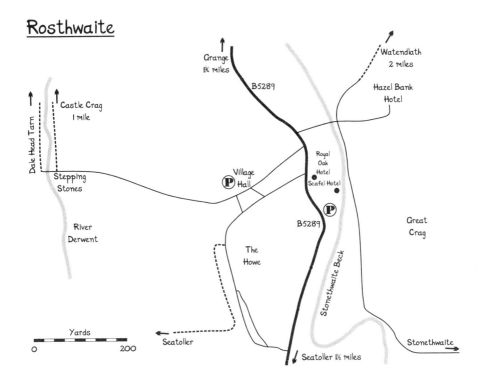

- Grange 1¾ miles
- B5289
- Watendlath 2 miles
- Hazel Bank Hotel
- Dale Head Tarn
- Castle Crag 1 mile
- Stepping Stones
- Village Hall
- Royal Oak Hotel
- Scafel Hotel
- River Derwent
- B5289
- Great Crag
- The Howe
- Stonethwaite Beck
- Seatoller
- Seatoller 1½ miles
- Stonethwaite

Yards
0   200

which can still be seen. There is access from here to Black Crag and King's How on Grange Fell.

Grange-in-Borrowdale [*OE. Monastic farm or Granary.*]

The monks of Furness Abbey built the 'grange' from which to administer their possessions in Borrowdale, the most remote of the abbey's estates.

The double-arched bridge, built over the River Derwent in 1675 offers a view, at its western end, of roche-moutonée (literally 'rock sheep') — smooth, rounded but ice-scraped volcanic rock. At one time, boats transported slate and wood from here to Crow Park at the northern end of Derwentwater.

From this bridge, old Mrs Wilson was thrown and drowned as a witch in Hugh Walpole's *Rogue Herries*.

Grange Methodist Chapel of 1894 replaced the Wesleyan Chapel of 1859. The remains of a non-conformist chapel, built by the Buttermere Slate Company at the time when immigrants from Cornwall and Wales were attracted to work in the local quarries, are visible near Mount View.

The Chapel of the Holy Trinity was built in 1861 from funds raised by Miss Margaret Heathcote who built Borrowdale Gates for herself and Castle Crag for the incumbent. She had sold paintings which she had done to raise money for the church and examples of her painting skills are displayed on the two panels in the sanctuary bearing the ten commandments. The communion silver was given in memory of Hugh Walpole of Brackenburn, about a mile away. Both inside and outside the decoration of imitation Norman dog-tooth is prominent. Upright slates form the churchyard wall.

Borrowdale Church, higher up the valley, pre-dates this church by nearly two centuries.

<u>Grange Farm,</u> in the centre of the village, off the tiny square, was a large sheep farm in the 13c, managed by Cistercian monks. Old houses in the square used to be farms and some dwellings in the village are barn conversions.

<u>Copperfields</u> was bought as a residence for the servants of Hugh Walpole for use whilst he was away in Hollywood writing the script for MGM's film *David Copperfield*. Walpole was cast as the Vicar of Blunderstone. The cottage was also a repository for part of Walpole's extensive collection of books and pictures.

<u>Grange Old School.</u> Pupils were first taught at Borrowdale Gates, where Miss Heathcote was the teacher, and later at Castle Crag. A tablet at Grange Old School, a village hall since 1933, records its origin: '*This school was erected to the memory of Miss Margaret Heathcote mainly by subscriptions of personal friends and others who thus recognised a life of good works spent among and for the inhabitants of this neighbourhood.* The first stone was laid on 4 October 1894 by Miss Langton of Borrowdale.

Grange Fell	3.3	Castle Crag	6.5
		Catbells	6.6
		High Spy	6.6
		Maiden Moor	6.4

<u>Jaws of Borrowdale.</u> The dale narrows dramatically into a ravine ¾ mile long between King's How on Grange Fell on the eastern side and Castle Crag to the west.

Thomas Gray, the poet, took one look through the Jaws of Borrowdale in 1769 and then withdrew from ' . . . *that ancient kingdom of mountaineers, the region of Chaos and Old Night*'. By contrast, Wainwright described this area as '*the loveliest square mile in Lakeland*'. (*Castle Crag 6.4*)

<u>King's How</u>, 1,100 feet, was bought in 1910 by the National Trust as a memorial to Edward VII. Just below the summit is a rock inscribed:

In loving memory of
King Edward VII
Grange Fell is dedicated by his sister
Louise
As a sanctuary of rest and peace.
Here may all beings gather strength and
Find in scenes of beautiful nature a cause
For gratitude and love to God giving them
Courage and vigour to carry on His will.

<u>Castle Crag</u>, 950 feet. This steep volcanic plug was given to the National Trust in 1920 by Sir William Hamer and his family in memory of his son and ten other men of Borrowdale who were killed in World War I. A plaque on the summit records this. A seat lower down bears the inscription, '*The land surrounding the summit of Castle Crag was given to the Nation in memory of Sir William Hamer, MA, MD, FRCP, by his wife Agnes, whom this seat commemorates. 1939.*'

The Crag was surmounted by an Iron Age fort, now completely obliterated by quarry workings. On the site, Roman Samian ware was found by Thomas West, the 18c antiquarian, and is displayed in the Keswick Museum.

The view qualified as one of West's Derwentwater 'stations'.

A quarried cave on the slopes of the Crag provided a home, with running water (from the roof) for the hermit of Borrowdale, Millican Dalton (1867–1947), the self-styled Professor of Adventure and lover of the outdoors, who sold camping equipment and guided parties of walkers. He was born at Nent Head, near Alston, Cumbria.

Below Castle Crag and Lobstone Band, the elevated side valley of

Broadslack Gill is an ice-marginal channel, etched out by a stream which ran along the upper edge of the glacier that once filled Borrowdale. It now forms part of the Allerdale Ramble.

From Grange, continue along the B5289 close to the River Derwent and through Low and High Hows Wood where red squirrels continue to survive.

<u>Bowder Stone</u> [Dialect for 'boulder'] This massive boulder of metamorphic rock, 30 feet high and 60 feet long, weighs an estimated 2,000 tons and balances on its edge in a seemingly precarious position. It either fell from the crags above or was deposited by retreating ice. Wooden steps give access to the top.

Towards the end of the 18c, the eccentric Joseph Pocklington built a small cottage nearby as a home for an old woman who became the official guide. He also cut the hole in the base of the boulder to enable visitors and the guide to shake hands from opposite sides.

The tale is told of the Borrowdale man building a wall close by. On being asked the purpose, the builder explained his desire to keep the cuckoo in Borrowdale, thereby retaining the spring-like weather all the year round, helped by rolling the Bowder Stone down to fill the gap in this narrowest part of the valley. To such simple minded is given the derogative dialect name 'gowk'.

The Bowder Stone car park at derelict Quayfoot Quarry was constructed by blowing up and collapsing the huge underground cavern.

This wooded area hides the crags above which provide sport for rock climbers.

Borrowdale opens out into a wide, flat, pastoral area at the confluence of the River Derwent and Stonethwaite Beck, where once was a post-glacial lake. Terminal moraines are prominent features.

The landscape reveals man's agricultural development of the valley, from the Viking 'thwaite', where trees have been cleared and obstructing boulders moved and used to build a patchwork of walls, to the modern up-dating of 17c 'statesman's' holding.

Rosthwaite [*ON. Clearing with a heap of stones.*]

This is the largest village in Borrowdale, with the only village store in the valley. Rosthwaite is clustered around The How, a rocky knoll with roche-moutonée visible towards the river.

Before the valley road for wheeled vehicles was constructed in 1842, Keswick was reached by the bridleway through Watendlath. Old Sally, Sarah Youdale, who lived more than a hundred years in Rosthwaite, (1768–1869) recalled, '*I paid one visit to Whitehaven; otherwise I was never out of the valley. There was no wheeled thing in Borrowdale in my youth.*'

The Royal Oak is presumed to be the Rosthwaite Inn where Wordsworth stayed in 1812 and had to share a bed with '*a Scotch pedlar*'.

The Scafell Hotel. A house that once stood on this site was reputedly built by Mary Barker, Dorothy Wordsworth's friend, but a similar claim has been made for Newton Place in Borrowdale. The house was later a vicarage, 1838–42.

Hazel Bank Hotel stands on the site of the fictional 'Herries' owned by Walpole's hero in *Rogue Herries*. From here, Judith Paris was rescued in the sequel of that name.

The Village Institute dates back to 1922. It was largely funded by the Simpsons of Hazel Bank, who owned most of Rosthwaite, and by the voluntary labour of local people. Highlights of the social calendar include Borrowdale Fell Races in August and the local Shepherds' Meet in September.

<u>Borrowdale Church of St Andrew</u>. A Chapel-of-Ease was consecrated in 1687 and replaced in 1762. From 1765, burials were permitted thus saving the twelve miles journey to and from Crosthwaite. By separating from Crosthwaite church in 1865, marriages could be solemnised.

A marathon runner, Bob Graham of Barrow House, was buried in the churchyard in 1966. For many years he held the Lake District record of 42 peaks, 32,000 feet and 130 miles in 23 hours 39 minutes.

When re-roofing became necessary in 1981, Chris Bland was sponsored to raise funds by climbing all the Wainwright summits in a week. In his effort, he climbed more than 100,000 feet and covered 308 miles.

The pulpit came from Mardale Church which was submerged when the Haweswater Reservoir was built in 1937.

<u>The School</u>. Provision was made in 1719 for the curate to conduct a free school inside the church. Not until c.1826 was a separate school building erected and later extended. A new school opened in 1968 and the old school site was redeveloped for housing local people.

A schoolmaster's house, 'Moraine' at Peat Howe, was provided in 1905 from a bequest of Abraham Fisher. It was sold in 1977 for the financial benefit of the school.

Grange Fell	3.4	Castle Crag	6.6
		Dale Head	6.8
Glaramara	4.5	High Spy	6.7

<u>Johnny Wood</u> (NT), west of Longthwaite, is notable for its sessile oaks and its rare mosses and lichens. Collectively, the valley woodlands are protected as Grade 1 Sites of Special Scientific Interest. Coppiced trees and flat pitsteads, where wood was turned

into charcoal for smelting metal ores, are reminders of an industrial past.

The valley divides round the great mass of Borrowdale Fells and Glaramara. The easterly branch leads to –

Stonethwaite [ON. Clearing amid stones.] The view up Stonethwaite Beck reveals a typical profile of an ice-carved U-shaped valley.

This Norse hamlet was included in the gift of the east side of Borrowdale to Fountains Abbey by Alice de Rumelli in 1195. The monks successfully raised a dairy herd and acquired more land in the process. This was the cause of a prolonged dispute with the neighbouring monks of Furness Abbey. To arbitrate in 1362, a lawyer, Sir Thomas de Eskhead, was appointed and the case referred to Edward III. The king forfeited the land on the grounds that his consent had not been sought for the judgement and was sold to the first bidder – the monks of Fountains Abbey – for forty shillings. Sir Thomas was rewarded with the benefit of Crosthwaite (1368–1390).

In winter, the valley lies in shadow until February. When the sun's rays once again touched the village, the women used to rejoice by turning out in clean white aprons to offer greetings.

Eagle Crag	3.3, 4	Bowfell	4.9
Great Crag	3.3	Gamara	4.6
Harrison Stickle	3.11	Rosthwaite	
High Raise	3.7	Fell	4.4, 3
Sergeant's Crag	3.4		
Ullscarf	3.8		

At Smithymire Island, the confluence of Greenup Gill and Langstrath Beck, iron ore from a mine at Ore Gap was smelted.

(*Bowfell 4.3*)

Greenup Gill, in a V-shaped valley, unusual in this heavily glaciated region, is part of the Coast to Coast Walk over Greenup Edge to Grasmere. This old packhorse route passes the foot of steep-sided Eagle Crag, where men were once lowered on ropes over the edge to destroy the eagles' eyries to protect their young livestock. (*Eagle Crag 3.3, 4*).

Langstrath Beck is '*the wildest, rockiest, most colourful and interesting mountain stream in England*' according to the Lakeland artist, W. Heaton Cooper. Closely following the beck, the old packhorse way over the Stake Pass into Great Langdale is now a six mile section of the Cumbria Way. Of the several rock pools, or dubs, the most impressive is Blackmoss Pot, a 20 ft deep rift in the rock beneath lofty Sergeant Crag.

A westerly diversion in Langstrath follows Angle Tarn Beck to its source at Angle Tarn.

Mountain View terraced cottages, on the B5289 at Strands Bridge, remain from the days when quarrymen working at Honister Quarries lived here.

Two tracks lead south up the hanging valley of Combe Gill. On the eastern side, an old corn mill, dated 1546, its machinery dating from the 1760s, retains its wheel and feeder leat. The other track enters the Combe, an awesome amphitheatre encircled by great crags with hummocky moraines underfoot.

From Strands Bridge, the Allerdale Ramble connects with Seathwaite in the south and crosses Folly Bridge, on the edge of Johnny Wood, to the north. On Folly Bridge is a verse by John Braithwaite (1781) who revealed his folly in building the bridge when lacking a male heir.

Combe Gill joins the River Derwent near Burthwaite Bridge where a morainic ridge is 30 feet high. A similar ridge is located opposite Longthwaite.

From <u>Seatoller Bridge</u> *on the B5289, an unclassified road leads to Seathwaite where there is parking space.*

<u>Thornythwaite Farm</u> [ON. *Clearing amid the thorns*], on the left, stands on the crest of a morainic ridge.

<u>The Borrowdale Yews,</u> on the right, is a relic yew forest that inspired Wordsworth to write his poem, '*Yew Trees*':

> ... *those fraternal Four of Borrowdale*
> *Joined in one solemn and capacious grove.*

Because of the ageing and damaged original, a replacement group has been planted.

<u>Seathwaite</u> [ON. *Clearing amid the sedges*] This tiny Norse hamlet in an ice-shaped valley is watered by Styhead Gill. Reputedly, it is the wettest inhabited place in England averaging 130 inches annually. The rainfall decreases by some 10 inches per mile in the eight miles to Keswick, where the average is 50 inches. In July 1966, four feet of flood water devastated Borrowdale, which was declared a disaster area.

The rain gauge stands in the grounds of Rain Gauge Cottage, formerly known as Beck Cottage, built in 1767 for a mine steward and facing west to provide a view of the plumbago mine. The cottage was gifted by the Bankes family to the National Trust in 1981.

<u>Plumbago</u> was a unique commodity mined in this country and plumbago mining relics remain on the slopes of Grey Knotts (7.5) at Wadhole Gill (OS. 232125) north of Sour Milk Gill.

Plumbago, variously known as graphite, black lead, black cawke and wad, was a remarkably pure form of carbon. Its presence is said to have been first revealed when an ash tree was uprooted in a storm. For a time, the only use was for marking sheep. There followed an expansion of uses: medication, glazing pottery, fixing blue dyes, lubrication, casting round shot and cannon balls and leading grates. To meet the increasing demand, mining developed from the end of the 16c to its optimum in the 18c and early 19c. Plumbago was the basis of the pencil manufacturing industry in the Keswick area from c. 1790.

Plumbago occurred in tubes, or 'pipes' in the Borrowdale Volcanic Series of rocks and was mined from horizontal shafts, or adits, tunnelled into the fellside. Lumps of plumbago varied in size from 1oz to 6lbs and occasionally up to 50lbs. Many of the miners lived at Seathwaite.

A notable mine owner in 1625 was Sir John Bankes, a London lawyer and son of John Bankes of Keswick. Plumbago mining under-pinned the Bankes family's fortunes for two hundred years. Sir John Bankes became Attorney General to Charles I and bought Corfe Castle in Dorset. During the Civil War, three years of siege left the castle in ruins. Following the Restoration of the Monarchy in 1660, the next Bankes, Sir Ralph, built Kingston Lacy. Ultimately, in 1981, these vast Dorset estates, the plumbago mine and property at Seathwaite were gifted to the National Trust. In celebration, a boundary marker stone was erected at the foot of the fell to replace one on the fellside, which had been destroyed by vandals. It is inscribed 'John Bankes Esquier 1752'.

The increasing value of plumbago from £13 per ton in 1597, to £3,500 in 1812 and to £5,200 in 1833 was maintained by periodical mine closures. Security against theft and smuggling became paramount, especially when William Hetherington tunnelled from his land into the Bankes' plumbago mine and 'pickers' searched for 'wad' in spoil heaps under cover of darkness. The Mine Act of 1752 made the breaking into a mine, or the stealing of 'wad' a felony, punishable by hard labour or transportation. At Gilbert Level, over the mine entrance in 1789, a security hut was built in which to search miners on leaving and to provide a guard house for armed guards, especially at night. A notorious smuggler was Black Sal. When the front of the cottage, where she was said to have lived, collapsed in the flood of 1898, a cache of 'wad' was revealed.

After 1833, imports of plumbago were cheaper, although of inferior quality. With no deposits of value left in the Borrowdale mines, closure was inevitable. From stock piles, Borrowdale plumbago was processed by Keswick's pencil mills for nearly forty years after the last mine closed.

The Pencil Museum in Keswick exhibits a replica 'wad' mine and a plaque outside the George Inn recalls the scene of illicit trading.

See: *Seathwaite Wad and The Mines of The Borrowdale Valley*. Ian Tyler (1995).

Seathwaite is an exceptionally popular starting point for walkers.

<u>*The Allerdale Ramble*</u> *begins here and continues north for more than fifty miles from mountainous country, along the foot of Borrowdale's western fells, across the pastoral Solway Plain, to the shores of the Solway Firth at Grune Point.*

<u>Sourmilk Gill</u>, pouring from its high corrie basin on Gillercomb, dropping 800 feet to the valley below, is a hanging valley below the summit of Brandreth. By crossing the footbridge over the River Derwent, provided as a war memorial by the Ramblers' Association, the track alongside the gill leads eventually to Green Gable and Great Gable.

Stockley Bridge [*OE. Clearing with the stumps*] is a restored packhorse bridge on the monks' route to Grange. Mounds of hummocky moraines are visible.

David Herries in Walpole's '*Rogue Herris*' fished here and met the pedlar who claimed to be the Devil.

The upward way now divides east and west of Seathwaite Fell.

To the East: Grains Gill and Ruddy Gill, and the track above Sprinkling Tarn, the source of the River Derwent, lead to Esk Hause, the meeting place of routes from Borrowdale, Great Langdale and Eskdale.

To the West: The old packhorse way up Styhead Gill to Sty Head [*ON. 'stee' = ladder*] passes Taylorgill Force falling over the ice-shaped rock step in the hanging valley on Base Brown before plunging 140 feet on its way to join the River Derwent. Sty Head is the meeting place of tracks from Borrowdale and Wasdale from which to reach Scafell Pike, 3,208 feet, the highest mountain in England.

The 1896 plan to commemorate Queen Victoria's Golden Jubilee, by constructing a 'carriage road' between Seathwaite and Wasdale over Sty Head, was defeated, thanks to the opposition of Canon Rawnsley and others.

Allen Crags	4.4	Base Brown	7.6
Esk Pike	4.9	Brandreth	7.7
Great End	4.6, 9	Great Gable	7.15, 16
Scafell Pike	4.15, 16, 17, 18	Green Gable	7.5, 6
		Grey Knotts	7.5
Seathwaite Fell	4.3		

From Seatoller Bridge, *the B5289 enters –*

Seatoller [*ON. The shieling with the alder tree.*] This hamlet expanded to house the workers in the neighbouring Honister Slate

Quarries. The two terraces of quarrymen's cottage are now mostly holiday homes.

<u>Seatoller House</u> gained the reputation of being a gathering place for academic and literary worthies since the Cambridge Apostles, G. M. Trevelyan, Ralph Vaughan Williams and others, first met here in 1895.

<u>Seatoller Barn</u> houses The Lake District National Park Information Centre which arranges informative exhibitions and special events. Car park.

<u>High Doat</u>, 927 feet, overlooks Seatoller. This isolated rocky volcanic knoll forms a side valley at 760 feet for the <u>Allerdale Ramble</u>. The side valley, an ice-marginal channel, continues northwards, squeezing between Castle Crag and Lobstone Band, where it is 100 feet lower.

Allen Crags	4.4	*Dale Head*	6.8
Esk Pike	4.9	*High Spy*	6.7
Great End	4.9		
Scafell Pike	4.15, 16, 17, 18	*Grey Knotts*	7.6

<u>Honister Hause</u> [*ON. Huni's settlement*] 1,176 feet.

The B5289 makes a 1 in 4 ascent of a glacial step, following Hause Gill through Little Gatesgarthdale to ease into a wide, moraine-filled basin which was the gathering ground of ice more than ten thousand years ago.

Beyond is Honister Pass and the descent into Buttermere.

An alternative way of ascent from Seatoller to Honister Hause for walkers is to use the old packhorse trail to the north of the road.

<u>Honister Slate</u>. At Honister Hause, the dramatically scarred fell-sides beneath Fleetwith Pike to the south, at Dubs and Honister

Crag and beneath Dale Head to the north, at Yew Crag, testify to the enormous amount of slate extracted over some 340 years.

The distinctive, durable, green slate of metamorphosed volcanic ash was first quarried to supply local needs c. 1643, although fragments of Honister slate have been found at such Roman sites as Hardknott and Ravenglass. The greatest demand from further afield arose as a consequence of the Industrial Revolution when roofing materials were needed for houses in the expanding communities in northern England.

Exposed veins were exploited first, followed later by driving horizontal tunnels into the veins and opening up huge chambers from which to extract the slate. 'Rock hands' quarried using basic tools until c. 1820 when locally produced gunpowder became available to increase the speed at which levels could be driven and underground rock faces worked. Large blocks of slate ('clogs') were reduced to manageable size by 'docking', using mallet and chisel or 'plug and feather' methods until 1856 when J.W. Greaves invented a rotary slate saw. After the 'docking' process, the 'river' split the slate to the required thickness and the 'dresser' 'dressed' the 'riven' slate to whatever shape and size was needed.

In the early days, the slate was 'dressed' underground where the waste material was discarded. The 'dressed' slate was then 'sledded' down the steep fell slope, from the working level to the Hause below, using a sledge with two inclined shafts. The quarryman between the shafts ran perilously in front of the sledge, which carried a quarter ton load, controlling the speed and direction of the descent. To return, he carried the sledge on his shoulders by a different route. Amazing stamina was demonstrated by Joseph Clark when he made 17 journeys from the quarry level to the Hause in one day, travelling more than 17 miles, half of them uphill carrying his 80lb sledge, and

304

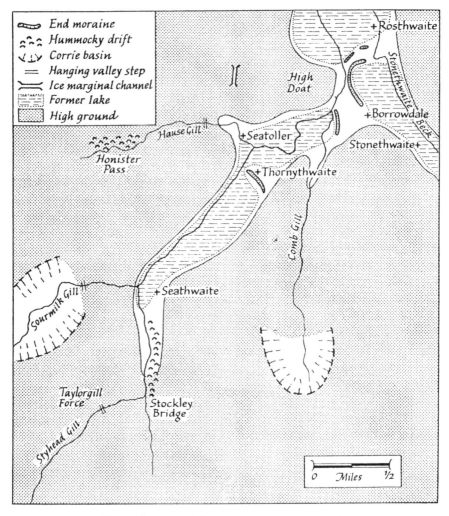

Glacial features of the upper part of Borrowdale.

Acknowledgement:

The Lake District, R. Millward & A. Robinson. Eyre & Spottiswoode

bringing down nearly 4.8 tons of 'dressed' slate.

Working high amongst the crags, exposed to turbulent gale force winds, driving rain, or ice and snow, or toiling underground by candlelight, sometimes supported by ropes and ladders, the quarry-men endured extremely hard, hazardous and dangerous conditions. Few could reach home at night because of the remoteness of their workplace. Many slept where they worked or in small communal huts nearby, only going home for a Sunday. One of the remaining huts on Dubs is now used by climbers.

Before 1851, the distribution of 'dressed' slate was by pack horse. The route to the coast for onward shipment became known as Moses' Trod, reputedly named after Moses Rigg, a quarryman and an illicit distiller of whisky who was also a smuggler. The track follows the west sides of Grey Knotts, Brandreth and Great Gable before dropping into Wasdale and continuing to Ravenglass, a total distance of 15 miles. (*Great Gable 7.7, 8*)

The packhorse route became obsolete after 1851 when the road into Buttermere and beyond to the coast was improved for transport by horse and cart. In 1907, a new road was constructed from Honister Hause, down the steep gradient to Seatoller, when a traction engine, and later a steam wagon, came into use to transport slate to Keswick and the railway network. The proposed rail link from Braithwaite, near Keswick, along the west side of Borrowdale to the Honister slate quarries, failed, fortunately, because of the lack of finance.

Changes in management and demand, interrupted by two world wars, did not prevent the introduction of improved production methods and working conditions. Up-graded and extended inclines, internal and external, provided better access to the working levels and facilitated the more effective removal of slate from the underground workings. Self-acting gravitational tramways, first introduced at Yewcrag Quarry in 1880, used the weight of descending laden trolleys to haul up the lighter empty ones. By 1926, an aerial ropeway, powered by electricity, was carrying blocks of slate from Honister Quarry to the newly constructed processing sheds at Honister Hause making the primitive and dangerous practice of 'sledging' obsolete. When new accommodation for quarrymen was provided at Honister Hause, Seatoller and Mountain View, living at the quarrying levels was no longer the only option.

The inevitable outcome of modernisation and mechanisation was a reduction in the strength of the workforce, from 100 at Honister Quarry in 1900 to about 30 at closure in 1985. Yewcrag Quarry had closed in 1966. See: *Honister Slate The History of a Lakeland Slate Mine.* Ian Tyler (1994).

The Kimberley Mine reopened in 1997. From a viewing area, visitors are able to see the huge 'clogs' arrive in their waggons, the two powerful electric saws at the cutting tables and the 'riving' and 'polishing' processes. Refreshments are available at the shop.

See: *Honister Slate. The History of a Lakeland Slate Mine.* Ian Tyler (1994).

A Youth Hostel opened at Honister Hause in a building designed to be similar in appearance to the old barracks which accommodated the quarrymen. Car Park.

On the fellsides, clearly visible, are the lines of tunnel mouths across the crag faces, identifying the course of slate veins, and the external inclines which connected them. The bed of the old gravitational tramway, which linked Dubs Quarry with the Hause, has become a fellwalkers' track.

Dale Head 6.7 Brandreth 7.4

Fleetwith Pike 7.5

Great Gable 7.17

Green Gable 7.4

Grey Knotts 7.7

Haystacks 7.7

Buttermere

[*ON. Buthor's mere. Buthar, a Norse settler.*]

From Honister Hause, the B5289 descends between the heights of Fleetwith Pike and Dale Head, passing through a wilderness of boulders as it follows Gatesgarthdale Beck in a landscape typical of that before medieval reclamation began.

Into view comes the Vale of Buttermere, a V-shaped valley profile modified into the U-section of a glaciated valley. To the east, are the rounded fells of Skiddaw Slate — Robinson, Whiteless Pike, Grasmere and Whiteside. To the west, a line of rocky summits enclose a succession of corrie basins — Haystacks (at Innominate Tarn, Wainwright requested that his ashes should be scattered), High Crag, High Stile and Red Pike.

<u>Gatesgarth Farm</u> [*ON. Pass of the goats.*] This is a typical fell farm of 2,700 acres, some of it 'inland', or fenced-in valley land, but most consisting of wild, rough fell, on which 2,500 sheep graze, many of them the Herdwick breed. The old salving, or sarving house survives. The salve of Stockholme tar and lard was applied to the skin of the sheep before the days of sheep dipping. Gatesgarth's most famous Herdwick breeder was Ned Nelson (d. 1887), a regular prizewinner at agricultural shows.

Scarth Gap Pass provides access on foot to Ennerdale.
From Ennerdale, Black Sail Pass leads to Wasdale.

Buttermere

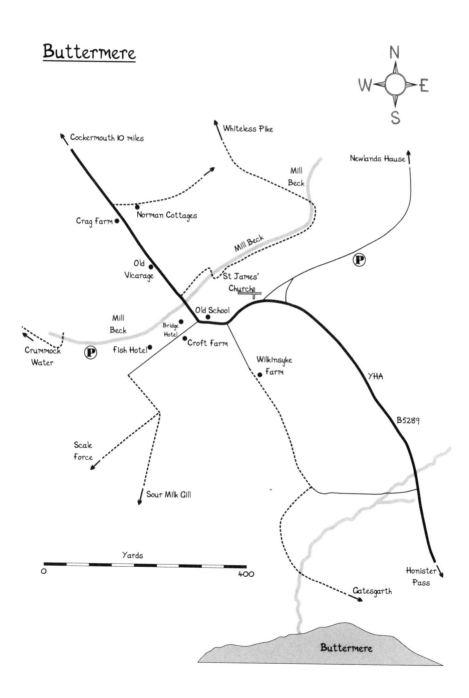

Hindscarf	6.7	Brandreth	7.5
Robinson	6.9	Fleetwith Pike	7.6
		Great Gable	7.18
		Haystacks	7.5, 6
		High Crag	7.5
		High Stile	7.8

<u>Lower Gatesgarth</u> was built in 1910 by the Cambridge economist, Arthur Cecil Pigou, a pioneering thinker about the Welfare State. He held climbing parties here during university vacations and climbed with George Mallory. At a party in 1953, guests included Wilfred Noyce's family whilst Noyce, Hunt and others helped Hilary and Tensing make the first successful conquest of Everest.

Another pioneering thinker who spent holidays here was Alan Turing, the brilliant mathematician who participated in breaking the German 'Enigma' code in World War II. As early as 1936 he had published a paper on 'computable numbers', the theoretical basis of the modern computer.

<u>Buttermere</u> (Lake). This imposing 1¼ miles long, comparatively narrow (½ mile) lake is shallow at the lower end, but has a maximum depth of 94 feet. Gatesgarthdale Beck is gradually building out a promontory of debris.

Buttermere was once one lake with Crummock Water but alluvium deposited by Mill Beck on the intervening rock sill has formed a delta flat, about a mile long, which frequently disappears under flood water after heavy rain. (cf. Derwentwater and Bassenthwaite Lake.)

<u>Hassness</u>. The owner of Hassness House in the 19c, George Benson, had this 40 yards long tunnel blasted through rock to avoid blocking the path round the lake and to keep his workmen busy during the winter.

Robinson   6.8

<u>Buttermere</u> (Village). The village is situated beside Mill Beck on the level strath between Buttermere Lake and Crummock Water, at the foot of Newlands Hause, which provides access to Keswick.

Buttermere Dubs connects the two lakes after falling steeply as Sour Milk Gill out of Bleaberry Tarn on Red Pike. From the summit of Red Pike five lakes can be seen on a clear day. The reddish colour of the rock debris is due to granophyre – an igneous rock similar to granite – which outcrops up the length of the gill.

<u>The Church of St James</u> is perched above the village on a rock shelf. It was built in 1840 with stone from Sour Milk Gill. The wrought iron gate into the porch shows a shepherd with his ewe and lamb. Inside the church is a memorial tablet displayed at a window,

Pause to Remember
Alfred Wainwright
Fellwalker, Guide Book Author
and Illustrator
Who Loved This Valley
Lift Your Eyes to Haystacks
His Favourite Place
1907–1991

Twin bells hang in the bell turret. There is no burial ground. Burials are conducted at Lorton about five miles away.

The small building below the church, constructed in 1871, was a schoolroom until 1950 when it became the church hall.

<u>The Bridge Hotel</u> was formerly the Victoria Hotel, but operated as a corn mill until 1735. At the rear, the rock cut away for the water wheel in the stony gorge can be seen. In the wood above the village the mill pond and race are still visible.

<u>The Fish Hotel</u> (formerly The Fish Inn) has catered for tourists since the 18c.

A tourist in 1792, Joseph Budworth, 'discovered' the landlord's daughter, Mary Robinson, and eulogised her beauty in a publication entitled, *A Fortnight's Ramble in the Lakes.* Mary soon became a tourist attraction known as 'The Beauty of Buttermere'.

In 1802, a visitor, who made himself known as the Honourable Colonel Alexander Augustus Hope, MP for Linlithgow, stayed at the inn for the char fishing. There followed a courtship of Mary lasting six weeks, ending with marriage at Lorton Church.

The whole affair was reported by Samuel Taylor Coleridge, who was then a correspondent for the London newspaper, the *Morning Post.* On reading the news, doubts were raised by Charles Hope, the Earl of Hopetown, who explained that his younger brother, Alexander Augustus, was not in Lakeland but was touring in Europe.

When the honeymoon couple returned, the groom was exposed as John Hatfield, a noted swindler, confidence trickster and now a bigamist. The outcry was nationwide. Hatfield fled and evaded arrest before being caught in Wales. He was brought to trial at Carlisle Assizes, where Wordsworth and Coleridge visited him.

For his many crimes, including falsely assuming the name, title and character of the Honourable Colonel Alexander Augustus Hope, MP, issuing forged and counterfeited bills of exchange, avoiding the payment of postage on letters (an MP's privilege) and, of course, bigamy, Hatfield received the sentence of death by hanging.

Novels and plays based on this sad incident have helped to immortalise it. Wordsworth wrote in *The Prelude* (1805)

> *... unfaithful to a virtuous wife,*
> *Deserted and deceived, the Spoiler came*
> *And wooed the artless daughter of the hills,*

And wedded her, in cruel mockery
Of love and marriage bonds . . .

Mary was left with a child. Happily, she married a farmer from Caldbeck, Richard Harrison. They lived at Todcrofts Farm, where Mary bore four children before she died at the age of 58. She was buried in Caldbeck churchyard.

Melvyn Bragg recreated the whole of this story in *The Maid of Buttermere*, Hodder & Stoughton, 1987.

When Nicholas Size was the landlord of The Fish Inn, he wrote historical novels about the neighbourhood, receiving advice and encouragement from Hugh Walpole. *Shelagh of Eskdale* described the Norse settlers who built the water-powered corn mill at Buttermere. *The Secret Valley* (1929) included the Battle of Rannerdale.

<u>Norman Cottages</u> are named after a former resident, John Norman, who sailed on HMS *Bounty* of mutiny fame.

Rannerdale Knotts	6.3	Great Borne	7.4
Robinson	6.7	High Crag	7.6
Wandope	6.5, 6, 7	High Stile	7.7
Whiteless Pike	6.3	Mellbreak	7.7
		Pillar	7.14
		Red Pike (B)	7.5, 6, 7, 8

Crummock Water

[OB. Crooked water.]

From Buttermere.

<u>Crummock Water</u>. This picturesque lake lies in the same glacial valley as Buttermere with only a narrow strip of alluvium separating the two lakes.

The lake is 2½ miles long and comparatively narrow at ½ mile. The maximum depth is 144 feet. It is home to greylag geese in the season whilst red squirrels inhabit the woods. Char, landlocked here since the Ice Age, as in Buttermere, live in the cold depths but swim into shallower water to spawn.

The western fells of Skiddaw Slates have craggy upper slopes. The screes of conical-shaped, 'sugar lump' Mellbreak sweep down to the water's edge.

Scale Force, on the northern shoulder of Red Pike, is the highest waterfall in Lakeland with a spectacular single fall of 172 feet and two others of 20 feet each.

The opposite shore of Crummock Water is dominated by the massive fells of Grasmoor.

Mellbreak.   7.6

<u>Rannerdale</u>. [ON. Valley of the ravens with shieling.] This is the site of a deserted settlement uninhabited for two centuries.

A local legend records that a chantry chapel was built here, to the east of Rannerdale Farm. It was the daughter church of the church at Brigham, Keswick, and was built to celebrate the victory of a Saxon Earl, Boethar, over the Norman army of William Rufus. The Normans were massacred in the narrow cul-de-sac of the Rannerdale Valley after being falsely informed that it was a pass. This defeat for the Normans was only a temporary set-back as eventually all this land was ruled by the Normans from Egremont. (Rannerdale Knotts 6.1).

This battle was featured in *The Secret Valley*, a novel written by Nicholas Size, a former landlord of The Fish Inn, Buttermere.

Hause Point is named after the small-scale 'hause', or pass, over the top of this craggy promontory.

Rannerdale Knotts	6.2

Cinderdale Common. Parking and picnic places are provided with access to the shore of Crummock Water.

Eel Crag	6.5
Grasmoor	6.7, 8

Lanthwaite Green [*ON. The long clearing*.] Car park.

This is the site of a settlement marked 'Homestead' on the OS. map. Mounds of hut circles and banked enclosures are visible.

Grasmoor	6.5, 6
Whiteside	6.8

From Lanthwaite Green, Gasgale Beck leads to Coledale Hause.

Eel Crag	6.9
Grasmoor	6.11
Grisedale Pike	6.11
Hopegill Head	6.8
Beck House.	
Whiteside	6.7

Loweswater

[ON. Leafy lake.]

From Crummock Water.

Loweswater

<u>Brackenthwaite</u> is the start of the ridge route to Whiteside, Hopegill Head, Hobcarton Crag, Grisedale Pike and Braithwaite.

<u>Scale Hill</u>, or Lanthwaite Hill, 674 feet. Car park and viewpoint.

<u>Loweswater</u> (Village) is situated in the broad valley between Crummock Water and Loweswater, alongside Park Beck.

Kirkstile Inn.

St Bartholomew's Church was built by the villagers in 1827.

St Ringan's Well (= Ninian's Well) is on the old church land.

Blake Fell	7.5
Gavel Fell	7.5
Great Borne	7.4
Hen Comb	7.3
Low Fell	7.3
Mellbreak	7.5
Starling Dodd	7.4

<u>Loweswater</u> (Lake) This is the third of the lakes lying in the same glaciated valley, and one of the least visited. It has the uniqueness

of being the only one of the sixteen lakes whose waters flow inwards towards the centre of the Lake District. The outflow from Loweswater by Park Beck is eastwards into Crummock Water, which is about 100 feet lower.

Loweswater is 1½ miles long and ⅓ mile wide and about 60 feet deep. It is overlooked by Darling Fell and Carling Knott, whilst Holme Wood on its southern shore provides much of its leafiness. There is a striking contrast between the higher and more rugged fells at the southern end of the lake and the gentler, lower hills at its northern end.

It is a favoured haunt of waterfowl and part of the shore is fenced off to protect the nesting sites.

> <u>Waterend</u>
> Burnbank Fell   7.3
>
> <u>Fangs</u>
> Burnbank Fell   7.2

Newlands Valley

[ME. Newly taken into cultivation.]

The Newlands Valley is an illustration of the individuality of Lakeland valley landscapes. Unlike neighbouring Borrowdale, there is no lake, although the Newlands Beck flows throughout the length of the valley. Missing also are the knobbly, precipice riven romantic qualities of Borrowdale Volcanic rock. Newlands Valley is Skiddaw Slate country, more rounded, smooth and gentle. There are no Victorian plantations of rhododendrons and exotic trees. There is next to no tourism. But, in days gone by, there was intensive mining in the valley.

Road access to the valley from the north is via Portinscale or Braithwaite.

Uzzicar *[OE. Patch of cultivated land near a farmhouse.]* The 'new lands' of this valley were created to provide better cultivation by draining the Husakar or Uzzicar Tarn in the 13c. The Tarn was thought to have been artificially created, caused by a Roman embankment carrying a road across the marshes from the foot of the Whinlatter Pass. At this lower end, the valley today is lush with green farmland and woods mostly on the eastern side. Uzzicar Farm is a typical statesman's long house.

Barrow Mine *[AS. Hill, or long ridge]* Uzzicar is overlooked by Barrow, which Wainwright described as *'the shivering mountain of Lakeland. The great fan of spoil from the old mines on the Newlands face sweeps down to the road near Uzzicar and is prevented from burying it in debris only by a retaining parapet with a cleared space behind to accommodate major falls. The spoil is a sandy gravel constantly in slight motion, and the rustle of movement on the slope (no more than a whisper) can be heard on the road below. Note also an airshaft in a small field south of Uzzicar.'* (Barrow 6.2, 4).

The life of this lead mine probably extended over three or four centuries. In the early days, the old miners sometimes illicitly secreted little piles of ore in the innermost recesses of the mine as an investment for the future, to be retrieved at a later date. At least two such storage places have been unearthed in Barrow Mine where, for reasons unknown, the caches had remained hidden.

In the latter days, Barrow Mine operated under different ownership and the spoil heaps date from the phase which ended in 1883, at the time when a 60-foot water-wheel dominated the site.

<u>Stonycroft Mine</u> was less extensive than Barrow. In the words of Wainwright, *'Traces of the old Stonycroft Lead Mine are seen upwards from the bridge. The ore was first discovered in the bed of the gorge and a shaft sunk here after damming and diverting the beck (the race can be seen, now dry).'* The old water-cut *'can be traced up, first carved in the rock and then following the contour of the fellside, with the gorge steeply below. The old level . . . half hidden by gorse, is alongside the cut in its top part.'*

'There is a story of a tragic accident here centuries ago, when the dam burst and many lives were lost below the flooded shaft; the bodies were entombed and never recovered.' (Barrow 6.6, 2) Years later, the mine was re-opened and deepened. No human remains were found – only tools and a chain. Even by installing a water-wheel to pump the water and another to crush the ore the mine could not be made profitable.

The old mine road provides an easy way into the hills.

<u>Stair</u> stands astride Newlands Beck. Stair House, marked 'FF1647'

above the door, was traditionally thought to have been the home of
General Thomas Fairfax, who commanded Parliamentry forces during the Civil War. The initials were those of his father, Ferdinando.
Alternatively, however, Frances Fairfax, a local lady whose marriage
is recorded in the Crossthwaite Church Register, lived here. The old
mill and mill cottages now cater for holiday activities.

Barrow	*6.6*
Causey Pike	*6.4*
Eel Crag	*6.6*
Outerside	*6.4*
Sail	*6.3*
Scar Crags	*6.2*

Skelgill Farm [*ON. Scale = spreading of waters.*] Since the 14c, the
Grove family has made this their home.

Beatrix Potter's Mrs Tiggy-Winkle washed the '*woolly coats belonging to the little lambs at Skelghyl*'. Here also was located Lucie's home,
but the actual building which Beatrix illustrated was Little Town Farm.

At Skelgill Farm, Stephen Spender, aged 9, stayed during the summer of 1918. His father read to him poems by Wordsworth and perhaps induced in Stephen an inclination towards poetry.

From the car park ½ mile away:

Cat Bells	*6.7*

Little Town. Beatrix Potter spent several summer holidays in rented accommodation around Newlands and Derwentwater, and wrote
about a hedgehog washerwoman, *The Tale of Mrs Tiggy-Winkle* (1905).
The story also concerned a small girl called Lucie, who lived at Little
Town. The book was inspired by a meeting between the daughter of
the vicar of Newlands, the Rev. Carr, and Beatrix Potter's tame and

much-travelled hedgehog, Mrs Tiggy-Winkle. The pet hedgehog was taken almost everywhere in a cardboard box to be a model for her drawings. '*Mrs Tiggy as a model is so comical, but if she is propped up on end for more than half-an-hour, she begins to yawn pathetically,*' wrote Beatrix Potter.

In the story, Lucie met Mrs Tiggy-Winkle who worked in a kitchen behind a small door on the side of Cat Bells. There are references in the story of other local places, such as Skelghyl and Gatesgarth, and many of the illustrations in the book were made near Little Town.

Catbells	*6.7*
Dale Head	*6.6*
High Spy	*6.8*
Maiden Moor	*6.5*

<u>Yewthwaite Mine</u>. The site can be identified by the spoil heaps around Yewthwaite Gill on the Newlands side of Cat Bells.

The mine operated between the late 18c and the late 19c extracting mainly lead and zinc ores. (*Catbells 6.2, 3, 4*)

The early workings near the surface were achieved without machinery. The quality of the ore was the incentive to reach a greater depth by driving a flank level. Valuable deposits were found shortly after Goldscope was discovered and Yewthwaite was neglected in favour of its more wealthy rival. Subsequently, further levels were driven at Yewthwaite and for many years the mine remained most prosperous.

<u>Goldscope Mine</u>. Goldscope was a corruption of the word 'Gottesgab' = God's Gift, the name given by the German miners on discovering the richest deposits of copper then known in Lakeland.

The mine had been opened in the 13c for the extraction of copper, but the most significant developments occurred in the reign of Queen Elizabeth I. She granted Letters Patent in 1564 to Thomas

Thurland and his German partner, Daniel Höchstetter, '*to search, dig, try, roast and melt all manners of ores of gold, silver, copper and quicksilver*'. Experienced German miners were attracted to come over in 1565 and work on a vein up to 9 feet thick. As mining operations expanded, the Company of Mines Royal was formed to oversee the development from 1568.

It was during the reign of Queen Elizabeth I that the royal prerogative was exercised. When the gold and silver extracted from copper or lead was greater in value than the copper or lead, then the mine became a Royal Mine. A dispute over this arose between Queen Elizabeth I and Thomas Percy, Earl of Northumberland, culminating, after failed litigation, in armed rebellion by the Earl. He was defeated, beheaded, and his head was displayed on one of the gates of York.

In early days, before the introduction of gunpowder, the extraction of ore was a laborious process. Into a shallow hole bored into the rock two 'feathers' (iron plates used as wedges) were inserted. A 'stope' (thin, tapering rod) was hammered between them, like a chisel, forcing them apart and causing the rock to split. At the Stamp House, the broken rock was crushed into small pieces which were transported by packhorse to Copperhead Bay on Derwentwater. Then a boat carried the crushed ore across the lake to the smelter at Brigham, Keswick. Charcoal for the smelting denuded Borrowdale and neighbouring valleys of their trees as it took half an acre of trees to provide the charcoal for each ton of ore smelted.

The German miners mostly lived on Vicar's Island in Derwentwater, later known as Derwent Island, which they eventually purchased for £60 in 1569. Features of their lifestyle in the early days were isolation and independence. To avoid trading with unfamiliar currency, everything they used, from food to clothing and candles, was deducted from their wages. Integration with the locals developed gradually and ultimately many marriages with Keswick girls were recorded.

In 1593, a remarkable achievement at Goldscope was the chiselling out of an underground pit to house a waterwheel to remove water and to raise ore.

The Civil War interrupted operations in 1651 when Cromwell's troops destroyed the Brigham smelter and miners were drafted into the army.

Goldscope was re-opened in 1690 by a group of Dutchmen who came over with William, Prince of Orange. The mine was worked until all the accessible, worthwhile copper ore had been extracted. The final stage dated from 1852 when lead was discovered at a deeper level and was obtained by using a 40-foot wheel to pump out the water. The mine was abandoned in 1864.

Goldscope can be located where the spoil heaps are visible today, on the Newlands flank of Scope End, above Low Snab Farm. (*Hindscarth 6.2, 5, 6*)

<u>Castlenook Mine,</u> about a mile beyond Goldscope, beneath the prominent headland of Castle Nook butting into the mid-valley was another source of copper. (*Dale Head 6.1, 6. High Spy 6.4, 8*)

<u>Dale Head Mine,</u> at the Head of the Newlands Valley, was second only to Goldscope in the duration of its active life producing copper.

The mine was worked by the Germans under Daniel Höchstetter and afterwards by the employees of the Duke of Somerset and several others. (*Dale Head 6.3, 5, 6. High Spy 6.8*).

Between Goldscope and Dale Head there is evidence that furnaces for smelting the ore were erected by the Duke of Somerset. Unskilled operation of a furnace could result in the ore being burnt and rendered useless. This happened to fifty tons of Goldscope ore owned by the Duke of Somerset. A similar misfortune occurred at Dale Head when Mr Barron of Keswick was the proprietor.

Return to Little Town and Chapel Bridge.

<u>Newlands Church</u>. A memorial east window is dedicated to the Rev. John Monkhouse for his work in having the church restored in 1843. The village school made use of the premises until it closed in 1967.

Hindscarth	*6.6*
Robinson	*6.5*

<u>Rigg Beck Bridge</u>. *This is the start of a footpath route between Newlands and Buttermere. The clearly defined path, up steepening fells, follows Rigg Beck to its head-waters. From the watershed, Sail Beck runs alongside the path down to the village of Buttermere.*

Ard Crags	*6.3, 4*

At <u>Birkrigg</u> a small relict woodland survives.

<u>Keskadale Farm</u> [ON. *The valley of Ketil's shieling*] also has a remnant of natural woodland with ancient sessile oaks at 500 feet above the road.

This is last farm at the head of the valley.

Knott Rigg	*6.4*

<u>Newlands Hause</u>, 1,096 feet. The ascending road follows the glaciated trough of Keskadale Beck. In this former medieval deer forest of Copeland there is an absence of stone walls.

At Newlands Hause, the morainic bar, almost in the valley floor, is cut by Moss Beck, which flows from Moss Force. Two corries are in the north-facing slope of Robinson.

Knott Rigg	*6.3*
Robinson	*6.6*

The road then descends through Skiddaw Slates scenery to Buttermere, following Sail Beck, which changes its name to Mill Beck.

Whinlatter Pass
and Lorton Vale

Leave Keswick on the B5289/A66 (T).

Braithwaite [*ON. Broad clearing*] is situated on the delta plain of rocky knolls and flowing drumlins between Derwentwater and Bassenthwaite, enclosed by a horseshoe of six fells. It is the gateway to the Newlands Valley and the Whinlatter Pass.

Force Crag Mine. The pleasant village of Braithwaite, watered by Coledale Beck, displays many different architectural styles from the 17c onwards. A row of miners' cottages dates back to the days of Force Crag Mine at the head of Coledale, about 2½ miles away. The mine opened in the 19c and during its intermittent years of production, depending on the prevailing economic conditions, manganese, zinc, iron, lead and barytes were extracted.

In the mid-19c, the ores were carted to Maryport and then shipped to Liverpool. Ironically, when the railway first reached Braithwaite in 1865 the mine was closed due to the falling prices of lead.

On reopening, the main purpose was to extract barytes which had largely been discarded in the earlier years. Industrialists now required barytes for such diverse products as plate glass, paint and explosives. Equipment for grinding and bleaching the mineral was erected at the mine and in the village of Braithwaite.

326

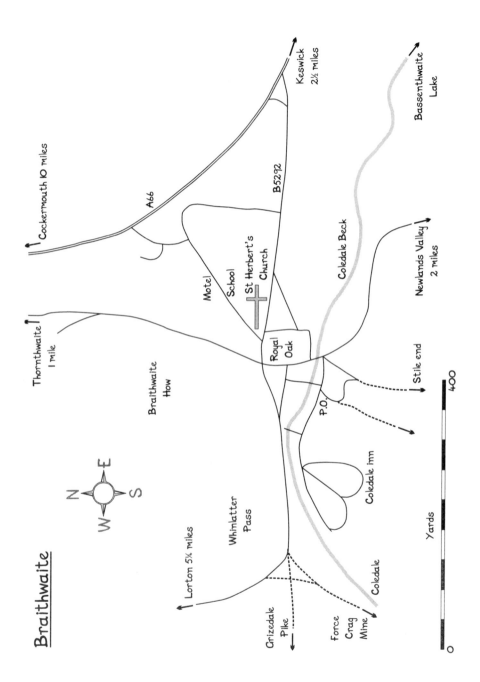

As the lower workings became less economical, new higher levels at High Force were opened, to which the lower workings were connected underground by La Porte Incline. Ore from High Force was flushed down wooden flumes to the mill below and an industrial tramway, two miles long, was built to Braithwaite.

The pattern of intermittent working continued. Two World Wars created renewed demands. During World War II, a new mill and an aerial ropeway from High Force to the mill were constructed. Traces of these remain.

In 1947, severe snow storms caused flooding in the mine but several companies in succession continued the attempt to extract barytes. In 1990, a massive collapse in the working levels caused the mine finally to be abandoned. It was the last mine to close within the Lake District National Park.

   (Grisedale Pike 6.3, 4, 5. Eel Crag 6.4, 7)
   See: *Force Crag.* Ian Tyler. 1990.

The Cumberland Pencil Co. began in Braithwaite in 1868 using plumbago obtained from Seathwaite in Borrowdale. After a fire in 1898, the manufacturing moved to new premises in Keswick.

St Herbert's Church is dedicated to the Derwentwater hermit. It was built in 1900 to replace an old mission room and has no church-yard.

Barrow	6.5
Causey Pike	6.5
Eel Crag	6.7
Grisedale Pike	6.8
Outerside	6.5
Sail	6.4

<u>Woodlands</u> has a car park and a viewpoint.

<u>Whinlatter Pass</u>, 1,043 feet. The Romans built a road through the pass starting from their fort at Papcastle, outside Cockermouth, to connect with the road running south-west from their fort at Old Penrith. Father West, the Jesuit priest who wrote the first guide book to the Lake District, thought that the two roads must have met at a fort at Keswick, but no evidence of this has been found.

The pass formed part of the 1761 turnpike road from Kendal via Ambleside and Keswick to Cockermouth. During 1947 the pass was blocked by snow for six weeks.

<u>Thornthwaite Forest</u> to the north, and the Hospital Plantation to the south, close in on the B5292 along which are car parks and picnic sites.

The first trees of Thornthwaite Forest were planted on the summit of the pass in 1919. Some of the original Sitka Spruce can still be seen.

<u>The Penrith Hospital Plantation</u> was planted in the 19c by the Marshall family. It was later acquired by the Forestry Commission to become one of the earliest and worst planned schemes of afforestation in Lakeland. Thousands of conifers gave the appearance of the Canadian backwoods.

<u>The Whinlatter Visitor Centre</u> is at the top of the pass where a forest trail leads into Comb Plantation.

Grisedale Pike	6.10
Hopegill Head	6.9
Lord's Seat	6.9
Whinlatter	6.4

<u>Scawgill Bridge</u>

Graystones   *6.7*

<u>Lorton Vale</u> is the vale of the River Cocker, which flows north carrying the overspill from Crummock Water into the River Derwent at Cockermouth. Wordsworth loved the unspoilt beauty of the vale.

<u>Hopebeck</u> is a village on a tributary of the River Cocker, Hope Beck, which rises at Hopegill Head.

Hopegill Head   *6.11*
Whiteside   *6.6*

Low Lorton

<u>Lorton Mill</u> on the River Cocker, is now a private residence.

<u>Lorton Hall</u> stands on a site which has been a dwelling place since pre-Norman times. It is a manor house, dated 1663, incorporating a pele or look-out tower. Traditionally, the house is said to be haunted by a woman holding a candle. A beech tree was planted in the ornamental gardens by Mary Winder, who reputedly entertained the future Charles II whilst he was secretly raising opposition to Cromwell's Commonwealth in 1653.

Several cottages in the main street date from the 17c and 18c.

<u>St Cuthbert's Church</u> *can be reached by a fieldpath from near the Wheatsheaf Inn.* The present church originated as a medieval chapel, a daughter church of the mother church at Brigham. Traditionally, this was one of the resting places of the body of St Cuthbert when his body was carried to safety by monks fleeing from the Danes c. 850.

In 1802, the imposter John Hatfield married Mary Robinson, 'the Beauty of Buttermere', here. The chapel was rebuilt in 1857 and reconsecrated in 1965.

In the churchyard, beneath a large beech tree, the gravestone of

High and Low Lorton

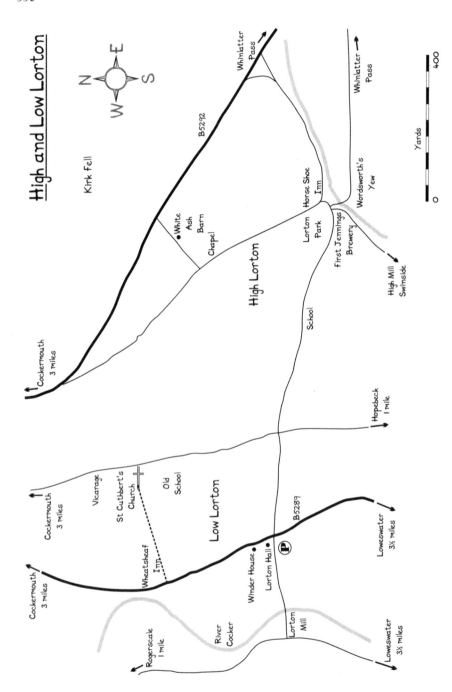

Daniel Fisher has the inscription:

> *On tombstones, praise is vainly spent*
> *Good work is man's best monument.*

<u>The Old School</u> next door, dated 1857, has been expertly converted into a private dwelling.

Fellbarrow   7.5

High Lorton

<u>Lorton Park</u> lies behind a high wall, with a tiny castellated tower to one side of the house.

<u>The Original Jennings' Brewery</u> was on the corner, by the bridge, in what is now an unusual village hall.

The Jennings' family was living at High Swinside Farm when they gained the reputation of brewing the best beer in the district. To meet popular demand, the family bought the old linen mill and converted it into a malt house. Success continued and the brewery moved to bigger premises in Cockermouth. The three Jennings brothers lived well into their ninety years of age.

<u>The Yew Tree</u>, over the beck, is where George Fox, founder of the Society of Friends, is said to have preached to Cromwellian Roundheads in 1653.

Wordsworth wrote a poem in praise of the tree:

> *...a Yew tree, pride of Lorton Vale,*
> *Which to this day stands single, in the midst*
> *Of its own darkness, as it stood of yore:*
> Wordsworth considered the tree:
> *Produced too slowly ever to decay; and*

> *. . . too magnificent/To be destroyed.*

But the ravages of time and weather brought about its end.

Terraced cottages line the main street at the southern end of which stands a row with stone steps leading up to the high-level doors.

The Horse Shoe Inn is an old pack-horse inn.

Broom Fell	6.5
Hopegill Head	6.10
Lord's Seat	6.8

<u>Armaside</u>. The former valley glacier dumped some of the debris it had gathered by its erosion. The small moraine is now capped with trees where the glacier temporarily halted and began to melt.

Graystones	6.6

<u>Thackthwaite</u>
Fellbarrow	7.6
Low Fell	7.4

Cockermouth

EC. Th. Mkt. M. [OB. Crooked steam]

The Roman fort of Derventio, 2c AD, near Papcastle, established a link with Alauna at Maryport, with Luguvalium at Carlisle and Hadrian's Wall and, over the Whinlatter Pass, with Keswick and Brocavum at Penrith.

Derventio stretched from the hill top down to the river bank, the whole site enclosed by a rampart and ditch. By 3c, a civil settlement had grown up outside the fort. Most of the remains of the fort and the settlement have been obliterated with the passing of time.

The town of Cockermouth became established on a strategically superior site a mile to the east of Derventio.

As its name implies, Cockermouth is located at the mouth of the River Cocker, which flows from Buttermere and Crummock Water to join the River Derwent from Bassenthwaite Lake.

It lies also at the junction of Skiddaw Slate and limestone and at the meeting place of six roads, just outside the boundary of the National Park.

In 1582, William Camden, an Elizabethan map maker, described Cockermouth as *'a populous and well trading Market Town neatly built but of low situation between two hills upon which is a church and upon the other against it is a very strong castle'*. This description is equally applicable today.

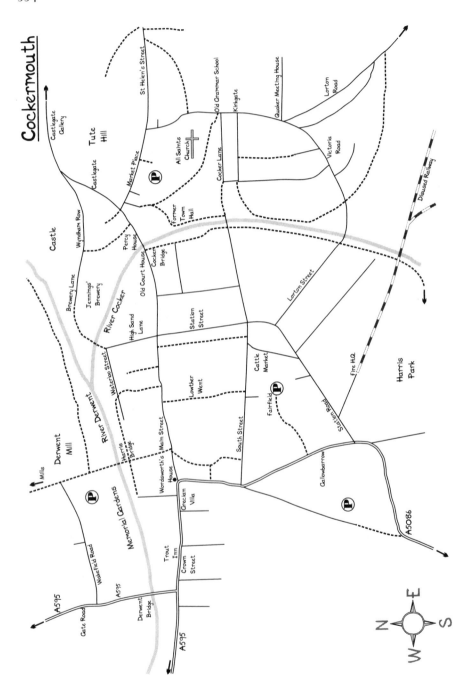

Cockermouth

From Wakefield Road car park –

<u>The River Derwent industrial development</u> took place hereabouts in the 18c and 19c when water and then steam provided the motive power. At the beginning of the 19c, the town had more than forty industrial sites.

<u>Low Gote Mills</u> were used for grinding corn and for the manufacture of textiles. Harris Linen Company occupied one of the mills from 1820 to 1847. Flax was dried in a nearby building, now a private residence called The Hospice. The mill buildings have been preserved by conversion into flats, even to the inclusion of the water-wheel outside one of them.

<u>High Gote Mill</u> once ground corn.

<u>James Walker's</u> modern factory manufacturers seals and gaskets.

<u>Derwent Mill</u> with its tall chimney, occupied a prominent position on the river bank. Embroidery silks and threads were manufactured here by Harris Linen until the 1930s. After World War II, Millors, the shoe company, took over until closure in 1990.

From the <u>Memorial Gardens,</u> cross the River Derwent by Harris Bridge to –

<u>Main Street</u>. This broad thoroughfare flanked by lime trees is enhanced by central flower beds. Many of the shops and offices have preserved their 19c facades and are cheerfully colour-washed.

<u>The United Reformed Church,</u> built in 1851 by Charles Eaglesfield of Maryport, had its Gothic-style facade added five years later.

<u>Six inns</u> congregate on the opposite side of the road.

<u>The statue,</u> erected in 1875, honours Richard Southwell Bourke, sixth Earl of Mayo, once MP for Cockermouth. In 1872, he became the only Viceroy of India to be assassinated when he was stabbed to

death by a convict in the Andaman Islands.

Other Cockermouth celebrities have included John Grave, thrice Lord Mayor of Manchester, who gave Manchester the idea of turning Thirlmere into a reservoir. The remarkable achievement of Richard and Adrian Crane was to run 2,000 miles through the Himalayas for charity in 1983.

Cockton's Yard and King's Arms Yard are attractive modern conversions into developments of small shops.

High Sand Lane leads to Waterloo Street, which once had an 1820 linen mill. Waterloo Bridge spans the River Cocker.

Brewery Lane. The ruined windmill once ground bark for a tannery.

Jennings Castle Brewery. Since the castle was built, there has always been a brewery taking advantage of its ample supply of pure well water.

The Jennings family brewery outgrew its 1828 origin in the village of Lorton and moved to Castle Hill in 1887, making use of a former cotton mill situated at the confluence of the River Cocker and the River Derwent. Guided brewery tours are available during the holiday season and there is a Visitor Centre with a Museum of Brewing.

Castlegate was for years the main road to Keswick and is still flanked by elegant 17c and 18c houses.

Cockermouth Castle provided protection for the early establishment of the town. The site was presented as a gift to Ranulf des Meschines and, later, it came into the possession of Waltheof, first Lord of Allerdale. According to tradition he built the first Norman castle c. 1140, supposedly in the enclosure of the Roman fort of 'Derventio'. A century later, c. 1250, the present castle at Cockermouth, protected on two sides by rivers, was built by William de Fortibus II, using building materials from the ruins of Derventio.

Over the centuries, the castle has been added to by different owners. The coats of arms of five of them hang on the 13c outer gatehouse.

<u>Cockermouth Castle</u> has been involved in the turbulent events of English history. In the 14c, it was attacked by Scots on several occasions and in the 15c, during the Wars of the Roses, it was captured from the Lancastrians by the Yorkists.

In 1568, Mary Queen of Scots is said to have lodged here for the night on the way to Carlisle and imprisonment following her escape after her defeat at Langside and an overnight stay at Workington Hall. Noting her travel-stained clothing, her temporary gaoler presented her with several yards of crimson velvet. This act of kindness was acknowledged by her son when he became King James I of England.

In 1648, the Royalists besieged the castle when the Percy family held out as a Parliamentary enclave in a strongly Royalist county during the Civil War.

Following the Civil War, the castle was partly dismantled and fell into disrepair. One wing was rebuilt in the 19c to house the Egremont family and the offices of the Egremont Estate Company. Turner stayed in the castle in 1809 and painted a picture of it.

During the Cockermouth Festival held in July, the castle is open to the public. The 'oubliette' dungeons, so called because the prisoners were locked up and forgotten, and the curiously named Mirk Dirk, a vaulted underground chapel, may be seen.

<u>Castlegate House,</u> a listed Georgian building, dated 1739, exhibits paintings and crafts.

<u>Market Place</u>. The town rapidly developed as a trading centre and

became second only to Kendal for its wool trade. Henry Ⅲ granted the market charter in 1221 and an open air market is still held on Mondays. The Market Bell or 'Butter Bell', which hangs from a nearby building, was traditionally rung to signal the start of the market.

<u>Opposite The Ship Inn</u> stood an Elizabethan mansion, Fletcher Old Hall, until it was substantially demolished in 1973. The claim is made that Mary Queen of Scots stopped here overnight and not at the castle in 1568.

<u>Tute Hill</u> overlooks the Market Place and offers a fine viewpoint.

<u>Kirkgate</u> broadens into a cobbled square, shaded by chestnut trees and lined with 18c Georgian houses.

<u>All Saints' Church</u>, with its 150 feet tall tower, was rebuilt in the Early English style in 1854 after a fire had destroyed the 1711 building which William Wordsworth had attended. The poet is commemorated in the east window. There is a plaque to Thomas Wilson, a local hat manufacturer, who financially supported the church.

In the SE. corner of the churchyard, Wordsworth's father, John, is buried, (1741–83). He died at the age of 42, five years after the death of his wife, Anne, aged 30. On the north side is a memorial stone to Fearon Fallows, mathematician and astronomer (1787–1831).

<u>The Old Grammar School</u>, in the churchyard, was demolished in 1896 and replaced by the Church Rooms.

Three scholars who became famous, attended the school.

William Wordsworth spent a little time at the school. After his mother died in 1778 he was sent at the age of 8 to live with an aunt in Penrith and, soon after, to attend the Grammar School at Hawkshead.

Fletcher Christian, who later led the mutiny on the 'Bounty' was

Wordsworth's senior by six years.

Dr John Walker (b. 1759) was the son of a local blacksmith. At the mature age of 40, he qualified as a surgeon and served on The National Board with Edward Jenner, who pioneered vaccination.

The Quaker Meeting House, at the top of the hill, dates from 1884.

From Victoria Road, turn back along a footpath alongside the River Cocker. At Cocker Lane, cross the footbridge, from where there are fine views over the town, and follow the riverside path upstream to Harris Park *and to the fountain with a statue of Dorothy Wordsworth as a child.*

Return to Cocker Lane, where the stone archway is the remnant of the entrance to a factory yard. Walk through.

The River Cocker industrial development took place here in the 18c and 19c like its counterpart on the River Derwent. Relics of the past include Cocker Bridge Textile Mill and, on the opposite side of the river stood Thomas Wilson's hat factory which used to manufacture 4,000 hats a week. The car park was once a drying area for Sanderson's woollen mill.

The local Cumberland and Westmorland Fusiliers once used the two-storey building as an armoury.

Cockermouth Town Hall, originally a Wesleyan Chapel, built in 1841, became the offices of the Town Council in 1933 when the Wesleyans moved to new premises in Lorton Street. Following the 1974 reorganisation of local government, Workington became the administrative centre and after the Planning Department's departure, these premises were most elegantly converted into a Tourist Information Centre.

Percy House, by Cocker Bridge, was built in 1598 by Henry Percy, ninth Earl of Northumberland. An upstairs room still bears the Percy coat-of-arms in plasterwork and, incorporated in the ornate design of the ceiling is the date 1598. The earl's bailiff used to live in the house.

Cocker Bridge, at the end of Main Street, was swept away by floods during its construction in 1826. In 1966, such serious flooding occurred in neighbouring streets that boats were the only means of transport.

The Old Court House dates back to 1828.

The Black Bull Hotel's rear yard was the scene of Reuben Herries' intervention in the bear-baiting in Hugh Walpole's *Judith Paris*.

The Globe Hotel, 1750, stands on the site of an earlier wooden inn.

Station Street, where the old cinema building is now a vet's surgery, leads to Station Road and as its name implies, to the railway station, which has been replaced by the Cumbria Fire Service Headquarters.

The Cockermouth and Workington Railway, 1847–66, nine miles in length, was constructed primarily to carry coal from local pits for shipment from Workington.

The Cockermouth, Keswick and Penrith Railway opened for mineral traffic in 1864 and subsequently for passengers in 1865, thus completing the cross-Lakeland link along forty miles of track through scenic countryside. Through services continued for 101 years until the closure of the Keswick-Workington section for goods and passengers in 1966. The passenger service between Penrith and Keswick survived until 1972.

South Street's Cattle Market holds auctions on Mondays and alternate Wednesdays, with additional sheep sales on Fridays in the autumn.

<u>Lowther Went Shopping Centre</u>, a supermarket development, gives access to Main Street and its continuation, Crown Street.

<u>Crown Street</u> is noted for –

<u>Wordsworth House</u> (NT). This fine Georgian house was built in 1745 for Joshua Lucock, High Sheriff of Cumberland. John Wordsworth, William's father, lived here when he was the estate and land agent for Sir James Lowther, Lord Lonsdale, the rich landowner, who controlled half the coal and iron industries in Cumbria.

All five Wordsworth children were born here: Richard in 1768, William in 1770 and Dorothy a year later. John and Christopher followed in 1772 and 1774.

It was here that William was introduced to poetry by his father. He later wrote about his childhood in *The Prelude*, playing in the terraced garden with Dorothy, or reminiscing about '*The Sparrow's Nest*', butterflies or Cockermouth Castle in three of his sonnets.

William's mother, Anne Cookson, the daughter of a Penrith draper, died in 1778, so William and his sister were sent to live with relatives in Penrith. Five years later, William's father died, by which time William was attending Hawkshead Grammar School.

The rooms of Wordsworth House are furnished in the 18c style and contain a few personal effects of the poet, including Crown Derby crockery (Morning Room), long case clock (stairs), settee (Drawing Room) and bureau bookcase (Study). There is a landscape by Turner, who once stayed at Cockermouth Castle with his patron, Lord Egremont.

A video presentation in the stable sets the scene and refreshments are available.

In 1937, there were plans to demolish the house and to replace it with a bus station. Fortunately, the National Trust saved the property.

Facing the house, across the road, is a bust of the poet, unveiled in 1970, the bicentenary of his birth.

The Grecian Villa was built in 1847 for Thomas Wilson, the hat manufacturer whose factory stood by Cocker Bridge. At various times since then, the Rural District Council and the Cumbrian Fire Service have made use of the building.

Harford Cottage, on the corner, across Low Sand Lane from Wordsworth House, was the birthplace of Fearon Fallows, mathematician and astronomer (1787–1831), who became the director of the new Cape of Good Hope Observatory where he compiled the first catalogue of southern hemisphere stars.

The Trout Hotel reminds customers, by a display of photographs and a letter, of the regular visits made by the late Bing Crosby, the crooner, on his angling holidays.

Cross Derwent Bridge to return to Wakefield Road car park.

The town's museums include –

The Western Lakes Motor Museum, in the former maltings building of Jennings Brewery.

The Toy and Model Museum, off Castlegate.

The Printing House Working Museum of Printing, on Main Street.

The Mining and Geology Museum in Crown Street.

In 1983, Cockermouth was twinned with the town of Marvejols in the Lozère district of South Provence.

Bassenthwaite

EC. Th. Mkt. M. [Anglo-French surname: Bastun. ON, thwaite = a clearing.]

Leave Keswick at the roundabout junction of the A66 (T) and the A591.

<u>Ormathwaite</u>. The Hall was the home of William Brownrigg (1711–1800), a physician and scientist. He experimented with gases and coal-derived chemicals at his Whitehaven laboratory. On Derwentwater, he demonstrated with Benjamin Franklin that oil could calm agitated water.

Later, the Hall was the home of Joseph Wilkinson, the artist for whose landscape engravings Wordsworth wrote the commentary which became his *Guide to the Lakes*.

A side road leads to the car park for Skiddaw.

Skiddaw	5.11

<u>Applethwaite</u>. The village was built on a terrace cut out of the mountainside in the 13c to preserve the Derwent basin below for agricultural purposes.

Sir George Beaumont, founder of The National Gallery, gave a plot of land surrounding Applethwaite Ghyll to William Wordsworth in 1802 to enable Wordsworth to live near Coleridge whose residence was Greta Hall. Wordsworth never lived here but his sonnet, 'At Applethwaite, near Keswick' commemorates this event. The slate cottage which now stands on the site was not built until 1867.

| Skiddaw | 5.14 |
| Skiddaw Little Man | 5.9 |

<u>Millbeck</u>. The former woollen mill has been converted into private dwellings.

From here, the Allerdale Ramble ascends Skiddaw.

Carl Side	5.5, 6
Dodd	5.11
Skiddaw	5.13
Skiddaw Little Man	5.7, 8, 12

<u>Dancing Gate</u>
| Dodd | 5.10 |

<u>Little Crosthwaite</u>
Carl Side	5.4
Dodd	5.9
Long Side	5.4

<u>Bassenthwaite Lake</u>. This most northerly lake in Lakeland, beneath the western slopes of Skiddaw, claims to be the only 'lake' in the Lake District because the other stretches of water are called 'mere' or 'water'. Wordsworth called it 'Broadwater'.

Elongated in shape, 4 miles long by ¾ mile wide, it has an average depth of 15 feet, maximum 75 feet. The road distance all round is 18 miles. The lake is fed by the River Derwent which flows from Derwentwater into and out of Basenthwaite Lake on its way to Cockermouth, Workington and the sea. Newlands Beck is the other main feeder stream.

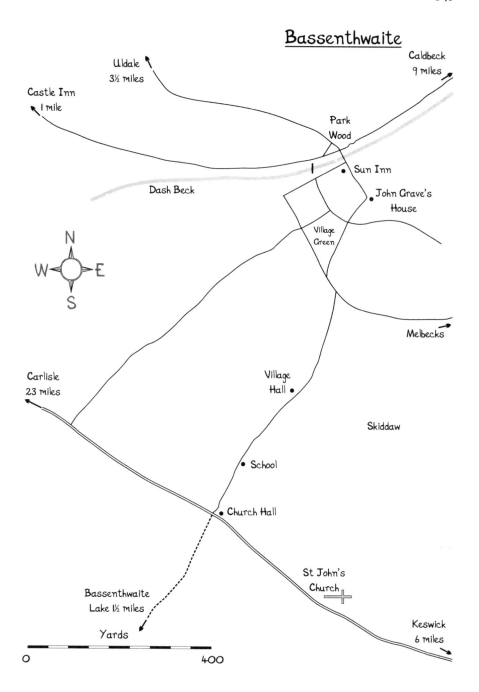

Bassenthwaite

Caldbeck
9 miles

Uldale
3½ miles

Castle Inn
1 mile

Park
Wood

Sun Inn

John Grave's
House

Dash Beck

Village
Green

N
W E
S

Melbecks

Carlisle
23 miles

Village
Hall

Skiddaw

School

Church Hall

Bassenthwaite
Lake 1½ miles

St John's
Church

Keswick
6 miles

Yards

0   400

The shape of the lake suggests that it was scooped out by a glacier as a distinct hollow, quite separate from that containing Derwentwater. At Bowness and Broadness, the ice left behind hillocks of Boulder clay which extend into the lake on either side of Bowness Bay.

At one time, Bassenthwaite Lake and Derwentwater formed a single large lake, but the subsequent deposition of alluvium, brought down by the River Greta and the Newlands Beck onto the rock bar between the two basins, led to their separation.

There is now 21 feet difference in level between the two lakes so that the River Derwent which joins them is rather sluggish, except after heavy rains. When these occur, the level of the lake may rise as much as 9½ feet. One result of the changing levels is that the lake is fringed by a wide storm beach which can be washed by sizeable waves when strong winds blow.

The alluvium plain belonged to Alice de Rumelli, who gave it to Fountains Abbey in 1195, together with the valleys of Watendlath and Langstrath. Later, the Egremont Estate became the owners, but to pay off death duties, ownership was transferred in 1979 to the Lake District Special Planning Board.

The first regatta on a Cumbrian lake took place on Bassenthwaite in 1780, an innovation which continued well into the following century. Today, power boats are banned and there is limited access for use of the lake in an attempt to protect the environment and to preserve wild life.

The busy A66 (T) hugs the western shore, following the line of the old Cockermouth, Keswick and Penrith Railway. The railway company became part of the London Midland and Scottish Railway in 1923, then British Rail in 1948. Rail traffic declined significantly and the line was closed in 1972.

<u>Dodd Wood</u> [*ME, rounded hill*] is leased from the Mirehouse estate. It is part of the Thornthwaite Forest which faces the forest of the same name on the opposite side of the alluvium flats.

A Forest Trail leads up to the conical-shaped summit of Dodd at 1,612 feet, from where there is a superb view over Bassenthwaite.

'Dodd Man', or the 'Skiddaw Hermit' were names given to George Smith of Scottish descent who made his home on the fellside here in the 1860s by building a huge tepee-like shelter of branches and bracken. He was able to pay for his drinks in the Keswick pubs by portrait painting.

<u>The Old Sawmill Information Centre</u> and café are housed in the original mill building which was built c. 1880 and still contains a water-powered saw and a collection of vintage forest tools.

<u>Mirehouse</u>. This manor house was built originally as a hunting lodge by the 8th Earl of Derby in 1666. It was later sold to his agent, Roger Gregg, and passed through his family until 1802 when it was left to John Spedding of Armathwaite Hall. It has remained in the Spedding family ever since.

John Spedding spent six years in the same classroom as Wordsworth at Hawkshead Grammar School. His younger son, James, was a noted literary figure in the 19c, the author of a fourteen volume biography of Francis Bacon. He was a close friend of Thomas Carlyle and Alfred Lord Tennyson and with his brother, Thomas, was host to some of the great literary figures of his day.

Edward Fitzgerald, who translated the *Rubaiyat of Omar Khayam*, was a visitor. So was Thomas Carlyle, who described Mirehouse as '*beautiful and so were the ways of it ... not to speak of Skiddaw and the finest mountains on earth*'.

While staying at Mirehouse, Lord Tennyson worked on his poem,

Morte d'Arthur, which he was to use in the *Idylls of the King*.

Many of the portraits and mementoes of the guests who stayed at Mirehouse are on display. Letters from Wordsworth, Robert Southey and Hartley Coleridge can be seen.

<u>St Bega's Church</u> is Bassenthwaite's old church, situated three miles south of the village and romantically sited in splendid isolation on the shore of Bassenthwaite Lake.

St Bega was traditionally of noble birth, the daughter of an Irish chief. She fled to England rather than marry the Norseman chosen for her by her father. She landed at St Bee's Head and founded a Benedictine nunnery there c. AD 650.

The present Bassenthwaite church dates back to Norman times. It was altered in the Victorian era, but retained the 12c chancel arch. The circular graveyard suggests that previously it may have been a pagan, perhaps a Druid, site.

The church is said to have inspired Lord Tennyson when he was working on his poem *Morte d'Arthur* in which he described the death of King Arthur and the throwing of the sword 'Excalibur' into the lake:

> *I heard the ripple washing in the reeds,*
> *And the wild water lapping on the crag.*

St Bega's is the '*chapel in the fields*' to which Sir Belivere carried King Arthur before the black barge bore away his body across '*the great water*'. At the spot where the poet felt inspired to write *Morte d'Arthur*, a little open air theatre by the lake was constructed in 1974 by the Tennyson Society.

<u>Ravenstone Hotel</u>
Long side   5.5
Ullock Pike   5.6

<u>High Side</u>
Carl Side	*5.7*
Skiddaw	*5.15, 16, 17*
Ullock Pike	*5.5*

<u>Bassenthwaite Village</u> is located on the old coaching route from Keswick to Carlisle.

Old cottages stand in a corner of the tree-lined village green. A plaque on a corner house, near the car park, states, '*This house done by John Grave, 1776.*'

The stone bridge over Dash Beck was built by the landlord of the Sun Inn to give coaches access to his hostelry.

St John's Church, with its pencil-shaped spire, was completed in 1878.

<u>Park Wood</u> is an attractive forest in a small valley with fine views over Bassenthwaite Village to the lake and to the wooded hill sides of Scab Fell beyond.

<u>Castle Inn</u>. *Digress to Caermote Roman Fort, off the A591 past Bewaldeth.*

Caermote Hill.	*OFOL 206.*

<u>Armathwaite Hall,</u> a large Victorian, neo-Tudor mansion is now a luxury hotel.

It was the family home of the Speddings before they inherited Mirehouse. The superb view of the lake from the terrace was the first 'station' recommended by West.

<u>Ouse Bridge</u> is where the River Derwent, on its way to Cockermouth, drains out of Bassenthwaite Lake.

Digress to Blindcrake

   <u>Isel Church of St Michael</u>, largely of Norman origin, is situated by Isel Bridge. The Triskele Stone, next to the chancel window, is part of an early Christian cross.

   <u>Isel Hall</u> overlooks the River Derwent and consists of a mansion built onto a pele tower.

<u>Blindcrake</u>

Clints Crag	*OFOL 204.*

<u>Embleton</u>. Higham Hall is where Cumbria County Council holds its summer schools.

   <u>Elva Hill Bronze Age Stone Circle</u> is 110 feet across, formed by 15 stones with a single outlier to the south-west.

Graystones	*6.5*
Watch Hill	*OFOL 202*

<u>Wythop Mill</u> was originally a corn mill on Wythop Beck. It became a sawmill around the mid-1800s. On display is the vintage water-powered woodworking machinery together with craftsmen's old tools. Refreshments are available.

Broom Fell	*6.4*
Ling Fell	*6.3*
Sale Fell	*6.10*
<u>Wythop Valley</u>	*Sale Fell 6.2, 3, 4, 6, 7, 8*
<u>Wythop Wood</u>	*Sale Fell 6.5*

<u>Castle How Iron Age Hill Fort</u> encloses 1½ acres with the steep hillsides north and south affording protection. Below the outer bank, the slope has been artificially steepened. At the east end are two banks, ditches and counterscarp banks. The inner ditch is vertical-

sided, flat bottomed and 6 feet deep. On the side exists an original entrance.

The Pheasant Inn at the foot of Castle How is a reminder that game birds were once reared in this area.

    Sale Fell   6.9

Beck Wythop promontory was West's fourth 'station' for viewing Bassenthwaite.

    Sale Fell   6.5, 7, 8.

Woodend has a car park and there is access to the lakeshore.

    Beckstones. Legend tells of a man who, for a wager, attempted to ride a horse up the fan-like screes on Barf. Half way up, beyond the worst stretch, the horse and rider fell and were killed. At that point, a white-washed rock commemorates the event. The OS map names this rock 'The Bishop'.

    An alternative version of the legend relates that it was a bishop who attempted this feat to demonstrate his faith in God!

    The publican from the Swan Hotel is traditionally responsible for the 'raiment' of white-wash on 'The Bishop' although a change of colour to red, white and blue took place on the day of the silver Jubilee in 1977.

    Beneath is a lesser known rock called 'The Clerk', who sits 'listening' to the interminable sermon from 'The Bishop' on high. Appropriately, above them both rises Lord's Seat.

    Barf.   6.2, 3, 4, 5

Thornthwaite. With increasing population in the valleys in the 12th and 13th centuries, and to overcome the defects of huge parishes with distant churches reached only by rigorous journeys, chapels were built as part of the process of land clearance and settlement.

Thornthwaite Chapel was built in 1240 by Thomas de Workington following a grant of freshly cleared land from Alice de Rumelli, who gave so lavishly in the Derwent Valley to Furness and Fountains Abbey. The present building, alongside Chapel Beck, was restored in 1760 and has twice been remodelled.

Thornthwaite Mines. Lead mining in this area was taking place in Elizabethan times. But profitable mining has been intermittent, depending on economic factors, such as demand, availability of capital, costs, and also on the development of mining engineering equipment and techniques.

Thornthwaite Mines gradually covered an extensive area including, from north to south, Beckstones, Rachel Wood, Thornthwaite and Ladstock. Of these, Ladstock was the oldest mine, pre-dating the use of gunpowder.

Amongst the variety of valuable ores extracted lead and later, barytes predominated.

Ores were extracted from 'adit levels' (horizontal tunnels) with shafts sunk to reach different levels within the interior of the mines. Thornthwaite Mine was an exception. It benefited from the introduction of more powerful machinery which enabled a main shaft to be sunk to a depth well below sea-level, serving several long galleries at different depths.

The ore was extracted from these mines by the 'cut and fill' method, where the dislodged mineral ore was sorted where it fell. The waste was left to accumulate on the floor and the ore was thrown down a 'mill' (chute, sometimes of brick, constructed through the waste rock debris) into wooden 'hoppers' (slides) below, which controlled the flow of the ore into the tubs for transportation.

The large quantity of ore raised warranted the erection of smelt-

ing works which were in use until the middle of the 19c. Water supplies came from Comb Beck where a dam provided a reservoir. During
the profitable years around the turn of the 20th century, as many
as 90 men were employed in these mines and on the surface. (Lord's
Seat. 6.5, 6)

Barf.	6.4, 5, 6
Grisedale Pike.	6.9
Lord's Seat.	6.7

Braithwaite. See *Whinlatter Pass.*
Portinscale. See *Around Derwentwater.*
Keswick.

Skiddaw Forest and
Caldbeck Fells

The northern fells in the Skiddaw-Blencathra range are composed of Skiddaw Slates, the foundation stone of Lakeland, seldom found outside the county. These shales with occasional grit bands were formed from silt and mud deposited at the bottom of a great expanse of water 500 to 600 million years ago. The resulting landscape is typically a huge rounded hump of bare fells, unvaried and repetitive.

Blencathra [OB. Welsh 'blaen' = summit; 'cateir'? = a chair) is aptly named, descriptive of its appearance, but its other name, Saddleback, is more instantly appropriate from some viewpoints. Its south-facing corries are exceptional features.

On the summit, Frau Hostetter was burnt as a witch in Hugh Walpole's *The Bright Pavilions* (1939) and her daughter, Catherine, was saved from the mob by Gilbert Armstrong, who claimed to be her fiancé.

Off the A591, eastwards from Keswick –

Castlerigg Stone Circle is a slightly oval shaped arrangement of 38 upright, glacial erratic boulders, approximately 110 feet in diameter, with an unusual rectangle of 10 stones inside the SE sector and thought to be 3–4,000 years old – older then Stonehenge. (Blencathra 5.2)

Castlerigg possibly inspired Keats to describe the fallen Titans in

CASTLERIGG MEGALITHIC STONE CIRCLE
12/98

his poem 'Hyperion',

> ... like a dismal cirque
> Of Druid stones upon a forlorn moor.

The setting is superb, with views of Latrigg, Blencathra, the Castlerigg and Derwent Fells as one turns full circle. The field in which the circle stands was bought in 1913 by Canon Rawnsley to prevent damage or exploitation.

Supporters of 'Ley Line' theories explain that a line drawn from the two highest visible summits of Skiddaw and Helvellyn passes the centre of the circle marked by the two tallest stones. Another line, drawn eastwards from the SW perimeter stone, and at right angles

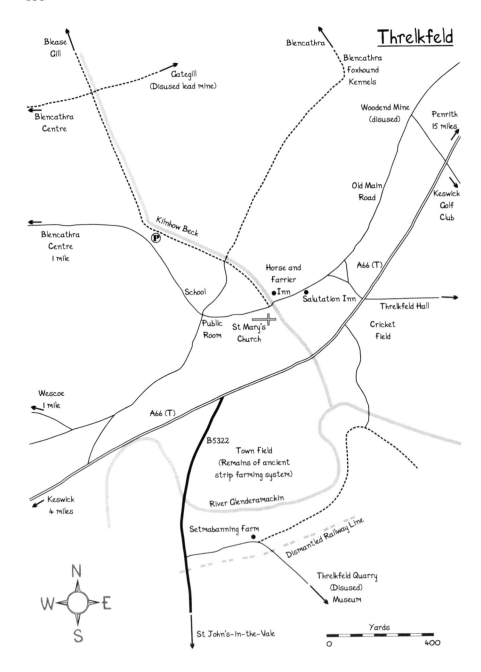

Threlkfeld

Blease Gill

Gategill (Disused lead mine)

Blencathra Centre

Blencathra

Blencathra Foxhound Kennels

Woodend Mine (disused)

Penrith 15 miles

Old Main Road

Keswick Golf Club

Kilnhow Beck

Blencathra Centre 1 mile

School

Horse and Farrier Inn

Salutation Inn

A66 (T)

Threlkfeld Hall

Public Room

St Mary's Church

Cricket Field

Wescoe 1 mile

A66 (T)

B5322

Town Field (Remains of ancient strip farming system)

River Glenderamackin

Keswick 4 miles

Setmabanning Farm

Dismantled Railway Line

Threlkfeld Quarry (Disused) Museum

St John's-in-the-Vale

N W E S

Yards

0

400

to the first line, goes directly to the stone circle of Long Meg, NE of Penrith, and marks the position of the rising sun on May 1st.

Continue eastwards.

Threlkeld [*ON. Thor's clearing*]

<u>Threlkeld Bridge</u> is where the River Glenderamackin [*W? glyndwfr = river valley; mochyn = swine*] from Mungrisdale is joined by St John's Beck from St John's-in-the-Vale, carrying the surplus water from Thirlmere. From here onwards the combined waters become the River Greta.

The village of Threlkeld, dominated by Blencathra, stands astride the old, twisting main road from Keswick to Penrith.

Boom time followed the discovery of lead, iron and zinc on Blencathra. At the end of the 19c, about 100 men were employed at <u>Gategill Mine</u> beneath Gategill Fell [*OE 'gat' = goat*]. Terraced houses were built for the miners using slate from the mine workings. At a later date, barytes ores were extracted by the 'cut and fill' method which enabled the waste material to be stacked underground. The interlinking mine at *Woodend* was even more productive until mining at Threlkeld ceased c. 1910. *(Blencathra 5.15, 16, 17)*.

<u>St Mary's Church</u>, built in 1777, has a squat bell tower remaining from an earlier, 13c, thatched structure. Parish records date back to Elizabeth I. An old village custom may still be perpetuated at Weddings. During the service, the churchyard gates are closed and tied with rope. The newly married couple are then held hostage until the bridegroom pays the ransom by throwing a handful of coins, for which the youths of the village eagerly scramble.

In the churchyard is a special memorial to 45 veterans of the hunt, contemporaries of John Peel. Among them, John Crozier was Master of the Hunt for 64 years up to his death at the age of 80.

> *The Forest music is to hear the hounds*
> *Rend the thin air with lusty cry,*
> *Awake the drowsy echoes and confound*
> *Their perfect language in a mingled cry.*

The kennels of the Blencathra fox hounds, which hunt the John Peel country, are situated at Gategill. The men hunt on foot in a uniform of grey.

The school was built in 1849 to replace an earlier one. Under the will of the Rev. Christopher Cockbain, who had retired to Threlkeld where he was born, a bequest was made to enable each child to receive a copy of The New Testament on leaving the school at the age of eleven.

Two inns remain. 'The Horse and Farrier', one of the oldest in Cumbria, has an inscription over the door, CIG 1688. The initials are those of Christopher and Grace Irton, then living at Threlkeld Hall. The Salutation Inn is of a much later date.

Threlkeld Hall, now separated from the village by the A66 (T), to the east, was once a fortified manor house. It is now a farm. According to legend, this was the locality where the young Lord Clifford, disguised as a shepherd, was hidden during the Wars of the Roses. Wordsworth referred to the story in 'Benjamin the Waggoner' and again in 'Song at the Feast of Brougham Castle'.

Blencathra Centre is a mile north-west of Threlkeld, along Blease Fell Road. It opened in 1904 as a TB Isolation Hospital, the second in England after Meathrop, Grange-over-Sands. It later became a hospital for the elderly and infirm before closing in 1975. The Lake

District National Park Authority has converted the buildings into hostel and self-catering accommodation.

Blencathra.   5.9, 10, 12, 13, 16, 17, 20

The Glenderaterra Valley is the northern end of the great fault which runs through the length of Windermere, Rydal, Grasmere and Thirlmere. Near the foot of Thirlmere, the fault divides into the two branches, one passing along the Vale of St John and the other along the Vale of Naddle. (*Great Calva 5.10*).

Ores from the Glenderaterra Mine (Blencathra 5.34) included lead, copper and barytes.

Lonscale Fell   5.5, 6
Mungrisdale Common   5.5

The Cumbria Way along the Glenderaterra Valley leads to Skiddaw House, one of the most isolated buildings in England, in a wild and desolate location at the 'back o' Skidda'.

The house, now a Youth Hostel, featured in the novels of Sir Hugh Walpole. In *The Fortress*, Uhland and John Herries made their separate ways to the deserted Skiddaw House on a damp and misty day to '*have it out, the two of us, once and for all – alone*'. In that great empty house, Uhland, armed with a gun, murdered his unarmed uncle and then killed himself. Skiddaw House was also the model for 'Green House', where Robin Herries attended a secret celebration of Mass in *The Bright Pavilions*.

Walpole would have known of the solitary shepherd, Pearson Dalton, who occupied part of the house for 47 years, 1922–1969.

Great Calva   5.6
Skiddaw   5.6, 8, 10, 21.
Skiddaw Little Man   5.10

From Threlkeld's main street, turn west, uphill to –

<u>Wescoe</u> [*ON. Western wood*] The family of W. H. Auden (1907–73), the British-born American poet and essayist, had a holiday cottage adjoining 'Far Wescoe', where Auden wrote several of his poems. Following his return here from the Spanish Civil War, when Christopher Isherwood stayed with him, he wrote his celebrated poem, '*Spain, 1937*'.

Nearby, Colin Welland, playwright and actor, has made his home.

> Latrigg   5.6

From the A66(T) take the B5322 (St John's-in-the-Vale.)

   <u>Threlkeld Town Field</u> lies between the village and the River Glenderamackin, just east of the B5322. The walled rectangular enclosures were built on the site of the former open field. In 1849, 14 acres, 11 strips, were farmed by 5 owners. The shared cultivation ceased and the strips were enclosed by 1860.

Cross Townfield Bridge, travelling south on the B5322, following the <u>Threlkeld Quarry</u> *sign to the* <u>Museum of Lakeland Mines and Quarries</u>.

   Threlkeld Quarry opened in the 1870s and closed finally in 1982, extracting granite continuously apart from the years 1937 to 1949. Granite was supplied for building material, road making, railway ballast, Manchester Corporation's Thirlmere waterworks scheme and for the tarmacadam plant in the quarry. Concrete flagstones were made in the flagsheds which, following sensitive restoration, now function as the *Blencathra Business Centre*.

   <u>The Museum</u> in the former quarry canteen displays an informative collection of small mining and quarrying artefacts, photographs, maps and charts which illustrate the hardship endured by

the miners and quarrymen of Cumbria. The geology of the Lake District is wonderfully represented in the Geology Room. The shop stocks beautiful minerals, gemstones jewellery and books on mining, geology and mineralogy.

The quarry was well served by the former <u>Penrith to Workington Railway</u>, which operated from 1864 to 1972. Threlkeld station was ¾ of a mile from Threlkeld village but well-sited for transporting quarry products and workmen. A narrow gauge tramway incline conveyed truck loads of crushed granite to the standard gauge sidings below. The quarry engine shed has survived and now contains locomotives, mine tubs and machinery.

Today, the Penrith to Workington railway track has been abandoned, or has been used as the basis of the A66 trunk road, with the exception of a 4 miles stretch between Threlkeld and Keswick, which has become a scenic walk through the narrow Greta Gorge.

On the A66 (T), in the direction of Penrith –

<u>Scales</u>. A gated road leads from the White Horse Inn at Scales to the Mill Inn at Mungrisdale.

<u>Scales Tarn,</u> formerly Threlkeld Tarn, lies at the foot of precipitous Sharp Edge on Blencathra. (*Blencathra 5.26*).

Bannerdale Crags	*5.7*
Blencathra	*5.21, 24, 25, 27*
Souther Fell	*5.6*

Turn north off the A66 (T) into –

<u>Mungrisdale</u>. [*ON. Grisdale = valley of the pigs. The reference to St Mungo was added later.*]

<u>Souther Fell</u> [*ON. Shoemaker's fell*] is almost surrounded by the River

Glenderamackin. *(Souther Fell 5.3)*.

On Midsummer Eve in 1745, at least 26 reliable people witnessed a ghostly army marching over the steep sides of the fell. Investigations made on the next day revealed no traces of the event. Subsequently, it was discovered that Bonnie Prince Charlie had been manoeuvring his troops far away on the Solway Firth prior to marching on London. Some kind of image, or a 'vaporous reflection' onto clouds might explain this strange phenomena. *(Souther Fell 5.7)*.

<u>Redmire Farm</u> *is signposted about 1½ miles from the A66 (T), along the Mungrisdale Road, where there is space for roadside parking.*

Walk up the farm track, skirt the farm and discover two of <u>Andy Goldsworthy's</u> sheepfolds: Single Fold (OS. 372296) and Boulder Fold (OS. 375294).

These sheepfolds were the first part of Cumbria County Council's Public Art Development Service. The project started in January 1996 for the Year of Visual Arts in Cumbria. By December 2000, an estimated 100 sites will have been utilised to create

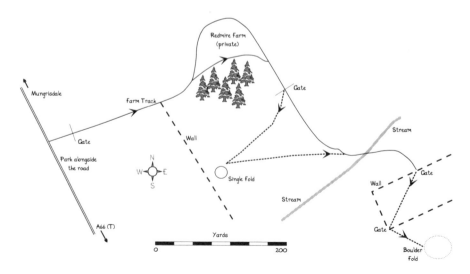

environmentally responsive sculptural works. By using existing sheepfold, washfold or pinfold sites and restoring or rebuilding the structures, Andy Goldsworthy has committed himself to working closely with the region's landscape and farming history.

Mungrisdale Village Church, built in 1756, is dedicated to St Kentigern, the saint who came to Carlisle and Cumbria from Glasgow, where he was known as St Mungo. It has boxed pews and a flagged floor. There is a memorial plaque to Raisley Calvert, Wordsworth's great friend, whose bequest supported the poet's career.

Coleridge reported the story of two local Quakers, John Slee and Isaac Ritson, who, with others, removed the church bell and buried it, fooling the parishioners into searching for it in strange places. Slee later taught mathematics at Kendal and Ritson, his pupil, became a poet and a writer.

The Mill Inn, 16c, has retained its mill sluice controlling the waters of the River Glanderamackin. The inn was patronised by Charles Dickens and Wilkie Collins during their tour in 1857.

Bannerdale has been unfrequented since the closure of the lead mine. (*Bannerdale Crags 5.3, 4*). Small deposits of 'wad' (graphite) were mined in the mid-19c.

Bannerdale Crags	*5.6*
Blencathra	*5.28*
Bowscale Fell	*5.5, 6*
Souther Fell	*5.5*

Bowscale stands in the mainly featureless divide, which once contained a lake, between the Glenderamackin and the Caldew rivers. Bowscale Tarn is referred to by Wordsworth in '*Song at the Feast of Brougham Castle*' where he recalled the local tradition that two immortal fish lived in the tarn. They were named Adam and Eve, but nobody was known to have seen them and the water was said to be too cold for fish.

>   *Bowscale Fell*   5.7

At the eastern boundary of The Lake District National Park, <u>Eycott Hill</u> marks the NE extremity of the Borrowdale Volcanic Series, composed of lavas with elongated crystals of felspar. The weathering of the softer beds on the western slopes has caused a terraced appearance. On the summit are bare rock ribs and marshy hollows.

From here, an escarpment of Carboniferous Limestone, covered in boulder clay, extends north through Hutton Roof [*OE, settlement on the summit of the hill*], with a 200 feet drop to the valley floor, on the boundary of The National Park.

<u>Mosedale</u> [*ON. Valley with a bog.*] Skiddaw slates now terminate against the rugged upthrust of igneous rock – not the Borrowdale Volcanic Series, but a complex sequence of granite and white felspar crystals, resistant to erosion, resulting in rocky crags.

<u>The Quaker Meeting House</u> was built in 1702, enlarged in 1884 and restored in 1973.

>   *Carrock Fell*   5.7
>   *Knott*   5.9, 10

<u>Carrock Fell</u> [OB. Rock] The Iron Age hillfort on the summit was possibly built by the Brigantes (Celts) shortly after the Roman Conquest. (*Carrock Fell 5.2, 10*).

On the lower slopes, facing east, is a group of over 200 small Bronze Age cairns, including examples of ring-cairns.

When Charles Dickens and Wilkie Collins climbed Carrock Fell, they got lost in the mist and rain. Dickens broke his compass. Collins fell into a ravine and sprained his ankle.

The Caldew Valley road is suitable for cars and penetrates two miles into the mountain fastness. A track continues to follow the River Caldew, leading to the Cumbria Way and onwards almost to the source of the river near Skiddaw House.

Carrock Mine, in the deep-sided valleys of Grainsgill Beck and Brandy Gill, tributaries of the River Caldew, was the only locality in the country, outside of Devon and Cornwall, to have produced tungsten (wolfram). This heavy metal is used in the manufacture of tungsten high-speed steel, cutting tools and the very fine filaments in light bulbs, vacuum and X-ray tubes. In nuclear reactors, tungsten became important as a cladding for fuel rods, because it is non-reactive, has a high melting point and is a good conductor of heat.

The mine opened in 1854 and was easily worked by a series of adit levels driven into the valley sides. However, the mine was worked only when the price of tungsten was at its peak, usually when imported supplies were threatened by wars. Closure came in 1981 and subsequently the site has been cleared of all equipment and buildings. Only the concrete bases of hoppers remain. (*Carrock Fell. 5.2, 4, 5. Knott 5.9*)

Stone Ends. Here, the escarpment of Carrock Fell is formed of 'gabbro', a dark coloured, coarse, igneous rock, ideal for climbing. cf. The Black Cuillins of Skye.

Carrock Fell   *5.8*

The Caldbeck Fells have been a rich mining area since Elizabethan times. At least ten major mines have produced a wide variety of minerals, including copper, lead, zinc, iron pyrites, manganese and barytes.

Barytes, once discarded as a waste material, came into great demand as a filler in the cloth and paper industries and as a lead substitute for paint. Barytes mud adds weight to the drilling lubricants in the boreholes of oil companies and is mixed with concrete in nuclear installations. From barytes, barium meals are derived for internal X-ray examinations.

The extraction of the mineral by high explosives and the use of hoppers (chutes) to remove the ore, enabled the waste rock to be stacked underground.

Barytes mining started seriously in the Caldbeck Fells in the 19c within a narrow belt of decomposed volcanic rock on the slopes of High Pike in a complex of workings largely between Calebrack and Fell Side. Typically, a series of intensive working periods were followed by interludes of idleness.

Two of the richest barytes mines were Potts Gill and Sandbed.

Mining in the Caldbeck Fells ceased in 1966 when Sandbed was the last mine to close. (*High Pike 5.2, 3, 5, 6*).

Three main starting points give access to the Caldbeck Fells and the major disused mines:

Calebrack

Driggeth Mine, reached by following Carrock Beck, had veins in line with Roughtongill Mine, a mile and a half to the east. Large quantities of lead and copper, and smaller amounts of barytes were extracted using three adits.

Sandbed Mine, opened c. 1844, took on a new lease of life with the recovery of barytes in the mid-20c. Huge pillars of white and yellow barytes were left to secure the safety of the mine when the mineral was dislodged by explosives and the 'cut and fill' technique allowed the waste debris to be stacked underground.

Carrock Fell   5.9

> *High Pike*   5.10 (Mines: Driggeth, Dry Gill,
>   Sandbed).

Nether Row is on the Cumbria Way.

Potts Gill Mine like Sandbed, opened c. 1844 and commenced the extraction of barytes in the 1940s.

> *High Pike*   5.9 (Mines: Driggeth, Potts Gill).

Fell Side

Hay Gill Mine originated in the 'stope and feather' days yielding copper ore of very good quality.

Red Gill Mine was also worked by the 'stope and feather' method and was once operated by the Company of Mines Royal. The mein ranked next to Roughtongill in the variety of ores produced, chief amongst which were lead and copper. It became famous for its rare deep azure blue crystals of linarite, specimens of which are in the Natural History Museum.

Roughtongill Mine was the most productive mine in the Caldbeck Fells both in the quantity and in the variety of the raw materials extracted. It yielded twenty-three minerals, chiefly lead, copper and zinc ores, together with manganese, iron pyrites and barytes. It was also the oldest of the mines in this group having been cut extensively by 'stope and feather' before the introduction of gunpowder. In Elizabethan times, the mine, like Red Gill, was operated by the Company of Mines Royal. In 1794, a smelting works replaced the adjacent ancient smelting hearths but the smelter soon fell into disuse and was converted into cottages which have long since disappeared. Although the mine closed in 1853, it took on a new life in 1888 for the extraction of barytes and umber before its final demise. (*High Pike 5.4, 7*).

<u>Silver Gill</u> was one of the larger mines involved in the extraction of copper.

Brae Fell	5.4
Great Sca Fell	5.5 (Mines: Hay Gill, Red Gill, Roughtongill, Silver Gill.)
High Pike	5.8 (Mines: Hay Gill, Potts Gill.)
Knott	5.7, 8 (Mines: Hay Gill, Red Gill, Roughtongill, Silver Gill.)

<u>Hatcliff Bridge</u>. The River Caldew cuts through a small limestone gorge. In dry weather, when the water level is low, much water disappears down swallow holes, leaving only large pools in the river bed.

<u>Hesket Newmarket</u> [*ON. Place overgrown with ash trees.*] This is one of several 'decayed' market centres in the area. Its market was 'new' following the granting of its Charter in 1751. Trade in animals and produce continued until the middle of the 19c. The four circular stone pillars of the 18c market cross are a reminder of the former trade.

Hesket Newmarket

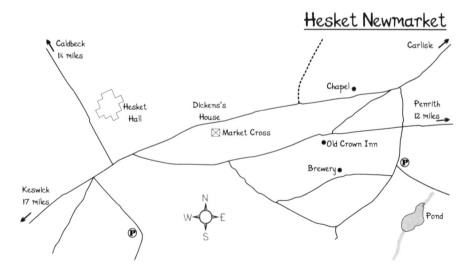

<u>Dickens's House,</u> directly behind the market cross, was formerly the Queens Head Inn, where Wordsworth and Coleridge stayed in 1803 and Charles Dickens and Wilkie Collins in 1857. The latter described their walking holiday in the Lake District in an article called '*The Lazy Tour of Two Idle Apprentices*' in Dickens's publication *Household Words*.

Overlooking the long green, which extends down the middle of the village, where a row of houses once stood, are numerous attractive buildings including the <u>Old Crown Inn</u> with its own brewery.

<u>Hesket Hall,</u> at the top end of the village, was built in the 17c by Sir Wilfred Lawson. Its peculiar features include the pyramid-shaped roof and the large square central chimney. The angular shape of the building was designed, we are told, so that the shadows from the twelve corners could act as a sundial.

<u>Caldbeck</u> [*ON. Cold Beck, or stream*]. This grey stone village lies in a limestone basin at the northern tip of the National Park.

It takes its name from the River Caldew which once provided the power for the important industrial development of the 17c and 18c. Corn mills, woollen mills, bobbin mills and a paper mill, together with a brewery, all contributed to the local prosperity. In the fells above Caldbeck, mining expanded during the reign of Queen Elizabeth I, with the most prosperous periods during the 17c and 18c. From a rich variety of minerals mined, the most significant were lead, copper and barytes. The last mine closed in 1966. An old proverb recorded the wealthy situation:

Caldbeck and Caldbeck Fells
Are worth all England else.

Caldbeck itself provides a fascinating retrospective view of its industrial past when there were 1,500 inhabitants and 13 ale houses compared with half that population today and just one pub. The industrial past is reflected in the preservation of several old mill buildings, which have been put to new uses and in the many disused mine workings on Caldbeck Fells.

Alongside the industrial aspect of Caldbeck's history, fell farming has always been a major occupation. It remains an important industry in the area today.

The Village Green is flanked by Ratten Row where the former Wheatsheaf Inn has become a private residence. Facing the duck pond, the National School built in 1865 became a Police Station before becoming privately owned.

The Old Rectory, now a private house, was built in 1785 on the site of a 12c hospice for travellers founded by monks from the priory at Carlisle. Friar Row and Friar Hall Farm retain a link with the past, albeit by name only.

The Church, built in 1112, is dedicated to St Kentigern (or Mungo) who had preached here in AD 553 during his flight from the King of Strathclyde. Just behind the church, on the river bank, is St Mungo's Well, a spring made holy by St Kentigern.

The churchyard has three graves of interest.

The parents of John Dalton, the originator of the atomic theory, are buried here.

Mary, 'the Beauty of Buttermere', courted and illegally wed by a rogue who was finally hanged at Carlisle in 1803, shares a grave, to the west of the side path, with her lawful husband, Richard Harrison, a Caldbeck farmer.

Carved with hunting symbols is the grave, to the left of the church door, of John Peel (1776–1854), the fox-hunter immortalised in the song.

> *D'ye ken John Peel with his coat so grey?*
> *D'ye ken John Peel at the break of day?*

D'ye ken John Peel when he's far far away
With his hounds and his horn in the morning?

According to John Woodcock Graves (1795–1886), John Peel's drinking crony and a Caldbeck millowner, the ballad was composed one snowy evening *'in a snug parlour'* at his house. Originally, Graves set the words to the tune of *'Bonnie Annie'* a traditional Scottish song. The better known, more lively tune was adapted from *'Bonnie Annie'* by the choirmaster of Carlisle Cathedral, William Metcalf, fifteen year's after John Peel's death.

John Peel, a contemporary of William Wordsworth's, was born in a cottage at Park End Farm. He grew to be more than six feet tall. Portraits of him show a cold hard eye, a long nose and a mean tight-lipped mouth.

At the age of twenty, he followed the example of his father when he eloped to Gretna Green with an eighteen-years old girl, Mary White. Their marriage was solemnised in Caldbeck Church in 1797. The couple lived at Upton where their thirteen children were born. In later life, Greenrigg Farm, Ruthwaite, was their home.

John Peel's passion for fox-hunting, to the detriment of business and parental concerns, prompted him to keep his own pack of hounds for 55 years so that he could always go hunting, on foot, or on his horse called 'Dunny'. After hunting, he often drank at the Sun Inn, Ireby.

John Peel died at the age of 78 after a hunting accident. Although he was laid to rest in Caldbeck's churchyard, he was not allowed to rest in peace. In 1977 his grave was desecrated by anti-blood sports protestors.

His friend, John Woodcock Graves, emigrated with his wife and four children to Tasmania, where John lived the life of a 'ne'er-do-well.'

<u>Priests Mill</u>, near the church, was built in 1702 by the rector who also built the church tower in 1727. This former corn mill and saw

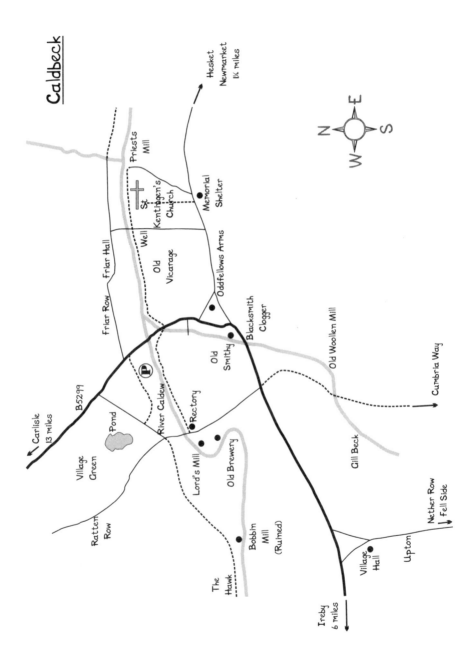

Caldbeck

mill has become a craft workshop. The waterwheel and mill race continue to function. Refreshments are available.

The Memorial Shelter was built in memory of John Peel and John Woodcock Graves. A shop occupies the premises.

The Oddfellows Arms used to be The John Peel Inn and before that The Rising Sun. It is the only one of the original 13 pubs still surviving. A portrait of John Woodcock Graves is on display.

Gate House, where John Woodcock Graves lived, is just west of the inn and marked 'BTB 1718' over the door.

The Old Woollen Mill, behind the clog maker's shop on Gill Beck, was built in 1862 and employed 20 villagers. At the mill, owned by John Woodcock Graves, a heavy cloth for overcoats known as Ivenson Grey was manufactured – the '*coat so grey*' worn by John Peel in the ballad. The mill is now a private house and business premises.

Beneath the cobbler's shop wool was 'fulled', that is, cleansed of grease and tar, before dyeing took place nearby.

Lord's Mill, is distinguished by its chequered-brick chimney. In 1704, it was grinding corn. Then it was rebuilt in 1830 and used as a mill until 1914.

Next door was a wheat mill dating back to 1670, but by 1810 it had become a brewery. As industrial activity declined, so the brewing ceased by the end of the 19c.

The elegant house close by, dated 1690, is typical of a former mill owner's house of which there are several similar examples in the village.

The Howk [*Cumbrian = to dig out with a pick or spade*]

This spectacular limestone gorge with two deep swallow holes is approached from the south corner of the village green, through a farm gate and along the north bank of the River Caldew.

The ruins of the former water-powered bobbin mill, which closed in 1920, carry a date-stone inscribed '1857'. Sixty men and boys were employed here at one time. Its 42 foot diameter wheel named 'Red Rover', one of the largest in the country, was scrapped for the war effort in 1940.

After viewing the falls, return to the wooden footbridge, from which a field path runs SE to Todcrofts, once the home of Mary Harrison (neé Robinson), the 'Beauty of Buttermere'. In the barn gable, a stone is carved 'RH 1852', the initials of Mary's husband, Richard Harrison.

Faulds Brow   OFOL 210.

Chris Bonington, the Everest climber, made his home a mile from Caldbeck at the foot of High Pike.

<u>Whelpo</u> [*ON. Hills of the whelps, or pups.*] Across Parkend Beck can be seen the pattern of lynchets, farmers' cultivation terraces on the hillside.

<u>Parkend</u>. The River Caldew abruptly disappears after its journey of 14 miles from its source near Skiddaw House.

A series of rectangular enclosures are evident on the former common field.

Parkend farm cottage, adjoining the restaurant, was the birthplace of John Woodcock Graves who wrote the words of '*D'ye ken John Peel?*'

> <u>Greenhead</u>
> *Brae Fell*   5.4
>
> <u>Longlands</u>
> *Great Sea Fell*   5.7
> *Knott*   5.6
> *Longlands Fell*   5.3

Meal Fell   5.4

Direct Route to Keswick

<u>Over Water</u> is a tarn in a depression cluttered with smooth, green hummocky drumlins and overlooked by Great Cockup Fell. The tarn is used as a reservoir.

This is the start of the Twenty Seven Lakes Marathon Fell Run, which involves 18,000 feet of ascent. Jos Naylor OBE of Wasdale Head has run the 106-mile course in 19 hours.

<u>Orthwaite</u>. Orthwaite Hall is 17c. Little Tarn is nearby.

<u>The Cumbria Way</u> leads to Whitewater Dash waterfall, where the little Dash Beck pours out of the heights of the Skiddaw Forest. The forest was once a hunting preserve and not a forest in the arboreal sense. <u>The Cumbria Way</u> continues to Skiddaw House and from there to Keswick or Mosedale.

Great Calva	5.5
Great Cockup	5.4
Great Sca Fell	5.6
Knott	5.5
Meal Fell	5.3

<u>From the road to Skiddaw House:</u>

Bakestall	5.4
Skiddaw	5.20

<u>Melbecks</u>

Skiddaw	5.19

High Side
Follow the A591 to Keswick.

Alternative Route to Keswick

Aughertree Iron Age Settlement. [*OE. Old cottage on the boundary. Pronounced 'Affertree'.*] There are traces of three ancient circular enclosures and tumuli. The enclosures are about 70 yards in diameter.

> Longlands Fell   5.6

Uldale is situated on an ice-eroded col with views of the Uldale Fells and the north face of Skiddaw Forest.

The rectangular pattern of enclosures of the former common field can be seen here.

St John's Church is almost a mile away at Uldale Mill. A triangular monument stands to the memory of the Reverend Jonathan Cape FRS (1793–1868), the author of mathematical text books and trigonometrical tables.

Sir Hugh Walpole set much of the action in the *Herries Chronicles* around Uldale. Uldale Mill Farm became Fell House, David Herries' farmhouse, in *Rogue Herries*. Here, David Herries died from a stroke on hearing that his son Francis supported the French Revolution. This fictional farm was burnt to the ground in *Vanessa*. Walpole repeatedly had fictional buildings destroyed to avoid conflict with the real topography.

Ireby. [*ON. Settlement of Irishman*] A Moot Hall butter cross stands in the market square, symbolic of the Market Charter granted in 1237. The Moot Hall itself has been converted into cottages. The fair, which impressed the poet John Keats on a visit in 1818, no longer takes place.

The Sun Inn was John Peel's favourite drinking place after a hunt.

All that remains of the old parish church, at some distance from the village on the Torpenhow road, is the 12c chancel. The nave and north aisle were demolished when the new church was built more conveniently in the centre of the village.

Reuben Sunwood, the nephew and friend of Judith Paris in Sir Hugh Walpole's novel of that name, was buried in the old churchyard after being shot during an attack on Fell House by a mob from Cockermouth.

<u>Boltongate</u> church has a stone-vaulted nave which is unique in England. The vaulting technique originated from Burgundy and was first used in Scotland at the Cistercian Abbey of Melrose. Bishop Goodwin remarked in the 19c, *'mathematically it ought to have fallen down, because the weight of the massive stone roof should have forced the walls out.'* Local tradition credits Michael Scott, a 13c Scottish wizard, with building the church in a single night. Others attribute the construction to imported French builders.

<u>Torpenhow</u>. The Norman church, more than a mile from Ireby, has a crude arch around the door, a fine chancel arch supported on carved capitals and a 17c painted wooden nave ceiling, said to have come from the headquarters of a livery company.

<u>High Ireby</u>. The Grange, once the home of James Gurney, was a Victorian mansion represented as Walter Herries' house, The Fortress, in Walpole's novel of the same name. After the death of James Gurney in 1933, The Grange was allowed to deteriorate until a fire in the 1950s destroyed most of it and demolition followed. The ruins are accessible through a large white gate by the telephone box.

In his novel, Walpole moved the position of The Fortress about a quarter of a mile to the hill above the old lime kilns, so that Walter Herries could look down on his cousins at Uldale in the valley below.

Melvyn Bragg, the Cumbrian-born broadcaster and novelist, chose High Ireby for his Cumbrian home.

> *Binsey*   5.6

<u>Ruthwaite</u>. John Peel Cottage, on the north side of the road, was the farmhouse of the famous huntsman during his late life. He died here in 1854 at the age of 78.

His wife, Mary White, came from this hamlet.

<u>Binsey Lodge</u>. Five roads meet in the vicinity.

> *Binsey*   5.5

<u>Bewaldeth</u>

> *Binsey*   5.4

> *Follow the A591 to Keswick.*

Troutbeck

Holehird, south of the village (OS. 410008), and approached from the A592, is where Beatrix Potter stayed with her parents during the summers of 1889 and 1895. Although she wrote of the poor weather, she was successful in searching for fossils and fungi.

In 1945, Edward Leigh Grove bequeathed the mansion and estate to be used '*For the better development of the health, education and social welfare services of the County of Westmorland*'. The house has become a Cheshire Home and the gardens, maintained by The Lakeland Horticultural Society, are open to the public throughout the year.

This Victorian mansion was built in 1854, reputedly on the site of an older farmhouse, 'Hird's Holding', named after the grant bestowed by Edward VI on Hugh Hird (or Herd), the amazingly strong 'Cork Lad of Kentmere'. (See: Kentmere Hall).

The same claim of origin is made for Hird House, north of the village (OS. 418057). One version of the story relates how Hugh Hird took possession of an empty house which became forfeit to the crown. When a new tenant arrived, Hugh prevented his entry. To answer this contempt concerning crown property, Hugh was summoned to appear before Edward VI. There, Hugh took the opportunity to demonstrate his incredible strength. The King was so impressed that he granted him a boon. Hugh asked for this Troutbeck cottage with one field near it for cutting turf and permission to cut wood in Troutbeck Park.

Troutbeck, a hillside village on the old packhorse route from Ambleside to Kentmere, extends for more than a mile along a narrow, undulating road above the valley floor of Trout Beck, which flows down from the Kirkstone Pass area to Lake Windermere.

There is no centre to the village, which consists of a series of some twenty 'statesman' houses, originally sheep farms with cottages and barns built of slate, grouped around a line of road-side wells which, until recently supplied all the water. The whole village of 17c and 18c properties, some with bank barns and spinning galleries, was declared a Conservation Area in 1981.

The township was once divided into three parts: Town Head, Longmire Yeat and Town End. Each part was called a 'Hundred' and

ROBIN LANE TO TROUTBECK

10/98

JB

had to maintain a bridge, a bull and a constable:

> *There's three hundred brigs i' Troutbeck,*
> *Three hundred bulls,*
> *Three hundred constables,*
> *And many hundred feuls.*

'The Hundreds' off Nanny Lane and 'Hundreds Road' off Robin Lane are marked on the OS map.

<u>Town End</u> (NT). *The National Trust Handbook* describes this property as, '*An exceptional relic of Lake District life of past centuries: a 'statesman' (wealthy yeoman) farmer's house, built about 1626, containing carved woodwork, books, papers, furniture and fascinating domestic implements of the past, collected by the Browne family who lived here from that date until 1944.*'

TOWN END HOUSE - TROUTBECK
10/98

In 1626, the former Chase (royal hunting preserve) was divided among local people by Charles I. The Browne family of yeoman wool farmers built on the site of an earlier house and lived in their house for thirteen generations. During the 17c, the Brownes were High Constables of Kendal Ward and other members of the family entered the professions of law and medicine.

Nothing was thrown away from the Browne's house and nothing was modernised so that Town End has remained an enthralling time warp, without electricity.

Across the road is a 17c bank barn with a spinning gallery where the Browne family stored fleeces.

<u>Thwaite,</u> at the foot of Robin Lane, is another example of a 17c 'statesman's' house.

<u>The Village Institute,</u> built in 1869, has a ground floor reading room and an entrance from the hillside to the public hall on the upper floor.

<u>Three Wells</u> on the roadside, St John's, St James's, and St Margaret's were built by the Dawson Family, formerly of Birkhead.

<u>Longmire Yeat,</u> inscribed GB 1649 on the chimney stack, was the home of Margaret Longmire who died in 1868 at the age of 104. She is buried in the churchyard. ('Yeat' is Cumbrian for 'gate'). Several attractive houses cluster nearby.

<u>Nanny Lane</u> rises over Wansfell, 1,597 feet, to Ambleside. Here, Beatrix Potter left her pony and went in search of fossils.

Wansfell   *2.5*

<u>Mortal Man.</u> This inn was originally The White House, a cottage inn built in 1689. A new inn sign, painted c. 1800 by a local customer, Julius Caesar Ibbetson, heralded the name change. One side showed the pallid face of a teetotaller and the other a jolly red-nosed individual. From their mouths come the words:

Troutbeck

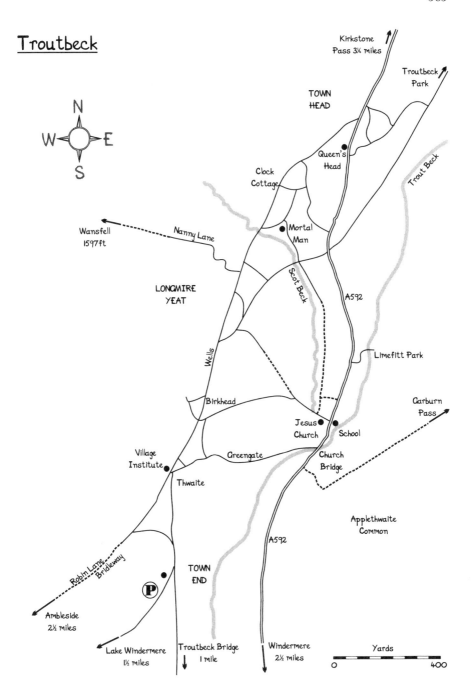

N W E S

Kirkstone Pass 3¼ miles

Troutbeck Park

TOWN HEAD

Queen's Head

Clock Cottage

Trout Beck

Wansfell 1597ft

Nanny Lane

Mortal Man

Scot Beck

A592

LONGMIRE YEAT

Wells

Limefitt Park

Birkhead

Garburn Pass

Jesus Church

School

Village Institute

Greengate

Church Bridge

Thwaite

Applethwaite Common

Robin Lane Bridleway

TOWN END

A592

P

Ambleside 2½ miles

Lake Windermere 1½ miles

Troutbeck Bridge 1 mile

Windermere 2½ miles

Yards

0   400

O mortal man, that lives by bread,
What is it makes thy nose so red?
Thou silly fool that looks so pale
'Tis drinking Sally Birkett's ale.

The landlord at that time took away the original sign when he retired, but the replacements have retained the features of the first.

Clock Cottage at High Green, one of a group of old farm buildings, has a clock on the gable end that stopped at 10.45.

Many of Troutbeck's most attractive buildings have interesting features such as round chimneys, crow-stepped gables and outside stone staircases.

Queen's Head Hotel. When stray sheep were brought down from the hills for identification and collection, Shepherds' Meets were held here.

Almost annually since 1780, a 'Hunting Mayor' has been elected. Although his main duty is officially to send off the local fox hounds on their first hunt of the season, he officiates also at evening celebrations from the 'Mayor's Chair' which is kept at the hotel.

The bar is said to have been constructed from a four-poster bed.

Troutbeck Park Farm, consisting of two thousand acres, was bought by Beatrix Potter in 1923. This started her lifelong enthusiasm for the native breed of Herdwick sheep. The farmhouse, the farm dogs and the surrounding features in the countryside were used by her for several of the illustrations in *Fairy Caravan*.

The farm was left to The National Trust in her will with the stipulation that the wild creatures she loved so much – the hare, the fox, the otter – should never be hunted on the estate.

from Limefitt Park

Caudale Moor	2.7	Sour Howes	2.2
Froswick	2.2	'Old Roads of	

High Street	2.7	Eastern Lakeland:
Ill Bell	2.5	Garburn Pass' 42
Thornthwaite Crag	2.5	
Troutbeck Tongue	2.2	

<u>Jesus Church</u>, below the village by Trout Beck, is unusual in not being dedicated to a patron saint like most churches.

The church existed in 1506 but was rebuilt in 1562 and again in 1736. The massive beams are believed to be from the 16c church. The imposing stained glass east window was designed in 1873 by the pre-Raphaelite Sir Edward Burne-Jones, assisted by William Morris and Ford Maddox Brown who, according to a local tradition, happened to be on a fishing holiday together at the time. The old oak panelling in the chancel came from Calgarth Hall.

In the churchyard, near the east end of the church, is the grave of Parson Sewell, who was the incumbent at Troutbeck for 42 years until his death in 1869. In 1840 he instigated the building of the inn at the summit of the Kirkstone Pass following the deaths of a number of winter travellers.

Buried nearby was Margaret Longmire, the villager who died in 1868 at the age of 104.

Across the main road is the former <u>village school</u> of 17c foundation.

Kirkstone Pass

The A592 links Windermere with Ullswater by climbing and descending about 1,000 feet over the Kirkstone Pass. The summit at 1,489 feet is the highest Lakeland Pass for motorists.

The very steep rise of the minor road from Ambleside to the pass is known as 'The Struggle'. Carriage passengers in the 19c had to alight and walk part of the way.

<u>The Kirkstone Pass Inn,</u> formerly The Travellers' Rest, is the highest pub in Lakeland. This old coaching inn near the summit was built in 1840 at the prompting of Parson Sewell of Troutbeck following a series of tragic deaths on the rugged mountain roads in the depths of winter. The pass is usually the first to get snow and skiing is popular on the neighbouring slopes. Overlooking the pass, on Caudale Moor, is a memorial cairn to Mark Atkinson (d. 1930) for many years the landlord of the inn.

    Caudale Moor   2.5

<u>Kirk Stone.</u> Half a mile north of the inn is the highest point of the pass from which to admire the extensive views down into Patterdale. Nearby, beneath Red Screes, is the Kirk Stone, a huge boulder 10 feet high, resembling a church steeple when approached from the north. De Quincey referred to it as '*this massive church*'. Wordsworth wrote:

> *This block – and you whose church-like frame*
> *Gives to this savage pass its name.*

Patterdale

Follow the A592

> <u>Brotherswater Hotel</u>
> Caudale Moor   2.6
> Hartsop Dodd   2.2 (Caudale Bridge)

Take the footpath from the hotel, through Sykeside camp site to reach –
   <u>Hartsop Hall</u> (NT) 15c. Three harts' heads adorn the family's coat-of-arms.

Just south (OS. 398117 marked 'Settlement') are faint traces of an oval-shaped enclosure and rampart, with the outline of three huts.

> Hartsop above How   1.2
> High Hartsop Dodd   1.2
> Little Hart Crag   1.4
> Middle Dodd   1.2

On the Caiston flank of Middle Dodd in 1948, nineteen Patterdale men struggled for fourteen days to rescue two terriers which had gone to earth down a vixen's bolt-hole.

<u>Brothers Water</u>. This small lake, ¾ mile by ¼ mile and 70 feet maximum depth was an unprecedented gift to the National Trust from the Treasury which had received it in 1947 from Lord Lonsdale in lieu of death duties.

Originally it was called Broad or Broader Water. The name change took place following a second tragic drowning c. 1785 of two brothers when the ice broke beneath them. On an earlier occasion, an identical fate in the same place had been suffered by another two brothers. Dorothy Wordsworth wrote about this terrible coincidence.

Caudale Moor   2.4

Hartsop [*OE. Valley of the deer.*]

This secluded hamlet, known sometimes as Low Hartsop, is situated off the A592 at the valley exit from Hayeswater.

When Hugh de Lowther was given the demesne of Hartsop in 1463, the Lowther family became Lords of the Manor.

Hartsop today belies its industrial past. The Romans found gold and silver. The Elizabethans mined lead and zinc. Quarried building materials and ores were transported out of the valley by pack horses along tracks used mostly now by hikers. The mining community was served by corn and cloth mills, blacksmiths, cobblers, and tailors, making Hartsop at that time the biggest settlement and industrial centre in Patterdale.

Mining and quarrying ceased long ago. Today, the haphazard cluster of blue-slate 17c 'statesman's' farmsteads and cottages are all that survive from the past. Even Wordsworth in his *Guide to the Lakes* described 'Hartshope' as a '*decaying hamlet*'. There is no church, no shop and no pub, although 'The Bunch o' Birks Inn' once stood at Fell Yeat (= Gate) on the packhorse route to the Kirkstone Pass.

What was once a Norman hunting forest is now traditional sheep farming country. One Hartsop farm has 1,300 sheep on 1,700 acres, but the sheep farming business has to be heavily subsidised to survive.

There remains much that is pleasing in Hartsop. Even neglected

Hartsop

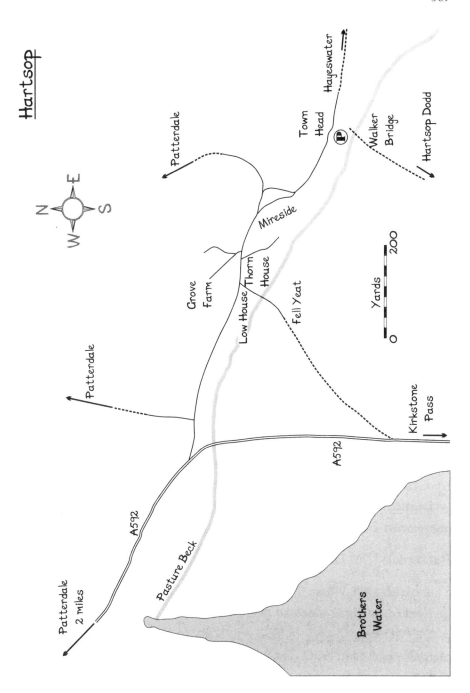

N W S E

Patterdale

Patterdale

Town Head

Hayeswater

Mireside

Walker Bridge

Hartsop Dodd

Grove Farm

Low House

Thorn House

Fell Yeat

Yards

0   200

Kirkstone Pass

A592

A592

Patterdale 2 miles

Pasture Beck

Brothers Water

and overgrown properties have their appeal in this attractive setting. Refurbished buildings have been sympathetically restored many of them further enhanced by landscaped gardens. Low House, Thorn House and Mireside have spinning galleries from which fleeces were once displayed for the inspection of wool merchants from Kendal. Delightful surprises include the remains of a corn mill drying kiln c. 1600, on the corner of the road to Grove Farm. An oven, with a heavy metal door, set in an outside wall, is used now as a place to leave bottles of milk.

Brock Crags	2.2	The Knott	2.3
Caudale Moor	2.4	Rampsgill	
Gray Crag	2.3	Head	2.5
Hartsop Dodd	2.2	Rest Dodd	2.3
High Raise	2.5	Thornthwaite	
High Street	2.5	Crag	2.4

The A592 continues to follow Goldrill Beck, the outflow from Brothers Water.

Lining the eastern side of the valley are 17c statesman's farms – Dubhow, Beckstones, Crookabeck and Rooking. On the opposite side are Lane Head, Greenbank and Noran Bank, fronted by the relict pattern of the former open field. Some Lakeland farms are bought today by outsiders who have little or no interest in farming as a living.

<u>Deepdale</u>. Just within the valley, near Deepdale Bridge, are two abandoned Iron Age village sites.

Patterdale [*ON. Patrick's Valley.*]

This slate-built village at the head of Ullswater, beside Goldrill Beck, is flanked on three sides by mountain ranges.

<u>St Patrick's Church</u> in 1853 was built to take the place of the 14c chapel replaced in 1600. The land for the present church was donat-

Patterdale

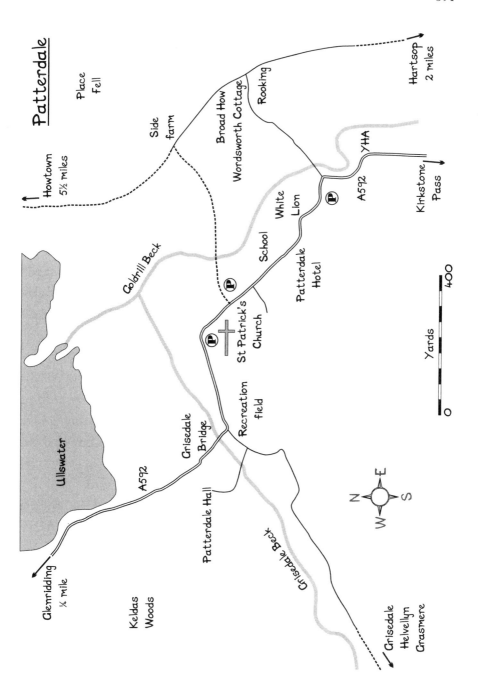

Ullswater

Place Fell

Howtown 5½ miles

Side farm

Broad How

Wordsworth Cottage

Rooking

Hartsop 2 miles

Coldrill Beck

School

White Lion

Patterdale Hotel

YHA

A592

Kirkstone Pass

St Patrick's Church

Recreation field

Grisedale Bridge

A592

Patterdale Hall

Keldas Woods

Grisedale Beck

Glenridding ¼ mile

Grisedale Helvellyn Grasmere

Yards

0   400

N
W   E
S

ed by the Marshall family of Patterdale Hall.

St Patrick, the Patron Saint of Ireland and founder of Christianity in 5c Celtic Britain, was said to have been shipwrecked on Duddon Sands whilst returning to Ireland and to have walked the thirty miles to Patterdale.

From the earlier churches came the Norman font and two bells. The white ensign on display was flown at the Battle of Jutland. The Communion Plate of Glenridding silver was presented in 1850 by the Greenside Mining Company which, in 1890, supplied the church with electric lighting, making it the first church in the country to be lit in this way.

Ann Macbeth's richly coloured tapestries were created when she lived at Wordsworth Cottage, the view from which, towards Kirkstone, is shown in the background to '*The Good Shepherd*'. Below this tapestry is the score of Parry's setting of William Blake's '*Jerusalem*'.

Side Farm was the home of Captain and Mrs Luff, with whom William and Dorothy Wordsworth stayed when visiting Patterdale. According to Dorothy's *Journal of a Mountain Ramble*, they were staying here in 1815 when they heard the news of the victory at Trafalgar and the death of Nelson.

Broad How, a Victorian house, stands on land bought by William Wordsworth in 1805 with help from his patron, Lord Lowther. After deciding not to build on the site, the poet sold the land in 1834 to the publican of the local White Lion.

Wordsworth Cottage next door but one, is a large, white-rendered stone cottage built in 1670. It has been confused with Broad How, but was the home of Ann Macbeth (1875–1948), the embroidress whose tapestries are displayed in Patterdale Church.

<u>The Patterdale Hotel</u> grew with the tourist trade from its small beginnings as The King's Arms.

<u>Patterdale Hall</u> in the 17c was the home of John Mounsey, a glutton and a miser, who owned the largest farm in the dale. Its remoteness helped him to avoid paying taxes. He was known as the 'King of Patterdale' following his victory over Scottish raiders at Stybarrow Crag. The 'title' became hereditary.

When the Hall was re-built in 1796, a very strong protest about its colour by Dorothy Wordsworth brought about a colour change.

The Mounsey dynasty ended in 1824 when the Hall was sold to William Marshall, a wealthy wool merchant from Leeds. The present house, built by the Marshall family, is now a residential centre.

<u>St Patrick's Well</u>, a mile north of the village, marks the spot where St Patrick is believed to have baptised the local inhabitants.

Arnison Crag	1.2	Angletarn pikes	2.5
Birks	1.4	High Raise	2.5
Dove Crag	1.4	High Street	2.5
Fairfield	1.7	Place Fell	2.5
Hart Crag	1.6	Ramsgill Head	2.5
Hartsop above How	1.3	Rest Dodd	2.3
Helvellyn	1.15		
Little Hart Crag	1.4		
Red Screes	1.6		
St Sunday Crag	1.5		

<u>Glenamara Park,</u> on the slopes of Birks, has an abandoned Iron Age village site.

<u>Grisedale</u> [*ON. Valley where young pigs are reared.*] This ancient route

from Ullswater to Grasmere follows Grisedale Beck into its upper reaches, passing Ruthwaite Lodge, once a shooting lodge now a climbing hut, and Grisedale Forest, which once belonged to the barony of Kendal.

Grisedale Beck flows out of the corrie basin of Grisedale Tarn, which is over 100 feet deep, and follows a fault line.

The Brothers' Parting Stone, just below the outlet from the tarn, bears an inscription commemorating the leave taking in 1800 between William Wordsworth and his brother John, captain of the 'Earl of Abergavenny', an East Indiaman. John was drowned five years later without William ever seeing him again. John's ship, on voyage to India was driven by a gale onto rocks near Portland Bill, Dorset, and sank with the loss of 300 passengers and crew. The effect of this tragedy on William was so shattering that it became a turning point in his life. Canon Rawnsley was responsible for having the inscription put on the stone.

The summit of the route is Grisedale Hause at 1,929 feet. Thereafter, the only track descends to Mill Bridge at Grasmere.

Birkhouse Moor	1.5
Dollywaggon Pike	1.7
Helvellyn	1.13
Nethermost Pike	1.6

Ullswater

[ON. Ulf's Lake – the first baron of Greystoke.]

Wordsworth, in his *'Guide to the Lakes'*, describes Ullswater
'like a magnificent river' winding its way through the landscape.

Lakeland's second largest stretch of water, 7½ miles long by ¾ mile
wide, is a glaciated, modified, submerged valley with three distinct
sections, each having a change of direction. The depths of the lake
vary on average between 50 feet and 100 feet, the greatest depth
being 205 feet opposite Birk Fell.

At both points where Ullswater changes directions there is a rock sill
coinciding with a col of pre-glacial times. Between Glencoyne and Silver
Point, the rock bar breaks the surface at Norfolk Island. Between Skelly
Nab and Hallin Point, the rock sill is totally submerged, but the water
along it is 75 feet deep compared with 125 feet on either side.

Skelly is a kind of freshwater herring, which used to be caught by
stretching a net across the lake from Skelly Nab at the lake's narrowest point. At one time it was feared that the skellies had been
killed off by pollution from Glenridding mine workings (now disused),
but the skellies survived. Normally, this is a deep water fish which
swims into shallow water to spawn in January and February.

At the head of the lake, towering above and behind, are the steep
slopes and the bare craggy outcrops of the Borrowdale Volcanic
Series. Included are the Helvellyn and Fairfield groups which reach
the west shore of the lake at Glencoyne, and the High Street range

which reaches the eastern shore at Hallin Fell. From Glencoyne and Hallin Fell, a continuous strip of easily eroded Skiddaw Slate extends on both sides of the lake to the lower end, giving rise to a gentle land-scape. Around Sandwick is an additional pocket.

The waters from at least twelve becks from twelve dales supply Ullswater at the upper end: Aira Beck from Matterdale; becks from Glencoyne, Glenridding, Grisedale, Deepdale, Dovedale and Caudale all meet in Patterdale; becks from Martindale Forest – Boredale, Bannerdale, Ramps Gill and Fusedale. The River Eamont is the out-let at the lower end.

After Windermere, Ullswater is the most landscaped of lakes, with extensive woods and substantial Victorian houses many of which have been converted into hotels.

In 1955, Sir Donald Campbell gained his first water speed record of 202.32 m.p.h. on the lake in his jet-propelled 'Bluebird'. Far more sedately, the motor yachts 'Lady of the Lake' and 'Raven' operate a passenger service along the length of the lake.

Glenridding

[OB. Bracken valley.]

This once prosperous, lakeside mining village, shut off to the east and west by high fells, has become a centre for boating and climbing now that mining activities have ceased.

Glenridding Beck is fed by the outflow from the corrie basin of Red Tarn and descends along a line of faulting. Near Red Tarn in 1805, the remains were found of a young man, Charles Gough, whose body had been guarded for many weeks by his faithful dog. Above, on the main summit ridge of Helvellyn, the Gough Memorial Stone records that Gough was killed by a fall. (*Helvellyn 1.21*). Sir Walter Scott

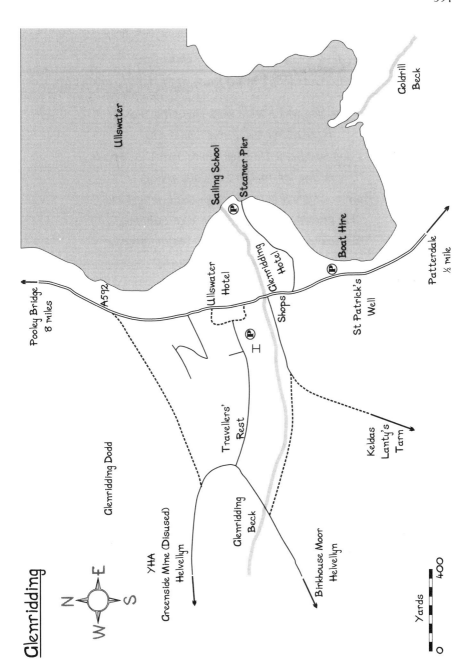

Glenridding

Pooley Bridge
8 miles

A592

Ullswater

Coldrill
Beck

Sailing School

Steamer Pier

Ullswater
Hotel

Glenridding
Hotel

Boat Hire

Shops

St Patrick's
Well

Patterdale
½ mile

Glenridding Dodd

Travellers'
Rest

Keldas
Lanty's
Tarn

YHA
Greenside Mine (Disused)
Helvellyn

Glenridding
Beck

Birkhouse Moor
Helvellyn

Yards

0   400

described the event in his poem:

'*I climbed the dark brow of the mighty Helvellyn.*'

Wordsworth also recorded it in his lines on '*Fidelity*', which conclude:

> The dog which still was hovering nigh,
> Repeating the same timid cry,
> This dog had been through three months' space
> A dweller in that savage place.
> How nourished here through such long time,
> He knows, who gave that love sublime,
> And gave that strength of feeling great,
> Above all human estimate.

Glenridding Beck has been kept in check by reinforced banks since the disastrous floods in 1927 when Keppel Cove Tarn, which served as a reservoir for the Glenridding lead mine, burst its earthen dam following torrential rain. Thousands of gallons of water hurtled down the valley carrying uprooted trees and boulders. The flood waters and debris crashed down onto the village of Glenridding leaving behind a trail of utter devastation. Rattlebeck Bridge was swept away and furniture from flooded houses and shops was washed far out into Ullswater. Livestock perished but no one was killed. This disaster almost forced the closure of the Greenside Mine as the Company had to pay compensation. (*Catastycam 1.5*)

The concrete replacement dam in nearby Brown Cove was partially breached in 1931 but without a repeat of the previous devastation.

Over countless years, the Glenridding Beck had formed a delta where it entered the lake. The flood disaster added masses of stony debris to form a peninsular which is now used as a car park by the Ullswater Navigation and Transit Company.

The Ullswater Navigation and Transit Company has operated since 1855 when it began by carrying goods, mining equipment, mail and passengers between Pooley Bridge and Glenridding. The 'Lady of the Lake' and the 'Raven' were built near Glasgow by Thomas Seath and Co. and transported in sections by rail to Penrith and by horse-drawn drays to Pooley Bridge for assembling and launching. The 'Lady of the Lake' was launched in 1877 and the 'Raven' in 1889. Both 'steamers' were converted to diesel oil in the 1930s. During the holiday season, these same vessels continue to operate a regular daily passenger service sailing the length of the lake in just under one hour and calling at Howtown.

Greenside Lead Mine. Greenside Road rises past 'The Travellers' Rest' and the slate-built miners' cottages, which are now used mostly as holiday accommodation. Higher up Glenridding Valley, at about 1,200 feet, are the remains of Greenside Lead Mine.

Although mining began with the discovery of outcrops of lead high on the fells in the 1650s, it was not until the Greenside Mining Company was formed in 1822 that full-scale mining activities took place.

A system of leats conveyed water to power water wheels making possible more extensive workings in the valley of Swart Beck, particularly at High and Low Horse levels.

From c. 1835, a smelting mill became operational at the mine. Smelting one ton of ore yielded about 80% lead and 250g silver. During the smelting process, highly toxic fumes were removed by means of a flue more than a mile long.

Lower down the ravine of Swart Beck, the Lucy Tongue level was begun. It took 16 years to complete and became one of the longest crosscuts in Lake District mining history.

In the 1890s, under the management of Captain William Henry

Borlase, Greenside was one of the first mines to instal hydro-electric power. An electric locomotive was introduced. To power the turbines, an adequate water supply was provided by constructing dams at Red Tarn and Keppel Cove.

In 1895, the workforce numbered 157. Fifty years later, that number had been halved. Eventually, reserves of ore were worked out and the mine closed in 1962, but not before the Atomic Weapon Research Establishment had simulated an atomic explosion in the mine using TNT.

Greenside holds the reputation of being the greatest and the last of the Lakeland lead mines after nearly 2½ million tons of lead ore and 2 million ounces of silver had been extracted over a record period of 150 years.

The scars of the mining activities are very much in evidence today. Attempts have been made to stabilise and landscape the huge heaps of spoil. Some of the former mine buildings have been converted into hostels, including a Youth Hostel. On the lower eastern slope of Raise are the remains of a stone aqueduct, the mile long smelter flue and a derelict chimney (*Raise 1.3, 4, 6*)

From the Glenridding Valley the ski slopes on the side of Raise (1.8) can be reached.

See: *Greenside,* Ian Tyler, 1992.

Birkhouse Moor	1.6
Catstycam	1.4
Glenridding Dodd	1.2
Helvellyn	1.16
Raise	1.6
Sheffield Pike	1.4
White Side	1.6

Continue along the A592, which hugs the lake shore.

<u>Stybarrow Crag</u>. Part of the crag was blasted away in 1920 to make space for the metalled road along Ullswater's shore.

It was here John Mounsey of Patterdale Hall gained the title of 'King of Patterdale' by repulsing the raid of the Scottish marauders.

In *The Prelude*, Wordsworth recalled an awesome boyhood memory of gazing up at the *craggy ridge* of Stybarrow, dwarfed from behind by Glenridding Dodd, when rowing out of the lake one evening.

<u>Glencoyne</u>. [OB. Valley of reeds]. Here, the towering, steep and craggy slopes of the Borrowdale Volcanic Series, typical of the landscape at the head of the lake, meets the gentler scenery of Skiddaw Slate at the lower end of the lake.

OB GLENCOYNE FARM - PATTERDALE ROUNDED CHIMNEYS 'CROW' STEPPED GABLE ENDS
11/98

Glencoyne's solitary 'statesman' farmhouse with cylindrical chimneys, dates from 1629. The row of miners' cottages at the rear is appropriately named 'Seldom Seen'.

Glencoyne Park was once a Norman deer forest like its neighbour, Gowbarrow Park.

Sheffield Pike   1.5

Aira Force. [*ON. Gravel bank steam*]. The National Trust has provided a car park and a café just off the A592.

Wordsworth described Aira Force in his '*Guide to the Lakes*' as '*a powerful Brook, which dashes among rocks through a deep glen, hung on every side with a rich and happy inter-mixture of native wood.*'

Aira Beck, viewed from woodland footpaths, plunges over three waterfalls in less than half-a-mile. Aira Force has a spectacular 80ft drop. On the lower bridge is an inscription to Cecil Spring Rice, '*poet, privy councillor and H. M. Ambassador to the USA during the Great War*'. The upper bridge carries a plaque to '*Stephen Edward Spring Rice. CB. 1856–1902*'. The next waterfall is known as High Force and, finally, at the highest level, is an unnamed waterfall.

Wordsworth used the valley of Aira Beck as the setting of his poem '*The Somnambulist*', a romantic legend which ended in tragedy. Emma, the pretty daughter of a nearby Lord of the Manor, fretted for her lover who was away on a crusade. Her lover returned to find her sleep walking by the Force. He touched her, she woke up, but overbalanced and fell into the torrent and drowned. The distraught crusader became a hermit in a nearby cave.

Gowbarrow Fell   1.3, 6

Matterdale

[ON. Valley of the madder plant.]

Take the A5091.

<u>Dockray</u> *[OE. Corner of land overgrown with docks.]* Aira Beck, from the area of Great Dodd and Stybarrow Dodd, flows down secluded Deepdale, past Dowthwaitehead, through Dockray and over the waterfalls to Ullswater where it has formed a lake delta.

Near its source is Birkett Fell, renamed in honour of Lord Birkett who, in 1962, argued in Parliament against the proposal to turn Ullswater into a reservoir. In fact, water is taken, but the plans were substantially modified. The pumping station is hidden underground and the idea of having a pipeline down Longsleddale was abandoned.

<u>Cockley Moor</u>, the long stone house a mile along the unclassified road from the Royal Hotel at Dockray, was built as the Lowthers' shooting lodge. It became the home of Helen Sutherland, collector, patron of the arts and hostess to many notable guests from the world of art and literature. Later, Fred Hoyle, Astronomer Royal, lived here.

<u>The Old Coach Road</u>, once the main route from Penrith to Keswick, strikes out from here across the fells to Wanthwaite, St John's-in-the-Vale.

Gowbarrow Fell	*1.6*
Great Dodd	*1.6*
Hart Side	*1.5*
Stybarrow Dodd	*1.6*

<u>Matterdale End</u>. In 1639, Matterdale men protested against the threat to their common grazing and one man walked to London, a journey of some 300 miles, to give evidence.

The church, built with a thatched roof in 1573, was the outcome of a petition as the mother church at Greystoke was considered to be too far away. The slate roof and the tower with stepped gables are later additions.

Great Mell Fell 1,760', and Little Mell Fell 1,652'. These conical hills consist of a conglomerate of slate, volcanic chippings and a little sandstone which together form a gritty mass. Large cobbles give rise to a series of crags on the west of Great Fell. These basic materials were transported by powerful floods in the distant geological past.

The surrounding 17c settlements were reclaimed from the former deer forest.

Great Mell Fell	*1,2, 3*
Little Mell Fell	*1,2, 3*

Return to the A592 along Ullswater's shore.

Lyulph's Tower *[ON. L'Ulf, the first baron of Greystoke, after whom Ullswater itself is named.]*

The tower was built by the eccentric Charles Howard of Greystoke, later the eleventh Duke of Norfolk, as a shooting lodge c. 1780, on the site of an earlier tower.

The tower was mentioned by Wordsworth in his poem '*The Somnambulist*':

> *List, ye who pass by Lyulph's Tower*
> *At eve; . . .*

Sir Walter Scott also featured the tower and its owner in *The Bridal of Triermaine.*

Gowbarrow Park *[ON. Windy hill]*, like neighbouring Glencoyne Park, was once a Norman deer park. Gowbarrow Hall was landscaped with

Douglas fir and rhododendrons in Victorian times.

It was on the lake shore here that Dorothy Wordsworth saw the golden daffodils which, in her words, *'seemed as if they verily laughed with the wind'*. William Wordsworth immortalised the scene in his poem *'Daffodils'*:

> *Beside the lake, beneath the trees,*
> *Fluttering and dancing in the breeze.*

Skelly Nab, the lake's narrowest point, is named after Ullswater's unique deep water fish.

Watermillock [*W.OE. Little hill where wethers graze.*]

The Old Church, an outlying chapel of Greystoke, situated by the lake's edge, was converted into Old Church House and became the home of Cecil Spring Rice. It is now The Old Church Hotel.

The dark Victorian replacement church, a mile west up an unclassified road, was built when the new parish of Watermillock was created out of the older, larger parish of Greystoke.

At 900 feet is a meltwater channel extending north-east from Priest's Crag, past Bennethead Farm and across the col near Maiden Castle hill fort.

Dacre

[W. Teardrop. Trickling stream.]

According to the Venerable Bede's *Ecclesiastical History* of AD 731, there was a monastic settlement here, *'which being built near the river Dacore had taken its name from the same'*.

William of Malmesbury, in his history of England, dated 1125, recorded that this monastery was probably the meeting place in AD

Dacre

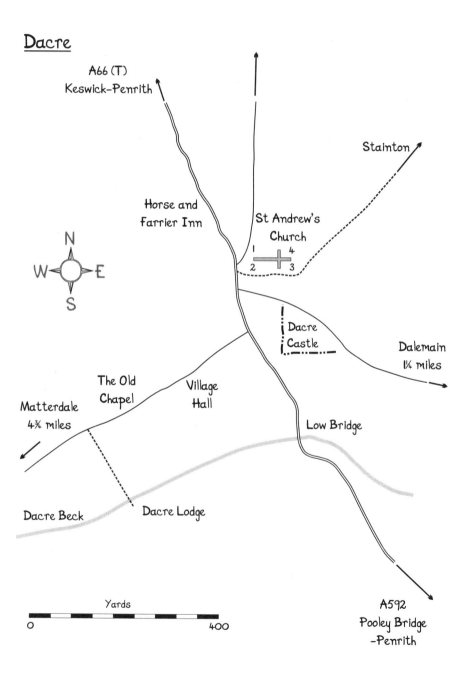

A66 (T)
Keswick–Penrith

Stainton

Horse and
Farrier Inn

St Andrew's
Church

1 4
2 3

N
W E
S

Dacre
Castle

Dalemain
1¼ miles

The Old
Chapel

Village
Hall

Matterdale
4¾ miles

Low Bridge

Dacre Beck

Dacre Lodge

Yards

0

400

A592
Pooley Bridge
–Penrith

926 of three kings: Athelstan King of England, Constantine King of the Scots, and Eugenius King of Cumberland. The Scottish and Cumberland kings paid homage to Athelstan and were baptised into Christianity. Legend claims that this 'Peace of Dacre' meeting took place in the 'King's Chamber' in the castle, but the castle had not been built.

Dacre Beck in 1307 drove the water wheel of a fulling mill, but no trace of the mill remains.

In 1802, Dorothy Wordsworth wrote in her journal of a visit here. The village today appears much as it did then, with 18c farmsteads and cottages built of pink-grey limestone, many of them grouped round the 'Horse and Farrier' inn.

<u>St Andrew's Church</u> is mostly Norman and is thought to be standing on the site of the former Anglo-Saxon monastery.

The chancel contains monuments to the Hasell family of Dalemain. The shaft of an 8c Anglian stone cross is carved with a creature resembling a winged lion. The 10c Viking shaft has been subjected to several interpretations. The lowest panel shows Adam watching Eve picking the apple. They leave the garden together in the panel next to the top. Animals of various kinds are shown on the intervening panels.

A lock in the south door bears the initials and date 'AP 1671'. The initials are those of Lady Anne Clifford, Countess of Pembroke, who owned properties throughout the north of England. Many of her properties were damaged during the Civil War and, following the restoration of the monarchy, she spent much of her later life having them repaired.

In the four corners of a rectangle around the church, stand four mysterious stone carvings of bears, each 3 feet tall. They are said to illustrate a story: (1.NW) Bear sleeping. (2.SW) Bear attacked by a cat or lynx. (3.SE) Bear shaking off the cat. (4.NE) Bear eating the cat. Their origin is unknown.

Dacre Castle is Lakeland's best example of a pele tower unchanged in its 14c simplicity.

It was built by the Dacre family, on the site of a Norman Castle, during the savage Scottish raids which followed the English army's defeat at the Battle of Bannockburn, 1314. The castle became one of a line of defences. The tower has walls 7 feet thick and elaborate turrets and battlements. Farm animals were originally housed on the ground floor and the inhabitants lived above.

In 1569, Leonard Dacre led an unsuccessful rebellion against Elizabeth I. In the 17c, when the dangers from Scottish raiders had receded, the fifth Lord Dacre added the large windows. When he died in 1715, the Dacre family possessions in Cumberland were sold off and the castle was eventually bought by Edward Hasell of Dalemain.

Return to the A592.

Soulby [ON. *Sula's farmstead.*] On the lower slopes of Soulby Fell, below the farms, is the site of the former open field, marked today by the hedged boundaries of the long rectangular early 19c enclosures.

Dalemain has been owned by the Hasell family since 1679. Sir Edward Hasell was the steward of Lady Anne Clifford.

In the middle of the 18c, Edward Hasell added the impressive Georgian facade onto the Elizabethan part of the house. The result is 'a glorious confusion of winding passages, quaint stairways, unexpected rooms'.

Access to the Elizabethan quarters is gained from the Norman pele tower, at the foot of which is a display of the regimental history of the Westmorland and Cumberland Yeomanry. This '*home full of surprises*' includes the panelled Old Oak Room, the Nursery and a priest's hole discovered in 1851.

There is a restaurant in the medieval Old Hall.

In the 16c great barn are displays by The Countryside Museum and the Fell Pony Museum.

The gardens are landscaped in the 17c and 18c style.

<u>Park House</u>, just west of Dalemain, was from 1804 the home of Wordsworth's brother-in-law, Thomas Hutchinson, who was often visited by William and Dorothy.

Ullswater East

Pooley Bridge

[O.E.ON. Formerly 'Pool How', the hill by the pool.]

<u>'Steamer' Pier</u>. From here to Glenridding, calling at Howtown, the M.Ys 'Lady of the Lake' and 'Raven' sail the length of Ullswater on a seasonal basis.

<u>River Eamont</u>. At the ancient crossing point and, more recently, at the county boundary between Cumberland and Westmorland, the River Eamont flows swiftly out of Ullswater beneath the narrow, three-arched bridge, constructed in 1763 at a cost of £400.

Millions of gallons of water from the lake are lifted, by enormous electric pumps, up and through the fells to top up the Haweswater reservoir. Pumping only takes place when the water is above a certain level and only at night when electricity is cheaper. For the construction of the unobtrusive underground pumping station near the village, Manchester Corporation won a Civic Trust Award.

<u>Village Square</u>. In times past, sheep, cattle and fish markets were held here.

For many years, until 1956, this was the venue for the Ullswater Sports, which included a regatta on the lake. The Sports were supported by Lord Lonsdale, who was known also as the Yellow Earl because of his passion for that colour. In 1923, he arrived at the Sports riding

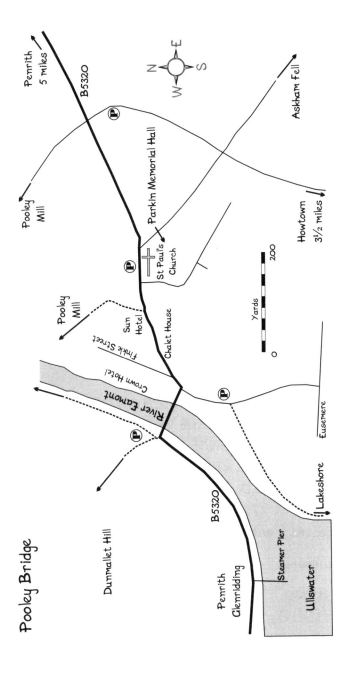

in a canary-coloured carriage with postilion-ridden horses.

The Sun, The Crown, The Chalet Hotel, cafés and shops cluster round this central area.

<u>St Paul's Church</u>. Pooley Bridge was once part of the vast medieval parish of Barton. Until 1868, when St Paul's was built with its lofty roof, bell tower and stubby steeple, parishioners had to travel two miles to Barton.

Next door is the Victorian Parkin Memorial Hall.

<u>Eusemere House</u> was built by Thomas Clarkson who, with his wife Catherine, lived here from 1796 to 1804. He worked with William Wilberforce for the abolition of slavery. William and Dorothy Wordsworth were very close friends of the Clarksons and stayed with them on several occasions, even for as long as a month. Dorothy complained in her journal that she could not see the lake for the trees. William's sonnet: *'Clarkson! it was an obstinate hill to climb...'* celebrated the passage of the bill which abolished the slave trade in 1807.

> *Loadpot Hill*   2.7

<u>Dunmallet Hill</u> (OS. Dunmallard) [*OB.G. Mallock's Fort or Cursed Fort.*] This conical, steep-sided knoll was reviled in Wordsworth's *Guide to the Lakes* for being disfigured by the symmetrical planting of conifers in avenues, resulting in an artificial rather than in a natural appearance. Deciduous trees predominate today.

The hill fort at 775 feet encloses about one acre, defended by a bank, ditch and traces of a counter scarp bank.

> *Dunmallet*   OFOL 214

Take the B5320.

Barton [*OE. Barley farm*] The Norman church of St Michael, built c. 1150, is sited on a mound with a circular churchyard which is indicative of possible pagan origins. It was the medieval parish church for a vast area bounded by High Street, the Kirkstone Pass and the summit of Helvellyn, with outlying chapels in Boredale and Bannerdale.

The chancel was extended between 1318 and 1536 when the church was in the care of the Augustinian canons of Water Priory near York, resulting in a rare double chancel arch cut into the squat, square tower to improve sight lines and access.

In the 17c, a coach house and stables were built for the use of long distance travellers. The vestry now occupies this site.

The Vicar's stipend in 1730 was £5 per annum, and included such privileges as free accommodation in the parish for a week at a time, a coarse linen shirt and the right to feed his goose on the common.

Richard Wordsworth (1690–1760) was buried in the chancel. He was born in Yorkshire, became Clerk of the Peace and from 1723 to 1738 was in charge of Lord Lowther's estates. During the 1745 Jacobite Rebellion, when he was Receiver General of the County, he took the precaution of hiding a considerable amount of public money in Patterdale until times became more peaceful. His married life was spent at Sockbridge Hall, now Wordsworth House. Richard was William's grandfather.

In the chancel also is a memorial to Ann Myers, the daughter of Richard, the poet's aunt. Her husband was the curate of Barton and headmaster of Barton Grammar School. Their son John, and William his cousin were studying at St John's College, Cambridge when she died in 1787.

The Lancaster Chapel carries the shield of the arms of Lancaster on the capital and at the base of the arch. Three memorial tablets are to John Wordsworth, William's cousin, his first wife Anne and his second wife Elisabeth. John became a sea captain for the East India Company and died of yellow fever.

Externally, above the keystone of the porch, is the Lowther shield of arms. On the east wall, the shield of the Hartsop family of Hartsop Hall has three stags' heads.

Glebe Farm, next to the church, is dated 1637.

<u>Kirkbarrow House</u>, rebuilt at the end of the 16c, retained the cruck framework of its medieval forerunner.

Thril [*ON. Shieling built of fir.*] This is where the Roman Road descends from High Street, en route to the Roman fort of Brocavum at Penrith.

<u>Old Friends' Meeting House</u>, built in 1733, on the corner of Quaker Lane, is now a private residence. The small field in front was the old burial ground where many Quakers were buried in unmarked graves. These include Charles Gough, who died on Helvellyn in 1805, and was commemorated in the poetry of Wordsworth and Scott. Thomas Wilkinson, who advised Lord Lonsdale on landscaping when Lowther Castle was rebuilt, 1806–11, is also buried here.

<u>Wordsworth House</u> (or Sockbridge Hall), at the top of the lane, has DRE 1699 over the door. Wordsworth's grandfather, Richard, lived here and then his father, John. Later it became the property of Wordsworth's brother, Richard, who was visited on several occasions by William and Dorothy.

Yanworth [*OE. Flat or level woodland.*]

<u>Yanworth Hall</u> has a 14c pele tower which was erected by John de Sutton as a protection against marauding Scots. A 15c hall is attached.

<u>The Grotto</u> was the residence of Thomas Wilkinson, (1751–1836) landscape gardner, Quaker poet and friend of the Wordsworths. His underground retreat attracted many visitors.

Return to Pooley Bridge. Continue along the east side of Ullswater. There are no through routes for motorists.

Manchester Corporation's Pumping Station lies underground, sympathetically landscaped with its surroundings.

Thwaitehill Neb shows evidence of a small moraine.

Sharrow Bay [OE. ON Boundary hill] is renowned for its prestigious reputation as the first Country House Hotel.

Martindale

[St Martin's Valley]

Swarthbeck Bridge [ON. Black stream] In the mid-19c, an iron marker was placed on the roadside here to indicate the entrance to Martindale.

Howtown, [OE. ON Settlement near the hill] is built on the delta plain of Fusedale Beck [ON. Valley with cattle shed] which flows down from Wether Hill on High Street.

Howtown is the regular calling place for the passenger boats to and from Glenridding and Pooley Bridge. Colourful buoys in the bay mark off an area for summer water sports.

The Howtown Hotel was originally The Buck Inn. Its history can be traced back more than 200 years.

A plaque was fastened to a crag overlooking the lake, dedicated to Lord Birkett of Ulverston, whose brilliant speech to the House of Lords reprieved Ullswater from being another reservoir for Manchester.

Arthur's Pike	2.3
Bonscale Pike	2.3
Loadpot	2.11

| Steel Knotts | 2.2 |
| Wether Hill | 2.7 |

<u>Martindale Hause</u>. *The road from Howtown rises steeply in zig-zags between Hallin Fell and Steel Knotts.*

<u>St Peter's Church</u>, at the top of the incline, is the 'new' church. It was built of red sandstone in 1880 by Colonel Parkin and his brother, local landowners, to replace the 'old' church of St Martin's which had become derelict. St Peter's was consecrated in 1882 on a day of great storms, which blew off St Martin's roof leaving it all the more desolate.

| Hallin Fell | 2.2 |

The road soon forks to Martindale or Boredale and Sandwick. Follow Howegrain Beck deep into Martindale.

<u>Cotehow</u> was formerly 'The Star Inn' and nearby private residences were once the village Reading Room built 1913, and a Methodist Chapel.

<u>St Martin's ('Old') Church</u> at Christy Bridge, which spans Howegrain Beck, was probably built during the reign of Elizabeth I (1558–1603) on the foundations of an older church which are visible protruding out of the ground on the south side. The porch and flagged floor of the church were probably the work of 1714 improvements and the old minstrels' gallery was removed in 1882. A stone, once used as a font, is thought to have come from a wayside shrine used by the Romans on High Street. The pulpit dates from 1634 and the pews are 17c also. Restoration of the once neglected and damaged church permits occasional services to be held during the summer months and especially on 4 July, St Martin's Day.

The first stipendiary priest was recorded in 1593. The first 'vicar', Richard Birkett, came in 1633. He arrived with two spare shirts and the clothes he was wearing, but by the end of his 67 years service he had saved £1,300. His stipend was £6 13s. 4d. which he supplemented by working as a schoolmaster, or a clerical worker, and even by lending money at 2s. in the pound interest – but never for more than a year. School fees were paid for in eggs and he was entitled to free board and lodging in the home of each scholar. He married at the age of 81 and his bride brought him a dowry of £60. She became a wealthy widow when he died on Christmas Day, 1699, although she soon married again. He left her £1,200. The remaining £100 he left to the parish to provide a better living for his successor. Richard Birkett was buried in the churchyard where the yew tree is said to be more than 700 years old.

Beda Fell	2.3
High Raise	2.6
Steel Knotts	2.2
Wether Hill	2.7

<u>Henhow.</u> Although a few 'statesman' farms remain in Martindale, depopulation is evident in such ruins as this.

The ghost of a poor girl haunts Henhow. She was seduced by a clergyman and given a 'potion' so strong that it killed her and her unborn child.

Near here is the confluence of Rampsgill and Bannerdale Becks which together form Howegrain Beck.

<u>Dale Head Farm,</u> at the end of the surfaced road, was rebuilt in 1666, retaining the stone pillars that once supported a spinning gallery. It was a former hunting lodge of the Hasells of Dalemain.

Angletarn Pikes	2.6	*The Nab*	2.2

<u>The Nab.</u> Uncontrolled public access into this area with the only remaining mountain deer in England (as opposed to woodland deer)

would be highly detrimental to its conservation. Permission to enter this unique deer sanctaury may be obtained by writing to Dalemain Estate Office.

The Nab causes Martindale to be split in two: Ramps Gill and Bannerdale.

Ramps Gill [*ON. Ravine with wild garlic*]. As its name implies, this valley is watered by Rampsgill Beck, which flows down from Rampsgill Head on High Street. It is a privately owned red deer forest. Tracts of relict oakwood are visible below Gowk Hill, [*ON. Cuckoo hill*] and above Rampsgill Beck.

The Bungalow is where the Emperor Kaiser William of Germany stayed before World War I when the Earl of Lonsdale transported him in one of his yellow phaetons.

The lower cottage at one time was the deer stalker's home with stables built by Lord Lonsdale.

Bannerdale [*ON. Valley with holly trees*] is a glaciated valley with steep slopes, extensive scree and hummocky drift at the base between Dale Head Farm and the foot of The Nab.

Bannerdale Beck rises from the craggy heights of Satura, Buck and Heck between The Nab and Beda Fell.

Near Heck Beck are the remains of a prehistoric settlement.

Boredale or Boardale

[ON. Valley with a barn.]

From the road junction on Martindale Hause, take the Boredale turn.

Like Bannerdale, this is a glaciated valley with an abrupt trough end.

Boredale Hause. The metalled road finishes at Boredale Head, but there is access on foot to Boredale Hause beyond.

This is the gathering ground for the waters of Boredale Beck.

At 1,200 feet on the hause, where five tracks meet, is the site of a 13c chapel now little more than a heap of stones. It was once in the medieval parish of Barton and indicates that the highest limits of settlement in the mountains was reached before the 15c.

Beda Fell	*2.3*
Place Fell	*2.3, 4*

Sandwick [ON. *Sandy creek*] Howegrain Beck from Martindale and Boredale Beck from Boredale merge to become Sandwick Beck before it enters Ullswater.

At Sandwick the road from Martindale Hause ends. A return to Pooley Bridge is the only exit for vehicles.

Access to Howtown on foot follows the lakeshore line at the foot of Hallin Fell. Ice shorn rock buttresses are evident at Kailpot Crag (cabbage pot), which has a hole just above the water line.

'The lakeside path from Scalehow Beck, near Sandwick, to Patterdale (in that direction) is the most beautiful and rewarding in Lakeland.' (Place Fell 2.3) The background to this lakeside walk is the rugged Borrowdale Volcanic Series landscape of Sleet Fell, Birk Fell and Place Fell, with magnificent views across Ullswater towards the Helvellyn range.

Beda Fell	*2.3*
Place Fell	*2.6*

Inglewood Forest

[OE. Forest of the Angles.]

Take the A66 (T) Keswick to Penrith road.

Troutbeck. The sites of three Roman camps and a Roman fort are close to the junction of the A66 (T) with the A5091 from Ullswater. A section of the old Keswick to Penrith highway cuts through some of these sites.

Troutbeck village was once served by the Penrith to Keswick railway which has now been dismantled.

Near the old railway station is Troutbeck's sheep market where Herdwicks and Swaledales, famous for their wool and hardiness on high pastures under harsh conditions, are bought and sold.

> *Great Mell Fell*   *1.3*

Turn left at the Sportsman Inn and first right onto the old Roman road to Voreda (Old Penrith) at Castlesteads (OS. 494383).

<u>Stone Carr Enclosures</u> (OS. 419283) This Dark Age (Celtic) settlement, on the edge of a limestone escarpment, is recognisable by its grassy, circular hollows and sunken trackways.

Field clearance and the use of the site for sports and games have together destroyed much of the evidence.

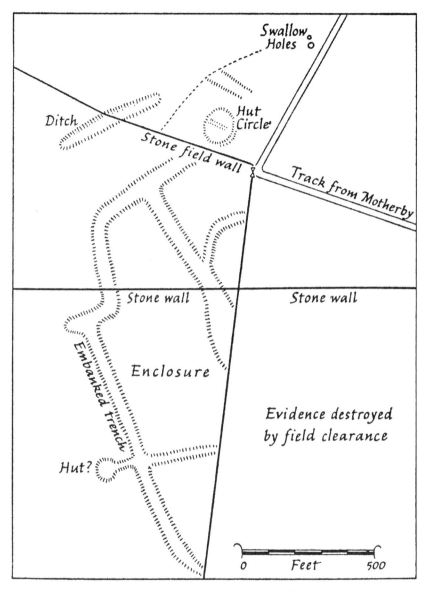

Enclosures at Stone Carr, near Motherby.
Acknowledgement:
The Lake District, R. Millward & A.Robinson. Eyre & Spottiswoode

Greystoke

[OE. Dwelling by the River Creik.]

Greystoke straddles the Roman road where cottages surround the triangular village green with its market cross, granted under royal charter in 1350. Through the village runs the stream, swollen by water from underground springs.

St Andrew's Church, 13c. On Church Road, behind a grille in the wall by the swimming pool, is a medieval sanctuary stone, which marked the boundary of church land, within which fugitives could claim the protection of the church.

The East Window. The lower panels illustrate the legend of St Andrew, who was guided to the city of Wronden where Matthew was imprisoned. Gaps in the medieval glass have been filled with substitute pieces from other windows because of breakages by Cromwell's men. The red devil at the feet of a bishop (far left, middle height) came from another window.

The 19c glass in the upper lights traces the arms of the nobility who patronised the church from the Greystokes through the Grimethorpes and the Dacres to the Howards.

The Greystokes. The earliest Greystoke tomb is that of John, the 10th Baron, who is buried on the north side of the altar.

In the south aisle are the effigies of William, the 14th Baron and John, his grandson, the 16th Baron.

The Chantries. William reacted to the Black Death in 1348, when a third of the population perished, including half the English clergy, by adding six chantries to the church, three on each side, and by founding a college to train priests. The chantries remained until the Reformation, when anti-Catholic pressure caused the removal of the oak screens that divided them leaving the impression of a very wide nave. Surviving piscinas mark the sites of some of the chantries.

The College, now Rectory Farm, consisted in the 14c of six chantry priests to sing masses and eight others under the leadership of a Provost or Master. The eight parish clergy undertook missions over a very extensive area. There may also have been a Master of Grammar to teach the boys of the parish. From such collegiate churches Eton, Winchester and the older colleges of Oxford and Cambridge originated. The College closed when chantries were abolished at the Reformation.

Responsibilities for the upkeep of the chancel was shared between the Barons and the Provosts. The Barons looked after the north side, where the stone corbels are helmeted, while the gentler features of the Provosts support the roof beams on the south wall.

The Modern College opened in 1958 to prepare men with little academic background for a full course of training at a theological college. The men lodged in the village and worked between studies to support themselves. About 90 were finally ordained before the college closed in 1979 because of a lack of applicants.

The Howards [*Hogward = pig farmer*] On the north side of the chancel, the Bestiary window, showing a variety of birds and beasts grouped around the Holy Trinity, is the oldest complete window in the church. Another window traces the descent of the Howards.

In the 16c, the male line of the Greystokes died out and the Duke of Norfolk took over the guardianship of the heiresses. He arranged that one should marry his son, thus enlarging the family fortunes of the Duke.

Charles, the 11th Duke of Norfolk, whose arms appear on the hatchment on the north aisle wall, succeeded in 1786. He enlarged Greystoke Park and whimsically built castellated farmhouses named after the battles of the American War of Independence (1775–83): Fort Putnam (battlements and turrets) and Bunkers Hill (six-sided tower). In response to a tenant farmer who declared that God's Word should be heard in the great outdoors, thus making churches unnecessary, the Duke built Spire House (polygonal with a spire). This same Duke was also responsible for designing Arundel Castle and its library in West Sussex.

Medieval relics include the rood beam bridging the chancel arch adorned with a floral design representing the five wounds of Christ; the oak choir stalls with carved misericords; the late 14c oak table from the college refectory; and the 15c fireplace and glazed squint in the vestry.

Modern sculptures include the Madonna and Child in the Lady Chapel, carved by a World War II German prisoner at the castle; and the figure of Christ crucified, the work of Josephine da Vasconcellos.

A plague stone, hollowed out at the top for cleansing coins in vinegar to avoid the risk of transmitting disease at a time of plague, is situated by the footpath 100 yards north of the church.

The racing stables of the late Sir Gordon Richards are just outside the village.

Greystoke Castle. The Viking leader, Lyulph, from whom Ulph's, or Ulls-water takes its name, is credited with being the first to build a fortress here.

The castle has a 14c pele tower to which an Elizabethan style Victorian house has been attached. Since Thomas Howard acquired the castle in the reign of Queen Elizabeth (1558–1603) it has survived two disastrous fires. During the Civil War (1642–49), the Parliamentarians set alight this Royalist stronghold. In the 19c, it caught fire during extensive work by the architect Salvin.

The castle remains a Howard property under the influence of the Duke of Norfolk, although Edward Rice Burrows, in his novel, made *Tarzan* the heir to Greystoke Castle and estates.

Inglewood Forest

[OE. Forest of and Angles.]

On a plateau of carboniferous limestone, covered by heavy boulder clay, oak woodland once flourished. Deer, wildboar and hawks provided the sport. By the reign of Henry II (1154–89), this had become the largest Royal Forest hunting ground in England, extending 40 miles from the River Eden to the Skiddaw massif, and 25 miles from Carlisle to Penrith.

The privilege to hunt was reserved exclusively for the king. Restrictive forest laws were imposed under threat of severe penalties. No forest land could be cultivated. The felling of trees, or the building of huts or shelters, was forbidden. Anyone carrying a bow and arrows, or with a dog, was excluded.

The 12c settlers followed in the wake of the army of William II, the Conqueror's son. According to *The Anglo-Saxon Chronicle*, William '*marched north to Carlisle with a large army, and re-established the fortress, and built the castle, and drove out Dolfin who had previously ruled the land there, and garrisoned the castle with his men, and afterwards returned to the south, and sent thither very many peasants with their wives and stock to dwell their to till the ground.*'

These early settlements can be identified by place names, where the Norman French personal name is attached to the suffix 'by', meaning '*settlement*'. Johnby is the settlement of John, Lamonby of Lambert, and Ellonby of Alein (Breton). Another group settled around Carlisle, colonising the frontier approach from England to Scotland. Upperby is Hubert's settlement, Harraby is Henry's, Etterby is Etard's and Aglionby (Agyllum's).

The 14c was troubled by disputes and border conflicts between England and Scotland. Grants of land for farms resulted in farmers' claims overtaking those of huntsmen. The piecemeal clearance of the forest is indicated by the widespread farms today.

The 18c. Gone now are the systems of medieval use when farmers shared intermixed strips of land. The landscape today retains the 18c grid of long straight enclosure roads, formal rectangular fields, neat hedgerows planted with trees, neatly grown spinneys, isolated and widely spaced Georgian farmhouses, the outcome of enclosing common land and apportioning it among the farming community.

Hutton-in-the-Forest. Legend would have us believe that this historic house was the site of the Green Knight's Castle in the Arthurian tale of *Sir Gawain and the Green Knight*.

It is one of three manor houses in the Royal Forest of Inglewood and was once held by the chief forester.

The Hutton family built the 14c pele tower. Since 1605, the house has belonged to the present owners' family, Lord and Lady Inglewood, and the building, with its furnishings, reflects the different tastes and styles of this one family through four centuries.

In the 17c, the Fletchers, wealthy merchants from Cockermouth became the owners and transformed the fortress into a mansion with a baroque facade. The panelling in the gallery dates from the 1630s and came from Torpenhow church. The Hall, built in the 1680s, is dominated by the Cupid Staircase which leads to the 18c rooms above. The 19c interiors, notably the Drawing Room and the Library, span the reign of Queen Victoria (1837–1901). The 19c owner acquired wallpapers and fabrics personally designed for him by his friend

William Morris. The castellated appearance was added at this time.

On display is the only contemporary portrait of John Peel.

Topiary terraces, originally laid out in the 17c, a walled garden built in the 1730s, and fine specimen trees in the woodland form part of the attractive setting.

There are limited times of opening.

<u>St James' Church</u> is ¼-mile north of Hutton-in-the-Forest.

The church was completely rebuilt in 1714 and greatly altered in 1868 when the architect, Anthony Salvin, transformed the building from its Georgian appearance to the Victorian Gothic seen today.

The oldest feature, dating from c. AD 1000, is a section of the shaft of a Viking cross built into the outside north wall of the nave.

Thomas de Hoton, Lord of the Manor of Hutton-in-the-Forest, built a chantry chapel in 1358 on the south side of the church. A chantry normally contained the founder's tomb, but a medieval tombstone in the churchyard (*north side of the path to the west door*) bears the coat of arms of the de Hoton family. The carving of a horn on the tombstone was indicative of a forester or a ranger. Chantries in England were suppressed in 1549 when an Act of Uniformity prohibited the Catholic mass and ordered the removal of statues of saints and icons from churches. There is no way of confirming whether or not the churchyard tombstone is Thomas de Hoton's.

Penrith

Ec. W. Mkt. T.S. [OB. Penrhudd = the red hill.]

Since earliest times, Penrith has been a market town bridging the River Eamont.

It stands at the crossroads of the main westerly route from England to Scotland and of the trans-Pennine route from Cumbria to Yorkshire.

In the 9c and 10c, Penrith was the capital of the old kingdom of Cumbria, then part of Scotland.

The town was part of Scotland when Edward I captured it in 1295. There followed many years of border disputes, skirmishes and raids. Penrith's role as a central refuge can be imagined by the town's layout of small squares and yards, where inhabitants and livestock could be sheltered, defended by a complexity of narrow streets, passages and alleyways.

The worst devastation came in 1347 when 'Black Douglas' descended on the town. He laid the town to waste and took away all able-bodied survivors as prisoners.

Resulting from this and from other raids by the Scots, permission to erect a castle was obtained. The town was fortified and, although the town gates have been demolished, their names have remained: Castlegate, Middlegate, Stricklandgate, Sandgate, Friargate and Burrowgate.

Penrith Castle

The ruins were bought in 1910 by Penrith Council from the Lancaster and Carlisle Railway Co.

In 1399, after repeated attacks on the town by the Scots, William Strickland, Rector of Horncastle, who later became Bishop of Carlisle, obtained a licence to extend an existing pele tower into a castle keep — which still stands today.

The castle was later enlarged by Richard Neville, Earl of Warwick, known as 'the Kingmaker'. It was used by his son-in-law Richard, Duke of Gloucester before he became Richard II in 1483 only to be killed two years later at the Battle of Bosworth Field. As Duke of Gloucester, he was Lord of the Western Marches and the Governor of Carlisle Castle. During this period, a magnificent banqueting hall was added.

By 1550, the castle was in ruins and the sandstone was being plundered as building material. In 1648, the Cromwellian General Lambert demolished the castle still further.

The castle grounds have been neatly landscaped into gardens and recreation areas.

Robinson's School, Middlegate.

The school was founded in 1670 by a local man, William Robinson, who made his fortune selling groceries in London. The purpose of the school was *'for the educating and bringing up of poore Gerles ... to Read and Seamstry works or such other learning fitt for that sex.'* The poorest scholars were stigmatised by having to wear the letters PS, which allowed them to beg in the streets.

The school closed in 1970 and the building now contains Eden Council's Tourist Information Office and local history exhibition.

Thacka Beck, behind the courtyard, flows under much of the old town. It was cut in 1382 as a clean water supply from the River

430

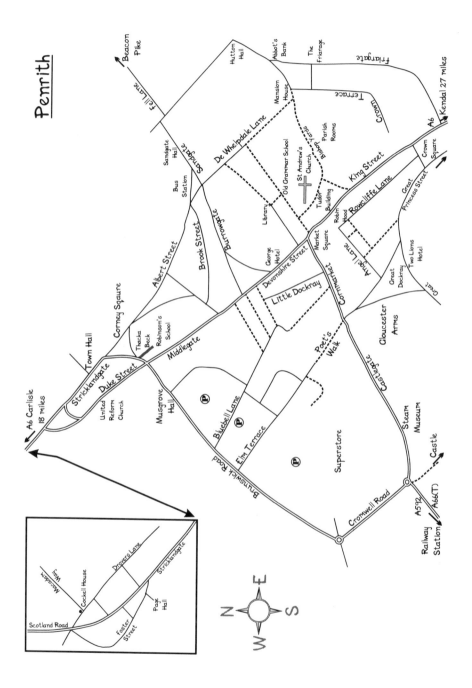

Penrith

Pettril in the north to the River Eamont in the south, a distance of four miles.

Musgrave Hall was once the town house of the Musgraves of Edenhall, benefactors of Penrith. Their family coat of arms is on the building. In the 1920s, the hall belonged to Countess Ossalinsky, whose family sold Thirlmere lake to Manchester Corporation for a water supply.

The United Reform Church, in Duke Street, was attended by Mary Wilson, wife of Harold Wilson, the former Prime Minister. Her family had long been associated with Penrith.

Page Hall, in Foster Street, off Stricklandgate, was the home for ten years of Samuel Plimsoll (1824–98), who later became a social reformer, Member of Parliament and deviser of the 1875 Merchant Shipping Act. This required every ship owner to paint a circle with a horizontal line through it on all ships to indicate the maximum depth to which the vessel could be loaded. This became known as the Plimsoll Line.

Cockell House, at the corner of Macadam Way, off Drovers Lane, was the home for a while of John McAdam (1756–1836). Born at Ayr, he travelled to New York to make his fortune, but returned to Scotland to devise new ways of constructing roads. After great success in Bristol, he was awarded a government contract in 1827 to improve the roads in Britain.

The Town Hall, in Stricklandgate, was created in 1905 by joining together two Adam-style houses constructed in 1791. One of the houses was owned by William Wordsworth's cousin, John, (d. 1819).

Sandgate is in the oldest part of town dating back to the 13c. In this open space bull terriers were once used for bear baiting. Inns like the Druid's Arms and the Grey Goat have survived from that era.

Sandgate Hall, now a row of three cottages, was once the town house of the Fletcher family of Hutton-in-the-Forest.

In 1745, the Duke of Richmond stayed here whilst pursuing Bonnie Prince Charlie back into Scotland.

<u>Hutton Hall</u>, in Benson Row, is notable for its pele tower.

<u>Friargate</u> is named after the Augustinian Friary established here in 1291. The end came in 1536 when the friars joined the rebellion against Henry VIII's demand for an Oath of Supremacy. Three years later, the King avenged himself on the rebels. The friars fled and no trace of the Friary remains.

<u>Abbot's Bank</u> stands on the site of the Abbot's House. Whilst digging the foundations in 1820, part of the Friary was revealed.

<u>The Friarage</u> was built on the site of the Friary in 1717.

<u>De Whelpdale</u> Lane is named after John de Whelpdale.

<u>The Mansion House</u> was built in Georgian style in 1750 for the Whelpdale family. Since 1919, it has been the headquarters of Eden District Council.

The <u>Queen Elizabeth Grammar School</u>, of which John de Whelpdale was an original governor, was founded by Royal Charter in 1564. The present building replaced the original in 1857, as recorded in Latin above the door. In 1915, the school was moved to a new building in Ullswater Road.

<u>Bishop Yards</u>. The crescent appears to be aligned along the ditch and rampart of ancient earthworks, perhaps the 10c site of the capital of Cumbria, Owen Caesarius's kingdom.

Part of the <u>Tudor Building</u> is thought to have been Dame Anne Birkett's School, where William and Dorothy Wordsworth and local tobacconist's daughter, Mary Hutchinson (27 years later to be William's wife) attended as young children.

<u>The Parish Rooms</u> stand on the site of a cock-fighting pit.

<u>Parish Church of St Andrew</u>. The sandstone church dates from 1133, but was rebuilt c. 1720, retaining its massive Norman tower, built by the Nevilles, whose arms, the bear and ragged staff, are visible on the north-west corner.

There are royal portraits in the stained glass of the church windows. King Richard II (1377–1399), who granted the town to the Nevilles as Lords of the Manor, displays his crown and sceptre. Richard, Duke of York, is shown. He married Cecily Neville, the Rose of Raby, who was the mother of two Plantagenet kings: Edward IV (1461–70)(1471–83) and his brother Richard III (1483–85). She lived through the Wars of the Roses (1455–1485) amidst the slaughtering of kings, princes and half the noble families in the north. When widowed, she became a nun – the Abbess of Barking.

A wall plaque commemorates the 2,260 people who perished in the plague of 1597.

The two brass chandeliers in the nave were bought with the gift of fifty guineas donated by the Duke of Portland in gratitude to the people of Penrith for their support against the 1745 Jacobite Rebellion.

<u>The Giant's Thumb,</u> in the churchyard, consists of two holes at the top of a stone column which has pre-Norman carvings. It is considered to be the remains of a Saxon cross.

<u>The Giant's Grave</u> was thought at one time to contain the bones of Owen Caesarius, King of Cumbria, AD 920–937.

Another belief was that Sir Lancelot du Lac killed the giant Torquin whose corpse was buried here.

In fact, the grave is an arrangement of four 10c Norse hog's back tombstones flanked by two 11 foot tall crosses.

<u>Burrowgate</u>, like Sandgate, is in the oldest part of the town. It was

formerly the site of the horse market. The rows of open butchers' shops which once stood here were known as the 'Shambles'.

The Dog and Duck is one of the 57 public houses recorded in 1829 for a population of 5,383.

The Co-operative Society has become a vast store where once it was a line of small shops – grocers, bakers, butchers and chemists.

Arnison's store, alongside 'the Narrows' in Devonshire Street, stands on the site of the former Moot Hall which consisted of five shops and a courtroom with prison cells underneath.

A wall plaque records that William Wordsworth's grandparents, William and Ann Cookson, lived in a building on this site.

It was here that tragedy struck the Wordsworth family. William Wordsworth's mother, Ann, caught a chill during a visit to London. Whilst travelling home early to Cockermouth her condition deteriorated. She was able to reach her parents' house here in Penrith, but died soon after. An entry in Penrith's Parish Register for 1778 reads, '*March 11th Mrs Wordsworth, wife of John Wordsworth Esq. of Cockermouth, aged 30. Buried.*' Her burial place is unknown. William was eight years old at the time. A year later he was separated from his brothers and sister Dorothy when he was sent to school at Hawkshead, boarding out with Mrs Anne Tyson.

Five years later, tragedy struck the Wordsworth children again. Their father died in Cockermouth, aged 42. William was able to continue his schooling at Hawkshead, cared for by Mrs Tyson, but his sister Dorothy came to live in Penrith with an uncle.

The George Hotel was owned by the Duke of Devonshire after whom the street is named.

In 1745, Bonnie Prince Charlie made this his first headquarters in England on his march south to claim the throne.

<u>The Market Arcade,</u> approached through an archway, was built in 1860 and extended in 1866 for public meetings.

<u>The Musgrave Monument</u> (T'Clock). The Musgraves were benefactors of the town and erected this monument in memory of their eldest son, Philip, who died tragically in Spain, aged 26.

During the 18c, a Market Cross stood on this site. It was an open-sided shelter where butter and eggs were sold and where tradespeople ('hirelings') offered themselves for employment.

<u>The Robin Hood Inn,</u> in King Street, is where William and Dorothy Wordsworth experienced another sorrowful event. To help the recovery from consumption of their friend Raisley Calvert by seeking a more favourable climate, they set off together from Keswick for Lisbon. Sadly they only reached the Robin Hood Inn where young Raisley died. A plaque records the visits of the Wordsworths in 1794 and 1795.

<u>Mitre House</u> has a 1669 datestone and a British Legion wall plaque which records that Trooper William Pearson (1828–1903) lived here and survived the Charge of the Light Brigade in 1854.

<u>Lloyds Bank</u> occupies the site of the cottage where an unsuspecting carrier of the plague lodged in 1597 thus bringing devastation to the population of Penrith.

<u>A Plague Stone</u> stands in Bridge Lane, in the grounds of Greengarth Old Peoples Home.

In the 16c, appalling living conditions and primitive means of sanitation were conducive to the spread of the plague. Penrith suffered terribly. Even wealthy families like the De Whelpdales and Musgraves were not spared.

The stone is font-shaped and was used to wash money in vinegar on market days when farmers, fearful of entering the town during the plague, sold their produce on the outskirts.

<u>Angel Square</u> is a pedestrian area of attractive Victorian-style shop buildings painted in pastel colours.

<u>Angel Lane</u>. The inscription above the double door of one shop states that the building was acquired in 1722 by a merchant, Robert Miers and his wife, then rebuilt in 1763 by WM, possibly their son.

<u>Great Dockray</u>. This central open space was one in which inhabitants and livestock could take refuge in times of attack, defended by the narrow approach roads.

The Tuesday market originated in 1223 when Henry III granted the Market Charter. During the 18c, the town's Cattle Market was held here also.

<u>The Board and Elbow Inn</u> stands on the corner.

<u>The Two Lions Hotel</u>, dated 1585, was formerly the town house of Gerald Lowther and has a beautiful plaster ceiling in the bar.

<u>The Gloucester Arms</u> was formerly Dockray Hall owned by the Docura family who gave their name to the house and to the open space in front.

The arms of Richard, Duke of Gloucester, later Richard III, hang over the entrance. He stayed at what is now the Gloucester Arms in 1471 while waiting for Penrith Castle to be made habitable for him. By marrying the daughter of Richard Neville, Earl of Warwick, the 'Kingmaker', he acquired the lordship and castle of Penrith which the Nevilles had held for over four hundred years.

Features include a 15c panelled room, a plaster ceiling with the Duke's arms and a four-poster bed dated 1477, its panels partly used in a cocktail bar.

The Steam Museum, in Castlegate, was opened in 1980 in the Castle Foundry. On display are agricultural engineering works, whose origins date back to the days of Jonathan Stalker in 1851. The foundry machine shop, the blacksmith's shop, steam engines, including Jennings Foden delivery wagon (1927, restored) and a three-roomed worker's cottage can be seen.

Poet's Walk is a pedestrian way lined with craft shops.

Cornmarket. Farmers once sold their grain from the front of an inn whilst stabling their horses at the rear.

Oats were sold between the Fish Hotel (now Poet's Walk) and the White Hart (now a florists); rye in front of the Black Bull (now a TV shop); wheat at The Black Lion (datestone 1624) and barley in front of The Griffin.

The Market Cross, similar to the one which stood where the Musgrave clock Memorial is now, was built in 1983.

Little Dockray. Once there were eight inns along this 80-yard length of lane.

Middlegate used to be inhabited by weavers, tailors and tanners. Near Woolworths is the entrance to William's Yard where the lintel is marked with a pair of shears and the date 1697.

Around Penrith

Ascend Fell Lane.

Beacon Hill at 931 feet is one of the series of sandstone hills that extend eastwards towards the Pennines. It is the hill referred to in the Celtic meaning of 'Penrith'.

The Lodge, now a private residence, was where visitors used to sign a visitors' book on entering the broad drive, which no longer exists, into the Lowther Estate plantation.

A beacon was recorded here in 1468. The present sandstone Pike dates from 1719 when it was built to enable a warning beacon fire to be lit in times of trouble. It was lit in 1745 when 'Bonnie Prince Charlie' marched on Penrith. It was restored in 1780 to commemorate the town's resistance against the Jacobite Rebellion. Sir Walter Scott claimed to have seen the beacon lit during the Napoleonic Wars. More recent beacon fires have commemorated special events. The view from the hill top reveals what a splendid look-out point this is.

Wordsworth's recollections of Beacon Hill appear in '*The Prelude. Books VI and XII*'.

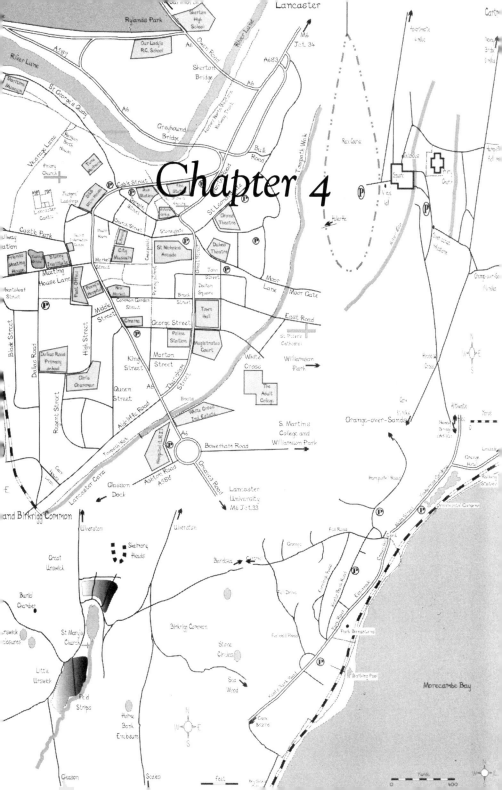

Chapter 4

Lancaster

[OE. Roman 'caester' = walled fortress; by the Lune.]

From the railway station, turn left up the footpath, then right.

<u>Lancaster Castle</u> stands on the hill top site of a Roman fort, established in AD79 by Agricola to guard the lowest crossing of the River Lune.

In Norman times, Roger of Poitou was awarded vast estates in return for helping William Rufus to capture Carlisle and thus to extend the northern limits of the kingdom. The responsibility of defending this area against attacks by the Scots prompted Roger of Poitou to build a motte and bailey castle on the Roman site c. 1093. At that time, the main west route to Scotland crossed the sands of Morecambe Bay visible from the castle.

Walk anti-clockwise round the castle where trees mark the remains of the castle ditch.

John O' Gaunt's Gatehouse carries his statue above the entrance (Shakespeare's *'time-honoured Lancaster'*) and the arms of his son, Henry IV, who built the gatehouse c. 1400. Since 1399, when Henry IV seized the throne from Richard II, his great estates in the Duchy of Lancaster have belonged to the Crown. *'The Queen, Duke of Lancaster'* is the Loyal Toast.

The Governor's House and the high walls belong to the era when the castle was used as one of H.M's Prisons.

The Well or Witches' Tower contains two of the castle's wells and

Lancaster

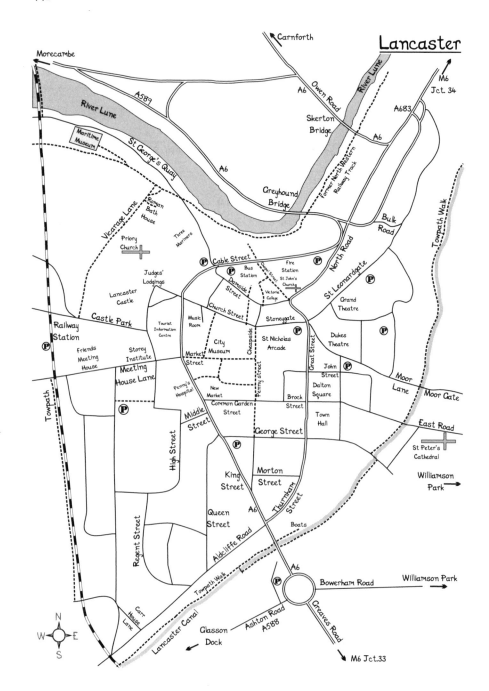

the dungeons where the Pendle Witches were said to have been imprisoned before their trial in 1612.

The massive quadrangular Keep or Lungess Tower of 1102 was strengthened in 1586 when invasion by the Spanish Armada threatened.

During the Civil War in 1643, Parliamentary troops garrisoned the castle and a month later the Royalists plundered the town. In 1651, Charles II was proclaimed King here before marching to his defeat by Oliver Cromwell at Worcester.

In 1715, James Edward Stuart, the 'Old Pretender' was proclaimed James III by the Scottish Jacobites at the market cross. Thirty years later, in 1745, his son Charles Edward, the 'Young Pretender', advanced and retreated through Lancaster until he was finally defeated at Culloden Moor.

From Easter to September, guided tours enable visitors to see Thomas Harrison's beautifully vaulted 18c Shire Hall with its magnificent display of heraldic shields dating from the 12c.

Visited also are the Crown Court and the Grand Jury Room furnished by Gillow of Lancaster. County Assizes, established here from 1166, were held three times a year until 1972. The prison cells are shown, the Drop Room where condemned criminals were prepared for the gallows, and the Execution Yard where public hangings took place between 1800 and 1865 until stopped by an Act of Parliament in 1868.

The Priory Church of St Mary shares Castle Hill with the Castle.

The Priory of Benedictine monks was founded by Roger de Poitou in 1094. Wars with France in 1414 severed links with its mother church, the Abbey of St Martin of Sées in Normandy, and Henry V handed the Priory to the nuns of the Convent of Syon and Isleworth, Middlesex, in 1424.

When the Priory's monastic function ceased in 1430, it became the

Parish Church of Lancaster, the focal point of a very extensive parish.

The present building dates mainly from the late 14c and early 15c, with later additions such as the tower (1754), the vestry (1827) and the Memorial Chapel of the King's Own Royal Regiment (1903). Many gravestones relate to Lancaster's maritime past.

The church treasures include the fourteen wooden choir stalls, misericords and canopies, each carved differently c. 1345. Modern needlework in the cushions and tapestry backs depicts local scenes, such as crossing Lancaster Sands at low tide. There are fragments of Anglo-Saxon crosses, a Crusader's casket, brass Abyssinian Coptic Crosses and The King's Own Regimental Chapel.

A Refectory and shop serve visitors.

Views over the city from this high point extend to the five arch, 600 feet aqueduct, built by John Rennie and Alexander Stevens, carrying the Lancaster Canal across the River Lune.

Descend Vicarage Lane footpath.

<u>Roman Bath Houses</u>. Excavations in 1974 revealed these remains which were part of an inn for official travellers situated outside the Roman fort.

Turn left along the old North Western railway track, now a cycleway.

<u>St George's Quay</u> was constructed on the tidal River Lune between 1750 and 1755 to handle the great influx of trade. Most of the imported goods came from the West Indies: sugar, rum, cotton, tobacco and mahogany as ballast.

To serve the growing port, a <u>Custom House</u> with offices of the Port Commission opened in 1764, designed by Richard Gillow of furniture fame.

Since 1985, the Custom House and part of the adjoining warehouse have become the <u>Maritime Museum</u>. Displays illustrate the history of the Port of Lancaster, the Lancaster Canal, local fishing methods and the Morecambe Bay Gas Field.

There is a cafeteria and a shop.

Fronting the river, the 18c warehouses, now converted into residences, still feature the loading doors with a gantry above.

The Easter Maritime Festival is a celebration of The Golden Age of maritime trade.

The port's decline came as a consequence of the Napoleonic Wars and the growth of Liverpool's docks capable of handling larger ships. Coastal trade diminished with the development of the railways and the end came with the construction of docks at Preston (1892) and Heysham (1904).

Upstream from the quay the river is spanned by Greyhound Bridge and by Skerton Bridge designed by Thomas Harrison and opened in 1788 to replace the medieval bridge.

Pass under the bridge on Damside Street.

<u>The Three Mariners</u> is Lancaster's oldest inn and claims to be the second oldest in Britain with a history of smugglers, press gangs and highwaymen. The river used to flow past the front door.

Divert to the corner of Chapel Street and North Road.

<u>St John's Church</u> dates originally from 1754–55 with later additions of both the tower and the spire by Thomas Harrison. The church, no longer in regular use, is cared for by the Redundant Churches Fund. It is occasionally opened for special events such as the summer series of lunchtime music recitals.

Church Street.

<u>The Conservative Club</u> is a fine Georgian house, originally built c. 1740 for the Dukes of Hamilton who lived at Ashton Hall, just south of Lancaster. The conical snuffer on the wrought-iron railings was used to extinguish burning torches.

Adjoining is the town house built for the Wilson family of Dallam Tower in 1775.

Castle Hill.

<u>The Judges' Lodging House</u> was built in 1662 by the Cole family on the site of the residence of Thomas Covell who was Governor of the Castle at the time of the trial of the Pendle Witches (1612). During the early 19c, the property was purchased to provide accommodation for visiting judges at the Lancaster Assizes, an arrangement that ceased in 1975.

As a museum, the dining room, billiard room, kitchen and bedroom are arranged to display examples of furniture made by Gillow, Lancaster's famous firm of cabinet makers.

On the top floor, the <u>Museum of Childhood</u> includes the Barry Elder Doll Collection.

The cross outside the house commemorates Thomas Covell.

<u>The Cottage Museum,</u> part of a larger house (1739) and divided in two (c. 1820), is furnished as an artisan's house about the time of William IV (1830–37).

<u>The Tourist Information Centre</u> was formerly a wine warehouse.

<u>Robert Gillow's first furniture workshop</u> was at No. 85. He moved from Great Singleton to Lancaster to take advantage of the mahogany timber which was shipped to Lancaster's port as ballast. By the early 19c the reputation of the Gillow family was firmly established.

<u>The Storey Institute</u>, donated by Sir Thomas Storey, manufacturer of oilcloth and linoleum, was built on the site of the old Mechanics Institute. It contained a Free Public Library, a Technical School and a School of Art. Exhibitions and lectures are held.

<u>Castle Park.</u>

<u>A former Dispensary</u> facing the castle dates from 1785. It provided free medical help for poor people.

<u>Castle Park House</u> bears a 1720 datestone.

<u>The Quaker School</u> is named after George Fox, the founder of the Quaker Movement. He preached here in 1652 and was twice imprisoned in the castle for his religious beliefs.

<u>King Street.</u>

<u>Penny's Hospital.</u> In accordance with the will of Alderman William Penny, tiny cottages, situated around a central courtyard with a chapel at one end, were built in 1720 to provide accommodation for twelve poor men.

<u>Middle Street and High Street.</u>

This was another prime residential area during Georgian times. The Georgian buildings reflect the great age of prosperity when trade, especially with the West Indies, enriched the merchants of Lancaster.

John Rawlinson, a lawyer, had a particularly impressive house built in the High Street in the prosperous late 18c.

Many of the 18c buildings provide the background for Lancaster's Georgian Legacy Festival when costumed re-enactments of life in Georgian times take place.

Common Garden Street and Brock Street.

<u>Dalton Square</u> was originally the site of a Dominican Friary, established c. 1260. Following the Dissolution of the Monasteries, the

land was bought by the Dalton family of Thurnham Hall.

Palatine Hall, on the north side, was built as Lancaster's first Roman Catholic Church in 1798.

The Statue of Queen Victoria was a gift from Lord Ashton. On the sides of the plinth, notable personalities of the day are depicted: Benjamin Franklin, Isaac Pitman, General Gordon, Rowland Hill, Florence Nightingale, Lord Macaulay, Charles Dickens and many more.

The Town Hall, designed by E. W. Mountford, was another gift from Lord Ashton, who opened the building in 1909. The pediment features a statue of Edward VII flanked by the figures of Loyalty and Justice.

Nelson Street.

The Lancaster Canal threads through the city providing interesting walks along the tow path, past homes, warehouses, converted cotton textile mills and waterside inns.

Punts are for hire at Penny Street Wharf and a choice of craft offer cruises.

The canal brought a reduction in the cost of transporting coal to Lancaster's mills and factories. Locks were avoided by following contours and a fast packet boat service, at speeds up to 10 m.p.h., was provided to Kendal and Preston.

East Road.

St Peter's Roman Catholic Cathedral, with its impressive 240 ft spire, was designed by E.G. Paley of Lancaster and built in 1859.

Notable features include the marble altar designed by G. Gilbert Scott, the triptych inspired by the designs of Albert Dürer and the stained glass of the English Martyrs' Window, the Rose Window and the West Window.

Continue one mile east of the city.

Williamson Park was a gift of 38 acres from James Williamson, oilcloth and linoleum manufacturer. He provided employment for local cotton mill workers during the cotton famine caused by the American Civil War (1861–65) by having the park constructed on the site of a disused quarry from which the stone had been removed for most of Lancaster's historic buildings.

During the summer months, open air events and theatrical performances take place.

The Ashton Memorial is a domed Baroque Folly described by Pevsner as *'the grandest monument in England.'* It was commissioned by the son of James Williamson, Lord Ashton, as a tribute to his late wife, designed by John Belcher in 1904 and built of white Portland stone (1907–09). The Memorial dominates Lancaster's skyline as it rises 220 feet above its hill top setting. From its galleries there are spectacular views of the Lake District, Morecambe Bay and the Isle of Man.

It is used for exhibitions and concerts.

Adjacent to the Folly is the Edwardian Palm House, home of The Tropical Butterfly House, a Mini-Beast Centre and a Foreign Bird Enclosure.

The Pavilion Café overlooks the Conservation Garden and there is a gift shop.

Return to the city along Moor Gate and Moor Lane.

The Duke's Playhouse was converted into a theatre from a former Georgian church.

The Grand Theatre, round the corner in St Leonardgate, claims to have been in continuous use for 200 years. Its Edwardian interior is supposedly haunted by the ghost of the actress, Sarah Siddons.

Pedestrianised City Centre

Market Street.

The ancient toll booth in the Market Square was replaced in 1668 by a Town Hall and this, in turn by the Georgian Sessions House, known also as the Old Town Hall, built 1781–83 to the design of Major Jarret and James Harrison.

The City Museum has occupied the building since 1923, illustrating the archaeology and social history of Lancaster.

The King's Own Royal Regiment, raised in 1680 and based in Lancaster from 1880, has pictures, documents and medals in the museum relating to three centuries of history.

Lancaster was granted its first charter when it became a borough in 1193 and gained the right to hold a weekly market on Saturdays. This paved the way for Lancaster's commercial prosperity.

Only since 1937 has Lancaster been a city, granted by royal charter on the morning of George VI's coronation.

The Music Room, possibly a corruption of 'Muses Room', built c. 1730, served as a pavilion in Oliver Marton's garden which has now been built over. In the 19c it became part of a stained glass factory. The Landmark Trust rescued it from collapse in 1974 by buying the adjacent buildings on all four sides, including a toy warehouse, and demolishing them to give the builders access.

The exceptional Baroque plaster work in the restored music room depicts the muses, with Apollo over the fireplace.

Meeting House Lane.

The Friends' Meeting House, dated 1707, was later extended. Quakers have worshipped on this site since 1677.

Return to the Railway Station.

Kent Estuary

Take the A 591 south from Kendal.

<u>Sizergh Castle</u> NT. [*ON. Sigrid's shieling.*] The Strickland family has owned this property since 1239. The lands were inherited from Gervase Deincourt to whom they had been granted by Henry II.

Members of the Strickland family have helped to shape English history, fighting at Hastings and during the Wars of the Roses, as well as at Agincourt and Edge Hill. For strongly supporting the Stuarts, most of their wealth was confiscated after 1688. One of the Stricklands, Joan, married Robert de Wessington, an ancestor of George Washington.

The oldest part of the house is the pele tower, nearly 60 feet high with walls 9 feet thick at the base, built in 1340. A Great Hall was attached in 1450, followed by Elizabethan and Jacobean additions containing kitchens and workshops to fill the sides of a courtyard.

The interior of the house has hardly changed since the 16c. The Elizabethan rooms include some fine Tudor panelling, overmantels and furniture, although some of the best panelling was sold to the Victoria and Albert Museum in the 19c. There is a large collection of Stuart portraits and relics and a two-handed sword which is as old as the pele tower. There is tradition that Catherine Parr, a cousin of the Stricklands, slept in one bedroom in which are examples of her embroidery.

The terraced gardens above the ornamental lake were added in the

18c and a limestone rock garden was created in the 1920s.

In 1950, the house was given to the National Trust with the family continuing to occupy the north wing.

Continue south to the A6.

<u>Levens Hall</u>. [*ON. Leofa's, or leafy headland.*] The 13c, five-storeyed pele tower, which guarded the ford across the River Kent, was possibly built by Matthew de Redman, who was responsible for mustering local fighting men whenever they were needed to resist the Scots. He took the family name from their Yealand Redmayne estates. The family shield had three cushions which were a reminder of the occasion when an ancestor had almost missed combat because he overslept due to the comfort of his bed.

The pele tower was incorporated into an Elizabethan mansion in 1586. In 1652, Alan Bellingham acquired the property and installed magnificent oak panelling and fine plaster ceilings. Other features include leather wall coverings and the earliest English patchwork. The family fortune came from the Dissolution of the Monasteries. But '*Levens was lost by the ace of hearts*' when it came to paying off gambling debts. A cousin, Colonel James Graham, bought the estate in 1688. He was responsible for the superb Charles II walnut dining chairs and for the topiary garden. The present owners are the Bagot family.

The house is said to be haunted. Tradition tells of a gypsy woman who was denied refreshment at the Hall and put a curse on the family to the effect that no male heir would be born to Levens Hall until the River Kent ceased to flow and a white fawn appeared in the Park. The curse ran true for many generations but was fulfilled in 1895 when the River Kent froze solid and a pale coloured fawn appeared in the Park. In the following year, Alan Desmond Bagot was born. The gypsy lady in grey haunts the house.

The topiary garden was devised in 1692 by Guillaume Beaumont, who came to England after training under Le Notre at Versailles and had designed Hampton Court Gardens for James II. The Umbrella tree is about 900 years old.

The old brewhouse now contains working models of static steam engines, each with an intriguing history. One engine was built to power the balloon used to relieve the siege of Paris in 1871.

Limited opening times apply. Refreshments are available.

Levens Park is separated from the house by the A6. Guillaume Beaumont designed the Park to enhance its natural beauty. He planted an avenue of trees to follow the line of the river and trees to emphasise the depth of the gorge.

Free public access can be gained on either side of the River Kent. *Continue south on the A6.*

Heversham. This mile long village has been by-passed since 1927 by Prince's Way, named after and opened by the Duke of Windsor, when he was Prince of Wales.

The Church has an Anglian cross in the porch and an oak screen dating from 1605.

The Old Grammar School, 1613, beyond the church, stands near the remains of a cock-fighting pit. Cockfighting was legal until 1835.

Milnthorpe. [*OE. Hamlet with a mill*] This former Westmorland port had a member of the Clifford family appointed Admiral of the River Kent. The port declined in importance with the building of the railway viaduct at Arnside and with the silting of the River Kent.

The Market Cross, to which miscreants were once shackled, was given a new head in 1964.

Owlet Ash. The authoress Constance Holme lived here. Her father was the agent for the Wilsons of Dallam Tower and this link with the gentry is evident in her novels. The Kent Estuary provided the background for her novel '*The Lonely Plough*'.

Turn west onto the B5282.

The Road from Milnthorpe along the estuary shore was built in 1859 by the Furness Railway Company.

Dallam Tower was the 1720 home of the Wilson family who built the brewery in Kendal. The road through the park and the footpaths alongside the River Belah are open to the public.

Sandside was once a tidal ford for crossing the estuary. When the tide was high a ferry boat was available. This area is rich in bird life, ducks and waders being the most numerous. Peter Scott shot geese here in his younger days. Salt water anglers catch fluke, a flat fish which feeds when the tide is in.

Arnside [ON. *Arnulf's settlement*] was probably founded by Norsemen from Ireland or the Isle of Man.

It originated as a tiny fishing village, built on a steep wooded slope above the sandflats overlooking the Kent Estuary. Boat building, including Arthur Ransome's dinghy, 'Swallow', and the export by water of locally produced gunpowder added to the occupations, but it really benefited from the arrival of the railway linking Carnforth with Barrow in 1857 and became a small holiday resort.

The Furness Railway Co. built the impressive Kent Viaduct over the estuary, 522 yards long, 50 spans each of 30 feet, supported on hollow iron piles embedded 90 feet deep, with broad iron discs at the bottom. The presence of the viaduct accelerated the natural process of silting and the channel of the River Kent moved westwards in the 1920s. Through the arches of the viaduct surges a tremendous tidal bore.

From the promenade and embankment, built c. 1897, there are spectacular views of the fells across the estuary. The salt marshes are covered only by the spring and autumn equinoctial tides and watching out for wigeon and mallard, curlews and oyster catchers is a fascination. Shelduck gather in the late summer before migrating to the Heligoland Bight.

Crossing the sands of Morecambe Bay from Arnside to Kents Bank. At low tide, 120 square miles of sand are exposed, but quicksands, shifting river channels and the tide coming in at a speed faster than a man can run, make the crossing perilous unless accompanied by the offical guide, who has previously marked the route with branches of laurel sticking out of the sand.

Stage coaches used to cross from Hest Bank to avoid bad roads and turnpike tolls. Such events have been featured by Turner in his paintings and by Melvyn Bragg in his novel *The Maid of Buttermere.*

Walk to Silverdale along the shore at low tide viewing Britain's largest wader population in the estuary and the variety of seashore plant life.

Arnside Knott, 522 feet. This limestone outcrop dominates the village and provides glorious views across the Lakeland Fells and to the Pennines.

Arnside Tower was a five-storey pele tower built by the Stanleys in the 13c for '*the defence of the coast against invasion of foreign and domestic enemies.*' The tower was destroyed by fire in 1602 and stands in ruins overlooking Morecambe Bay.

The countryside around Arnside has been designated an Area of Outstanding Natural Beauty.

Continue south from Arnside.

<u>Silverdale</u> [*ON. Sigward, a personal name*] This was a small farming and fishing village until a copper smelting works was built in the 18c. The ore came from Crag Foot and the Cove.

Silverdale was also one of the starting points for crossing the sands of Morecambe Bay. To provide for stage coach passengers, the Silverdale Hotel was opened in 1836. Twenty years later, the railway brought an increasing number of visitors. Coasters and pleasure boats from Morecambe used to call until the channel of the River Kent became silted.

Verdant expanses of sea-washed turf at the foot of the limestone cliffs have become the habitat of such plant life as thrift, sea aster, sea purslane and white goosefoot.

<u>Gibraltar Farm and Tower House</u> – named after the 19c three-storey stone tower in its garden – frequently provided holiday accommodation for Mrs Elizabeth Gaskell with her young family and nurse. Written here were part of her *Life of Charlotte Brontë* (1855) and her novels *Ruth* (1853) and *Sylvia's Lovers* (1863).

<u>Jenny Brown's Point</u> was named after an old lady who lived in the 18c in a large house on the shore and kept pigs.

A chimney at the edge of the bay once served Silverdale's copper smelting works. The limestone wall extending into the bay is all that remains of the 1864 scheme to reclaim Silverdale Sands.

<u>Leighton Moss,</u> an area of reed beds and meres, where the natural stages of development from fen to woodland can be seen, is leased to The Royal Society for the Protection of Birds. The rare bearded tit and the bittern breed here whilst ospreys, marsh harriers and others may be seen in passage. There are otters and red deer also. A half-mile public causeway crosses the middle and an observation hide is provided.

<u>Carnforth</u> was mentioned in the Domesday Book under the name Cliseneford.

It was a small port and shipbuilding centre until great changes took place with the construction of the Lancaster Canal in 1797 and the railway in 1846.

The Lancaster Canal stimulated the working of sand and gravel in the area, and is navigable from Tewetfield Locks in the north to Preston in the south. This distance of 41 miles is the longest lock-free length of canal in the country.

The railways provided access to iron ore from the Furness area and coke from the Durham coalfields to enable an iron works to be started in 1864. Carnforth then grew into a small town. The iron works continued in production until its demolition in 1931.

<u>Carnforth Railway Station</u>, on the west coastline between London and Glasgow, was the setting in 1945 for David Lean's classic film *Brief Encounter*. In the refreshment room, Trevor Howard began the romantic relationship with Celia Johnson, having removed a piece of grit from her eye.

<u>Steamtown</u>, took its name from the railway centre which, for many years, attracted visitors to see the restoration and preservation of vintage rolling stock in the former British Rail engine shed and in the sidings.

Turn right off the coast road at the sign for Morecambe Lodge and Red Bank Farm.

<u>Hest Bank</u>, for the northbound traveller, was a popular starting point for the hazardous crossing of the sands of Morecambe Bay to Kents Bank, near Grange-over-Sands, a distance of 8 miles. Mule trains, stage coaches and travellers on foot used this route, with the essential help of a guide, to avoid a much longer journey on poor

roads with costly turnpike tolls.

The trade across Morecambe Bay increased with the use of the Lancaster Canal, but the construction of the railway made the crossing unnecessary. The crossing became even more hazardous when the River Kent shifted its bed in 1980.

Turn back north along the A5105 and the A6.

<u>Warton</u> nestles at the foot of Warton Crag on the summit of which are the remains of a Brigantes hill fort.

<u>St Oswald's Church</u>, 14c, has associations with the family of George Washington, the first President of the United States of America (1732–99). The first Washingtons came from County Durham. John de Washington arrived at Warton c. 1350. In 1475, Robert Washington paid for the building of the church tower from where the American flag flies on Independence Day, 4th July. His coat of arms, three mullets and two bars, carved in stone in the belfry wall, is said to have inspired the design of the 'stars and stripes'.

<u>The Old Rectory</u>, 14c, in ruins opposite the church, had a ground floor service area above which was a large dining hall, a building style which was to be the forerunner of many great medieval and Tudor houses.

<u>Washington House</u>. A date stone registers 1612, but the present house was rebuilt in the 18c. Lawrence Washington lived here before moving, c. 1560, to Sulgrave Manor in Northamptonshire.

<u>The Shovel Inn</u> was where the Manor Court or Court Leet met after the decay of the Old Rectory.

<u>The School</u> was founded as a Grammar School in 1594 by Matthew Hutton, Bishop of Durham, '*For God and good education*'.

<u>The School House</u>, 17c, across the road, is where the Grammar School boys boarded.

Yealand Conyers [*OE. Yealand = high land.*] During the 13c, the Yealand estate was divided between two daughters whose surnames became Conyers and Redmayne when they married. Two attractive villages are named after them. Both villages are situated on the lower slopes of Warton Crag. Occupations of the village have been as diverse as farming, quarrying limestone, lime burning and flax weaving.

The Friends' Meeting House in Yealand Conyers has remained undisturbed since it was built in 1692 at a little distance from the main road. Earlier, Richard Hubberthorne had left Yealand to follow the teachings of George Fox, but Richard died for his beliefs in Newgate prison in 1662.

The Manor House, 19c, was built by wealthy shipowners, the Fords, who arranged to be summoned to meals by the ringing of a ship's bell.

Yealand Redmayne, on a lower level, consists of one long street.

Leighton Hall is set in a broad expanse of park land with a background of wooded fells.

The building of 1763 was replaced by an Adam-style house, which in turn was modified in the early 19c by Thomas Harrison, who added the neo-Gothic facade of white limestone.

In 1822, Richard Gillow, the grandson of Robert, the founder of the famous furniture firm of Gillow & Co. in Lancaster, took possession and the house came into the ownership of the Gillow-Reynolds family.

Inside, visitors can see some fine examples of Gillow furniture. There is also a collection of English and French clocks.

In the grounds, where birds of prey are kept, displays of flying eagles take place. Attractive gardens, woodland walks, a gift shop and tea room are welcoming features.

Beetham [*ON. River Bela settlement*].

The Saxon Church was desecrated by the Parliament forces under General Fairfax during the Civil War when horses were said to have been stabled there. Amongst the fragments of fine glass that remain is a portrait of Henry IV.

Beetham Hall is now a farm incorporating a former 14c pele tower, one of the most southerly. The 14c Great Hall is used as a barn.

The Fairy Steps are approached from the west of the church through the woods. The 'Steps' form a natural staircase in a narrow cleft in a steep limestone crag. Locally it is said that if you descend the steps, without touching the sides, your wish will come true.

This is part of 'The Limestone Link', a waymarked walk through the limestone country of South Cumbria, from Arnside, ½ mile from the railway station in Black Dyke Road, to 'The Devil's Bridge' at Kirkby Lonsdale, approximately 13 miles. The first section, from Arnside over Whin Scar, is known as 'the coffin route', along which the dead were carried for burial in Beetham's churchyard before Arnside's church was built in 1866.

The Heron Corn Mill was built c. 1750 on the site of a mill on the west bank of the river Bela and operated commercially until 1955. Following restoration, the 14-foot water wheel now turns four pairs of millstones producing stone ground flour and oatmeal whilst visitors watch.

On the opposite bank is the Henry Cooke Waterhouse Paper Mill A Museum of Papermaking shows both historic and modern production methods.

Cartmel Peninsula

[ON. Rocky sandbank]

Leave Levens Bridge west on the A590.

The Long Causeway is the former foot and bridleway over Foulshaw Moss, the marshes of the Kent Estuary. When it was built in 1816, it was known as The New Causeway, 'The Corsair'.

Nether Levens Hall, alongside the River Winster, dates from 1188 when the lands were divided in two. Over Levens became Levens Hall and Nether Levens became the property of the Preston family.

In the 15c, a pele tower was built, followed by an oratory. A curtain wall, part of the medieval great hall, and the pigeon house remain alongside the Tudor buildings with their enormous cylindrical chimneys.

Sampool Bridge, or Gilpin Bridge, crosses the River Gilpin which flows through the Lyth Valley.

For the Lyth Valley and Windermere, turn off here onto the A5074.

Whitbarrow, 706 feet, is the limestone mass with fan-shaped scree and White Scar on its southern edge, part of a narrow belt of carboniferous limestone which encircles Lakeland. Woodlands cover the lower slopes. At the highest point, around Lord Seat, a Nature Reserve has been established in memory of Canon G.A.K. Hervy (1893–1967), founder of the Lake District Naturalists' Trust.

OFOL 36

Turn off for the Winster Valley.

Wilson House is now a dairy farm, but in 1748 it was the forge and furnace of John Wilkinson whose father had been overlooker at Machell's iron forge at Backbarrow. It is claimed that John built the first iron boat and tested it locally on Helton Tarn in the Winster Valley. He moved to Wolverhampton and Bilston and then to Coalbrookdale in Shropshire to work with ironmaster Abraham Darby, who first smelted iron using coke as a fuel. Such contracts were completed as a 40 mile iron pipe system for water in Paris and the casting of parts for the construction of the first iron bridge in 1779 across the gorge of the River Severn at Coalbrookdale. The Bridge stands today as a symbol of the birthplace of the Industrial Revolution.

Turn onto the B5278.

Lindale [*ON. Valley of lime trees*] George Fox spoke here during his first journey through this area in 1652.

John Wilkinson's Obelisk, transferred from Castlehead gardens, is cast iron, and commemorates the achievements of this great ironmaster (1728–1808), sometimes referred to as 'the father of the English iron industry', or 'Iron-Mad Wilkinson'. Inscribed are the words, '*John Wilkinson, Ironmaster, died July 14th 1808, aged 80. His different works in various parts of the kingdom are lasting testimonies of his unceasing labours. His life was spent in action for the benefit of Man, and, as he presumed humbly to hope, to the glory of God. Labore et Honore.*'

The old mill pond and associated buildings have long been part of the village scene.

Castlehead, close to the River Winster, is where John Wilkinson once lived. He created the garden from barren rock by having loads of soil transported in panniers by pack horses. His wish was to be buried in a cast-iron coffin in the garden with an iron obelisk over the grave.

With some difficulty his wish was carried out. The cast-iron coffin was almost lost when the hearse stuck in quicksand during the crossing of Morecambe Bay. The first coffin was too small; the grave for the second was too shallow. Twenty years later when the estate changed hands, the new owners had the coffin removed to an unknown plot in Lindale churchyard. The obelisk was discarded and lay in a hedge for more than thirty years. In 1863, the obelisk was salvaged and erected in its present position. Repairs were necessary after it had been struck by lightning, but it is now classified as an Ancient Monument.

Castlehead became an adult education centre.

Newton Fell   *OFOL 52*

Grange-over-Sands

[OE. Monastic granary or farm – belonging to Cartmel Priory]

From the 13c, the major route to and from Lancaster was 'over the sands', across Morecambe Bay, hence the words added to the name 'Grange'. Guides on the 'oversands' journey have always been necessary and were first provided by the Prior of Cartmel.

The Monastic Grange is thought to have been located in the vicinity of Yewbarrow Gardens. A vineyard was maintained by virtue of the southern aspect and the mild climate, comparable in winter with southern England. Coal for the Priory was unloaded at a small harbour near to the site of the Grange Hotel today.

The town owes its development to the coming of the Furness railway in 1887. The railway hugs the seashore and a wall was built to protect it from tides. Along the top of the wall in 1904 a mile long promenade was completed, providing extensive views across the bay where the coast line has lifted itself away from the sea. Instead of the usual margin of 200–300 yards between high and low tides, a

Grange-over-Sands

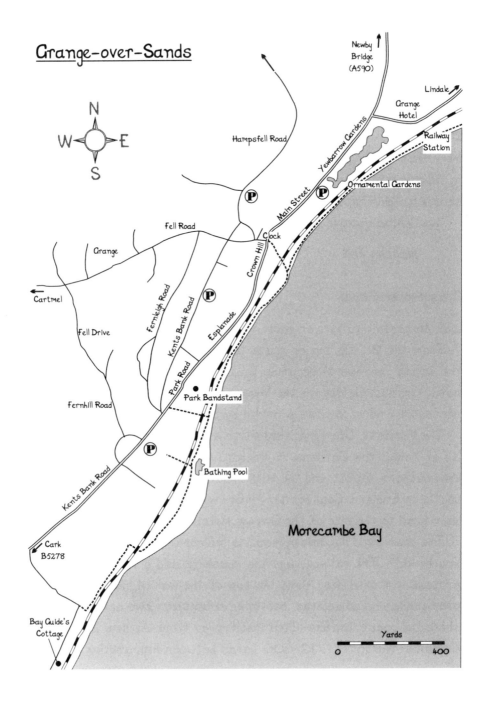

vast area is covered by the sea. Then, six hours later, an enormous expanse of sand banks and mud flats, saltings and marshes, begins to appear, attracting bird life of many kinds.

The railway brought wealthy merchants from Lancashire and Yorkshire who built large houses. Hotels followed, catering for visitors, and Grange became a fashionable watering place when promoting the waters from the Holy Well at Humphrey Head.

Ornamental gardens and a salt water open air swimming pool – preferable to the dangerous currents in the estuary – added to the attractions, although the swimming pool is now closed.

Hampfell Hospice [*ON. Hamr's fell*] (OS. Hampsfield).

Approach from Grange Fell Road or Hampsfell Road.

This Victorian, limestone tower, with an outside staircase to the flat roof, was built on the fell 727 feet above Grange-over-Sands. The founder, Rev. G. Remington of Langlands, used to climb Hampsfell every morning before breakfast. The hospice was constructed for the '*shelter and entertainment of travellers over the fell.*' Painted boards display amusing verse or moral sayings.

'*All persons visiting this Hospice by permission of the owner are requested to respect private property, and not, by acts of wanton mischief and destruction, shew that they possess more muscle than brain. I have no hope that this reasonable request will be attended to, for as Solomon says, "Though thou shouldest bray a fool in a mortar among wheat with a pestle, yet will not his foolishness depart from him."' G. Remington.*

From the crags and limestone pavements on the summit an exceptional view unfolds across Morecambe Bay and towards Lakeland's southern fells.

Hampsfell.   OFOL 58

<u>Kents Bank</u>. Packhorse trains once crossed the sands from here to Hest Bank, north of Morecambe, a distance of eight miles. This saved a journey of twenty miles along bad roads and the cost of turnpike tolls.

In the 18c, the journey across the sands was a popular part of the Lakes Tour and there was a regular service by stage coach making the crossing from the Kings Arms in Lancaster to the Sun Inn at Ulverston.

A guide has always been necessary as the sands are criss-crossed with deep channels and there are quicksands and a swift in-coming tide to avoid.

<u>Guide's Cottage</u>, in Carter Road, has been the home of the 'over-sands' guides since the 16c. The road is named after 'Carter', the first guide to have held this office.

The original guides were appointed by the Prior of Cartmel, but after the Dissolution, the service was continued by the state. It became the responsibility of the Duchy of Lancaster to provide a guide at a salary of £15 per annum paid for from a charitable trust.

Today, Cedric Robinson guides tourists across the sands at low tide.

<u>Humphrey Head</u> [*OE. Humfrith's headland*] *Walk from Kents Bank.*

The limestone cliffs, 173 feet high, are the only sea cliffs of any size between North Wales and St Bees Head.

According to tradition, Sir Edgar Harrington of Wraysholme Tower, now a farmhouse with a Tudor pele tower, killed England's last wolf here in the 14c. However, a ballad of 1821 ascribes this feat to Sir John De Lisle whose reward was to marry Harrington's daughter.

<u>The Holy Well of St Agnes</u> is a mineral spring at the foot of the cliffs on the west side. This was once a place of pilgrimage. Lead miners from Alston drank the waters to counteract the effect of the poi-

sonous metal as the waters were sold as a cure for health problems.

<u>Grand Arch or Fairy Church</u> is a bridge-shaped rock formation where a hole from the top of the cliff emerges through its side.

Humphrey Head.   *OFOL 66*

<u>Flookburgh</u>. Although situated a mile from the sea, Flookburgh has always been a fishing community.

The first part of its name is derived from the flook or flounder, a small flat fish, caught in a stake-net. Some people point out that a flook adorns the weather vane on top of the church tower, but others see it as the hook of an anchor. The second part of the name refers to Flookburgh's status as a borough granted by Edward I.

Trawling for shrimps takes place using a tractor and trailer dragging the net along at the edge of the tide. As the lower beam at the mouth of the trawl reaches the shrimps, they jump upwards and are caught in the net.

Cockles are caught by pounding the sand with a 'jumbo' – a broad board with two long handles – forcing the cockles towards the surface to be scooped up with a fork-like implement called a 'croam'.

<u>Cark</u> was once a shipbuilding and shrimp packing village at the mouth of the River Eea.

<u>Cark Hall</u>, 17c, was the home of the Rawlinson family whose coat of arms is carved above the door. The estate passed to the Rigge family, but Fletcher Rigge's young bridge was so appalled at the desolation of the Eea Valley after the terrifying journey over Tow Top (gradient 1 in 4) that she refused to live at Cark. Northallerton became their home instead.

<u>Holker Hall</u> (pron. Hooker) was built on land belonging to Cartmel

Priory at the end of the 16c by George Preston, the restorer of Cartmel Priory after the Dissolution. Holker Hall then became the home of the Dukes of Devonshire for more than three centuries, continuing with the Cavendish family today.

The Hall was rebuilt in 1840 in a style resembling the original by the seventh Duke of Devonshire who said, '*Chatsworth is my palace, but Holker is my home.*' After a disastrous fire in 1874, the Hall was restored once more to the design of architects Paley and Austin. The result is an architectural mix of the 16c, Georgian and Victorian.

The interior offers much of interest. The library is said to be one of the finest in the north. The cantilevered staircase, with each of its hundred or so balusters carved differently, leads up to the long gallery. Radiators blend with oak panelling and switches are behind dummy books. Furniture, paintings and family memorabilia infuse a 'lived-in' atmosphere.

The 25 acres of formal gardens were laid out with a topiary in the 1720s. Advice was received from Joseph Paxton, the gardener at Chatsworth and the designer of Crystal Palace. *The Good Gardens Guide* describes them as, '*Amongst the best gardens in the world.*'

Herds of fallow and red deer and a flock of Jacob's sheep graze in the 125 acres of parkland, where events take place regularly involving historic vehicles, horse-drawn carriages, and hot air balloons.

Permanent tourist attractions include the Lakeland Motor Museum where The Campbell Legend Bluebird Exhibition is featured.

Return to Cark. Take the minor road to Cartmel.

<u>Headless Cross,</u> just outside Cartmel, is where four roads meet. It was formerly South Cross where pilgrims thanked God for a safe crossing of the sands.

CARTMEL GATE HOUSE
12/98

A milestone on the edge of the village indicates 'Lancaster-over-sands 15 miles' and 'Ulverston-over-sands 7 miles'.

Cartmel

<u>Cartmel Priory Church</u>. The earliest mention of 'Cathmell' was in AD 678 when Egfrith, the King of Northumbria, granted this district to St Cuthbert, the Bishop of Lindisfarne. To serve this widespread area of scattered settlements, a chapel was built, possibly at Allithwaite. There was as yet no village of Cartmel.

According to legend, some Irish monks received a divine message to build a priory on a spit of land between two streams that flowed in opposite directions. The marshy ground between the River Eea and Mere Beck fulfilled this criteria.

According to history, the Priory was founded on this legendary site in 1188 by William le Marechal for the Canons Regular of the Order of St Augustine. William, who later became Earl of Pembroke and Regent of England, had acquired this area as a gift from Henry II.

The land donated by Henry II extended between the River Winster and the River Leven, continuing as far north as the River Brathay. Included were the sheepwalks on the Cartmel and the Bigland Fells, water mills at Newby Bridge and Backbarrow, fishing rights along the coast, and the responsibility for the employment of 'oversands' guides.

A chapel was built and the 'black canons' began 350 years of influence throughout the region. The building of the Priory was a continuous process extending over many centuries and involving architectural styles from the Norman to the Perpendicular.

In 1280, the canons constructed a tiny harbour at Grange-over-Sands, under licence from the King, to import goods from Ireland and coal for the Priory. The gatehouse was added c. 1330 in response

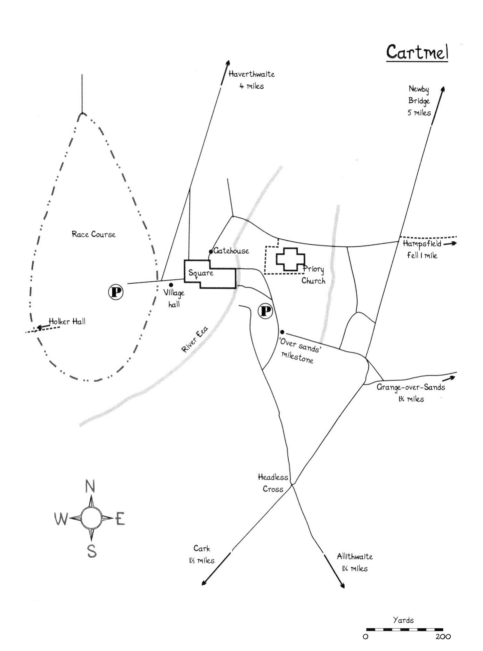

Cartmel

to the threat of Scottish raids. About the same time, Lord John Harrington arranged for the rebuilding of the chapel. The belfry tower, c. 1410, is unique as it was built diagonally on top of the original, low, lantern tower. Some original monastic walls have survived.

The Priory Church of St Mary and St Michael only survived Henry VIII's Dissolution of the Monasteries because part of the south choir aisle, or Town Choir as it was known to locals, had been used as a parish church. Unfortunately, whilst awaiting the outcome of appeal, removal of the roof and windows went ahead. The church stood roofless for 80 years until George Preston of Holker Hall had it restored, 1610–23.

A further setback took place in 1643 when a group of Cromwellian soldiers camped in the church for the night. The organ was smashed and some of the furnishings. The south-west door was peppered with bullets.

In the churchyard, near the gate from the village, is the grave of William Wordsworth's teacher, William Taylor, 1754–86, headmaster of Hawkshead Grammar School. The epitaph is from Gray's 'Elegy'. Wordsworth in *The Prelude' Book X*, recalled a visit to the grave.

Of interest inside the Priory Church are:

The stained glass in the great east window, c. 1425, inspired by a window in York Minster. Some medieval stained glass from Cartmel was installed in St Martin's Church, Bowness-on-Windermere.

The medieval choir stalls and misericords, c. 1450.

The carved screen and canopies behind the choir stalls, c. 1620.

The tombe of Lord Harrington and his wife, 1347, with a wolf (?) or lion (!) beneath his feet.

The tomb of the first Prior.

In the transepts, the blocked doorway of the 'night stairs'.

The intricately carved 17c Preston screen.

The Victorian memorial to Lord Frederick Cavendish, murdered in Phoenix Park, Dublin, in 1882.

The tombstone of two who were drowned on the sands.

The sculpture, *They fled by night* by Josephina de Vasconcellos.

The Priory Church has continued to serve as the centre of a large parish, as a place of worship and as a venue for concerts and special events.

Cartmel Village grew up around its famous 12c Priory on a 22 acre site, with access at one time only through the 14c Gatehouse. Until the 19c, the village was known as 'Cartmel Churchtown'.

The Market Square, with its obelisk replacement of the market cross and village pump and trough, is enclosed by Georgian style, creeper-clad houses, inns, a hotel and shops.

From the square, narrow streets and alleys reveal delightful, 17c and 18c, grey-white limestone cottages and houses with stream-side walks following the River Eea.

The Priory Gatehouse (NT) was built c. 1330 in one corner of the square as the entrance to the Priory precincts. It housed the Manorial Courtroom in its upper room until 1624 when it was converted into a Grammar School, followed by a Methodist Chapel and a warehouse. In 1946 it was given to the National Trust and is now an artist's shop and gallery, which features the work of Helen Bradley.

Through the archway is Cavendish Street with its Georgian terrace and the Cavendish Arms, the oldest inn in Cartmel.

Helen Bradley. The artist moved to Cartmel in 1966 at the age of 60. A talent for painting had been revealed in her childhood days in Lees, Oldham, helped by her uncle, Charles Edward Shaw, RA. But Helen's father would not permit her to go to art school. She married an artist and that may partially explain why she did not take up painting again until late in life. Encouragement came from another Lancastrian, L.S. Lowry, but whereas his paintings frequently depicted the greyness and drabness that he grew up with, Helen

Bradley's paintings tell stories from her childhood memories of a gen-
teel, colourful, well-dressed Edwardian age. Her painting life extended over fourteen years until her death in 1979, a week before she was
to receive the M.B.E.

The Park is leased from nearby Holker Hall and Cartmel Races
have taken place on this site since 1856. It is the smallest National
Hunt course and holds race meetings on the Spring and late Summer
Bank Holidays.

Cartmel Show is held early in August, on the Wednesday after the
first Monday.

The Vale of the River Eea [OE. River]

The River Eea, which flows through Cartmel to reach the sea at
Cark, passes between the limestone upland of Hampsfield Fell and
the Silurian slates of Bigland Heights.

This is the same geological two-tone pattern as the Winster Valley.

Hampsfield Hall lies beneath the wooded slopes of Hampsfield Fell.
On the fell side are two stones, Robin Hood and the Little John,
probably way marks.

Aynsome Hall, [OE. Eea's holm (riverside flat ground or island)],
was built by the Marshall family, descendants of William le Marechal,
founder of Cartmel Priory. There was once a Priory corn mill here.

*Through a maze of twisting country lanes the picturesque hamlets
of Field Broughton, Barber Green, Settle and Ayside are reached.*

Newton Fell.   OFOL 52.

Bigland Hall, on Bigland Heights, offers visitors country sports
activities, such as horse-riding, fishing in Bigland Tarn and clay
pigeon shooting.

Furness Peninsula

Continue west along the A590.

<u>Greenodd</u> [*ON. Green point*] is situated at the mouth of the River Crake, which drains from Coniston Water, at its confluence with the tidal River Leven from Lake Windermere.

It is recorded that Antony Tissington built the brigantine *Fortune* here in 1770 and that it was shipping ore in 1780. Ores of copper and lead were exported from this busy little harbour, as well as slate and timber. Imports included cotton for the mill at Backbarrow. Such trade had ceased by the end of the 18c because of silting. Only rotting staithes and the Ship Inn remain as evidence.

The former railway station overlooking the Leven Estuary, on the branch line of the Furness Railway from Ulverston to Windermere, which opened in 1868 and closed in the 1960s, is now a picnic site attracting anglers and bird watchers.

<u>Hoad Hill,</u> 435 feet, is surmounted by a 100 ft replica of the Eddystone Lighthouse, built in 1850 at a cost of £1,250. It is a memorial to a local celebrity, Sir John Barrow (1764–1848), whose birthplace in Dragley Beck is marked by a plaque. He was an Arctic explorer and a naturalist who became Secretary to the Admiralty for 40 years. He founded the Royal Geographical Society and was the author of *Mutiny on the Bounty*. Named after him are Point Barrow in Alaska and a sea duck, Barrow's Golden Eye.

The lighthouse is open to the public whenever its flag is raised.

Ulverston

[ON. Ulfr's settlement]

Ulverston lies at the junction of the Silurian Slates of Kirkby Moor and the limestone of Birkrigg Common.

There is mention of Ulverston in the Domesday Book, 1087. In the 12c, the landowner was Henry I's nephew, Stephen, who later became king. From then onwards ownership passed to the monks of Furness Abbey until the Dissolution of the Monasteries.

Raiders from Scotland under Robert Bruce twice burned the town, in 1316 and in 1322. More destruction was inflicted during the Civil War when both sides fought over it.

By the 18c, Ulverston had become a thriving port backed by extensive copper and iron mining and, from 1770, by smelting furnaces. It was also an important stopping place for the mail coach from Lancaster which had taken that short route across the sands of Morecambe Bay. The turnpike road from Kendal opened in 1763 and contributed further to making Ulverston a busy trading centre, for which it became known as '*the London of the Furness*'.

When shifting sands silted up the harbour, the Ulverston Canal was built, supervised by John Rennie and opened in 1796. This link between the town and the sea at Canal Foot was said to be the shortest (1½ miles), the widest, the deepest and the straightest canal in England. The canal gave Ulverston nearly another century as a profitable port, trading mainly in iron and coal and as a shipbuilding centre.

With the establishment of the railway by 1857, a decline in shipbuilding set in and closure followed in 1878. Blast furnaces were demolished soon after and the foundry was transferred to Millom.

The canal fell into disuse in the 1940s and the seaward end was sealed off. It is now used as a water tank by Glaxo Laboratories which manufacture pharmaceutical products.

Ulverston

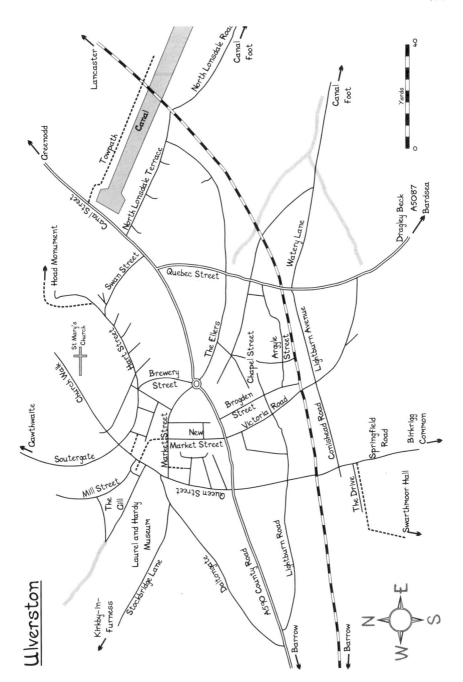

<u>Canal Foot</u> has become a haven for anglers and for bird watchers. At Guides House lives the official guide for the route across Cartmel Sands. Like the crossing of Morecambe Bay, a considerable road journey was saved, especially in pre-turnpike days.

Ulverston, once part of Lancashire, passed into Cumbria with local government reorganisation in 1974.

<u>The Town Centre</u>, with its cobbled main street, has an 18c and 19c appearance.

Coaching inns, such as the King's Head, the Sun Inn and Braddly's Arms date from the middle of the 17c. Hartley's Brewery continues to supply locally brewed ale.

In the <u>Market Place</u> stands a medieval style market cross designed by W. G. Collingwood.

The Market House dates from 1736.

A Market Charter was granted by Edward I to Roger de Lancaster in 1280 and Ulverston now boasts the biggest and most colourful street market in South Lakeland. Market days are Thursdays and Saturdays. The livestock market, known as 'L'ile Pig Day', is held on Thursdays at North Lonsdale Road.

The Charter Festival is celebrated during the week which includes the 11th September.

<u>Theatre Street</u> is named after the Theatre Royal where Sarah Siddons once performed but the theatre no longer exists.

<u>Furness Galleries</u> occupy a former 18c Commercial Bank and Sherry Warehouse. The recesses for the safes and the shelves in the cellar where the sherry was stored have been retained. This arts and crafts centre specialises in dolls' houses and furniture.

In Lower Brook Street, off Buxton Place, is <u>The Ulverston Heritage Centre</u>, a registered charity which displays information, pictures and memorabilia about the history of Ulverston.

Upper Brook Street houses <u>The Laurel and Hardy Museum</u> originated by an ex-Mayor of Ulverston, Bill Cubin. Particularly honoured is Stanley Jefferson – Stan Laurel, 'the thin one' of the famous duo, who was born in Ulverston at No. 3 Argyle Street in 1890 and lived in the town for five years. Personal mementoes and rare photographs are exhibited and a small 1920s style cinema shows classic Laurel and Hardy films.

<u>The Gill</u> is the venue for the annual Whit and Michaelmas fairs. It is also the start of the Cumbrian Way to Carlisle. <u>Ulverston Point</u> is a converted granary attached to the old town watermill. The three-storey building and former wagon yard accommodate a Crafts Centre and furnishing items. Ship paintings and documents display the maritime history of the town.

<u>Heron Glass</u> produces a unique range of glass by the ancient art of glass blowing.

Lightburn Road, in the old cattle market, is where <u>Cumbria Crystal</u>, *'The Choice of British Embassies'*, offers factory tours and sales from the factory shop.

<u>St Mary's Church</u> is known as the 'Four Ones Church' from the date of its foundation in 1111. The Elizabethan tower was built with stones from Conishead Priory following the Dissolution of the Monasteries. Restoration took place in 1866 and a new chancel was added in 1902. The main treasures are the Norman south doorway and the north-west window of stained glass dating from 1805.

The footpath beyond leads to the Hoad Monument.

<u>Swarthmoor Hall</u> *can be reached by a footpath adjacent to The Drive,*

off Springfield Road.

This Elizabethan manor was built c. 1586 by Judge Thomas Fell, an ardent Puritan. His wife, Margaret, having heard George Fox preach, persuaded her husband in 1652 to give sanctuary to the 'Man in Leather Breeches', who would give allegiance to none but God Himself.

George Fox was the founder of the Quaker Movement, The Society of Friends, and consequently the recipient of much hostility. He wrote, '*Justice Bennet of Derby was the first to call us Quakers because I bade him quake and tremble at the work of the Lord.*'

Because of Judge Fell's position and influence, the Quakers were spared persecution, but on his death in 1658 that protection ended. Although Margaret once obtained the release of 4,000 Friends from prison by pleading with Charles II, she was later imprisoned for four years.

Eleven years after the Judge's death, Margaret married George Fox and together they promoted the Quaker Movement in spite of opposition.

The Hall is owned by The Society of Friends and is open to the public. It contains some fine panelling and a rare newel staircase, centred around a wooden cage. A 'trip step' was deliberately built higher than the rest so that an intruder would stumble and alert the occupants. Some of Fox's possessions are displayed and there is a small library.

A notable visitor to Swarthmoor Hall was the Quaker William Penn, who sailed to America in 1681 to found the colony of Pennsylvania, where Swarthmore College is named after this Cumbrian manor house.

George Fox bought a small property, about a mile from Swarthmoor Hall, called Petty's and converted it in 1688 into a Friends' Meeting House, which is still in use today.

From Ulverston, take the A5087 coast road.

<u>Conishead Priory</u> began as a hospital founded during the reign of Henry II (1154–1189) by a Norman nobleman, Gamel de Pennington. Augustinian monks provided the care.

The hospital became a priory and continued to function until the Dissolution in 1536–37. Rebuilding followed and occupation by a succession of families.

From 1821, Colonel T.R.G. Braddyll began a major reconstruction in the Gothic Revival style, but unfortunately he became bankrupt, unaware of the iron ore deposits beneath his estate. Subsequent owners used the premises as a Hydropathic Hotel and as a convalescent home for Durham miners.

Today, Conishead Priory has reverted to the care of monks – a Buddhist community, the Manjushri Institute of Tibetan Studies.

Visitors are invited to be shown round the premises and to enjoy following a Nature Trail through the woodland which extends to the seashore.

From the pebbly beach, <u>Chapel Island</u> can be seen with the ruins of <u>St Catherine's Chapel</u>. Wordsworth refers to these in *The Prelude, Book X*, where he describes his crossing of the estuary at low tide on his way to Aldingham.

<u>Bardsea Country Park</u>, on the edge of Morecambe Bay, provides car parks, picnic spaces, information boards and coastal walks.

Further north, a nature trail passes through Sea Wood, which was originally planted with oak trees to provide timber for the masts of ships built at Barrow. The wind blown trees lean inland at an acute angle.

Turn inland up a minor road.

<u>Bardsea Village</u> stands on a hill overlooking the coast.

<u>Holy Trinity Church</u>, like much of the village, is built with silvery-

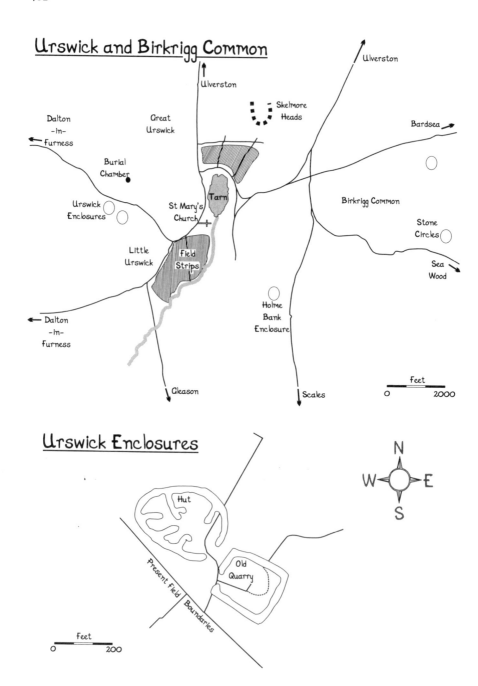

Urswick and Birkrigg Common

Ulverston

Ulverston

Skelmore
Heads

Dalton
-in-
Furness

Great
Urswick

Bardsea

Burial
Chamber

Tarn

Birkrigg Common

Urswick
Enclosures

St Mary's
Church

Stone
Circles

Little
Urswick

Field
Strips

Sea
Wood

Holme
Bank
Enclosure

Feet

0   2000

Gleason

Scales

Dalton
-in-
Furness

Urswick Enclosures

N

W   E

S

Hut

Old
Quarry

Present Field Boundaries

Feet

0   200

grey limestone.

The Ship Inn, 18c, was once a barn.

From Bardsea take the minor road to Great Urswick.

Birkrigg Common [*ON. Ridge with birch trees*] is one mile from Bardsea, on the left.

On the common is a graveyard where George Fox's widow, Margaret, is buried, north of High Sunbreck farmhouse.

This bare, rounded, limestone upland divides the coast from the little valley of Urswick. It is known as the Bronze Age capital of Furness due to the number of Bronze Age and Iron Age barrows, burial mounds and stone circles. These can be seen before the summer bracken obscures them.

Stone Circles (OS. 292739) This double circle has two non-concentric rings of stones, no more than 2 feet high. The inner circle contains 10 stones and has a diameter of 30 feet; the outer circle has 15 stones and a diameter of 85 feet. Within the inner circle were five cremations, one in an inverted collared urn.

A 'platform' cairn (OS. 282740) stands one foot high and measures 50 feet across. The surface is level and large limestone blocks are visible around the edges. Ten cremations were found in the mound.

Four tiny barrows (OS. 286742) have been excavated without any revelations.

A mound (OS. 285744) is 3 feet high and 40 feet across. A large angled stone at the centre resembles the capstone of a possible rifled cist.

A mound (OS. 289743) 2 feet high and 40 feet across contained three skeletons and a bronze awl. Near the east side were deposits of black earth covered by stone slabs. A circle of boulders encloses the mound.

A mound (OS. 288746) 2 feet high and 27 feet by 30 feet had seven cremations in the north-east corner, three of them in cordoned urns.

Two enclosures (OS 288746) are probably of a fortified homestead and a cattle pound. The north-east enclosure is roughly oval, 300 feet across with a surrounding bank 2 feet high and 10-15 feet across. Inside the interned entrance to the east are three depressions, probably hut circles. The south-west enclosure is oval also, but much larger with a less conspicuous bank and an entrance to the north-west.

Great Urswick [*OE. urs = bison lake, the old name for Urswick Tarn. wie = dairy farm; village.*]

The Church of St Mary, 13c, contains fragments of a 9c Saxon cross, said to be part of a monument to Tuthred, the Saxon Earl of Urswick. Stained glass windows were brought from Furness Abbey.

Urswick Tarn is overlooked by the church.

Urswick Enclosures (OS 260741). These two Iron Age enclosures are probably a family settlement and an adjacent animal pound.

The roughly oval westerly enclosure covers 1½ acres and is surrounded by a stone wall 1 foot high and 10-12 feet wide. The entrance in the south-east is obscured by a later field wall which passes through it. Inside, at the centre, are five hut circles, 20-30 feet across, with entrances facing east. There are a number of rectangular cattle paddocks with stone walls 4-5 feet thick.

The rectangular south-eastern enclosure has a bank no more than 2 feet high and 15-20 feet wide, with an entrance at the south-east corner.

An associated cultivation terrace 500 feet long lies to the

north-west and north-east of the enclosures.

<u>Neolithic Burial Chamber</u> (OS. 262744) lies ¼ mile north-west of Little Urswick, just north of the minor road to Dalton-in-Furness.

Two large boulders, strengthened by packing stones, support a capstone. More stones nearby were probably part of the chamber.

<u>Holme Bank Iron Age Enclosure</u> (OS. 276734) is west of the minor road from Ulverston to Scales.

This five-sided enclosure measures 60 feet by 160 feet. It consists of an earth and stone bank revetted on both sides by large upright slabs up to 14 feet wide and 2–3 feet high, with an entrance at the east where a slight ditch is discernible. Inside are traces of two huts, 15–25 feet in diameter and, to the north, a cross-bank, probably for livestock.

Another hut site, with a bank and ditch round its north side, is located about 25 yards to the north-west.

<u>Gleaston Castle</u> stands in ruins on the minor road between Scales and Gleaston.

During the 14c, the Lordship of the Manor passed from the le Flemings to the Harringtons who built the castle for protection against Border raiders.

<u>Gleaston Water Mill</u>, built in 1774 on the site of an earlier mill, has been restored to full working order.

Return to the coast road, the A5087, at Aldingham. This road was built during the 1920s to provide employment for local workers during the depression.

<u>Aldingham</u>. *[OE. The 'ham' of the descendants of Alda.]*

<u>Castle Mound</u> at Moat Farm is the site of the Norman castle of

Michael le Fleming, military overlord, who was granted a large tract of 'border land' along Morecambe Bay by Henry I (1100–35). Traces of the small motte and bailey and the old moat can still be seen.

Most of the village was washed away in the tidal storm of 1553, leaving the church very close to the sea.

<u>St Cuthbert's Church</u> is named after the 7c saint who brought Christianity to Cumbria. The 12c church, begun by Michael le Fleming on an earlier Saxon foundation, is largely built with rounded stones from the beach. It is said to be on the site where St Cuthbert's body was placed whilst his bearers rested on their long journey from Lindisfarne to escape from the Danish invasion of Northumbria in AD 875.

<u>Newbiggin</u>. On the seaward side of the coast road is Seed Hall, once a Monastic Granary.

Continue along the coast road, the A5087.

<u>Rampside</u> has a single main street along the shore. It was once a port with its own station for boat trains which connected with a steamer service across Morecambe Bay to Fleetwood. The former station house and traces of the old platform can still be seen. The station's original name of Concle (= *whelk*), from nearby Conc Hole Scar, is continued in the name of the Concle Inn. Rampside has now became a yachting centre, sheltered by the causeways to Foulney Island and Roa Island, which are islands no more.

<u>Rampside Hall</u>, 16c, is distinguished by a row of tall, diagonally set Elizabethan chimneys, known locally as 'The Twelve Apostles'.

On the seashore stands a curious Victorian lighthouse.

<u>Rampside Church</u>, about a mile inland, was built in 1840 on the site of a 17c chapel where George Fox converted the priest, Thomas Lawson, to Quakerism in 1652. In the churchyard are the graves of mariners who perished at sea. A Viking burial, with a sword, was dis-

covered in 1909.

Foulney Island is a causeway, more than a mile in length, leading to a Nature Reserve, the home of large nesting colonies of terns during spring and summer.

Roa Island. John Abel Smith built the half-mile causeway in 1847, capable of carrying a railway to his deep-water jetty on Roa Island to link with his steamer service. The scheme never materialised.

At the end of the causeway, the small village of 19c terraced houses includes an old Customs House, a Gothic style watch tower and the Marine Villa, built originally for the wealthy Victorian industrialist, H.W. Schneider. The Bosun's Locker café advertises details of the ferry service across to Piel Island.

The tip of Roa Island is the start of the Cumbria Coastal Way which continues to Carlisle, a distance of 124 miles.

Piel Island is named after its castle, but it is known also as Foudrey Island [*ON. Fodder Island*] on account of the good grazing.

It lies half-a-mile off Roa Island from where it may be reached by ferry boat. (Tel 01229 833609).

The island was given by King Stephen to the Savignac monks in 1127. Their merger with the Cistercians in 1147 and the growth of Furness Abbey furthered the need for a local harbour. Piel Island was chosen and the motte and bailey castle with defence ditches was built in 1327.

The castle was used as a fortified warehouse to protect cargoes, especially wool, from raiders and pirates. By avoiding customs men and tariffs a lucrative smuggling trade sprang up. The Abbot of Furness was charged with wool smuggling in 1423.

A rare invasion of England took place from the island in 1487. Richard III had been suspected of eliminating rival claims to the throne by having the two princes, Edward, Earl of Warwick and his brother Richard, Duke of York, murdered in the Tower of London. Lambert Simnel, the son of an Oxford baker, was persuaded to impersonate the Earl of Warwick with the aim of seizing the throne from the new king Henry VII. Lambert Simnel allowed himself to be crowned Edward VI in Dublin Cathedral. He landed on Piel Island with his mercenaries and marched south on Henry VII only to be defeated and captured at Stoke Field, near Nottingham. Henry spared his life and put the youth to work in the royal kitchens.

Following the Dissolution of Furness Abbey in 1539, Piel castle fell into ruin, but the island's harbour continued in use for shipping and smuggling. By the 18c, 250 ships were recorded at anchor in Piel harbour and revenue officers had been appointed. In the late 18c, the Furness iron industry was developing, more ships were trading and cottages for ships' pilots and a public house were built on Piel Island. They are occupied today.

The landlord of the Ship Inn is traditionally known as the 'King of Piel', a title which dates back to when Lambert Simnel declared himself king. Anyone who sits in the ancient oak chair becomes a 'Knight of Piel' in a ceremony performed by the 'King' or another 'Knight'. The duties of a new 'Knight' are to buy everyone present a drink, to be a moderate smoker, an ardent lover of the opposite sex and of good character. Should ever a 'Knight' be shipwrecked on Piel Island, he may demand a meal and a night's lodging, free of charge, at the Ship Inn.

Barrow-in-Furness

EC.Th.   Mkt. W, S. [ON. Barr-ey. 'ey' = island]

In 1851, Barrow was a small, insignificant farming and fishing community on the shore of Walney Channel, with a population around 500.

Although there were known deposits of rich haematite in the Furness area, the vast change in Barrow's fortune was brought about by Henry Schneider's discovery of the largest and richest 'strike' of all at Park Mines near Dalton, just north of Barrow, where production continued for almost seventy years, until closure in 1921.

The sharp rise in iron ore production imposed a severe strain on the existing rail and shipping network resulting in the construction of the Furness Railway from 1845. Its General Manager, James Ramsden, persuaded the company to purchase land at Hindpool, on the shore of Walney Channel, for the construction of improved harbour facilities and for shipbuilding docks, all served by the Furness Railway. Ramsden also encouraged Henry Schneider to build his iron works in this area.

Schneider, Hannay & Co. Ltd had built the first blast furnaces for their ironworks by 1859. Five years later, Ramsden, Schneider and the Earl of Burlington, who became the seventh Duke of Devonshire, formed the Barrow Haematite Steel Company Ltd to convert the pig-iron from the ironworks into steel, using the new Bessemer process, on a site alongside the ironworks.

The unprecedented development of the iron and steel industry made the Furness Railway one of the richest companies in the country as it went ahead to build and operate four docks: Devonshire (1867), Buccleuch (1873) Ramsden and Cavendish (1879). From these, the Barrow Iron Shipbuilding Company (BISC) operated until Vickers Shipbuilding and Engineering Ltd. (VSEL) took over. Ships, especially for the Royal Navy, have ranged from the earliest ironclads to the modern HMS *Invincible*; from Britain's first submarine to the nuclear-powered Trident submarine of today.

By 1881, Barrow claimed to have the largest iron and steel works

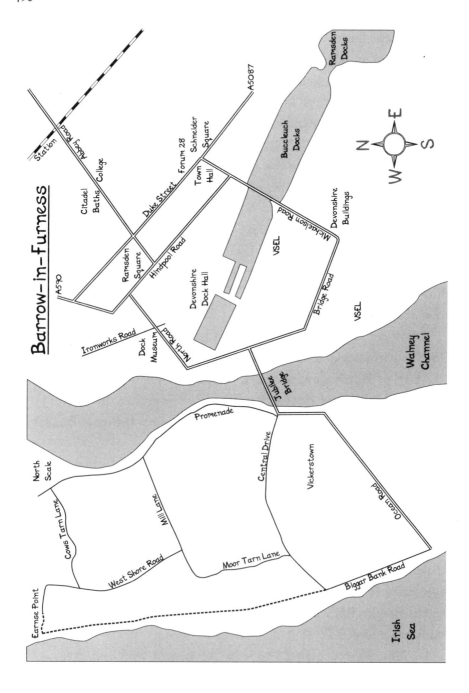

Barrow-in-Furness

in the world, employing 5,000 people.

Within thirty years the population had increased to 48,000.

To provide some diversification and alternative employment, especially for women, James Ramsden founded the Flax and Jute Company in 1870.

But Ramsden's dream of Barrow as a port to rival Liverpool in importance was never realised due largely to the expensive problem with silting in the Walney Channel.

During the 20c, local reserves of iron ore became exhausted and competition from other steelworks intensified. Armament production for two World Wars and post-war rebuilding sustained the iron and steel industry for a while, but the ironworks closed in 1963 and, twenty years later, due to overcapacity in the industry, the steelworks closed also.

Within little more than a hundred years the iron and steel industry had come and gone, leaving only the shipbuilding and the railway with historic links with the past.

Following the establishment of Barrow as a Municipal Borough in 1867, the planning of the town around the iron and steel works was largely a joint venture between James Ramsden, the first mayor, and the Earl of Burlington. Broad, straight, partially tree-lined streets and squares remain characteristic with blocks of flats for the workers to the south-west at Vickerstown on Walney Island.

From the railway station turn left into <u>Abbey Road</u> *where stands the Salvation Army Citadel.*

The Technical College, designed by Woodhouse and Willownby in 1900, was used as a college until 1991. Two mottoes inscribed on the friezes read, 'Ais longa vita brevis' (art endures, life is short) and 'Labour omnia vincit' (effort overcomes all things.)

Ramsden Baths, opened in 1872, were the first swimming baths in the town.

Ramsden Square is named after James Ramsden, industrialist. He was the first Mayor of Barrow, a position he held for five successive years.

The Library (1915–20) and the National Westminster Bank (1875–1900) are notable buildings.

Turn left into Duke Street.

Forum 28, an award winning Arts Centre, includes one of the largest theatres in Cumbria and the Tourist Information Centre.

The Town Hall was built in 1887 to the winning design of N.A. Lyn of Belfast. The Neo-Gothic red sandstone building has a 'Big Ben' type of clock tower.

Schneider Square. Henry Schneider (1817–1887), industrialist, was Barrow's mayor for three years from 1875.

Turn right onto the bridge in Michaelson Road.

To the north-west is the Devonshire Dock and, to the south-east, the Buccleuch, the Ramsden and the Cavendish Docks. Greatly in evidence are the VSEL shipbuilding works.

At the corner of Bridge Road are two large tenement blocks built for the workers in 1884 and named Devonshire Buildings.

Turn right into Bridge Road.

Pass the assembly sheds of VSEL.. Jubilee Bridge was built by Vickers in 1908 across Walney Channel to the Isle of Walney.

Isle of Walney

[OE. Wagen = quagmire, quicksand. ON. ney = island]

<u>Vickerstown</u>, built 1899–1904, was planned as a dormitory suburb of Barrow and owed much to Lord Leverhulme's pioneering model for housing factory workers at Port Sunlight on the Wirral, Cheshire.

Streets at Vickerstown are named after great admirals and ships built at Barrow.

After crossing <u>Jubilee Bridge</u>, turn left to reach <u>Ocean Road</u> which leads to the sea at <u>Biggar Bank</u>.

The eleven mile long, narrow strip of land of the Isle of Walney, curved at each end, shelters Barrow from the wild Irish Sea. Along this vulnerable centre of the island the monks of Furness Abbey built the raised causeway of Biggar Dyke against erosion by the sea.

To the south: The ancient village of <u>Biggar</u> [*OE. Barley garth*] served as a Grange for the monks of Furness Abbey, but smuggling was a profitable sideline. The beams of black Spanish oak in The Queen's Arms are said to have come from an Armada galleon wrecked on the coast.

Further south, *Sheep Island*, accessible at low water, was once a quarantine station for seamen.

South Walney Nature Reserve includes the largest colony of lesser black-headed and herring gulls in Europe and is of great importance for migrating and wintering birds.

At *Haws Bank*, evidence of prehistoric settlement has been uncovered.

<u>Walney Lighthouse</u> at Haws Point has been warning shipping since 1790.

From Biggar Bank, turn north along the beach to the caravan park at Earnse Point.

Beyond the World War II airfield lies –

<u>North Walney Nature Reserve</u> and a site of prehistoric settlement. The unique Walney geranium and the natterjack toad are

amongst the special attractions.

From Earnse Point, follow Cows Tarn Lane into the village of North Scale which has survived from Saxon times in spite of the devastation caused by Royalist troops in 1644 during the Civil War.

Turn south to join the Promenade. Cross Jubilee Bridge to the mainland. Turn left.

North Road

Devonshire Dock Hall, the enormous cream building, is where the Trident submarine is assembled.

The Dock Museum, straddles and incorporates a 33 feet deep Victorian graving dock – a dry dock for cleaning and repairing ships. Barrow's industrial and maritime history from the middle of the 19c to the present day is told using modern audio-visual technology.

Ironworks Road is a reminder of Barrow's industrial past. *Turn right into* Hindpool Road. Cornerhouse Park is now a retailing area on the site of the former steelworks. *Turn left into* Abbey Road. The Customs House stands at the roundabout. *Continue along Abbey Road to the starting point.*

Furness Abbey

The origin was at Tulketh, on the banks of the River Ribble near Preston, where land was given to the monks of the Order of Savigny in 1123 by Stephen, Count of Boulogne, who later became King of England (1136–1153). As the site was subject to flooding, the monks were given alternative lands in Furness, in the wooded valley of Bekansgil, the Vale of the Deadly Nightshade, an area rich in stone and minerals. In 1147, the Savigny monks amalgamated with the Cistercians.

In addition to building a magnificent abbey using local red sandstone, the monks farmed and made good use of the local iron ore, which they smelted on the Isle of Walney. They owned their own fleet of sailing ships and traded with the Isle of Man and with Ireland. The construction of Piel Castle guarded the entrance to Walney Channel whilst Dalton Castle offered protection against Scottish raiders. Into the monks possession came large estates in northern England and the Isle of Man with the consequent responsibility for law and order. By 1537, Furness Abbey was second only to Cistercian Fountains Abbey in Yorkshire, in wealth and in importance.

Henry VIII, having failed to have his marriage to Catherine of Aragon annulled, and desperate for a son, outraged Roman Catholic Europe by his twin repudiation of his wife, who was the King of Spain's aunt, and of the Pope. Fearing military invasion, Henry needed to increase defence spending. To raise taxes would only have made his break with Rome even more unpopular so, instead, he turned to the monasteries. Arguing that the monks were lazy, corrupt and immoral, he persuaded Parliament in 1536 to abolish nearly 400 smaller monasteries. The monks were turned out and allowed to become parish priests; the nuns had to live on meagre government pensions; the monastic treasures were seized and their estates were sold to raise money for a perceived threat of war. It was the biggest shift in land ownership since the Norman Conquest.

Opposition in southern England was slight, but rebellion broke out in the north. In October 1536, some 40,000 men joined the protest movement known as 'The Pilgrimage of Grace'. The rebel leader, Robert Aske, said that '*To the Statute of Suppression he did grudge against the same, and so did all the country, because the abbeys in the north parts gave alms to poor men and laudably served God.*' The monks of Furness and other abbeys took an active role in the rebellion. They became roving agitators recruiting for the rebels, marching with them or sending them supplies and money.

Eventually, Henry persuaded the rebels to disband by promising that the larger abbeys would be spared. Then he reneged on his word and sent an army of revenge into the north. The leaders of the revolt were hanged, along with monks from Furness Abbey. The suppression and the Dissolution of the larger monasteries, including Furness Abbey, went ahead in 1539. The buildings were pillaged for stone and lead and soon became deserted ruins.

The site of the Abbey and some of its lands were granted to the King's minister, Thomas Cromwell. In turn, these possessions passed through the ownership of the Curwen, Preston and Lowther families to the Cavendish family of Holker Hall until, in 1923, the Abbey ruins were placed in the care of the state, now English Heritage.

William Wordsworth wrote of boyhood visits to the Abbey in *The Prelude II*, 102–31, and composed a sonnet, 'At Furness Abbey' in 1840 and again in 1845.

The Abbey is included on the way marked walk 'The Cistercian Way'.

Visitors to the extensive Abbey ruins are guided and informed by the commentary on a portable tape recorder.

Leave Barrow-in-Furness on the A590 (Ulverston) road.

<u>Dalton-in-Furness</u> [OE. *Dale tun = dale town*] is now a small market town at the junction of two main roads, but was formerly the centre of intensive iron ore mining from 1712. It was at one time the 'capital' of Furness until superseded by Barrow-in-Furness.

<u>Dalton Castle</u> (NT) is a ruined 14c pele tower built by the monks of Furness Abbey for protection against Scottish raiders. The Abbot held court within the castle and its prison was in use until 1774.

<u>The Market Place</u> has held markets since 1239 and street markets continue on Tuesdays. From a curving line of old stone slabs fish

was offered for sale.

The cast iron fountain, erected for Queen Victoria's Jubilee in 1897, bears the inscription 'Keep the Pavement Dry'.

St Mary's Church of 19c design displays an unusual chequerboard pattern in its decorative stonework. The large nave and imposing west tower bear witness to the past prosperity of the town.

In the churchyard, a memorial plaque refers to the 300 victims of the bubonic plague which ravaged the town in 1631.

Nearby is the grave of George Romney (1734–1802), the portrait painter, who was born at Beckside, Dalton-in-Furness. The family moved to High Cocken, some two miles from Barrow, and Romney spent much time sketching at nearby Dendron where the 17c village chapel was the school in Romney's day. He began his working life as a cabinet maker, like his father, before being apprenticed to the Kendal artist Christopher Steele. After marrying a Kendal girl in 1756, he moved to London without her to establish his career and to rival Sir Joshua Reynolds as the most fashionable painter of the age.

Church Weint. A steep little lane below the church leads to Goose Green, where stray animals used to be confined in the old circular stone 'pinfold', or compound. The Brown Cow Inn is reputedly the oldest hostelry in Dalton. The local poorhouse has been converted into two attractive cottages and the town's Free School is now the Chequers Motel.

The South Lakes Wild Animal Park, just out of town, opened in 1994. Fourteen acres of parkland contain over a hundred species of animals and birds.

Leave Dalton on the A595.

Sandscale Haws (NT) [ON. Hamestead on the sands.] Signposted Roanhead. Miles of open sands on the edge of the Duddon Estuary are exposed at low tide, backed by sand dunes. This is a breeding ground for oystercatchers, ringed plovers, the little tern and the rare natter jack toad. Maritime plants and flowers include the Coral Root Orchid and the Burnett Rose.

<u>Iron Mining</u>. The limestone region around Dalton-in-Furness, including the villages of Lindal, Newton and Stainton, was very rich in scattered deposits of iron ore.

The prospect of finding a large deposit attracted Henry Schneider into forming a partnership with the landowner, the Earl of Burlington, who became the seventh Duke of Devonshire. Schneider invested £50,000 but after four years of exploration his geologists discovered little of value. A cash crisis arose, saved by a further investment from the Earl.

Another shaft was sunk at Park, between Dalton and Askham, near the shore of the Duddon Estuary. Again the money was exhausted, but the miners agreed to work for a further week without wages. In the last dramatic days, a rich vein of very high quality haematite was exposed, the second largest ever found in Britain. As a consequence, Park Mine produced more than seven million tons of ore from 1856 until closure in 1921.

To pump water from the mines, Cornish engines were installed and the influx of Cornish miners resulted in one mine being called 'Mousell', after Mousehole in Cornwall where the miners originated.

Today, the legacy of the 18c and 19c industrial boom years has left this area honeycombed with old mine workings and pit shafts. Spoil heaps, flooded craters and relics of large-scale quarrying, as carried out at Greenscoe, are scattered across the countryside. Derelict and flooded old workings have become unofficial nature reserves attracting wildlife, both flora and fauna.

At Park, mining subsidence was very extensive, indicative of the massive quantities of material removed from the mine. The consequent flooding is a further indication of the huge volume of water which had to be pumped continuously from the mine. This flooded area has become a trout farm.

Askham-in-Furness [*ON. Among ash trees*] became an industrial settlement as a direct result of the discovery of vast quantities of iron ore at Park. To smelt the ore, blast furnaces were built at Askham by Wakefield Mackinnon and Company. Smelting began in 1867 and continued until 1918. The iron works then stood idle for fifteen years before demolition in 1933.

Terraced houses built for the workers, remnants of slag tips and traces of railway track remain. The long, low pier extending into the Duddon Estuary is constructed of waste material from Askham's iron works. A cladding of wooden piles forms a quay.

Tytup Hall. SE from the Bay Horse Inn and ¼-mile beyond the Black Dog Inn is this large 17c house in attractive grounds. It was the home of Father Thomas West (1720–1779) a Catholic priest from Scotland who settled in Furness. He wrote two of the earliest and most influential books on Lakeland: *The Antiquities of Furness* (1774) and a pioneering *Guide to the Lakes* (1778) in which he recommended the best viewing points or 'stations'.

Marsh Grange dates back to the 12c when it belonged to Alexander Kirkby, Lord of the Manor. By 1552 the property was owned by the Askew family. Margaret Askew married Judge Thomas Fell and lived at Swarthmoor Hall. On her husband's death she married George Fox, the founder of the Quaker movement.

Dunnerholme, a low-lying limestone promontory on the Duddon Estuary has two old limekilns, accessible by means of a public footpath over the railway crossing and through the golf links.

Sandside, at the eastern end of the ancient crossing route over the Duddon Sands, has the old Ship Inn for the refreshment of travellers. Slate from Kirkby Moor was shipped from here in flat-bottomed boats called 'dolly flats' and loaded onto sloops at Haverigg or Millom.

<u>Kirkby-in-Furness</u> [*ON. Church hamlet*] To the north, extending as far as Foxfield, is lonely Angerton Moss, crossed by ancient peat-cutters' tracks.

To the east, rises the most westerly outcrop of Silurian Slate to a height of 1,000 feet. Dark blue slate was extracted from a complex of small quarries throughout the 17c by tenant farmers on land rented from the Burlington Estate. From c. 1760 the demand for roofing material increased on account of the Industrial Revolution and the need for more houses for the workers in the factory towns. Transporting the slate to distant places was facilitated by the construction of Slaters Road over Kirkby Moor to link with the Ulverston Canal which opened in 1796.

Around 1843, problems with overlapping tunnels and drainage in the quarries caused Lord William Cavendish (second Earl of Burlington), who became the seventh Duke of Devonshire in 1858, to take over all the workings. He was also the Chairman of the new Furness Railway Company which extended its line to Kirkby in 1846. This enabled Burlington slate, brought down to Kirkby station siding by a gravity incline system, to be transported to Barrow by rail for onward shipment.

The distinctive trade mark of blue grey Burlington slate was the 'roundhead' dressing as opposed to the usual square dressed slate. Natives of Kirkby came to be known as 'Roundheads'.

From these quarries has come the greatest production of roofing slate in the whole of England, Scotland and Ireland. The present huge Burlington quarry continues to be worked.

On Kirkby Moor, a Bronze Age ring cairn (OS. 251827), with a diameter of 75 feet, has a bank 2 feet high and 6 to 10 feet wide. The inner side of the bank shows the remains of a revetment circle of large stones. The entrance is to the south-east. To the north-east are three pairs of stones, each about 2 feet high, probably part of an avenue.

A Bronze Age round cairn (OS. 251830) is 80 feet across and 3 feet to 4 feet high. On the south-west sector, a stone cist originally contained a cremation.

Western Lakes and Coast
From the Duddon to the Esk

Many centuries of inaccessibility because of difficult routes across wide river estuaries or through Lakeland fells have left this western area of Lakeland relatively unspoiled and quiet.

A595/A5093 to Millom.

<u>From Duddon Bridge</u> the River Duddon widens into a broad estuary. At low tide a vast amount of sand is exposed, two miles across at the widest point. The mudflats are the habitat of large numbers of wading birds.

<u>Holborn Hill.</u> Until 1850, the Pack Horse route across the Duddon Estuary led to this small village.

<u>The Ship Inn</u> used to have a lamp burning in its window to guide travellers across the dangerous sands. A guide service was also available from the inn as the inscription above the door records:

> *William and Anne Barren live heare*
> *Who mostly keep good ale and beer*
> *You that intend to cross ye sands*
> *Call here a guide at your command.*

The route across the sands was curtailed when the railway link between Whitehaven and Furness was opened in 1851 to serve the iron mines and foundries in the area. A halt at Holborn Hill was established for the local mines.

<u>Hodbarrow Mines.</u> In 1855, Nathaniel Caine from Liverpool and John Barratt from Cornwall founded the Hodbarrow Mining Company and first extracted iron ore from the Old Engine shaft at Hodbarrow Point. Rent and tonnage royalties were payable to the Earl of Lonsdale.

By 1862, ore was being shipped from Borwick Rails. Vessels were assisted on the Duddon by steam tug and a lighthouse was built close to the point. A railway link with the Furness Railway in 1864 and a blast furnace, set up by the Cumberland Iron Mining and Smelting Company a year later, provided further outlets for Hodbarrow ore.

When huge pockets of extremely high quality haematite ore, up to 100 feet thick, were discovered at Hodbarrow, employment increased dramatically. Cornish and Irish men were recruited to work down the new shafts which opened successively from 1868 onwards. Eleven working shafts came into operation.

As a consequence of the rapid growth of mining and of iron smelting, a new town close to the old village of Holborn Hill came into being – Millom. Holborn Hill railway station was incorporated into the town to become Millom station and extensive sidings were built to deal with the products of Hodbarrow Mine and the iron works.

Flooding problems in the mine workings necessitated the erection of a sea wall. A wooden structure in 1885 was superseded in 1890 by an inner sea wall which is still visible today. But the sea broke through in 1898 and an outer barrier, over a mile long, from Haverigg to Hodbarrow Point, was completed in 1905.

The output figures made this complex the largest and busiest in Britain. In 1968, when the extraction of Hodbarrow's ore had become uneconomical, the mine closed. It had produced more than 25 million tons of very high grade iron ore during 112 years of operating. The

Millom iron works closed in the following year.

Millom [*OE. Settlement by the mills.*] A mile or more north of the present town centre are:

The Castle. This 14c defensive pele tower now has a farmhouse built into it. It was the fortified residence of the Lords of the Manor.

Holy Trinity Church. The restored Norman and 14c church is notable for its 'fish' window and for the Hudleston family monuments from the time that they lived at the castle.

On a 15c churchyard cross are carved the family arms of the Hudlestons.

Millom town owes its origin to the iron ore mining at Hodbarrow in the mid-19c and to the industrial and commercial activities which emanated from it.

Millom Folk Museum features the history of the local iron production. Among the exhibits are a replica of the working levels of the Hodbarrow Mine and a reconstruction of a room in a miner's cottage.

There is a tribute to local celebrity, Norman Nicholson, OBE (1914–1987), the distinguished poet and writer.

He was born in Millom and lived all his life at 14 St George's Terrace, just downhill from St George's Church where he is buried in the extended churchyard. His father was a men's outfitter and the building now bears a commemorative plaque.

At the age of 16, Norman Nicholson contracted tuberculosis and spent the rest of his days recovering. For nearly two years, he was almost unable to speak, except in a whisper, and this handicap possibly concentrated his mind on the written word.

In his attic bedroom he wrote about the history, the social issues and the industrial decline of Millom. It was the closure of Millom's iron ore industry which prompted the lines:

You and I know better, Duddon.
For I who've lived for nearly 30 years
Upon your shore have seen the slagbanks slant
Like screes into the sand.

Religious verse plays, topographical books on Lakeland, an anthology and an autobiography are indicative of the range and depth of his writings.

Millom Railway Station houses workshop units for a Craft Centre in the station buildings.

Hodbarrow, just south of Millom, is where iron mining took place for more than a century. Many scars remain. Rainwater has flooded behind the long sea wall which was built in 1905 to protect the mine workings from the sea. Hodbarrow Hollow Lake has resulted and is now an RSPB Nature Reserve. Waterfowl and waders, a varied flora and the rare natterjack toad are the main attractions which are best observed from the circular walk round the lagoon.

Haverigg [ON. *Hill where oats are grown*] has a large expanse of sand at low tide backed by sand dunes almost 70 feet high in places. To bind the soft sand, tenacious marram grass has been planted.

To the north is a modern open prison and a twelve-mile beach to the estuary of the River Esk at Ravenglass.

The RAF Millom Museum, founded in 1992, is housed on the former airfield at Haverigg where aircrew were trained during World War II.

Kirksanton [OE. *The church by the sandy farmstead*] is notable for the Lacra Bronze Age Stone Circles (OS. 150814). Remnants of five circles and possibly two avenues are visible.

The first circle is 50 feet across and has 6 surviving stones, 2 of them close together and facing east.

The second circle, to the south, has a diameter of 48 feet and has 6 stones remaining from 11 upright. A low central mound contained a cremation and once supported a circle of stones 14 feet across.

The third circle, to the east-south-east, originally measured 60 feet across, but only 4 stones remain, one of them 5 feet high.

The fourth circle, further east-south-east, is about 60 feet across with a large flat stone in the centre. A stone at the north side of the ring had collared-urn sherds at its base.

The first avenue of a ragged double line of stones runs east-north-east from the fourth stone circle. Outcrops of rock confuse the scene.

The fifth circle, 25 feet north-west of the fourth circle, has 6 stones. It is 16 feet across with a central stone.

The second avenue, to the south-west, is 50 feet wide and runs west-south-west for 230 feet although most of the stones on the north side are missing.

Giant's Grave (OS. 137811) is part of the Lacra complex and consists of 2 upright stones 10 feet and 8 feet high respectively. The larger one bears a cup mark, 3 inches across and 1½ inches deep.

Silecroft. Obtaining salt from sea water by a process of evaporation was once an industry here.

Whitcham [*OE. Homestead of Hwita's people.*] Victorian St Mary's Church was built on an ancient foundation.

    Black Combe   *OFOL 166*

Back along the A595, 2½ miles towards Duddon Bridge is – Beckside (OS. 152847).

    White Combe   *OFOL 172*

Continue towards Ravenglass on the A595.

<u>Gutterby Spa</u> [*ON. Godric's homestead*]. A narrow track leads to the wild open beach of sand and gravel backed by a line of cliffs, but there is no sign of the mineral spring.

<u>Holegill Bridge</u>, Bootle. (3 miles from Whicham; ¾ mile from Bootle).

Black Combe.   OFOL 168

<u>Bootle</u> [*OE. Dwelling house*] is recorded in the Domesday Book and its Market Charter dates from 1346.

<u>St Michael's Church</u>, although considerably altered, still retains characteristic Norman architecture in its chancel. There is a memorial to Sir Hugh Agnew, Henry VIII's cellarer, or keeper of the royal wines and spirits, who lived at Seaton Priory following its dissolution in 1541.

<u>Seaton Hall</u>, a mile north, incorporates the remains of Benedictine Seaton Priory, where Wordsworth once stayed on holiday.

Two lanes lead to the sea:

One lane leads to <u>Annaside</u>, named after the River Annas, which is crossed when approaching the shore. Hundreds of rock pools are exposed at low tide. A walk northwards leads to tiny <u>Selker Bay</u> where the River Annas flows into the sea.

The second lane leads to <u>Tarn Bay</u> with its very good beach.

Waberthwaite [*ON. Clearing with a hunting or fishing hut*] Richard Woodall's shop, famous for Cumberland sausage and home-cured ham, displays the Royal Warrant sign.

<u>Estuary of the River Esk</u>.

Wasdale

[ON. Valley with a lake.]

Take the A595.

The Lutwidge Arms Hotel stands on the site of the former
Holmrook Hall farm, the family home of the Lutwidges, cousins of
Charles Lutwidge Dodgson (Lewis Carroll, 1832–98), who visited fre-
quently in the 1870s.

*From the corner of the road, take the public footpath sign-post-
ed Irton Church.* Into view comes all that remains of Holmrook Hall
– an archway and a coach house. Some of the furniture and fittings
from the Hall were removed to the hotel.

*Continue along the footpath (¾m) to the remote St Paul's Church,
Irton (OS. 092005).*

A 9c red sandstone Anglian cross in the graveyard stands 10 feet
high, elaborately sculptured with knot work and scrolls. On its west
side, the runes read: *'Pray for ...'* It is thought that the cross was
erected for an Anglo Saxon thane or his wife.

Inside the Victorian church is a Burne-Jones window and a
memorial to Crusader Adam of Irton.

Return to the A595.

*Travel south alongside the River Irt for a little more than ½ mile
to the Gubbergill turn to Santon Bridge.*

<u>Irton</u> [*OE. Farmstead by the River Irt (Welsh 'ir' meaning 'fresh' or 'green')*] This is a widely scattered community around the River Irt which is the outflow from Wast Water.

<u>Irton Hall</u>, once a pele tower, became a special school for children.

<u>The River Irt</u> was famous at one time for its pearls. The Roman authors Tacitus and Pliny wrote about the pearls in the first century AD. William Camden in the late 16c explained, '*In this brook the shell fish eagerly sucking in the dew conceive and bring forth pearls or shell berries. These the inhabitants gather up at low water, and the merchants buy them of the poor people for a trifle, but sell them to the jewellers at a good price. Further mussel pearls are frequently found in the other rivers hereabout.*' Pearl fishing concessions were granted from the 17c up to the middle of the 19c. Since then, pearl fishing has been sporadic or non-existent.

<u>Santon Bridge</u> [*OE. Bridge by the sandy farmstead*] spans the River Irt near the junction of four minor roads in an area of glacial debris – huge roches moutonées and scattered moraine.

<u>The Bridge Inn</u> is the venue for 'The World's Greatest Liar' competition, held on the third Thursday in November.

The competition began in 1974 in memory of Will Ritson the Wasdale man and licensee of what is now The Wasdale Head Inn. He was renowned for telling tall stories. 'Auld Will' boasted that turnips grew so big in Wasdale that dales folk quarried them for Sunday lunch and used the remainders as shelters for their Herdwick sheep.

One competitor won by telling a TV crew covering the event that he was not taking part. They believed him and left without filming and he was judged to be the winner.

Competitors must be over the age of 18 and journalists, lawyers and politicians are excluded.

Irton Pike *OFOL 182*

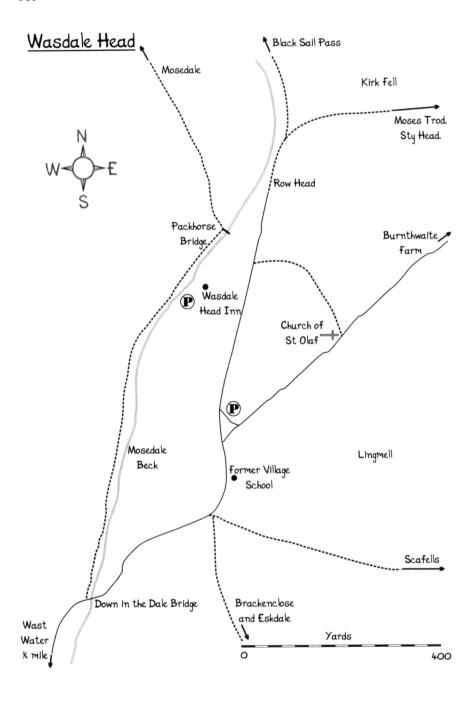

Wasdale Head

Mosedale

Black Sail Pass

Kirk Fell

Moses Trod.
Sty Head.

N
W E
S

Row Head

Packhorse
Bridge

Burnthwaite
Farm

Wasdale
Head Inn

Church of
St Olaf

Mosedale
Beck

Lingmell

Former Village
School

Scafells

Down in the Dale Bridge

Brackenclose
and Eskdale

Wast
Water
¾ mile

Yards

0   400

<u>Nether Wasdale</u> is another scattered community. In the 18c, the new techniques of the Agricultural Revolution enabled local farmers to plant more profitable crops, such as potatoes and turnips, in the deeper soil. Farm buildings constructed at that time bore evidence of the greater prosperity.

The maypole on the village green was erected to celebrate Queen Victoria's Jubilee in 1897.

<u>St Michael and All Angels</u> is a 15c Chapel of Ease to St Bees. Its aisle was added in 1830. Painted texts adorn the walls and , on either side of the altar are carved oak panellings salvaged from York Minster after a fire in the 17c.

Whin Rigg   4.5   *Seatallan*   7.5

<u>Wasdale</u> is regarded as the most austere of all the Lakeland valleys. Critics have harshly proclaimed it to be '*the last place God made and He had lost His touch.*' Its inaccessibility brings the benefit of quietness.

<u>Wast Water</u> (NT) was described by Wordsworth as '*long, narrow, stern and desolate.*'

It is probably the most awesome of all the English lakes, 3 miles long and ½ mile wide, gouged out by a glacier cutting deeply into the original valley floor, the deepening being the greater because the valley is restricted in width. Consequently, the maximum depth of the lake is 258 feet between Long Crag and Illgill Head, 58 feet below sea level, making it the deepest lake in England.

The glacier was fed by the snows of Kirk Fell [*ON. The fell above the church*], Great Gable [*ON. The shape resembling the gable end of a house*] and Scafell Pike [*ON. Fell with a bare summit*], England's highest mountain (3,210 feet), which together form the most impressive dalehead of any Lakeland valley.

An additional element of grandeur is the sheer 1,600 feet drop of the fan-shaped screes which extend along the full length of the lake on the eastern side. These loose stones, formed by glacial erosion and streaked with hues of red and brown, tumble spectacularly straight down into the dark waters below.

The redness of the stones on the screes was caused by deposits of iron. These stones were formerly the source of 'ruddle', a deep red paint produced by wetting and rubbing, used for marking sheep.

The lack of nutrients in the water means that it can be tolerated only by trout and char.

A pump house on the River Irt, opposite Low Wood, provides water from the lake for British Nuclear Fuels' processing plant at Sellafield. Not only is Wast Water the nearest lake to Sellafield but the high purity of the water decreases the damage to equipment. Plans to build a weir to provide Sellafield with more water were vigorously contested and defeated.

<u>Wasdale Hall</u> was built c. 1826 on the site of a farm for a Yorkshire wool merchant, Stansfeld Rawson. An accident by drowning in the lake of a child of the house gave rise to the notion that the area was haunted by the mother and child. After several subsequent owners, the Hall was bought by the National Trust in 1959 and leased to the Y.H.A.

Illgill Head	4.3, 4

Continue along the lake shore.

<u>Netherbeck Bridge</u> spans Nether Beck which descends from Scoat Tarn at an altitude of 1,956 feet.

Haycock	7.6
Scoat Fell	7.5
Seatallan	7.6

<u>Overbeck Bridge</u> gives access to Bowderdale, the valley of Over Beck which has its source at Dore Head.

Red Pike (W)	*7.5*
Yewbarrow	*7.5*

<u>Bowderdale</u> is an isolated sheep farm (OS. 165072) whose most famous occupant was the marathon fell runner Joss Naylor, MBE. His records included The Twenty-Four Hour Race covering 72 peaks of over 2,000 feet, a distance of 108 miles and climbing a total of 40,000 feet; The Three Peaks Race – Ben Nevis, Scafell Pike and Snowdon in 11 hours 54 minutes; and The Welsh Peaks Race – 14 peaks, mostly 3,000 feet high.

<u>Wasdale Head</u> is a small, isolated community in a flat amphitheatre almost entirely encircled by some of the most majestic mountains in Lakeland.

These are featured in silhouette behind Wast Water on The Lake District National Park's emblem: Great Gable flanked by Kirk Fell and Lingmell [*ON. Heather covered hill.*] At Wasdale Head, the high peaks of Pillar and Scafell Pike also contribute to the grandeur and scale of commanding splendour.

Settlement and land clearance on the flat valley floor between Mosedale Beck and Lingmell Beck began in the 12c. By the end of the 16c, an open field covered 345 acres, and 18 farmers held plots of 'arable and meadow', 3 to 10 acres in size. Today, the few scattered farms form a landscape pattern of small enclosures bounded by dry stone walls, with surplus stones piled in the corners.

Traditionally, it is claimed that the original flock of Herdwick sheep prospered here after being rescued from a stranded ship – possibly a Norse ship – in the early Middle Ages.

PACK HORSE BRIDGE AT WASDALE HEAD - GREAT GABLE BEYOND
12/98

So isolated is the settlement that electricity only reached it in 1979, the cable having been laid along the bed of the lake and underground.

The Wasdale Head Inn began as Row Foot, a small farmstead where William Ritson was born in 1808. In 1856 he extended the farmhouse, named it The Huntsman's Inn and obtained a licence to accommodate visitors at a time when tourism and rock climbing as a sport were beginning to increase in popularity. What remains of the old inn can still be seen as an annexe to the present hotel.

Will Ritson was well known as a huntsman, a wrestler and, above all, as a raconteur, who entertained Victorian visitors with his odd ways and humorous dialect speech. He boasted that Wasdale had the highest mountain (Scafell Pike), the deepest lake (Wast Water), the smallest church (St Olaf's) and biggest liar (himself). By comparing himself to George Washington, who could not tell a lie, 'Auld Will' is said to have won a lying competition!

Will Ritson retired in 1879 and died in 1890. He was buried at Nether Wasdale.

On the site of Will Ritson's The Huntsman's Inn was built The Wastwater Hotel in the 1880s. Further extensions converted it into The Wasdale Head Inn. A bar with climbing memorabilia at the inn is named after Will Ritson and also a waterfall in Mosedale Beck. In his memory, The World's Greatest Liar Competition is held annually at Santon Bridge.

Mountaineers regard The Wasdale Head Inn as a birthplace of the sport of rock climbing. From a group of Oxford undergraduates on their summer vacation here in 1881 emerged, in the following year, Walter P. Haskett-Smith together with his younger brother, Edmund, who began a systematic series of climbs. Although inappropriately dressed and ill-equipped by today's standards, they nevertheless pioneered rock climbing as a serious sport. The Abraham brothers, George and Ashley, used the inn as a base from which to climb and to take their remarkable photographs, several of which are on display at the inn.

A popular time for climbers, before World War I, was Christmas when the village schoolchildren would perform a pantomime for the visitors who devised an entertainment for them in return.

A further amusement was the Barn Door Traverse where climbers tested their skills up and over the barn door where the stone lintel is still marked 'Post Horses'.

For many years the inn has been featured in climbing memoirs and in fiction.

<u>St Olaf's Church</u>, dedicated to the IIc Patron Saint of Norway, was built c. 1552. It stands in a group of yew trees, a simple dale chapel, one of England's smallest, seating 39 people. On one of the windows is an etching of Napes Needle on Great Gable above the text from Psalm 121, 'I will lift up mine eyes unto the hills from whence cometh my help.'

Until this century, the chapel, which was in the medieval parish of St Bees, had no burial rights and coffins were carried on horse-back across Eskdale Moor for burial at Boot.

One legend relates how a procession of mourners were escorting the coffin of a young man strapped to a horse when the mist came down over the moor. The mist eventually cleared but the horse and coffin were nowhere to be seen. In vain the mourners searched before returning sadly home. Not long after, the mother of the dead man died from grief. The procession set out again over Eskdale Moor and once again the mist came down. When the mist eventually lifted, the horse was there – carrying not the coffin of the mother, but the coffin of the young man.

Burial rights were granted in 1889 and there are several graves of climbers who were killed on the dangerous heights of Pillar, Great Gable, Scafell – and the Himalayas. Alexandrina Wilson is recorded as the *'Last schoolteacher of the dale'* (d. 1947) and *'Climbed in these hills'* is the epitaph for the Shakespeare scholar, A.P. Rossiter.

The Village School, closed for many years, operated on 'Whittlegate' terms for the local schoolmaster who lodged at different farmhouses in turn, offsetting the cost by giving lessons.

Brackenclose, near the lakeshore, opened in 1937. It was the first base for the Fell and Rock Climbing Club.

Row Head, 17c. Sir Arthur Quiller-Couch brought Oxford students here during Easter vacations. They studied in the mornings and climbed in the afternoons whilst 'Q' occupied himself writing his first Cornish novel, *Dead Man's Rock* (1887).

Burnthwaite Farm is the last building at Wasdale Head en route to Sty Head Pass.

The Wasdale Show is held at Wasdale Head late in the year, on the second Saturday in October.

The Packhorse Bridge over Mosedale Beck is a reminder that, originally, Wasdale Head provided a resting place for pack men and sheep drovers, who travelled the early trails through the mountain passes to reach the coast.

In the 17c and 18c, packhorse trains of slate from Honister and wadd (graphite) from Borrowdale passed through Wasdale in one direction, whilst imported tobacco and spirits, as well as coal, were carried over the mountain passes in the opposite direction.

Mountain Passes

1.   Mosedale, Black Sail Pass to Ennerdale; Scarth Gap to Buttermere.

2.   Sty Head Pass to Borrowdale; or to Esk Hause and Eskdale; or to Rossett Pass and Langdale.

3.   The Burnmoor 'Corpse' Track to Eskdale.

Bowfell	4.6	Great Gable	7.20
Esk Pike	4.8	Green Gable	7.6
Great End	4.8	Kirk Fell	7.4
Illgill Head	4.6	Pillar	7.9
Whin Rig	4.8	Red Pike (W)	7.6
Lingmell	4.5, 6	Scoat Fell	7.6
Scafell	4.10	Steeple	7.6
Scafell Pike	4.13, 14	Yewbarrow	7.6

Return along the lake shore for 2 miles.
   Turn right onto the Gosforth road.

<u>Greendale Gill</u> descends from Greendale Tarn.

Haycock	7.5
Middle Fell	7.4
Seatallan	7.6

<u>Gill Beck/Harrow Head</u>

Buckbarrow	7.2
Seatallan	7.5

<u>Buckbarrow</u> [*OE. The hill of the buck or goat.*] This area of morainic debris heaped against a rock barrier from Yew Tree Farm (OS. 117055) to Easthwaite (OS. 137035) is a landscape of humps and hollows, of rocks and boulders, and very difficult to farm.

   Not until the 16c did colonisation of this wild country begin. It was

known as Copeland Forest and included the western fells south of
Bassenthwaite Lake and the River Derwent. The name is still print-
ed on the OS Map north-west of Wast Water. The Borough of
Copeland today extends from just north of Whitehaven to south of
Millom, bounded by the Irish Sea on the west and by Lakeland's high-
est fells to the east.

<u>Copeland</u> [ON. *'the bought land']* was originally one of several baronial
forests in Lakeland and its name probably originated when the Norse
settlers engaged in land transactions.

   <u>Sowermyrr</u>. Hugh Walpole, on holiday from his boarding school in
Durham, spent memorable summers here with his parents between
1893 and 1898 and developed a lasting love of Lakeland.

   At Wellington Bridge turn right for Blengdale.

<u>Blengdale</u> [ON. Valley of the dark river.] Afforestation from Bleng
Bridge ends on reaching <u>Stockdale Moor</u>.

   The moorland at 900 feet is littered with relics of antiquity, but
the clusters of pre-historic cairns, walled enclosures, hut circles
and evidence of former fields are difficult to distinguish.

   <u>Sampson's Bratfull</u> (*'brat'* = apron) is a huge mound of stones,
96 feet long, 39 feet wide and 6 feet high, tapering towards the west.
It may be a Bronze Age burial mound, although 'long barrows' are
more usually found only in southern England. Legend declares that
the Devil dumped the stones after carrying them in his apron.

   Caw Fell   *7.7, 8*

Western Lakes and Coast
From the Esk to St Bees.

Quiet beaches extend for 17 miles from the estuary of the River Esk to the red sandstone cliffs at St Bees Head, with the intrusion of controversial and formidable Sellafield.

Take the A595/B5344

Drigg [*ON. Place where boats had to be dragged or carried over unnavigable water – here the River Irt.*]

Sheltered by sand dunes from the Irish Sea is this breeding ground for colonies of black-headed gulls, terns, mergansers, shelducks and Britain's rarest amphibian, the natterjack toad.

Flotsam washed ashore at Drigg has traditionally belonged to the Pennington family at Muncaster Castle who hold the 'right of shipwreck'.

In complete contrast, solid low-level waste, such as protective clothing and used paper towels from Sellafield, and used radio therapy materials from hospitals, is disposed of in specially designed trenches.

Seascale, [*ON. Small hut by the sea.*] was originally built by the Furness Railway Company and now houses workers from the British Nuclear Fuel complex at Sellafield.

Grey Croft Bronze Age Stone Circle (OS. 034024) lies north-west of Seascale House Farm. The circle was restored in 1949 when standing stones, buried in the 19c, were located and re-erected. Of the original 12 stones, 10 varying in height from 4 feet to 7 feet, now form a circle 80 feet in diameter. Alongside one of the stones was found a partly ground stone axe from Langdale's Pike o' Stickle. A low central mound revealed some burnt fragments of bone and part of a jet ring.

Continue along the A595.

Gosforth [*OE. Goose ford.*]

St Mary's Church contains remarkable Saxon masonry and Norse carvings. The Fishing Stone shows Thor attempting to catch the Midgard Serpent. Two Norse hogback tombstones are thought to be memorials to 10c chieftains. One is in the shape of a thatched cottage. The other depicts a battle scene, where two groups of men are armed with spears and shields.

In the churchyard stands a 10c sandstone Celtic/Norse cross, 15 feet high, one of the finest in England. At the top of the pillar is a wheel cross and at the base a bark carving representative of the sacred ash tree. The carvings on the pillar illustrate how the Norsemen superimposed the old Norse religion, which they brought with them, onto the Christian beliefs which they found on arrival. On one side, the triumph of good over evil is recorded by the Nordic sagas, where Vidar is fighting a double-headed dragon-wolf and Heimdal, the hornblower, is guarding the rainbow bridge leading to the realm of the gods. On the other side, the theme of the supremacy of good is continued where a soldier at the Crucifixion is piercing the side of Jesus with a sword, leading ultimately to the Resurrection.

| *Caw Fell* | *7.8* |
| *Ponsonby Fell* | *OFOL 192* |

<u>Gretigate Bronze Age Stone Circles</u> (OS. 058036) are ⅓ mile west of Gosforth, north of the bridleway. The site contains 3 circles and 9 small cairns.

The south circle is 104 feet across. The middle circle to the north-west, is 72 feet across and has a low central cairn. The north circle is 24 feet across and also encloses a small cairn. Excavations of the site have been inconclusive.

<u>Calder Bridge</u> [*W. Bridge over a rocky or rapid-flowing river.*]

<u>Calder Abbey</u> can be seen, but not visited, from the footpath from the churchyard along the north side of the river.

It was founded in 1134 by Gerald and his twelve Benedictine monks of the Savignac Order from Furness Abbey. After being raided by the Scots four years later, the abbey was abandoned. The monks were reproached for cowardice when they fled to start a safer community at Byland in Yorkshire. In 1148, the abbey was rebuilt by Cistercian monks, under the rule of Hardred. Their monastic rules forbad them the use of fur and linen, and the eating of meat, except in times of life-threatening sickness. At the beginning of the 14c, Robert the Bruce attacked the abbey, but it survived until the Dissolution in 1536. Parts of the monastic building have been incorporated in the late 18c house to which a Victorian mansion has been attached.

<u>Coldfell Road</u>, a minor road leading to Ennerdale, is now the western boundary of The Lake District National Park.

<u>Sellafield</u>, on the flood plain of the River Calder, was historically two localities known as Low Sellafield and High Sellafield. Today, the Sellafield site of British Nuclear Fuels (BNFL) occupies the area formerly known as Low Sellafield. Three major, inter-related, production activities take place.

<u>Windscale</u>. Locals originally described this area as one of '*poor, rough grazing*'. Then industry arrived. A wartime munitions factory was built by the Ministry of Supply c. 1941.

Years later, there were munitions here of a very different nature. Windscale, recognisable by its tall concrete chimneys, opened in 1951 in the vicinity of Windscale Nook, producing plutonium for the British atomic bomb by means of nuclear power.

When Windscale's reactor overheated in 1957, Britain was faced with a well-publicised nuclear accident. Iodine 131, in gaseous form, by-passed the filter system and was released into the surrounding countryside. For a period of about two weeks, contaminated milk in the locality had to be poured away. Norman Nicholson wrote in his poem '*Windscale*',

> *This is a land . . .*
> *Where sewers run with milk, and meat*
> *Is carved up for the fire to eat*
> *And children suffocate in God's fresh air.*

Whether or not beef cattle had to be incinerated is a controversial point.

<u>Calder Hall</u>, recognisable by its four cooling towers, became operational in 1956 on a site adjacent to Calder Hall Farm. As a Magnox reactor, it uses uranium metal machined into rods and fitted into cylinders of magnesium alloy. The reactor had a dual purpose: optimised for producing plutonium, but supplying electricity as a very useful secondary product. This was the world's first industrial scale nuclear power station to supply electricity to a national grid. Changing needs have now made generating electricity the prime function.

<u>BNFL's Reprocessing Plant</u> at Sellafield is where spent fuel is

treated to separate the valuable, reusable uranium and plutonium (about 97%) from the waste products (about 3%).

The Fuel Handling Plant operates the first stage of the reprocessing. Used fuel is stored under water in 'ponds', until its most intense radioactivity has decayed. The removal of the cladding from spent magnox fuel is also carried out.

The B205 Magnox Reprocessing Plant has reprocessed Magnox fuel since 1964.

The Thermal Oxide Reprocessing Plant (THORP) has reprocessed uranium fuel pins from Advanced Gas Cooled Reactors (AGRs) and spent uranium oxide fuel from Pressurised Water Reactors (PWRs) since 1994.

THORP cost £1,650 million and is so huge that St Paul's Cathedral would fit into just one section.

Mixed Oxide (MOX) Fuel, a mixture of uranium and plutonium oxides recovered from reprocessing, has been produced at Sellafield since 1993.

Waste Management. About 3% of used fuel, when reprocessed, ends up as radioactive waste.

The Vitrification Plant converts highly active liquid waste into solid glass blocks, reducing the volume by about two-thirds. This process makes the waste more manageable to store as this must be done for a minimum of 50 years. By this time it will have cooled off sufficiently for disposal when a deep underground repository becomes available.

The Encapsulation Plant. Intermediate level waste from conditioned Magnox fuel cladding is encased in cement inside stainless steel drums. Surface storage awaits the development of a suitable underground site.

Drigg is where compacted low-level waste is sealed in cement, within freight containers, which are then stored in concrete-lined vaults. Low-level waste from hospitals and universities is also stored here.

The Site Ion Exchange Effluent Plant (SIXEP) reduces the radio-activity of liquid discharges into the Irish Sea.

Integrated with this plant since 1994 have been five additional effluent treatment plants, including the Enhanced Actinide Removal Plant (EARP).

The Sellafield Visitors' Centre, open daily, has an impressive exhibition area which initially cost £5 million. The complexities of nuclear energy are visually and aurally explained. There is also an organised coach tour of the site with video presentations in the coach of the processes taking place inside the various buildings.

An *unclassified road leads to –*

Beckermet [*ON. OE. Stream where the hermit lives.*]

St John's Church was originally built on the site of a small Celtic monastery. Rebuilding took place in 1811 and again in 1879.

Haematite. In an arc of limestone from the Beckermet area in the south to the Rowrah district in the north, the mining of high quality iron ore (haematite) began in the early 19c. The adjacent coalfield provided fuel for a local iron and steel industry and a network of railways was constructed along this industrial plain.

A population explosion took place and these heavy industries prospered and declined for more than a century, according to cyclical conditions. By the 1960s, local iron and coal mines had been abandoned and local furnaces and railways closed down. Only the legacy of these industrial years is seen by the tourist today.

St Bees lies in the sheltered valley of Pow Beck beneath the high cliffs of St Bees Head.

St Bees Priory Church is named after St Bega, an Irish princess who fled from her father rather than marry the heathen Viking warrior he had chosen for her. Her ship was wrecked here in AD 650 and shelter was given to the survivors at Egremont Castle. As a thanks offering for deliverance, St Bega and her followers wished to build a sanctuary. Lady Egremont set about persuading her husband to provide the land and the building materials. Lord Egremont agreed to give stones and timber, but offered the land only if it would be covered by snow the following morning. It was midsummer, but legend relates that part of the land between Egremont Castle and the sea was indeed covered by snow the next morning. This sign convinced Lord Egremont that the land should be given to St Bega.

In the 10c, St Bega's cell was destroyed by the Danes. In 1120, the Benedictines started a century of rebuilding and extension. After the Dissolution in 1539, the buildings were largely left in ruins, but by 1611 part of the priory was restored to become the parish church. During the 19c a college was established for the training of clergy – the first of its kind outside Oxford and Cambridge.

Wordsworth wrote about St Bega, the priory and the college in 'Stanzas Suggested in a Steamboat off Saint Bees Head'.

See: *Credo.* Melvyn Bragg. Sceptre.

Inside the church, under the chancel in a burial vault, a lead coffin was found in 1981. The well-preserved body of a middle-aged man, who had died a violent death, was wrapped in a shroud, which contained pollen grains from plants native to the Middle East, leading to the belief that he may have been a Crusader.

The west doorway of the Priory Church has retained its magnificent Norman arch, carved in red sandstone.

Opposite, in the churchyard wall, is a carved stone which was unearthed when the path by the doorway was laid. It has been named the 'Dragon' or 'Beowulf' stone and shows St Michael fighting the beast.

St Bees School was founded in 1583 by a local man, Edmund Grindall, who became Archbishop of Canterbury (1576–83). A replica of his coat of arms is carved on the ancient bridge. A plaque marks his birthplace not far from the Manor House Inn.

The School House and the clock tower in the courtyard are reminiscent of an Oxbridge college. Close to the gate the old village pump is preserved.

The school's fortune changed for the better when the Lowthers were compelled to pay for the coal they were extracting from beneath the school's land.

St Bees is now a small Co-educational Independent School.

St Bees Head is on the designated Heritage Coast. The 300 feet high sandstone cliffs, the highest on the Cumbrian coast, are topped by a lighthouse built in 1781. A cliff-top path continues to Whitehaven, and beyond, along the Coastal Way.

Colonies of sea birds, including black guillemot, razorbill and kittiwake, can be observed from the lookout points in the Nature Reserve of the RSPB.

Alfred Wainwright's long distance *A Coast to Coast Walk* (1973) of 190 miles to Robin Hood's Bay on the Yorkshire coast starts from the sea wall at St Bees and climbs to St Bees Head before turning inland.

Rottington. Legend claims that the bones of a Viking giant, Rottin by name, are buried here. He and his crew carried off several nuns from St Bees and kept them as slaves. One nun managed to drug their captors and to stab the Vikings to death. She released her sister nuns and they all escaped together.

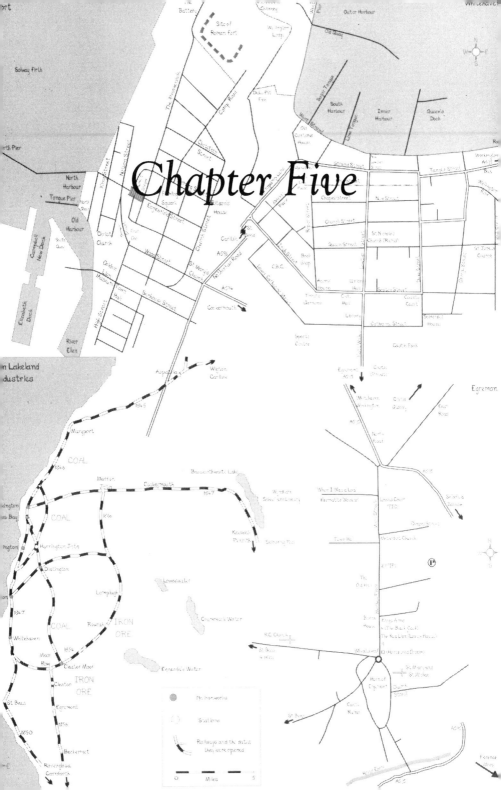

Chapter Five

Calder Bridge to
Ennerdale Bridge

From <u>Calder Bridge</u> [W. Rocky, or rapidly flowing river] on the A595, passing the ruins of 12c Calder Abbey, Coldfell Road, reputedly a Roman highway, climbs over Cold Fell to Ennerdale Bridge, a distance of 6½ miles. It is the shortest road link between Wasdale and Ennerdale and marks The National Park's western boundary for most of the way.

<u>Coldfell Gate,</u> now a cattle grid, is where minor roads from Egremont and Haile meet.

Follow the farm track and Friar Gill eastwards for ½-mile to reach <u>Monks Bridge,</u> known locally as Matty Ben's Bridge, a delightful packhorse bridge which spans the infant River Calder. It was possibly built by the monks of Calder Abbey.

Lank Rigg	*7.6*
Cold Fell	*OFOL 196*

<u>Near Thwaites</u> has a car park and picnic site.

Lank Rigg	*7.6*

<u>Kinniside Stone Circle</u> (OS. 060141) is not listed as an antiquity on OS maps because of its origin. One explanation is that twelve Bronze Age standing stones were removed by farmers many years

531

ago. Subsequently, the missing stones were recovered and re-erected on what is believed to be the original site.

Caw Fell	7.9
Grike	7.4

<u>Ennerdale Bridge</u> crosses the River Ehen, the outflow from Ennerdale Water.

The village inn has variously been called The Shepherds Arms and The Fox and Hounds.

St Mary's Church dates from 1543 although the main structure was re-built in 1858. Wordsworth, after a visit here with Coleridge in 1799, used the churchyard as the setting for his poem '*The Brothers*', where Leonard found his brother's grave.

Crag Fell	7.4
Great Borne (Herdus)	7.4
Grike	7.5

Turn off here for <u>Ennerdale</u>.

Ennerdale Bridge to Cockermouth

The road continues to mark the western boundary of The National Park at a higher level than the alternative A5086.

Above Ennerdale, on the remote fell sides, iron ore was extracted from open cast and drift mines until 1896.

<u>Croasdale</u> [*ON. Valley with a cross.*] The red spoil heaps are from the workings which extracted haematite on a commercial basis.

Gavel Fell	7.6

The Kelton Fell and the Knockmurton Fell Mines extracted

deposits of iron ore from Skiddaw Slate, not from limestone. At first, the ore from these high-level remote mines was carted to the railway at Rowrah, but in 1877 the Rowrah and Kelton Fell Railway connected with the mines. Kelton Mine was abandoned in 1913 and Knockmurton in 1923.

<u>Felldyke</u> has a car park for <u>Cogra Moss</u>, a tarn with a dam to form a reservoir, almost hidden by a dense conifer plantation.

<u>Lamplugh</u> [*Br. landa = sacred enclosure. The second element may be the name of an unknown holy person.*] is built not of the slate on which it stands, but of red sandstone.

Iron ore mining, particularly around Lamplugh Cross, took place from the mid-19c until 1931.

The church was designed by William Butterfield, the architect of Keble College, Oxford, re-using parts of the medieval chancel. Three gargoyles and an unusual double bell-cote are of interest.

Lamplugh Pudding, for which the village is famous, is made from hot spiced beer poured over oats or crushed wholemeal biscuits to which sugar and raisins can be added.

Blake Fell	7.6
Burnbank Fell	7.4

Fangs Brow is the junction of the road from Loweswater.

<u>Mockerkin Tarn</u> was formed by the ice which once covered the whole of Lakeland. As a glacier retreated a block of ice was left embedded in the silt and debris. Slowly, this huge ice-block melted, leaving a steep-sided hole, called a 'kettlehole', filled with water. With no inlet or outlet stream, the still waters provide a favourable habitat for

vegetation, for peat and sphagnum moss.

The A5086 runs north-east to Cockermouth.
From the A5086 several minor roads branch eastwards into Lorton Vale.
From the A5086, turn left.

Dean. St Oswald's Church dates from the 12c (Norman font and churchyard Preaching Cross base). The chancel was added in the 15c (windows) and the sanctuary in the 17c. The oak pews and the pulpit by Thompsons of Kilburn, Yorkshire, famous for their mouse trade mark, were installed during renovations, 1967–73.

Dean was the birthplace of Dr John Dalton (1709–63), a clergyman and poet. His popular adaptation of Milton's *Comus* had a prologue by Samuel Johnson. David Garrick performed in the title role in 1750. Dr Dalton also wrote '*A Descriptive Poem Addressed to Two Young Ladies at their Return from Viewing the Mines near Whitehaven*' (1755), the earliest poem to praise extensively the scenic beauty of Lakeland.

Eaglesfield has a claim to two famous sons.
On the A5086, ½ mile north of the Eaglesfield turn, a public bridleway signed 'Eaglesfield' leads to Morland Close Farm, the birthplace of Fletcher Christian in 1764. He was appointed chief mate under Captain Bligh and became the notorious leader of the mutiny on H.M.S. *Bounty.*

In Eaglesfield village, John Dalton (1766–1844), the mathematician and chemical philosopher, who propounded the Atomic Theory in a paper on '*the relative weights of the ultimate particles of bodies*' (1803), was born into a Quaker family at John Dalton House. He also wrote a paper on colour blindness from which he suffered. In 1781 he moved to Kendal and in 1793 to Manchester, where a city centre street has been named after him.

Minor road north.

Brigham. St Bridget's Church is dedicated to the Irish Saint, founder of the white-robed Sisters of Mercy. The original Norman church was restored by William Butterfield with a colourful Victorian painted ceiling and beams.

George Fox preached here in 1653 and John Wordsworth, the poet's son, was the vicar from 1833.

On the north side of the church, the Old Parsonage is now a farmhouse. The 'New' Parsonage, due east of the church, was built by John Wordsworth. His father, William, wrote about the house in his sonnet *'To a Friend on the Banks of the Derwent'*. He also wrote a sonnet, *'Nun's Well, Brigham'*, but there is no trace of the well today nor of the convent which used it.

The A66 leads to Cockermouth.

Ennerdale

[Valley of the River Ehen]

*[Ehen as a British river-name is probably based on
the Welsh 'iain' = cold: and ON. 'dalr' = dale.
Before the 14c, the valley was known as Anenderdale, or
Anand's valley, from an ON personal name.]*

From <u>Ennerdale Bridge</u> there are several roads to Ennerdale Water.

<u>Bleach Green Cottages</u> were named after the method in former times of washing and open-air drying to bleach freshly woven fabrics.

Electricity only reached this area in 1989.

Close to the car park, a weir forming a shallow dam enables the North West Water Authority to supply increasing industrial and domestic demands. The pumping station is nearby.

There is a splendid view of Ben Gill tumbling down the face of Revelin Crag, above Crag Farm House.

<u>How Hall Farm</u> has a stone plaque with the words, '*This house was built AD 1566 by Anthony Patrickson and Frances, his wife, daughter of Sir Thomas Swinburne of the Privy Council to King Henry VIII.*'

Beyond the farm, the National Trust car park is on the water-front site of the once famous Anglers' Hotel. The hotel was demolished in anticipation of the construction of a 10 foot high

536

embankment prior to raising the level of the lake by a further 4 feet to enable the North West Water Authority to extract more water. On this occasion, 1980, the protestors were successful in stopping the plan, unlike their predecessors who were unable to prevent the construction of reservoirs at Thirlmere and Haweswater.

Ennerdale Water. A full length view of the lake from the National Trust car park is framed by Anglers' Crag and Bowness Knott in the foreground which contribute to Wordsworth's description of the lake as 'fiddle-shaped'.

Ennerdale Water, the most westerly, the most remote, the most secluded and the least accessible of the lakes was formerly known as Broadwater. It is the only one of the sixteen lakes without a road along its length.

The lake, carved by glacial action, is 2½ miles long, roughly ½ mile wide, 368 feet above sea-level and 148 feet deep. In it, a cairn of stones rises from an underwater ridge.

Unusually, the lake lies at the outlet and not at the head of the valley. Inflowing is the River Liza [ON. *Bright water*], which springs into life below Windy Gap on Great Gable. Outflowing is the River Ehen, which wanders through Cleator and Egremont on its way to the sea near Sellafield.

This is a popular lake for brown trout and char fishing but, as it is a reservoir, no boats are allowed.

On the way to Bowness Knott, Whinis is the starting point of the Floutern Pass route to Buttermere. Wainwright descried the quagmire in the middle section as 'a mess.'

Bowness Knott is a Forestry Commission car park and picnic site halfway along the north shore. Beyond this point, the road is closed to all but authorised vehicles and walkers.

There is a dramatic view across the water to Anglers' Crag at the junction of the Skiddaw Slates and the Borrowdale Volcanic Series. The small grassy headland is named Robin Hood's Chair for no apparent reason. This is where local people used to pick bilberries on a commercial scale, using combs, 'pickers' and biscuit tins to gather the harvest. Carved initials on the rock date back to 1700.

At Bowness Knott the Ennerdale Show is held on the last Wednesday in August.

Two Forestry Commission waymarked trails start from the car park:

The Smithy Beck Forest Trail   *(1¼ miles).*
The Nine Becks Walk   *(9 miles).*

Ennerdale is on the route of Wainwright's
A Coast to Coast Walk.

Ennerdale was bare of trees until 1926 when the Forestry Commission began planting Norwegian and Sitka spruce, European and Japanese larch. The six miles of over-crowded, straight-line, regimented plantations on both sides of the valley, extending into the upper reaches, had a highly insensitive and totally alien effect on this wild and desolate landscape. The protests were vociferous. The consequences were twofold. Future plantings had to harmonise more with the surrounding landscape by following the contours and by using deciduous trees to soften the impact. The outcry also led to the agreement not to plant the central 300 square miles of The National Park.

An earlier battle had been fought and won by Canon Rawnsley and The Lake District Defence Society when they opposed the plan to run a railway through the valley.

<u>Low Gillerthwaite</u> [*ON. Clearing where snares are set*] has a field Centre.

Caw Fell	7.10
Haycock	7.7
Scoat Fell	7.7
Steeple	7.5

<u>High Gillerthwaite</u> has a Youth Hostel.

High Stile	7.9
Pillar	7.12
Red Pike (B)	7.9

In the field where the River Liza flows as Char Dub into the lake there is evidence of the foundations of Viking or Saxon homesteads.

<u>Memorial Bridge</u> is the 1939–45 War Memorial of The Fell and Rock Climbing Club. A plaque is attached to a nearby boulder.

Pillar	7.8, 13

From the smooth, rounded fells and rolling moorlands of Skiddaw Slates, a conspicuous change takes place at the head of the valley where the rugged masses of the Borrowdale Volcanic Series are very evident in High Stile, Haycock, Steeple and Pillar.

Pillar dominates the upper valley. Pillar Rock is said to be the tallest vertical crag in England and was climbed by a local shepherd, John Atkinson, in 1826. Pillar Rock's North Climb, which overhangs Ennerdale, was accomplished at the second attempt by W. Haskett-Smith in 1891. His first attempt nearly proved fatal.

Wordsworth featured Pillar Rock in his poem '*The Brothers*'.

<u>Black Sail</u> was a shepherd's bothy now converted into a Youth Hostel Hut, a humble, remote and isolated abode encircled by a great amphitheatre of magnificent peaks in an area of drumlins left by a retreating glacier.

There are two mountains passes:
Black Sail [*ON. Swampy hill*] to Wasdale.
Scarth Gap [*ON. Gap in a ridge*] to Buttermere.

Brandreth	7.6
Great Gable	7.19
Green Gable	7.7
Haystacks	7.8
High Crag	7.4
Kirk Fell	7.5
Pillar	7.10

Egremont to Cockermouth

Egremont

[Norman French. Possibly named after Aigremont in Normandy.]

This small, historic market town lies under the lea of Dent Fell beside the River Ehen. It is situated in the former Barony of Kaupland, which extended from the River Derwent in the north to the River Duddon in the south. Today it is administered by the Borough of Copeland.

The Castle, although in ruins, dominates the southern end of town. William de Meschines began to build a motte and bailey castle in 1120 on this prominent knoll overlooking a bend in the River Ehen, on the site of a former Danish stronghold. Surviving from a later building are the red sandstone gatehouse and part of the hall with three arched windows. Herringbone masonry provides a decorative effect.

Close to the entrance of the castle grounds, open to the public, is the stump of a cross found in the Market Place in 1922 and thought to be of 13c origin.

Two legends associated with the castle have been re-told by William Wordsworth.

In 'The Horn of Egremont Castle' (1806), the two sons of Baron Lucy of Egremont left home to fight in the Crusades. Both were captured by the Saracens who released the younger brother to enable him to return home and raise the ransom. On reaching Egremont and hearing of his father's death, he announced that his brother was also dead and assumed the title of Lord of Egremont. But he dared not attempt to blow the horn —

Which none could sound
Save he who came as rightful heir.

Meanwhile, the elder brother, with the help of the Saracen's daughter who had fallen in love with him, escaped, and together they travelled to England. When the elder brother sounded the horn, the younger brother realised that the rightful heir had returned to claim his inheritance and so he fled in fear of his life.

The second legend, '*The Force of Prayer*', features The Boy of Egremont, William de Rumelli, nephew of King David I of Scotland. William was out hunting with his greyhound on the leash when he came to The Strid where the River Wharfe in Yorkshire rushes through a narrow, rocky gorge some thirty feet below. He leapt across, but his dog held back and he was pulled down into the gorge where he drowned. With his death perished all family hopes for the future. His distraught mother, Alice de Rumelli, is said to have founded the Priory at Bolton Abbey in his memory, but as William's signature appears on the Priory deeds the legend has taken liberties with the sequence of events.

In the 14c, the town was ransacked by the Scots under Robert the Bruce and later by Lord James Douglas, 'Black Douglas', resulting in enormous loss of life.

In the 15c, the Castle was left empty for long periods and fell into disrepair. From the neglected Castle, stone was taken in the 17c to replace the timber and wattle of the town houses.

Industrial Development. Only a single road in West Cumberland, from Egremont through Whitehaven, Workington and Cockermouth to Carlisle, was indicated by John Ogilby in his road book of 1675.

At Egremont, early industrial development was powered by the River Ehen and included Corn Mills, Tanneries, Flax, Sailcloth and Flint Mills.

Egremont was the centre of the medieval iron industry. In the 14c, several iron forges were located near the Market Place where the ore was extracted from shallow pits.

In the mid-19c, rich deposits of high quality iron ore were mined at deeper levels in the neighbourhood and a railway network evolved to link the mines with local iron, steel and shipbuilding industries. One such railway ran from Whitehaven through Cleator and Moor Row to Egremont in 1856, with a subsequent extension to Rowrah and Lamplugh.

The new Bessemer process of making steel required phosphor-ous-free iron (haematite) and in the limestone of West Cumberland were the only major deposits in the country. Because of the ore's red colour, the landscape was covered with red dust and the miners were known as 'the red men of Egremont'.

In 1875, the Egremont Mining Company mined at Whin Pit adjacent to Egremont's cemetery. Subsidence occurred in the cemetery, an injunction was imposed and mining had to cease. No traces of this event remain.

Florence Mine, south-east of the town, was named after the Chairman's wife. It opened in 1914 and remains the last working deep haematite mine in Western Europe. The Florence Mine Heritage Centre with its cafeteria and shop is open to tourists.

Spoil heaps, worked-out mines and disused railway tracks remain from this great industrial era.

Egremont

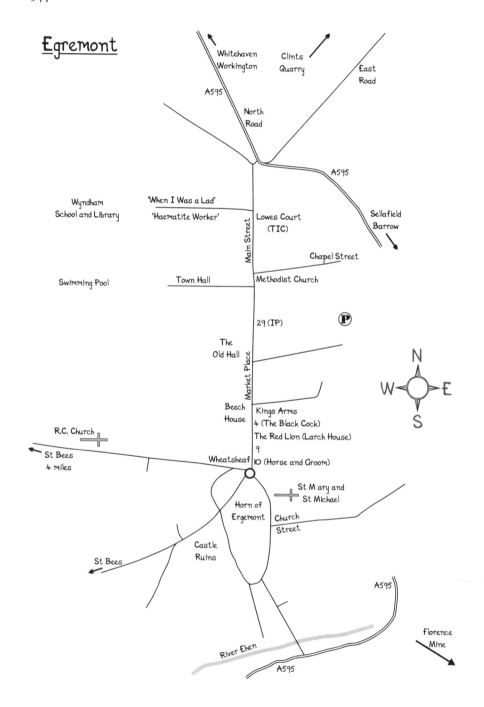

Whitehaven
Workington

Clints
Quarry

East
Road

A595

North
Road

A595

Wyndham
School and Library

'When I Was a Lad'

'Haematite Worker'

Lowes Court
(TIC)

Main Street

Sellafield
Barrow

Chapel Street

Swimming Pool

Town Hall

Methodist Church

29 (IP)

Ⓟ

The
Old Hall

Market Place

N
W — E
S

Beech
House

Kings Arms

4 (The Black Cock)

The Red Lion (Larch House)

9

R.C. Church

St Bees
4 miles

Wheatsheaf

10 (Horse and Groom)

St Mary and
St Michael

Horn of
Ergemont

Church
Street

St Bees

Castle
Ruins

A595

River Ehen

A595

Florence
Mine

The Parish Church of St Mary and St Michael was built on the site of an earlier chapel dating from 1130. The new church, with its unusual dual dedication, had two long chapels side by side separated by a wall. One chapel was dedicated to St Mary and controlled by the monks of St Bees before the Dissolution. The other was dedicated to St Michael. There were also two foundation stones: one laid with full masonic rites; the other blessed by the Church of England.

After 130 years the twin-structured church was demolished and replaced by the present red sandstone Victorian church, built by John Smith of Egremont to the design of Thomas Lewis Banks, a local architect, and incorporating four of the Early English windows in the chancel. The transept was built of stone from the former arcade and the ancient sedilia was placed in the vestry wall.

The southern approach to the town crosses:

Egremont Bridge, over the River Ehen. The bridge was opened in 1822 to replace an earlier structure.

The Horn of Egremont, facing the Parish Church, was formerly The Globe Hotel. It has survived from the time when Egremont supported as many as fifteen pubs, only a few of which remain.

Its Assembly Room was large enough to hold 450 people or more at such functions as 'Penny Readings' in 1865.

The Market Place. A charter to hold a weekly market in the town and an annual three-day fair was granted to Lambert de Multon in 1267, during the reign of Henry III. Lambert adopted the name de Lucy after his father-in-law, Reginald de Lucy, who completed the building of Egremont Castle.

The weekly market is held on Fridays.

The annual Crab Fair, which takes place on the Saturday closest to 19 September, derives its name from the traditional distribution of apples from a cart passing through the town. Fun and games include climbing a greasy pole, track and field sporting events, wrestling, pipe smoking and the singing of hunting songs. The day ends with the World Championship Gurning Contest, when competitors frame their heads in a horse collar and 'gurn' or 'grimace'. The one who pulls the most grotesque face is the winner. One year, a spectator was said to have won and he was not competing!

Walk up the east side of the Market Place and Main Street.

<u>Numbers 9 and 10</u> date back to the mid-17c and have a walled garden built on a burgage plot granted in the 12c. Such lands and tenements in towns were held on the basis of a yearly rent payable to the overlord.

<u>Number 10</u>, with a date stone 1667, was once a public house, named The Horse and Groom, which belonged to the Parton and Harrington Brewery.

<u>The Red Lion</u>, formerly Larche House, was also built on a burgage plot.

<u>Number 4</u>, formerly The Black Cock, was bought in 1718 by the Gaitskell family who were curriers in the leather trade and silk merchants. They owned the premises for 122 years until they moved to Yearton Hall to the south of the town. From 1955–63, Hugh Gaitskell was the leader of the Labour Party and his widow became Baroness Egremont.

<u>The Kings Arms</u> served not only as a coaching inn but also as a Court House. Those condemned to be hanged were transported from here to Gibbet Holme, a field at the top of Bigrigg Brow, where several skeletons have been found.

<u>Number 29</u>, dated 1662, carries the initials IP belonging to one of the Ponsonby family of Haile Hall. This town property was the home

of the Sheriff of Egremont for many years.

Next door, a well at the rear with an old pump, dated 1682, also carries the initials IP. This well was one of the sources of drinking water before the first standpipe was erected in Main Street to supply water piped from a reservoir at Howbank.

The Methodist Church, built in sandstone, 1874–77, was designed by the same architect as the Parish Church.

A succession of chapels have been built and replaced since Methodism first came to Egremont in 1794, when Dr Coke, accompanied by John Braithwaite from Whitehaven, delivered a sermon from the Calvary steps of the old Market Cross.

Lowes Court, a 16c building, houses an Art and Craft Gallery and the Tourist Information Centre.

Cross over Main Street and descend on the western side.

Two statues by Colin Telfer flank the road to Wyndham School and Library. '*When I Was a Lad*' is dedicated to the children of Egremont, 1993. '*Haematite Worker*' is dedicated to all the '*redmen*' of Egremont, 1992. These very attractive enhancements of an undistinguished street scene are reminders of recent history.

The Town Hall, built of sandstone in 1889, has a large hall at the rear which was formerly used as a Market Hall. Public meetings, concerts and social events take place here.

At the time of building the Town Hall, the broad Main Street was paved and trees were planted along each side.

The Old Hall has become a night club.

Beech House is a doctors' surgery.

The Wheatsheaf Hotel served as Egremont's first theatre when travelling players performed in the Assembly Room which stood at the rear of the premises.

<u>St Mary's R.C. Church</u>, in St Bridgets Lane (Brewery Lane) was built in 1977 in the style of an Early Basilica. The mosaic, in the semi-dome over the altar, depicts Christ as Lord of all Creation.

Various buildings in the town have been used previously for the dual purpose of worship and school, including a room above the Co-operative store.

<u>Clints Quarry</u>, to the north of the town, is a Nature Reserve.

This section is concerned more with the past

than with the present.

Follow the A5086

<u>Cleator and Cleator Moor</u> were at the centre of the early iron mining development and like the other industrial villages of Frizington and Arlecdon further north, grew in response to the demand for more labour than was available locally.

Most immigrant workers and their families came from mining areas in decline: tin miners from Cornwall, and copper miners from Ireland. Within forty years, 1840–1880, the population of the area exploded from 835 to 17,651 and the number of miners increased from 60 to more than 6,000.

Even though the iron mining industry ended for the most part shortly after World War I, the surnames of local people reflect their origins. Terraced rows of miners' cottages remain and the land-scape is scarred by the relics of the mines and the railways.

<u>Cleator</u> [*ON. Irish. Summer pasture*] Mining began here when Thomas Ainsworth (1804–1881) arrived from Lancashire, having acquired Cleator's linen mill and found iron ore on his land in 1846. The ore was extracted from a large opencast quarry, but dozens of pits

were sunk in the following years, ultimately connected to the Whitehaven, Moor Row, Cleator and Egremont Railway from 1854.

The Ainsworth family lived at the north end of Cleator in a large house named The Flosh, after a nearby stretch of water. Today, The Ennerdale private hotel occupies the premises and the large garden at the rear is now a public park.

The Lindow family were also pioneers in the mining of iron ore. Samuel Lindow (1799–1871) was born in a house in Main Street and his brother John (1804–1878) built Ehen Hall on the river bank at the south end of Cleator.

St Mary's Church has a grotto built with stone from the spoil heap of Parkhouse Mine by unemployed miners during the great depression of the 1920s.

Cleator Moor. This small town with a large square and a flour mill was planned as a mining community which developed in the latter half of the 19c.

'The town of Cleator Moor would not have existed had it not been for iron mining – built for iron, on iron, surrounded by iron and, eventually almost destroyed by iron. Here, at one stage, the iron deposit was so near the surface that the people living in the houses above could hear the blasting beneath them and feel the vibrations, yet the mining continued. Nowhere has subsidence affected a town as much as it affected Cleator Moor. The town was built over a large deposit of iron ore which was extracted from under it. A large part of the original town has disappeared due to subsidence. Streets and schools were abandoned. The effect of subsidence seems to have settled now, but it has left its mark on the town.'

See: *The Red Hills* by Dave Kelly, Red Earth Publications. 1994.

John Stirling, who came from Ayrshire to work in the Cleator linen mill, lodged with the owners at Cleator, the Ainsworth family, and his sister married Thomas Ainsworth. John had a strong association with Cleator Moor as a master of iron mines and as a Liberal concerned with local affairs.

John Stirling started The Montreal Mine which was said to contain one of the largest deposits of haematite in West Cumberland. Between 1870 and 1880 it produced two million tons and, remarkably, also raised coal from the same shaft. Altogether, twenty shafts had been sunk in The Montreal complex, some in the coal measures, by the time of closure in 1925.

Iron works at Cleator Moor were built in 1841 by local mine owners, the Ainsworths, the Lindows, the Stirlings and others, who formed the Whitehaven Haematite Iron Company, which continued in production until 1925.

Flat Fell and Dent   OFOL 198

<u>Frizington</u>. At Parkside Mine in 1862 the miners' first unified confrontation with the management took place. They demanded a reduction from ten-hour shifts, six days a week, to eight-hour shifts at four shillings (20p) per shift. The response was immediately to dismiss the miners but to offer protection for those who submitted to reinstatement under unchanged conditions.

At Parkside, one of the largest haematite deposits produced 150,000 tons in 1874.

<u>Rowrah</u> was almost at the limit of the haematite iron zone of West Cumberland. From Beckermet in the south to Rowrah in the north, this limestone area, ten miles in length and a mile and a half wide, was thickly studded with mines. The innumerable iron mines were the

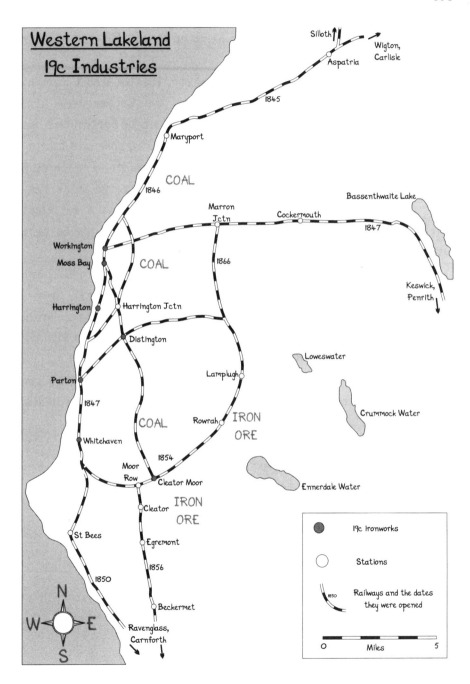

Western Lakeland
19c Industries

Silloth
Aspatria
Wigton, Carlisle
1845
Maryport
COAL
1846
Marron Jctn
Cockermouth
Bassenthwaite Lake
1847
COAL
Workington
Moss Bay
1866
Keswick, Penrith
Harrington
Harrington Jctn
Distington
Parton
Lamplugh
Loweswater
1847
Rowrah
IRON ORE
Crummock Water
COAL
Whitehaven
1854
Moor Row
Cleator Moor
Ennerdale Water
Cleator
IRON ORE
St Bees
Egremont
1856
1850
Beckermet
N
W E
S
Ravenglass, Carnforth

19c Ironworks

Stations

1850   Railways and the dates they were opened

0   Miles   5

main reason for the rail network being built and Rowrah was an important junction.

In 1866, the extension of the Whitehaven, Cleator and Egremont Railway northwards of Rowrah, to join the Cockermouth and Workington line at Marron Junction, opened up opportunities for long distance traffic. In an east to west direction, coke was transported from County Durham to Marron Junction and through Rowrah to Cleator Moor and Workington iron works and those further south. In the opposite direction, the products of West Cumberland's furnaces, iron ore mines and other industries were carried.

The Cleator and Workington Junction Railway opened in 1879 and ran from Cleator Moor to Workington on the jointly owned Whitehaven, Cleator and Egremont line. There were branch lines, amongst others, to Distington and Rowrah, which connected with the Rowrah and Kelton Fell Railway.

The railways connected the iron and coal mines with the iron and steel works, but as the mines were worked out the railways gradually closed until today only the main coastal line remains.

The A5086 continues to Cockermouth. It is joined by the road which marks the National Park boundary at the Mockerkin turn.

Whitehaven

[ON. Refers to the white stones on the headland to the south.]

In the 12c and 13c, the small fishing cove was the property of St Bees Priory and the monks used it to transport a modest coal production by sea. There were only nine houses here in 1633.

Whitehaven's transformation into a flourishing seaport was largely the work of the affluent Lowther family whose wealth was derived from land owning and coal mining. Ultimately passing into their possession, after the Dissolution of the Monasteries, was the Manor of St Bees.

The presence of local coal prompted Sir Christopher Lowther (1611–1644) to build Whitehaven's first pier in 1634 for coal to be transported by sailing ships.

His son, Sir John Lowther (1642–1705), introduced new engineering methods to increase the output of coal – and the wealth of his family. He improved the harbour facilities and extended the coal trade with Ireland, thereby increasing Whitehaven's shipping fleet. By attracting shipbuilders, he founded an industry which lasted for two hundred years.

During the lifetime of his son, Sir James Lowther (1674–1755), the Georgian town plan for Whitehaven was put into effect, based on a grid pattern of streets, inspired by Wren's plan for rebuilding London after the Great Fire in 1666. It was ' . . . *the earliest post-medieval planned town in England*' according to Sir Nicholas Pevsner. Building land was divided into 15 feet wide plots and buildings were constructed on a single or a double plot, sometimes terraced, occasionally

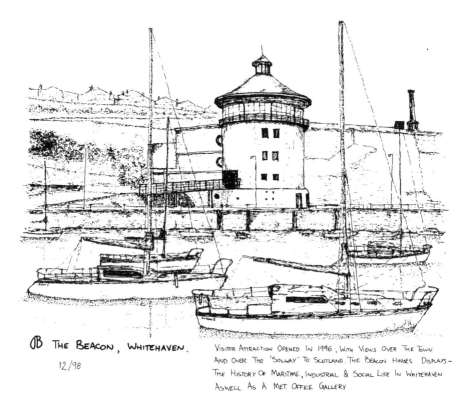

ᗞᗷ THE BEACON , WHITEHAVEN.

12/98

VISITOR ATTRACTION OPENED IN 1996 , WITH VIEWS OVER THE TOWN AND OVER THE 'SOLWAY' TO SCOTLAND. THE BEACON HOUSES DISPLAYS— THE HISTORY OF MARITIME, INDUSTRIAL & SOCIAL LIFE IN WHITEHAVEN ASWELL AS A MET. OFFICE GALLERY

detached. '*The builders were commonly obliged that they should not build their fronts under a certain height, and that they should make their doors and windows and ornaments to a rule laid down.*' This diversity with conformity still characterises the town. By 1693, the population had risen to 2,222.

In the 18c, coal mining, shipbuilding and a thriving sea trade, supported by the wealth of the Lowthers, made Whitehaven a larger port than Liverpool and third, after London and Bristol, in national importance. For nearly two centuries, Whitehaven was sustained as a port by importing tobacco from Virginia, sugar and rum from the West Indies, and by exporting coal to Ireland and the settlers emigrating to the New World. By 1762, the population had grown to 9,063.

David Brocklebank (1742–1801), an emigrant from West Cumberland to America, started to build ships at Maine. Disrupted by the American War of Independence (1775–1783), he returned to his homeland and settled at Whitehaven where he established his successful shipbuilding yard in 1782. Before he died, he built 27 ships and his sons carried on until 1865. The last of an estimated 684 vessels built at Whitehaven was the *Englehorn*, a four-mast barque launched in 1889.

Continuing industrial and commercial wealth into the 19c assured progress in the development of the town where wealthy merchants built elegant houses. By 1831, Whitehaven's population was 17,000.

The West Cumberland coalfield extended 14 miles from Whitehaven to Maryport with some of the mines running a mile or more under the sea. Increasing supplies of iron ore from the hinterland were processed by the Whitehaven Iron and Steel Company from 1841. Transporting these heavy products of the mines gave impetus to building up a network of railways:

1847. Workington to Whitehaven, connected with Cockermouth and Carlisle.

1854. Whitehaven, Cleator and Egremont, with subsequent extensions to Rowrah, Lamplugh and beyond.

1857. Through connections southwards from Whitehaven via the Furness Railway's coastal line to Carnforth and the main line from London to Scotland.

1864. Connections via Cockermouth, Keswick and Penrith to the east coast, London and Scotland.

In the 20c, the former prosperity diminished. The steady decline in coal and iron mining ended with the closure of these industries. Shipbuilding had already ceased and the expansion of the port for bigger modern ships was prevented by the tidal nature of the harbour. All but the coastal railway closed down. Whitehaven began to take on a rundown, neglected look. Accommodation for the rapid growth in population had been provided by building on the original, spacious, town gardens and filling in streets. Overcrowding and squalor followed, with some relief when a new council estate was built overlooking the town centre.

Whitehaven is now committed to divesting itself of the legacy of industrial and commercial decline by restoring much of the original town to its former splendour for the benefit of residents and tourists.

Proceed from the Rail or Bus Station to –
High Street.

At No. 7, the observatory built by John Fletcher Miller (1816–1856) has been demolished. As a pioneer meteorologist, he regularly made marathon walks throughout Lakeland, even to the top of Scafell, to site and to read his rain gauges. His published records inspired the idea of siting reservoirs in the Lake District to supply the needs of the growing cities.

St James' Church, built at the top of the hill in 1753, was designed by a mining engineer, Carlisle Spedding. Sir Nicholas Pevsner described it as '*the finest Georgian Church in the country.*' The altar painting of '*The Transfiguration*' is by Guilio Proccacini (1548–1626). The blue and white ceiling medallions, portraying '*The Annunciation*' and '*The Ascension*', are believed to have been designed by the Italian artists Arturi and Bagutti. Memorial Chapels commemorate the fallen in two World Wars and the men, women and children who were the victims of mining accidents. Appropriately, a miner's lamp serves as a sanctuary lamp.

Queen Street. *Turn right into* George Street.

The redeveloped housing area on the left is a blend of restored, listed and new buildings with courtyards.

Turn left into <u>Church Street</u>.

The terrace on the left won an award for its restoration in European Architectural Heritage Year, 1975.

Turn right into <u>Duke Street</u>.

In <u>Tangier Street</u> stands a 19c Italianate style of building, designed by Thomas Lewis Banks, the architect of several buildings in the town.

Turn left into <u>King Street</u>.

This main shopping street leading to the Market Place was pedestrianised in 1974.

Turn left into <u>Lowther Street</u>.

In <u>New Lowther Street</u> two terraces of early 18c buildings have been conserved. A sea captain in sailing ship days built the oriel windowed premises. Offices in the street are occupied by the Dutch and Danish Consulate.

From the harbour, 18c <u>Lowther Street</u> leads to Whitehaven Castle, the former home of Sir John Lowther.

On the left, the Regency style Trustee Savings Bank, built in 1833, won a Civic Trust Award in 1965.

Opposite, R. & H. Jefferson have been Wine and Spirit Merchants since 1785 when Whitehaven was importing rum from the West Indies.

<u>St Nicholas Church</u>, built in 1693 and rebuilt in 1883, was destroyed by fire in 1971. Only the red sandstone tower survived and now functions as a chapel in an attractive garden setting. George Gale of Whitehaven, on a visit to Virginia in 1700, married Mildred Warner

Washington, the grandmother of George Washington, America's first President. Mildred came to Whitehaven and was buried in this church.

Pass the Civic Hall, used as an entertainments centre, and the Library.

Flatt Walk

Flatt Hall, built in 1769, became Whitehaven Castle, the home of Sir John Lowther. It was sold in 1924 and converted into a hospital which closed when a modern replacement was built on the edge of town. Subsequently, it has been divided into flats. The 13 acres of Castle Park are open to the public.

Across the road is Whitehaven's Sports Centre.

Turn back along Flatt Walk. *Turn right into* Catherine Street.

Two terraces of late 18c buildings were formerly the town houses of wealthy merchants.

Somerset House, built by Samuel Martin, c. 1750, is now occupied by Cumbria County Council Social Services Department. A request for an Historic Building Grant towards its repair in 1972 involved the Historic Buildings Council which designated Whitehaven an 'Outstanding Conservation Area'.

Turn left into Duke Street.

The County Court, renovated in 1988, was formerly the Town Hall, and originally a three-storey mansion built by William Feryes in the early 18c.

Turn right into Scotch Street.

On the right-hand side, the restored terrace of 18c houses is typical of many in the town.

Turn back along Scotch Street, *crossing* Lowther Street.

Italianate Union Hall houses the Education Department of Cumbria County Council.

The adjacent terrace was built by merchants in the early 18c.

Opposite the entrance to Trinity Gardens, no.1 Scotch Street was built by Joseph Deane, a Tide Surveyor. He was a particular friend of George Washington's father.

Irish Street

The offices of Copeland Borough Council occupy the Italianate building designed by Sydney Smirke, who also designed the surface buildings of the Wellington Pit.

Turn back.

Turn left into Roper Street.

Michael Moon's Antiquarian Bookshop is the largest in Cumbria.

The restoration of many 18c houses has revitalised this once dilapidated area.

No. 30 has an acorn emblem in the pediment over the door. This is from the Spedding coat of arms. James Spedding, son of Carlisle, built the house in 1743, but 19c detail has been superimposed.

Market Place

Golden Lion House was Whitehaven's first Custom and Excise House, built in the early 17c. In the 1770s, the Controller of Customs was Richard Wordsworth, the uncle of William. As children both William and Dorothy stayed with him.

The restored Market Hall, designed by Thomas Lewis Banks and built in 1880, houses the Tourist Information Centre.

Michael Moon wrote the Monster Mosaic poem.

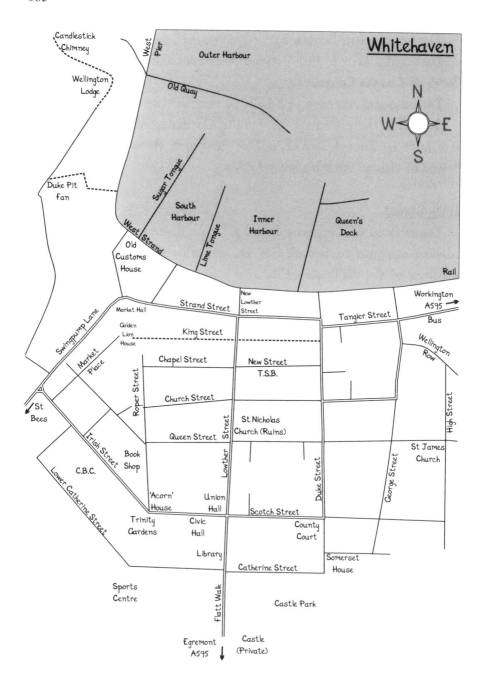

Street markets are held on Thursdays and Saturdays.

Turn left into <u>West Strand</u>.

The Old Custom House was built in 1811.

Climb up the steps to the <u>South Beach Recreation Area</u>.

This reclamation project from a disused coal mine won an award in the European Architectural Heritage Year. The viewpoints overlook the harbour, the town and the coastline.

To the left, is the preserved ruined fan chamber which drove fresh air into Duke Pit, sunk in 1749.

Wellington Lodge, now used as a café, was once the entrance and Miners' Lamp House to the Wellington Coal Mine, sunk in 1840 and closed in 1933 after a disaster which claimed 136 lives. On top of the air vent down into the mine stands the 'Candlestick' chimney. Lord Lonsdale is said to have agreed to the air vent whilst he was dining, providing that the top was built in the shape of the candlestick in front of him. The architect, Sydney Smirke, obliged.

The cannon nearby is thought to be from a ship sunk by John Paul Jones in 1778.

Beyond the Recreation Area, on the cliff top.

A private house was once the Red Flag Inn. The red flag was hoisted when the militia engaged in firing activities. Before that it was known as Bowling Green House where Jonathan Swift (1667–1774) lived as a small boy and revisited later. At the age of one year he was kidnapped by his nurse, who felt that she could not leave him behind in Dublin when she sailed to visit a relative in Whitehaven. Jonathan's mother insisted that no risk should be taken on a return journey until her son was better able to withstand the voyage. He stayed in Whitehaven for three years. It is thought that the idea for

Gulliver's Travels came to him after watching the tiny figures on the beach below gathering washed-up coal.

Descend the terraced paths to the <u>Harbour</u>.

West Pier was built by the Scottish engineer, Sir John Rennie.

West Strand. The stubby lighthouse, dating from 1739, known now as The Beacon, opened in 1995 to exhibit the mining, maritime and social history of the town and its environment.

The Old Quay. Sir Christopher Lowther built this pier, Whitehaven's first, in 1634 to enable coal to be transported by sailing ships.

During the American War of Independence in 1778, the harbour was raided by the privateer *Ranger*, whose captain, John Paul Jones, once apprenticed to a Whitehaven master seaman, made an unsuccessful attempt to set fire to the shipping. This was the last attack from the sea by an enemy power until a German U-boat bombarded the port in 1915.

Captain John Paul Jones became known as the founder of the American Navy and, later, he was an admiral in the Russian Navy.

Queen's Dock, in north harbour, was built for the iron ore trade near the site of the shipyards.

As the tidal harbour was basically designed for sailing ships, modern bulk carriers bringing phosphate rock from Morocco for the chemical works of Albright and Wilson at Marcham, were compelled to anchor off shore and transfer their cargo to smaller craft which were able to enter Queen's Dock for unloading.

Today, fishing smacks and pleasure boats share the harbour which has been declared a Conservation Area.

<u>Rosehill Theatre</u>, 2 miles north at Moresby, was founded in 1959 by Sir Nicholas Seckers, a local silk mill owner.

Whitehaven to Workington

Take the A595 and the unclassified road via Parton and Lowca.

<u>Moresby</u>. Sited here was a Roman coastal auxiliary fort, built in the last decade of Hadrian's reign, c. AD 128–138, and thought to have been called 'Gabrosentum'. It was one of a chain, linked with similar coastal fortifications at Burrow Walls, Maryport, Beckfoot and Bowness-on-Solway, to protect Hadrian's exposed western flank against seaborne raiders, especially the Celtic tribesmen from south-west Scotland.

The Fletcher family, on their Moresby estate, exploited the mining of coal Lowther opposition was overcome by 1705, a pier was built at Parton and Moresby coal competed with Whitehaven coal in exports to Dublin.

St Bridget's Church was rebuilt in 1822 when a medieval arch from the old church was re-erected in the churchyard. The rector from 1829 to 1833 was John Wordsworth, the poet's son. William visited in 1833 and wrote three 'Evening Voluntaries': 'By the Sea-Side', 'Composed by the Sea-shore' and 'On a High Part of the Coast of Cumberland'.

B5296.

<u>Harrington Harbour</u>. According to the chronicler Simeon of Durham, Bishop Eardulf and escorting monks embarked from this coast in AD 875 for the safety of Ireland, having fled from the Danes with the body of St Cuthbert and some of the monastic treasures. A violent storm arose and a precious illuminated copy of the Gospels, richly bound in gold and priceless stones, was washed overboard and lost. The voyage was abandoned. In a dream, St Cuthbert appeared to one of the monks and explained where the book could be found. It was discovered washed up by the tide but undamaged. The Lindisfarne Gospels now rest safely in the British Museum.

The first quay was built for the export of coal from Harrington in 1760 and there were two shipyards by 1829. From the expanded harbour in the 19c, the export of coal from John Christian Curwen's collieries at Harrington continued until coal trading ceased in 1929.

<u>Jane Pit</u>, sunk c. 1843 by Henry Curwen, has been preserved as a relic of the coal industry. Two castellated chimneys remain, one for the pump house, the other for the unusual, oval-shaped engine house. The crenellations match those of the Curwen family's home at Workington Hall. The pit ended its working days as a ventilation shaft for the neighbouring Buddle Mine.

Workington

[OE. 'Wyres' settlement – a local chief.]

The Romans built Burrow Walls coastal fort on the north side of the estuary of the River Derwent as part of Hadrian's defence against seaborne attacks. A chain of similar forts extended along this north-west coast.

In the 7c, a community of Angles settled on the south side of the River Derwent.

Following the Norman conquest, Workington grew as a small port and market town. A Market Charter was granted by Elizabeth I in 1573 and Wednesdays and Saturdays have become traditional market days.

Industrial development was largely the work of the Curwen family of Workington Hall, comparable with the achievements of the Lowther family at Whitehaven.

Henry Curwen, besides being an M.P. for 18 years, began coal mining and shipped coal to southern England or exported it to Ireland. In those early years it was not unusual for five-year-old children to be employed for thirteen hours a day carrying lights for the miners. By 1815, four pits were being worked and steam engines had been introduced for winding coal to the surface. Some coal was mined as far as three miles under the sea and tragedy struck John Christian Curwen's Chapel Bank Colliery at Workington in 1837 when the sea broke in and 27 men and boys and 28 horses were drowned. This was the only occasion when the sea inundated a Cumberland mine.

The original harbour of 1763–1769 was tidal and coal ships were loaded from staithes (raised wooden jetties) on the south side. In 1865, the Lonsdale Dock was opened for the iron and steel trade and enlarged in 1927 to become the Prince of Wales Dock, capable of accommodating ships of 10,000 tons.

A shipyard had been established by John Wood prior to the building of the harbour and it continued in production for 60 years. Between 1839 and 1938 more then 200 ships were built giving rise to the local manufacture of sails and ropes.

To transport coal and iron ore from the mines, a network of inter-connecting railways was built:

1845   Maryport and Carlisle Railway.
1846   Maryport and Workington Railway.
1847   Workington and Whitehaven Railway.
        Cockermouth and Workington Railway.

The demand for railway lines grew and Workington specialised in their manufacture. Exports were shipped across the world, particularly to Argentina and China.

The Moss Bay Iron Works of 1872 later developed into the Workington Iron and Steel Company when several of the region's ironworks combined. Derwent Iron Works was on an adjacent site. In 1883, advantage was taken of the high grade iron ore mined in the region to introduce the revolutionary steel-making process invented by the English engineer, Sir Henry Bessemer (1813–1898), in which iron is decarbonised by blowing a blast of hot air through the molten metal. Following a reconstruction of the works in 1932, Bessemer steel and foundry iron continued in production until 1975. British Track products then used the site for the rolling of rails using steel from Middlesborough.

Prosperity came to Workington from coal mining and coal exporting, from shipbuilding and shipping, and later from the production of iron and steel. The population increased from 5,716 in 1801 to 26,143 in 1901.

With the great decline in coal mining and in the iron and steel industry, Workington has been compelled to diversify into other areas of employment.

Proceed from the Railway or Bus Station via Station Road, Oxford Street, Murray Road and Ladies Walk. Park off Ramsey Brow (A66 Cockermouth).

Workington Hall was constructed around a 14c pele tower to become one of the finest manor houses in the county. The Lords of the Manor were the Curwen family and this was their home for more than 600 years.

The Hall was the first refuge of Mary, Queen of Scots, when she escaped from Lochleven across the Solway Firth in an open boat with thirty fellow refugees following her defeat in 1568 by the rebellious Scottish Lords at the Battle of Langside. From the Hall, she wrote in French to Queen Elizabeth asking for mercy and support. Next day, she was escorted to Carlisle, stopping at Cockermouth on the way. Wordsworth's sonnet, '*Mary, Queen of Scots*', commemorated this event. During her 18 years imprisonment, Mary became the focus for Catholic plots against Protestant Elizabeth who, in self defence, felt impelled to sanction Mary's trial for treason and ultimate beheading at Fotheringhay in 1587.

Architectural styles representing the different periods of building from the original pele tower, extended to become a castle, a late

Tudor mansion and then an 18c home, are evident in the masonry of the Hall. The present ruins are said to be haunted by the ghost of 'Galloping Henry Curwen', who was murdered in 1623.

Curwen Park is the arena for entertainments in the summer.

Cross Ramsey Brow to Park End Road.

The Helena Thompson Museum is housed in a fine, listed, Georgian house, the former home of the steward of the Curwen estate. The house was bequeathed to the town in 1940 by Miss Helena Thompson, the great-granddaughter of Charles Udale, the original owner.

There are mainly Victorian exhibits of ceramics, glass, silver, furniture, costumes and accessories. The Clifton dish, a local example of 18c slipware pottery, was acquired by auction in 1989. Links are shown with the famous Staffordshire pottery families, including the Wedgwoods.

The local history gallery explains the social and industrial history of the town with the emphasis on coal mining, shipbuilding, iron and steel.

Turn right into Elizabeth Street. Off to the right is . . .

Portland Square. This elegant, late 18c, tree-lined cobbled space, with streets of terraced houses leading off, was formerly the centre of the old town's social and commercial life.

The Assembly Rooms, in the top corner, founded by John Christian Curwen, were the venue for public meetings and concerts.

The Green Dragon Posting House, 1805, was a coaching inn. 'The Royal Mail' to Cockermouth, Keswick, Penrith and Kendal and 'The Royal Sailor' to Maryport and Carlisle, were services which dwindled and ceased with the coming of the railway.

The obelisk is dedicated to Dr Anthony Peat (1819–1877) who

Workington

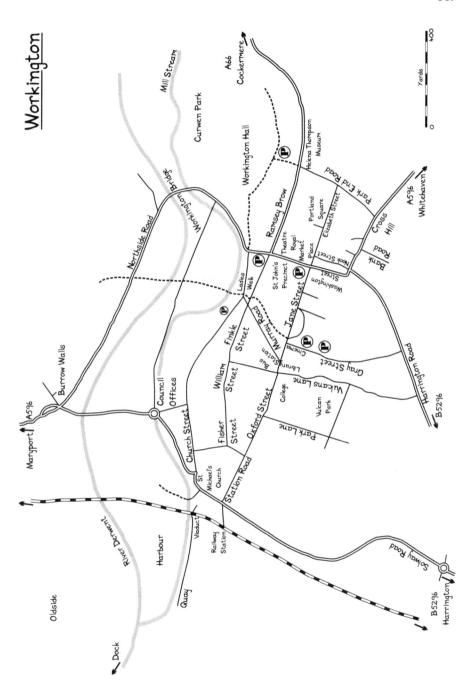

practised for 32 years from his dispensary in Christian Street. He particularly helped the poor, especially during the cholera epidemic of 1849.

No. 15 has a sundial high up on the wall.

No. 13 was formerly the Wheatsheaf Inn.

No. 6 was formerly the Coach and Horses.

Christian Street

No. 7 was the home and dispensary of Dr Peat.

The workshop at the end was Workington's first theatre, which closed in 1840.

Return to Portland Square and leave by Portland Street passing the entrance to the old Shambles. The Lowther Arms used to be a Posting House.

At Curwen Street, turn left.

Market Place. The Market Charter was granted by Elizabeth I in 1573. Wednesdays and, later, Saturdays became market days, but with the town expanding the present venue is on the site of the old Central Railway Station.

The small alley once led to the Slaughterhouse which, from 1861, became the glass-roofed covered market.

Leave by Nook Street. Near the end, on the right, is Ritson Street, where the small round-roofed building, erected by public subscription early in the 19c, was the former Lock-up.

At the main road (Guard Street) turn left and then right into Bank Road.

Church of Our Lady and St Michael. The Curwens brought Irish families to increase the workforce in their mines and on their farms.

To cater for their religious needs, John Christian Curwen appointed a Benedictine monk to be in charge of a small mission in 1811. This grew and developed into the present church, designed by E.W. Pugin and opened in 1876. The church is linked with Ampleforth Abbey.

Higher up the hill, on the right, where crosses are set into the wall, is Cross Hill, the site of a Chapel of Ease, originating from the 11c. It was situated on the old 'Corpse Road' to Camerton Church where Workington's burials took place until the 15c.

Descend Cross Hill and Guard Street to Washington Street. St John's Church, designed by Thomas Hardwick, was built in 1823 to commemorate the Battle of Waterloo. It resembles St Paul's Church in Covent Garden, London, the masterpiece of Inigo Jones, which Hardwick rebuilt to the same design after it was damaged by fire. Thin cast-iron columns support the gallery. The organ came from the chapel of Workington Hall.

Continue along Washington Street.

The Washington Central Hotel stands on the site of the Crown Inn from which 'The Defiance' stagecoach used to run to Penrith and Kendal.

The Theatre Royal began as The Lyceum in 1866. In spite of fluctuating fortunes, the Workington Playgoers' Club has ensured its continued growth and development.

The Tourist Information Centre is here.

The Harbour Area

Walk along Jane Street and Oxford Street, passing St John's Precinct and Arcade, the cinema and library.

Turn right into Vulcans Lane and the bus station.

Turn right at the end, onto Finkle Street, to the Carnegie Theatre and the Arts Centre.

Turn back along Finkle Street, along William Street to the end of Fisher Street. St Michael's Parish Church has stood here since the 7c, although a larger church was built in 1770.

Cross over Church Street and Mill Stream along the side of the railway viaduct.

Derwent Park is the venue for Workington's rugby league games, with a football ground and a greyhound track adjacent. An older ball game, 'Uppies and Downies', customarily played at Easter, involves any number of participants in two teams, using the town as a playing area, in an attempt to move the ball from one end to the other.

Across the River Derwent is the Roman coastal fort of Burrow Walls.

The harbour, quay and docks survive in this once thriving industrial area of Workington, north and south of the Derwent estuary, but not three of the original ironworks. To the west of the viaduct, the cramped Lowther Iron Works were in production 1873–1911. Further north, on the seaward side of the coastal railway, were Oldside Iron Works, 1841–1930, and on the east side of the railway, West Cumberland Works, 1862–1900, with steel production from 1870.

Take the A596 north.

Siddick Pond Nature Reserve, once a reservoir for ironworks, has a hide from where many species of migratory birds can be observed.

Turn right.

<u>Seaton</u> Pagan warrior burials, complete with swords and other equipment of Norse origin, have been found.

The most successful of all Cumberland's 18c blast furnaces was founded here by James Spedding of Whitehaven. The plant included two blast furnaces, slitting and rolling mills and a foundry in which were cast guns for ships, cannon, fire grates, hollowware and steam engines. Several hundred men were employed by 1794 when it became one of the largest iron manufacturing centres in the north of England.

<u>Camerton</u> St Peter's Church has been rebuilt many times, but the altar tomb, dated 1500, has remained. The effigy in black painted sandstone, dressed in warrior's armour, is commonly called 'Black Tom of the North', who was buried at Shap Abbey. Black Tom was related to the Curwen family of Workington and numerous legends and folk tales centre around him.

Return to the coast road, A596.

Maryport

This ancient seaport dates back to Roman times when the fort of Alauna was built to guard against seaborne raiders outflanking the defences of Hadrian's Wall which still extends across northern England from Wallsend on Tyne to Bowness on Solway.

Alauna was an integral part of Hadrian's 26 miles of coastal defences and the natural harbour was used to supply the fort and the town.

Until the mid-18c, Maryport remained a fishing village known as Ellenfoot, after the River Ellen which flowed into the harbour. Then in 1748–9, a local landowner and coalmine proprietor, Humphrey Senhouse II, began to develop the industrial potential of the harbour as a coal port and re-named it Maryport after his wife, Mary Fleming. He also created the town in the style of Whitehaven, adopting a grid-iron pattern of streets.

Maryport was situated at the northern limit of the Cumberland coalfield which extended southwards some 14 miles to Whitehaven. From this coalfield the coal trade with Ireland was a virtual monopoly in the 18c. The Senhouses coalmining enterprises in the Ellen Valley had not met with the very high level of success enjoyed by the Curwens in the Workington area, or by the Lowthers around Whitehaven. But success in developing Maryport's harbour stimulated further investment and by 1780 the Senhouse family had three collieries working outside the Ellen Valley.

A blast furnace began production on Mote Hill in 1752 and iron railway lines were shipped all over the world. More than 100 vessels registered at Maryport in 1794 exported a million tons of cargo annually. There was a substantial trade with America. By 1867, 3,000 vessels a year were making use of the harbour.

A shipyard at Workington established by John Wood was followed c. 1764 by a shipyard opened by his brother William at Maryport, which dominated shipbuilding at the port for more than a century. A second shipyard was in production at Maryport by 1829. Larger sailing ships had to be launched broadside into the River Ellen.

Coalmining, manufacturing and trade received a further stimulus when the Carlisle to Maryport Railway opened in 1845. Rail links with Workington, Whitehaven, Cockermouth, Keswick and Penrith soon followed. Glassworks, paper and cotton mills, tanneries and brewing added to the prosperity of the town.

As steam replaced sail, and iron replaced wood, the closure of Maryport's shipyards resulted. Bigger ships found the harbour too small and the building of a new dock at Workington reduced Maryport's trade. The coal and iron industries declined and the years of depression between the two World Wars brought unemployment to 80%. Hardship and neglect contributed to the silting up of the harbour and to its state of dereliction.

Gradually, a transformation is taking place. A huge construction programme in the harbour area includes waterfront houses, a hotel, shops, offices and a Heritage Park to recreate the historical and social development of Maryport.

The Maritime Museum and Tourist Information Centre stands where Humphrey Senhouse II, Lord of the Manor, started to construct the harbour and new town of Maryport. On the corner of the

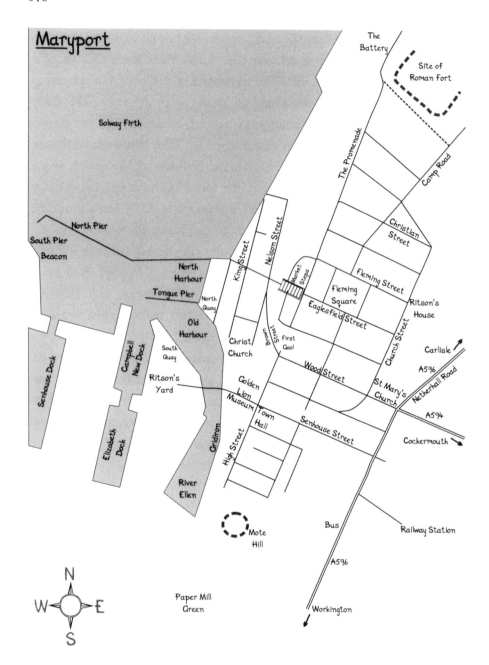

Maryport

Solway Firth

The Battery

Site of Roman fort

The Promenade

Camp Road

Christian Street

North Pier

South Pier

Beacon

North Harbour

Tongue Pier

North Quay

Nelson Street

King Street

Market Steps

Fleming Street

Fleming Square

Eaglesfield Street

Ritson's House

Church Street

Old Harbour

South Quay

Christ Church

Brown Street

First Gaol

Wood Street

St Mary's Church

Carlisle

A596

Netherhall Road

A594

Cockermouth

Senhouse Dock

Campbell New Dock

Ritson's Yard

Golden Lion Museum

Town Hall

Senhouse Street

Elizabeth Dock

Gridiron

High Street

River Ellen

Mote Hill

Bus

A596

Railway Station

Paper Mill Green

Workington

N
W E
S

building, a mosaic profile of Queen Victoria is a reminder that this was formerly the Queen's Head Inn.

Senhouse Street

Named after the founder, this is one of the 'grid' pattern of streets.

The Golden Lion Hotel was visited by George Stephenson during his planning of the Carlisle to Maryport Railway, and by the novelists Charles Dickens and Wilkie Collins.

Turn right into High Street.

No. 28. Born here was Isabella Harris, mother of Joseph, Lord Lister, the first English surgeon to use antiseptics.

No. 11. Greek Doric columns add classical features to a modest town house.

Return to Senhouse Street.

Next to the Town Hall lived the printer Robert Adair, who possibly printed some of Wordsworth's early poems. In 1833, he helped to organise what may have been the world's first secret ballot to elect members of Maryport Harbour's Board of Trustees.

The Carlton, opposite, Italianate in style, was once a bank and then a cinema.

Continue along High Street. Turn right into Wood Street.

Between Nos. 19 and 29a is the site of Whillens Yard where millionaire Thomas Henry Ismay was born in 1837. His White Star Shipping Line commissioned the ill-fated *Titanic*.

St Mary's Parish Church, rebuilt 1890–92, has Maryport's 'foundation stone', above a doorway in the south aisle, commemorating

Humphrey Senhouse II. A stained glass window in the War Memorial Chapel was installed by Ismay in memory of his parents. The organ came from Chester Cathedral. In the sanctuary is *The Good Shepherd* sculpture by Josephina de Vasconcellos.

On the outside north wall, at the east end, a plaque records that Joseph Peel, who lived through the reigns of eight monarchs to reach the age of 106, was killed when he fell from his horse after it took fright on being scratched by a cat that was being carried in a basket. 'Ten Shillings Smith' was washed up on the shore, unidentified, and named from the contents of his pockets.

Turn right up <u>Church Street</u>.

The former home of the Ritson shipbuilding family is on the corner of Fleming Street.

Turn left into <u>Christian Street</u>.

The street was named after Fletcher Christian, the leader of the Mutiny on the Bounty. His father's family lived at Ewanrigg Hall on the outskirts of Maryport. From the Hall and the Christian family came the mother of Edward Law, leading counsel for Warren Hastings during his impeachment for corruption and becoming, in 1802, Lord Chief Justice of England. Wilkie Collins based his novel *The Woman in White* on Ewanrigg Hall.

Turn right into Camp Road then left along the <u>footpath</u> *adjacent to a stone wall.*

<u>The Roman Fort of Alauna</u> was the Command Headquarters for Hadrian's coastal defence system. The double ditch, ramparts and the positions of the four gates of the 5¾ acre site can be identified, together with the parade ground and tribunal to the south of the fort

where Roman altars buried in pits were uncovered during excavations in 1870. In the extensive settlement outside the fort to the north, the foundations of houses, shops and taverns were discovered.

At the end of the footpath on the right –
The Battery, formerly a Royal Naval Reserve Station, houses the Senhouse Roman Museum, which opened in 1990. The Roman relics were first discovered during the reign of Elizabeth I by John Senhouse, Lord of the Manor. Succeeding members of his family over four centuries continued their amateur archaeology and built up a unique collection of Roman artefacts. As the collection began c. 1550, it is the oldest in the country. It contains the largest grouping of Roman Military Altar Stones and Inscriptions from any site in Britain.

Return to town along the clifftop Promenade. Turn left into Fleming Square.
The square is called after the maiden name of the wife of Humphrey Senhouse II. Formerly, it was Maryport's Market Place and the site of the old Goose Fair. Georgian and Victorian houses overlook this cobbled area.

Leave at the lower right corner. Turn right into Eaglesfield Street. Descend the Market Steps.
Near the top of Brown Street, to the left, was Maryport's first gaol.
Continue from the steps to King Street and turn left.
Christ Church was built in 1872 for residents in the lower part of town.
The huge anchor in front, estimated to be more than 200 years old, was fished out of the Solway Firth and is dedicated to the

Maryport mariners who perished at sea.

Follow North Quay to <u>*Tongue Pier*</u>.
No. I North Quay was the birthplace of Ned Smith who was award-
ed the Victoria Cross in World War I.
At the head of North Harbour, William Wood built Maryport's first shipyard.

Return along <u>*North Quay*</u>.
Next to The Sailors Return quayside inn, William Curry once kept
a lamp and oil shop. He used to light a lamp in one of his windows to
guide ships to the quay.
<u>The Maritime Museum</u>, on Shipping Brow, traces the growth of the
port from its earliest days.
The story is told of Fletcher Christian, leader of the mutiny on
the *Bounty*. A facsimile of Captain Bligh's logbook for the *Bounty* is
open on the fateful day of the mutiny in 1789.
Another local celebrity featured is Thomas Ismay, whose shipping
company, the White Star Line, included the *Titanic*, the biggest ship
in the world and described as 'unsinkable'. On her maiden voyage to
New York in 1912, she hit an iceberg and sank with the loss of 1,513
lives.
From the Museum, turn left upstream along the river bank. On the
'Gridiron', in the river bed, ships' hulls were cleaned or repaired at low
tide.
The inlet opposite is the site of Ritson's shipyard, where large
ships were launched 'broadside' as the River Ellen was too narrow for
conventional launchings.
Mote Hill was a Roman and Norman stronghold.
Paper Mill Green beyond is the site of a Paper Mill built in 1756.

Return to the Museum. Cross the River Ellen by the 1987 bridge and turn right along <u>South Quay</u>.

Nos. 4 and 7 have inscribed door lintels with a date, a number and the initials of William Blennerhasset, Lord of the Manor of Flimby, who exported coal from this quay in the 18c.

At the side of No. 4 is the entrance to the courtyard of the former Crown Inn.

Maryport's first dock, <u>The Campbell or New Dock</u>, was opened in 1836.

<u>Elizabeth Dock</u>, named after Humphrey Senhouse II's eldest daughter, opened in 1857. It was the first 'wet' (non-tidal) dock between the Clyde and the Mersey. Railway sidings were built for ships to be loaded from coal wagons on the dock side.

Two restored steamships occupy the dock. *The Flying Buzzard*, a Clyde-built 1951 tug, worked the Clyde for 11 years. The *Vic 96* was built as a naval inshore supply ship during World War II.

Continue round Elizabeth Dock to reach <u>Senhouse Dock</u>.

This was built in 1884 covering an area of six acres and named after Humphrey Senhouse II. From local iron and steel works, railway lines were exported round the world. When the dock was converted into a marina in 1989, commercial vessels were replaced by pleasure craft and a slipway, a chandlery and repair facilities were added.

On the <u>South Pier</u>, the iron Beacon Light is one of the oldest of its type, having stood here since 1846.

Nearby, on the sea wall, were the old Harbour Office, Customs House and a wartime Observation Post.

Return to the Museum.

Maryport to Carlisle

Take the A596 and A595 (Roman Road).

The Carlisle to Maryport Railway runs parallel with this route, which leaves Maryport by following the River Ellen.

At Crosby, divert right.

<u>Dearham</u>. St Mungo's Church (*St Kentigern*) dates from Norman times. Norman features are apparent in the doorways and windows. The castellated tower was added later in a defence against Scottish raiders. Further additions in 1882 revealed various sepulchral slabs and these were built into the walls of the church. Amongst the church treasures are the Norman font; the Adam stone depicting the Fall and Redemption of Man; and the Viking Cross, c. AD 700, with its ancient carvings.

When the Senhouse family expanded their coal mining activities into the Ellen Valley in the late 18c, Dearham had its own colliery.

Return to the main route.

<u>Aspatria</u> [*ON. Patrick's Ash*] The Patrick is presumed to be an Anglian chief, Gospatrick, Earl of Northumberland.

St Kentigern's Church (*St Mungo*), where he preached in the 6c, was rebuilt in 1847, retaining its Norman arch and a Viking hogback coffin. Sir Wilfred Lawson's memorial records that he served the area as a Liberal MP for forty years.

GEORGE MOORE MEMORIAL
12/98
– WIGTON MARKET PLACE. WEST CUMBRIA.
GATEWAY TO THE SOLWAY PLAIN AND WESTERN LAKES.

The coalfield in the Ellen Valley, on which the 19c prosperity of Aspatria was based, has been exhausted.

A Georgian model farm and corn mills, now converted, have survived from the past, although surrounded now by modern buildings.

The first Agricultural College in the north of England was established here in 1874 by Sir Wilfred Lawson. As an educational and research unit, the college developed new ways of feeding livestock. The college closed in 1925 and the Beacon Hill School took over the premises.

A very lengthy sporting tradition has been established by the Aspatria Rugby Union Football Club since it was founded in 1869.

Wigton. The commonly held theories concerning the migration of people and the pattern of settlement in the Lake District indicate that the original Anglo-Saxon farming community at Wigton was later dominated by the Vikings.

The right to hold a Tuesday market was granted in 1262. As a local market centre, Wigton gained in importance with the closure of Holme Cultram Abbey in 1538. A reduction in market trading took place from 1856 when surplus agricultural produce from the Solway Plain was diverted from Wigton to Carlisle on the newly opened Carlisle and Silloth Railway.

Scottish raiders burnt Wigton to the ground in 1315 and, thereafter, no significant development took place until late in the 18c. Then the manufacturing industry emerged, mainly of woollen, cotton and linen cloth. Today, the main employer manufactures cellulose film wrapping.

Manufacturing in London made a fortune for George Moore. His memorial in the town centre was erected in memory of his wife and is graced by Thomas Woolner's sculptures, *The Four Acts of Mercy*.

Overlooking the town is Highmoor House with its ornate tower, which once housed an 18 ton bell and carillon provided by the owners, the two Banks brothers, both of whom became High Sheriffs of Cumberland.

More recently, the broadcaster and author, Melvyn Bragg, was born here in 1939 and Anna Ford, the broadcaster, was brought up in the town.

Divert right off the A595.

Thursby is said to have been named after Thor, the Viking God of War. All the inhabitants were slaughtered by the Danes in the 9c. Born here was Sir Thomas Bouch who designed the Tay Bridge which collapsed in a gale in 1879.

Dalston. Turnips were a novelty when first grown here in 1794.

A two-storey, stonebuilt cotton mill, with a tall brick chimney and an extensive mill race, has survived.

Continue to Carlisle.

Solway Coast

From Maryport: A596 (Carlisle). Left onto B5300.

'The Allerdale Ramble' from Maryport follows a coastal route to the northern extremity of Grune Point, a distance of 15 miles, crossing the district of Allerdale, formed in 1974 and taking its name from a 12c Baron ruler. From the start of the Ramble, at Seathwaite in the mountainous area of Borrowdale, to the finish, the total distance is about 55 miles.

Crosscanonby Church of St John the Evangelist, 8c or 9c, has ancient connections with the Priory and Cathedral of Carlisle. Until 1908, it was the parish church of Maryport.

In the 18c, Humphrey Senhouse of Netherhall removed a Roman arch from the fort of Alauna at Maryport to serve as the present chancel arch. A minstrel's gallery was constructed in 1933 from the old Senhouse family pew.

Of interest are: a section of a carved sandstone Viking cross; a Viking hogback gravestone; and the grave of a Crosscanonby salt-pans inspector, John Smith (d. 1730).

Saltpans. The remains of this 17c site where salt was obtained is a link with a tradition which lasted nearly 700 years along this coast. The salters' cottages and stables were located at the foot of Swarthy Hill and the salt-making process was conducted above the shoreline as described by the plaques on the site.

Salt-laden sand (sleech) from the sea shore was heaped into a large, circular, clay-lined structure (kinch) with reeds acting as a filter across the bottom. Over the sleech was sprinkled fresh water or sea water which dissolved the salt as it trickled down into a brine pit. The process was stopped when the brine was concentrated enough to float an egg. The brine was then gently boiled in iron pans and the white of an egg was added to clear up any silt or scum. Slow heating evaporated the liquid leaving a residue of salt crystals.

From 1698 a salt tax was levied at source and abolished in 1824.

Milefortlet 21, on the cliff above the Saltpans, was initially discovered by aerial photography. It was one of a chain of small fortresses, each a Roman mile apart with two stone towers in between, built to protect the vulnerable flank of Hadrian's Wall. Excavations uncovered barrack blocks and stables of the 2c and 3c AD. Inscriptions testify to an infantry garrison one thousand strong in the 3c. Interpretive panels explain the site.

Allonby grew from the early settlement in the 12c to a village well-known for the construction of fishing boats, 'wherries', in the 17c. By 1775 it had become a fashionable sea bathing resort and it remains popular with holidaymakers today.

Christ Church has a memorial to Joseph Huddart who was born in the village in 1741. His work as a surveyor took him to the coasts and harbours of the Far East. The disastrous result of a cable breaking at sea prompted him to devise a method of rope making which ensured that the stresses between the fibres were evenly distributed. By becoming a rope maker in London he made his name and fortune and was buried at St Martin-in-the-Fields.

<u>The Ship Inn</u> in 1857 provided a place of rest for Wilkie Collins, who had sprained his ankle on Carrock Fell, whilst his travelling companion, Charles Dickens, explored the neighbourhood. Evenings at the inn were spent collaborating on the fictionalised account of their journey which was published in '*The Lazy Tour of Two Idle Apprentices*'.

<u>Salta Moss</u> is a Nature Reserve.

<u>Beckfoot.</u> The coast road, constructed along a raised beach with sandy cliffs on the landward side, is evidence of earlier, higher sea levels. Conversely at Beckfoot, a submerged forest, visible at low tide, is indicative of a much lower sea level at one time. The tide goes out more than a mile here exposing vast areas of sand and rock pools.

Fragments of a Roman fort, part of Hadrian's coastal defences, have been traced.

<u>Wolsty Castle.</u> Aerial photography revealed the site of an Iron Age settlement, c. 800 BC, in the shape of a circular wooden hut in an oval pallisaded enclosure.

Later, it became the site of a pele tower built to safeguard the Treasury and the Archives of Holme Cultram Abbey. Reputedly, Michael Scott, Wizard of the North, mathematician and philosopher, lived here during the 13c. In 1348, a licence to crenellate was granted.

Silloth

The town's name appeared in the 13c, derived from '*Sea lath*', meaning '*the barn by the sea*'. Cistercian monks from Holme Cultram Abbey established the barn on the coast to store their grain.

From only a few scattered farms in the mid-19c, Silloth developed into a commercial port and a seaside resort.

Continuing the monks' ancient tradition of grain storage by the sea, Carr's Flour Mill was built five storeys high in 1831 and located to receive imported grain directly from the ships. Later buildings and silos now surround the mill which has preserved some of its early machinery in the factory museum.

Land for the construction of a deep water anchorage was bought from the Joliffe Estate by the Carlisle and Silloth Bay Railway and Dock Company. The Railway reached Silloth in 1856 and Marshall Dock was completed in 1859. When the stone entrance wall of the dock collapsed in 1880, it was rebuilt by the Railway Company and, at the same time, the inner dock was completed by 1885. Until World War II there was a summer steamer service from Silloth to Dublin calling at the Isle of Man.

The Railway Company held a competition for the design and development of the town. Broad, tree-lined streets, paved with granite setts, were laid out in a grid pattern. Pleasant terraces, 'mildly Italianate' according to Pevsner, were separated from the seashore by 40 acres of lawns and flower beds, known as The Green. The Promenade was constructed in 1951. Splendid views of distant Galloway in Southern Scotland, dominated by Criffel, inspired the English landscape painter, J.M.W. Turner (1775–1851).

Although the railway closed in 1964 and the port was never able to compete with the facilities available at Workington and Whitehaven, the town continues to attract as a seaside resort.

Walk along the <u>Promenade</u> *in a northerly direction to enjoy both the spaciousness of The Green and the extensive views across the Solway Firth.*

At the tennis courts, turn right to enter the town.

The streets leading north and south are named after locally visible geographical features: Criffel, Solway and Skiddaw. The east and west streets are named after the rivers which flow into the Solway.

Petteril Street

The Good Companions Residential Home, originally built as a Vicarage, has variously been a residential private school, a children's wear factory, a hotel and a restaurant.

The old National School was built in 1857 by public subscription and grants from the Privy Council, sponsored by the National Society. Before Christ Church was built, services were held in the school.

The Secondary School was built in the late 1930s and the new Primary School in 1980.

Turn right into Solway Street.

The Fire Station bears an inscription recording the occasion when four firemen set out on a very wild night to rescue a man trapped by the incoming tide on the marsh. Tragically, all four firemen perished, but the fate of the trapped man is unknown. No one was ever reported missing.

This disastrous incident led to the formation of a lifeboat station at Silloth.

Pass: United Reformed Church of St Andrew, and Hall.

Christ Church Mission Hall, 1887.

Trinity Methodist Church, 1875.

Wampool Street

The Roman Catholic Church of the Assumption, in the eastern section of the street, was originally a Congregational Church, the first built in Silloth. The Congregationalists moved out to join the Presbyterians and become the United Reformed Church. The bell in

591

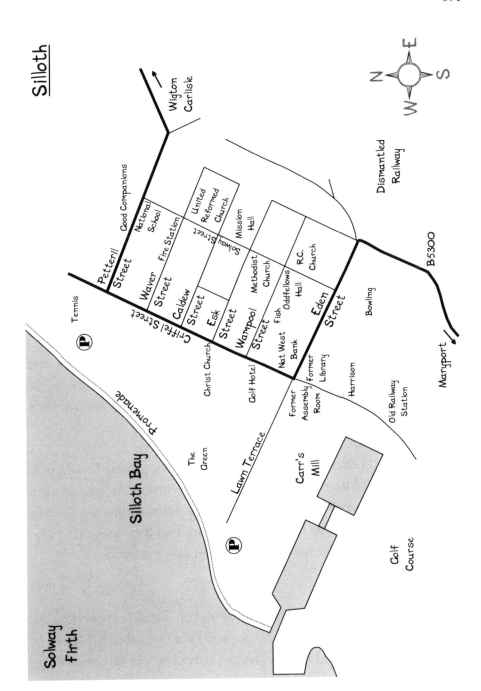

Silloth

the forecourt came from a buoy which marked the entrance to the channel into the port. The replacement in the channel operates electronically.

The houses past the church were among the first to be built and originally accommodated the coastguards. For the families of men who came to build the docks, Raglan Court was built, between Wampool Street and Esk Street.

The shop on the corner with Solway Street was built originally as the Oddfellows Hall in 1877 and later became the Majestic Cinema.

Along the western section of the street, the Fish Shop has remained in the ownership of the Lomas family since it opened in 1904. Two fishing boats owned by the family used to supply the fish, but now there is a regular delivery from Aberdeen.

Turn right, into Criffel Street.

Four-in-hand carriages needed wide streets in which to turn and the cobbles lessened the risk of horses slipping when pulling heavy loads.

Christ Church was built in 1870 of grey granite imported from Ireland. The clock was added in 1884.

Turn back down the street.

The Golf Hotel displays a collection of Old Silloth prints. It was privately owned until World War I when the government decided to curb the excess drinking of munitions workers by nationalising the Carlisle Brewery and the inns and hotels in the region. This unprecedented situation lasted until 1970 when privatisation was restored.

Eden Street

A plaque on the National Westminster Bank commemorates Kathleen Ferrier (1912–53), the singer who lived here when her husband was the bank manager, 1936–41. She celebrated her first competition win at Carlisle Music Festival in 1937.

On the opposite corner, the shop was originally built as the Library and Post Office.

Diagonally across, on the corner, stood the former Assembly Rooms, where dances were held.

Station Road and Docks

One of the Harrison family of jewellers invented a chronometer used to determine position at sea.

The Old Railway Station has been privately altered and the former marshalling yard is now the site of modern factory units.

To the Docks, ships bring cattle from Ireland. The cattle pens allow the imported cattle to be rested, fed and watered, before resuming their journey.

At various times, imports have included ingredients for animal feed from America, molasses from Jamaica and paper pulp from Spain. Exports have included food products such as milk powder to Saudi Arabia and El Salvador. Coasters carry cement and small boats fish off the coast.

Carr's Mill imports grain from Europe and Canada and manufactures animal feed.

Beyond the Golf Club House, towards the coast, stands The Cumberland and Westmorland Convalescent Home, opened in 1862.

On the coast, before World War I, guns were tested at the Battery.

Continuous efforts to stabilise the sand dunes and to prevent the erosion of the coastline have been made since the monks of Holme Cultram Abbey first built sea dykes or breakwaters.

Return past the Golf Course and Station Road to the starting point.

Solway Coast

Follow the unclassified road to –

<u>Skinburness</u>. During the military campaigns of 1300–1306 against the Scots, Edward I (1272–1307) developed Skinburness as a naval supply base for his army. In thankfulness, he granted a charter to the village making it a *'free borough, with all liberties and free customs for ever . . .'* These privileges were cut short by the devastating flood of 1303 which swept away most of the settlement. The surviving inhabitants moved to safer ground further inland at Newton Arlosh, [*New town on the Marsh*].

Today the sea has receded leaving a wide expanse of salt marsh, the grazing ground for sheep and cattle.

In later years, smuggling across the Solway Firth became a way of life. On one occasion, the ferryman's passenger was an Excise Officer, the great Scottish poet, Robert Burns (1759–96). Arriving at Skinburness, he accepted an invitation to be the guest of the regular customers at the Jolly Sailor Inn, where a fiddler was enlisted to provide entertainment. While the Excise Officer was convivially distracted, the ferryman made a quick and profitable return crossing of the water with a cargo of contraband.

A furtive way of smuggling illicit whisky from Scotland was by use of 'belly' cans, strapped round the waist and concealed beneath clothing.

Sir Walter Scott (1771–1832) wrote, *'Red Gauntlet'* while staying in the village at 'The Longhouse'.

<u>Grune Point</u>, a peninsula projecting into Morecambe Bay, offers wide views of the Solway Firth, the habitat of waders, wildfowl and salt marsh plants. A World War II Observation Post remains.

This is also the northern end of The Allerdale Ramble.

Aircraft hangars, widely dispersed against bombing attacks during World War II, now stand on disused airfields near Silloth, Kirkbride and Anthorn. Some hangars have been brought back into use housing small, commercial enterprises.

Take the unclassified road to the B5302.

Abbeytown

Abbeytown takes its name from <u>Holme Cultram Abbey</u>, founded in 1150 by Henry, Prince of Scotland, as a daughter house of Melrose Abbey. The Cistercian monks grew grain and raised large flocks of sheep on lands which extended from Workington to Galloway. They built sea dykes, drained marshes, established saltworks and developed the port of Skinburness.

The Abbey was not spared involvement in the tumultuous Border Wars. A Scottish raid in 1216 resulted in the loss of many valuable books and other treasures. The Abbey suffered also from the cost of provisioning the English armies. In 1300 and again in 1307, the armies of Edward I camped at the Abbey when he came to 'hammer' the Scots. The King acknowledged the hospitality by making Abbot Robert (Abbot from 1289–1318) a member of his Council, an honour incorporated in the Abbey's seal.

After the death in 1307 of Edward I whose entrails were buried at Holme Cultram Abbey, the Scots returned with a vengeance. Robert the Bruce showed no mercy when he sacked the Abbey in 1319, even though his father, the Earl of Carrick, one-time Constable of Carlisle, had been buried there since 1304. Villages and towns were burned, families slaughtered and churches destroyed, causing wealthy families to build pele towers for their future protection.

596

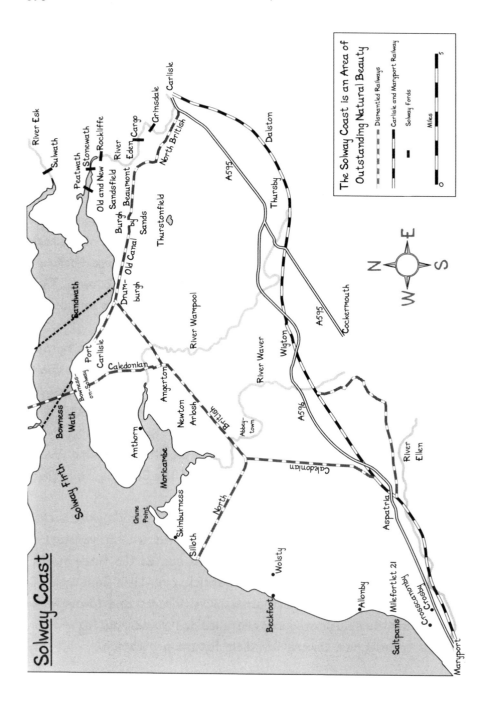

Solway Coast

The Solway Coast is an Area of Outstanding Natural Beauty

- Dismantled Railways
- Carlisle and Maryport Railway
- Solway fords
- Miles
  0 5

In the 15c, the Pope granted indulgences to Penitents who visited the Abbey and gave alms for its upkeep and repair. The end came in 1538 when Henry VIII suppressed the monastery in spite of the protest of Abbot Thomas Carter and others.

After the Dissolution, the Abbey's lands were eventually given to Oxford University but the parishioners successfully petitioned Chancellor Thomas Cromwell to retain the Abbey Church of St Mary as a place of worship and as a refuge against the Scots. The remains of the original Abbey Church, six bays of the Nave, have become the Parish Church and the tenor bell, c. 1465, which formerly summoned the monks to prayer, has been preserved.

The entrance is through a magnificent Norman doorway from the Tudor porch built by Abbot Robert Chamber in 1507. Within the church, a stained glass window set in an old cast-iron frame depicts St Mungo (St Kentigern). A memorial to Joseph Man records that he invented a primitive reaping machine in 1826. In the Ambulatory, opened by H.R.H. Princess Margaret in 1973, there are memorials to The Earl of Carrick, Father of Robert the Bruce; Matthias and Juliana De Keldsik, who are thought to have been related to Abbot Robert; and to Abbot Robert Chamber (a 'chained bear' = Chamber.)

Follow the B5307

Newton Arlosh [New Town on the Marsh] was founded c. 1305 by the monks of Holme Cultram Abbey after the disastrous flooding of Skinburness. The Abbot successfully petitioned the King to have the liberties and privileges bestowed on Skinburness transferred to Newton Arlosh and a fresh charter was granted to that effect in 1305. Despite permission to hold a weekly market, the settlement did not prosper. The village was safe from the sea but still exposed to the perils from Scottish raiders who crossed it.

The Church of St John the Baptist, dating from c. 1304, was built as a defensive stronghold as well as a place of worship. The walls are five feet thick. The narrow entrance, 2½ feet wide, permits only one person at a time to pass through and the windows are no more than arrow slits seven feet from the floor. The last place of refuge was the castellated tower. Access can be gained only from the Nave, through a narrow doorway, closed by an iron-framed heavy oak door. Only one person at a time can ascend the easily defended steep, narrow, twisting staircase and an alarm bell was accessible to ring for assistance.

After the Dissolution the church fell into nearly 300 years of ruin. Restoration in 1843 benefited from the generosity of Miss Sara Losh, an amateur architect and Principal of a school of carving and sculpture at Wray. Examples of her work include the lectern, the Bishop's chair, the old Communion table and stone rams' heads. From Holme Cultram Abbey came the early 13c font. The 1894 alterations removed the box pews and turned the seating to face a newly constructed Sanctuary and Altar on the north side.

Take the unclassified road left from Angerton.

Anthorn. The masts on the disused airfield are part of the Royal Navy's signals network.

Herdhill Scar, a short headland projecting into the Solway Firth, shoulders the remains of a 440 yard stone-faced embankment on which was the track of the Solway Junction Railway. From this approach, a 1,960 yards long iron railway viaduct, built in 1869 by James Brunless, crossed the Firth to the Scottish shore, south of Annan, establishing a direct link between the iron-ore mines of Cumberland and the smelting furnaces of Lanarkshire. Twice damaged by severe frost or drifting ice-floes, and expensive to maintain, the viaduct was declared unsafe in 1921 and demolished in 1934–5. Until then, thirsty Scotsmen could walk across the viaduct seeking a drink on Sundays when Scottish inns were closed.

Bowness-on-Solway

Bowness-on-Solway [*OE. ON. Bow-shaped headland*] is located at the western end of Hadrian's Wall. Along this section, the wall was only a turf rampart and few signs of it remain.

The Roman Fort [Maia], however, was the second largest on the wall and many houses in the village are built of stone from it. The north wall of the fort was eroded by the sea and the south wall has been located to the north of the church. The village now occupies most of this site. The fort was built where the Solway Estuary was fordable, a crossing known as the Bowness Wath to the English, or the Annan Wath to the Scots.

St Michael's Church was built largely of stones from the Roman Fort. Examples can be seen in the west wall and to the east of the window by the pulpit. Norman craftmanship is in evidence at the base of the Sanctuary window on the north side and also in the font.

The church bells were stolen in 1626 by a raiding party of Scots, who were halfway home across the estuary before they were nearly overtaken and had to abandon the bells in a pool now called Bell Dub. In retaliation, the bells from the villages of Dornoch and Middlebie, on the Scottish side of the Solway, were seized by Bowness men to re-equip their church. The Scottish bells are displayed in the church.

Many local Solway scenes are depicted as a background in the stained glass memorial windows.

In the churchyard by the Rectory door, under a Cypress tree, is the grave of Thomas Stoal. The Registers describe him as a 'Smuggler'. His wife is said to have had the headstone of Snaefell slate made in the Isle of Man and shipped to Maryport. As a penance, she then carried it on her back to Bowness. Sir Walter Scott, in his novel *Redgauntlet*, tells of smugglers from Annan who came from the Isle of Man.

Port Carlisle

Port Carlisle became what its name implies when its harbour for coastal shipping was built by the Earl of Lonsdale in 1819 and the 11½ miles canal link to Carlisle was completed by 1823. But the concept of this scheme bringing Carlisle access to the sea was short lived because of the railway construction boom and especially the opening of the Carlisle to Maryport Railway in 1845. Consequently, the canal was drained in 1854 and the Port Carlisle Railway track was laid on its bed to complete a metamorphosis. When the railway was extended from Drumburgh to Silloth in 1856 (the North British line), Silloth benefited as a port to the detriment of Port Carlisle. The final blow came with the building of the viaduct across the Solway Firth in 1869, to carry the Caledonian Railway, preventing sizeable ships from reaching Port Carlisle. The Drumburgh to Port Carlisle branch line operated for more than fifty years with a horse-drawn 'Dandy' carriage, then reverted to steam, before closing in 1932.

In this small village, the stone walls of the harbour and the lock entrance to the canal are still visible, but the canal basin has been largely filled in. The railway platforms are still discernible and the former goods yard is now a children's playground. It is still possible to trace the course of the old railway track back to Carlisle.

A traditional method of catching salmon, which swim up the Solway estuary to spawn in the Eden or the Esk, is by a 'haaf' net. [*ON. Heave or Channel*]. A three-sided rectangular wooden frame, to which the net is attached like a tennis net, is held by the wading fisherman against the force of the tide, assisted by the support of a long timber pole attached centrally to the horizontal spar.

<u>Drumburgh</u>. This small village occupies the site of a two-acre Roman fort on Hadrian's Wall. No visible signs of the fort remain, but the road through the village bends round the line of the outer walls.

<u>Drumburgh Castle Farm</u>, constructed as a pele tower c. 1307, was rebuilt in the early 16c by Thomas, Lord Dacre. Its purpose was to guard the Sandwath Ford across the Solway. The end wall with an outside staircase incorporates stones from the Roman fort.

<u>Drumburgh Moss</u>, a Cumbria Wildlife Trust Reserve covering 300 acres, is one mile south of the village.

The low sea wall stretching eastwards follows the direction of the Roman turf ramparts of Hadrian's Wall and the Roman ditch (vallum) behind the ramparts of the wall. Close by is the former Port Carlisle Canal, which was transformed into the Port Carlisle Railway and later, the North British Railway track.

<u>Burgh-by-Sands</u> (pron. Bruff) The village with thatched and clay dobbin (daub) whitewashed houses, unusual for Cumbria, is built on the site of a Roman fort [Aballaba] covering nearly five acres. The Roman bath house was destroyed during the construction of the Port Carlisle Canal.

<u>St Michael's Church</u>, 12c, stands within the site of the Roman fortress, stone from which was used to build the church. Like others along the coast, the church served the dual purpose of a place of worship and a defensive stronghold. The 14c pele tower, built as a refuge

with walls seven feet thick, can only be entered from the Nave through a heavily bolted iron gate, or 'yett'. The windows in the tower are narrow defensive slits. The remains of a second tower are at the east end.

<u>Thurstonfield Lough</u>, a tarn, lies 2 miles to the south.

<u>Burgh Marsh</u>. Edward I, '*the Hammer of the Scots*' set out to cross the Solway by the fords and suppress the rebellion of Robert the Bruce. On Burgh Marsh in 1307, the ailing King fell fatally ill and died, aged 68. His body was carried to lie in state in St Michael's Church at Burgh-by-Sands. A tall sandstone commemorative pillar was erected on Burgh Marsh in 1685.

At Monkill divert left.

<u>Beaumont</u> was the site of a Roman milecastle.

The 12c church is fortified like others along the Solway Coast.

Sea-washed turf from the Solway coastline has enriched the playing area of many sports venues, including Wembley Stadium.

Return to the original route, turn left, and after 3 miles join the B5307 to Carlisle.

<u>Historical Solway Fords</u>:

<u>The River Eden</u>

<u>Peatwath</u>, near the mouth of the river at Old Sandsfield, was where 2,000 Scottish soldiers drowned in 1216 whilst attempting to retreat after a border raid.

<u>Stonewath</u>, near New Sandisfield.

<u>Rockcliffe, Cargo and Grinsdale</u> were used by Bonnie Prince Charlie's army on the way to capture Carlisle in 1745.

The River Esk

Sulwath, near the mouth of the river. [ON. Sul = pillar, referring to the large, ice-borne granite boulder, Lochmaben Stone, which marked the Scottish end of the ford. Wath = a ford.]

Only for limited periods of time, at low tide, were these fords passable and an expanding road construction process contributed towards making them progressively obsolete.

Carlisle

EC. Th.   Mkt. W,S. [OB. Caer-Luel = hill fort.]

Carlisle, the administrative capital of Cumbria, was built on the foundations of the Roman town of Luguvalium, which supplied the nearby garrison at Stanwix and the western end of Hadrian's Wall. The inner city street pattern continues to follow the line of the original Roman town walls and Roman relics have been uncovered during excavations.

Carlisle Castle. William Rufus captured the Saxon stronghold here in 1092 and built a palisaded Norman motte and bailey castle on the mound overlooking the River Eden.

The castle became the focal point of the power struggle between England and Scotland for territorial control of the border country. Between 1122 and 1461 it was besieged nine times by the Scots; captured and re-captured four times.

The original wooden structure was enlarged and strengthened by King David I of Scotland, who died in the castle in 1153.

The English King, Henry II (1154–1189) built the keep and the curtain wall. Stone was readily available from Hadrian's Wall.

'The garrison building was transformed into a Royal Palace by Edward I (1273–1306) when he lived here for a time. The Long Hall, where he supervised three Parliaments, was demolished in the 19c. Also destroyed was the tower where Mary Queen of Scots was held

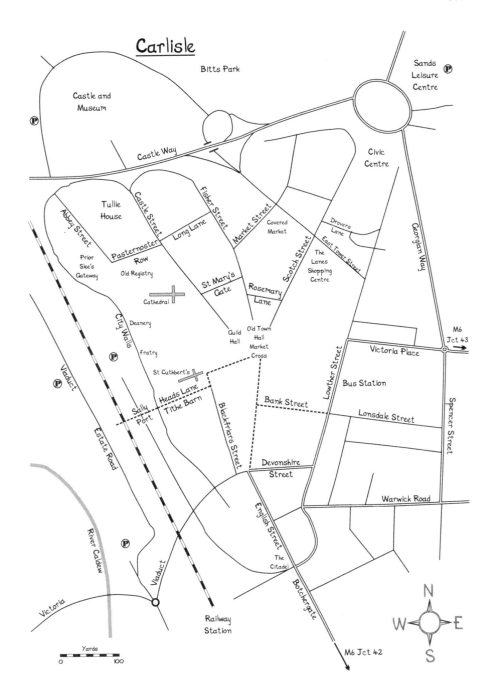

Carlisle

prisoner in 1568. She took her exercise below the castle's southern wall, which became known as Lady's Walk. After two months she was moved to the greater security of Bolton Castle.

During the Civil War, the castle was overcome after nine months by the Parliamentarians, then by the Royalists and finally by the Parliamentarians again.

In 1745, Bonnie Prince Charlie captured the castle on his march to claim the throne of England. The castle was re-captured within six weeks by the Duke of Cumberland for the last time in its long and turbulent history.

In spite of everything, the castle has retained its basic motte and bailey shape. The 12c keep, the 14c main gate and the dungeons remain. Part of the former Royal Palace now houses exhibits of the King's Own Royal Border Regiment.

From the high ramparts are views of Bitts Park, the River Eden and the Sands Leisure Centre. Across the Solway Firth lies Scotland.

Castle Street to Tullie House

This Jacobean town house, *'the most ambitious house in Carlisle'* (Pevsner) was built for the Tullie family in 1689, a date visible on the ornate lead downspouts. A large panelled room and a fine staircase belong to this Jacobean era.

The Tullie family left in 1817 and in 1893 the Museum and Art Gallery moved from Finkle Street Academy of Arts to display collections of Archaeology, Natural History, Fine and Decorative Arts and Social History.

After a £5 million refurbishment, Tullie House re-opened in 1991 to portray Carlisle's fascinating and turbulent place in Border history. Visitors are invited *'to begin a journey of discovery'* and to *'reflect back on the strife and struggle that were part of every day*

life of the people of Carlisle and the Borders.'
Tullie House stands on a former Roman road and the shrine in the grounds is the city's only permanent visible Roman structure.

Georgian Abbey Street to Prior Slee's Gateway (1527) and the Cathedral Precinct

The Old Registry (1699) is on the right.

The Deanery has a three-storey 13c pele tower, known as the 'Prior's Tower', formerly a place of refuge from Scottish raiders. In the Prior's Room, domesticated between 1500 and 1530 by Prior Senhouse, is a remarkable ceiling of 45 painted panels. The exhibits span eighteen centuries.

The Cathedral also had a defensive wall, a portion of which is identifiable by the massive sandstone masonry just beyond the tower.

The remains of the monastic buildings include the Fratry (Dining Hall) rebuilt in the 15c by Prior Thomas Gondibour, whose initials are in the vaulting of the first two bays of the Undercroft. The Undercroft has become the Cathedral's visitor centre and buttery.

Carlisle Cathedral is one of the smallest in England. It was built as part of a Priory, which Henry I granted to Augustinian canons in 1123. In 1133, he increased the Abbey's influence by establishing it as a base for the Carlisle diocese with the Priory Church of St Mary as its Cathedral. Henry I's confessor, Aethulwulf, became the first bishop.

In 1292, the Cathedral and Castle were largely rebuilt after a disastrous fire.

Here, whilst 'hammering' the Scots, Edward I ex-communicated Robert the Bruce, King of Scotland, with 'bell, book and candle'.

Following the Reformation, the Augustinians were replaced by a Dean and canons and the name of the Cathedral was changed to the Holy and Undivided Trinity.

Of special interest:

The east window, with its exquisite tracery, contains some fine 14c stained glass.

The choir, with a barrel-vaulted painted ceiling, has columns surmounted with carved capitals representing activities connected with the months of the year. The choir stalls and misericords are notable examples of medieval craftsmanship, c. 1400.

St Wilfred's Chapel has a magnificent, 16c, carved Flemish altarpiece known as the Brougham Triptych. It had been brought to England by Lord Brougham, one-time Chancellor, who installed it in the private chapel of his home at Brougham Hall, near Penrith until it was donated to the cathedral in 1979.

Two bays of the Norman nave and the Norman south transept remain from the original Priory completed in 1120. The north transept is late medieval, c. 1400.

In the north and south aisles, medieval paintings depict the life of St Augustine, the Legends of St Cuthbert and St Anthony and the figures of the Twelve Apostles.

From the west end, six bays were removed by the Parliamentarians during the Civil War when stone was needed to strengthen the castle and the city walls. The truncated nave was still in a poor state of repair when Sir Walter Scott was married in 1797. In 1949, the damaged area was restored by Dykes-Bower and dedicated to the Border Regiment.

The Cathedral bells were replaced eventually during the 19c after being removed supposedly for having welcomed Bonnie Prince Charlie in 1745.

<u>City Walls</u>. King David of Scotland first built walls round the city in 1126, enclosing an area of 45 acres.

The eastern ramparts disappeared with the expansion of the city, but the west walls survived virtually intact until the early 19c as the River Caldew limited expansion. Today, West Walls Road runs along the top of the old city wall.

The Sally Port was one of a number of secret gateways in the Wall that were used when the city was under siege. From these gateways, the defenders could 'sally forth'.

In later years, Sally Port gave access to the Tithe Barn without going through the city gates and having to pay tolls.

Visible from West Walls is Shaddon Mill, built of red sandstone in 1836. In its day, it was one of the largest cotton mills in England.

<u>Heads Lane leads to the Tithe Barn</u>, a 15c building, restored in 1971. It was used to store goods or grain paid as taxes to the church. These tithes represented one tenth of each man's income.

It is now the parish hall of St Cuthbert's Church. Medieval oak timbers support the sandstone flagged roof.

<u>The Sportsman Inn</u> is probably 18c.

<u>St Cuthbert's Church</u> pre-dates the Cathedral. There was a church here in AD 685 and a second in AD 870 to house the body of the saint who was Bishop of Carlisle in AD 680. The Normans built their church on the same site and this was replaced by the present structure in 1778.

A 14c window is set in the north wall. Inside is a gallery supported by Tuscan columns and a moveable pulpit (c. 1900) mounted on rails. The Mayor's official pew has ornamental wrought iron holders for the Civic Sword and Mace and incorporates a cross and four roses, which were the early arms of the city.

Note the commemorative plaque to William McReady's Theatre.

St Cuthbert's Lane and Castle Street lead to The Crown and Mitre
Hotel, 1902
On the corner of Castle Street and the Greenmarket is the build-
ing where Sir Walter Scott stayed prior to his marriage in the
Cathedral.
On the corner of Greenmarket and Fisher Street is The Guildhall,
the only surviving medieval timber-framed building in the area.
Richard of Redeness acquired the site in 1396 and by 1407 his
house was built. He bequeathed the house *'to the mayor and com-
munity of Carlisle'* and it came into use as a meeting place for the
city's eight trade guilds – the Butchers, Merchants, Shoemakers,
Skinners and Glovers, Smiths, Tailors, Tanners and Weavers.
Together, they formed the city corporation.
Brightly painted 'grotesques' peer from below the first floor windows. Inside, the medieval timber work is impressive and there are
examples of a ceiling lined with rushes and wattle and daub partition
walls.
The Guildhall Museum illustrates the history of the Guilds and the
city. On display are the city's stocks and pillory.

The Market Square. Plaques on shops and buildings commemorate
some of the notable people associated with Carlisle.
The Old Town Hall was built in 1717, partly on the site of an
Elizabethan building. The main chamber was the meeting place of the
City Council until the Civic Centre opened in 1964. It is now the
Tourist Information Centre.
The 'muckle bell', once housed here, but now in the Guildhall, was
an alarm bell which could be heard eleven miles away.

The market bell used to open the market at 8.00 a.m. Trading before the bell was rung could result in a fine for 'forestalling'. The Market Charter was granted in 1158.

The Market Cross, dated 1682, continues to be the city's traditional meeting place where public proclamations are read from the steps. From here, Bonnie Prince Charlie proclaimed his father King in 1745.

On top of the Cross, a lion holds the 'Dormant' Book of the city (dated 1561), which contains the 'byelaws' and lists of apprentices of that date.

English Street connects with The Citadel, built in 1542 on the orders of Henry VIII, to guard the southern entrance to the city. Its cannons were last fired in anger by the Scots against the Duke of Cumberland's English troops in 1745.

In the early 19c, the Citadel was partly demolished to provide easier access to the town. A Toll Board on the wall lists the charges made to bring livestock into the city, and a plaque commemorates the site of the city gaol, closed in 1922.

The Railway Station was built in 1847 by Sir William Tite. At one time a record number of seven different railway companies operated from Carlisle.

The Market Square to Castle Street
No. 21 is built of hand-made bricks laid in Flemish bond style.

Long Lane to Fisher Street. Turn right.
Carlisle Working Men's Club has a serpentine front.
Nos 18–22 opposite illustrate the distinctive patterned brickwork

of many 19c Carlisle buildings.

The Covered Market, 1887–9, has entrance columns with capitals carved with the heads of animals that represent the meat on sale.

Scotch Street. The Lanes Shopping Centre has attempted to retain the character of the area by renovating and repairing older buildings whilst adding new buildings designed in a sympathetic style.

Events

Cumberland Show. Cumbria's largest agricultural show. July.
Carlisle Great Fair. Established 1353. August 26th.

Abbreviations

EC	Early Closing	Mkt	Market Day
NT	National Trust	OS	Ordnance Survey
c	Century	OB	Old British or Celtic
Br	British or Celtic	W	Welsh
OE	Old English 5c–11c	AS	Anglo Saxon
ON	Old Norse	ME	Middle English, 12c–15c

Ill Bell 2.4   refers to "A Pictorial Guide to the Lakeland Fells" by A. Wainwright, Book 2 "The Far Eastern Fells", section Ill Bell, part 4.

OFOL   "The Outlying Fells of Lakeland" by A. Wainwright.

WFR   "Walks from Ratty."

Key to Maps

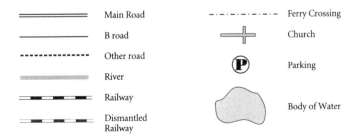

══════ Main Road	—··—··—··— Ferry Crossing
─────── B road	Church
------------ Other road	Parking
▓▓▓▓▓▓ River	
▬▬▬▬ Railway	Body of Water
▬▬▬▬ Dismantled Railway	

Selective Bibliography

M.J.B. Baddeley, *Guide to The Lake District.* Ward Locke, 1952.

Norman Nicholson, *The Lakers.* Hale, 1955, Cicerone Press, 1995.

A. Wainwright, *A Pictorial Guide to the Lakeland Fells.* Westmorland Gazette, 1955–66, (Seven Books) Michael Joseph, 1991.

Jessica Lofthouse, *The Curious Traveller Through Lakeland.* Hale, 1959.

Norman Nicholson, *Portrait of The Lakes.* Hale, 1963.

Molly Lefebure, *The English Lake District.* Batsford, 1964.

Jessica Lofthouse, *Countrygoers North.* Hale, 1965.

A.H. Griffin, *The Roof of England.* Hale, 1968.

Molly Lefebure, *Cumberland Heritage.* Gollancz, 1970.

Millward & Robinson, *The Lake District.* Eyre Methuen, 1974, Michael Joseph, 1991.

A. Wainwright, *The Outlying Fells of Lakeland.* Westmorland Gazette, 1974.

F.J. Carruthers, *Lore of The Lake Country.* Hale, 1975.

John Parker, *Cumbria.* Bartholomew, 1977.

William Rollinson, *A History of Cumberland and Westmorland.* Phillimore, 1978, 1996.

ed. Peter Bicknell, *The Illustrated Wordsworth's Guide to The Lakes.* Webb & Bower, 1984.

David McCracken, *Wordsworth and The Lake District.* Oxford, 1984.

Ordnance Survey, *The Lake District Landranger Guide.* O.S./Jarrold, 1988.

Colin Shelbourn, *Lakeland Towns and Villages.* Forster Davies, 1989.

Jim Watson, *Lakeland Villages.* Cicerone Press, 1989.

ed. Tim Locke, *The Holiday Which? Guide to The Lake District.* Consumers' Assn., 1989.

Hugh Owen, *The Lowther Family.* Phillimore, 1990.

Ron & Marlene Freethy, *Discovering Cumbria*. John Donald, 1991.

Jim Watson, *Lakeland Towns*. Cicerone Press, 1992.

Tom Fletcher Buntin, *Life in Langdak*. Titus Wilson, 1993.

Hunter Davies, *The Good Guide to the Lakes*. Forster Davies, 1993.

Grevel Lindop, *A Literary Guide to the Lake District*. Chatto & Windus, 1993.

Pearson, Warner & Warner, *Borrowdale*. Mikes-Eyre, 1995.

Robert Gambles, *The Story of the Lakeland Dales*. Phillimore, 1997.

References to other books are made within the text.